D1616599

# THE ARCHAEOLOGY AND POTTERY OF NAZCA, PERU

# The Archaeology and Pottery of Nazca, Peru

## ALFRED L. KROEBER'S 1926 EXPEDITION

Alfred L. Kroeber and Donald Collier

EDITED BY
Patrick H. Carmichael
with an Afterword by
Katharina J. Schreiber

A DIVISION OF SAGE PUBLICATIONS, INC.
Walnut Creek • London • New Delhi

*Published in cooperation with*
*The Field Museum, Chicago, Illinois*

For information address:

AltaMira Press
A Division of Sage Publications, Inc.
1630 North Main Street, Suite 367
Walnut Creek, CA 94596
explore@altamira.sagepub.com

SAGE Publications Ltd.
6 Bonhill Street
London EC2A 4PU
United Kingdom

SAGE Publications India Pvt. Ltd.
M-32 Market
Greater Kailash I
New Delhi 110 048 India

LIBRARY OF CONGRESS CATALOGING-IN-PUBLICATION DATA

Kroeber, A. L. (Alfred Louis), 1876–1960.
The archaeology and pottery of Nazca, Peru: Alfred L. Kroeber's 1926 expedition / by Alfred L. Kroeber and Donald Collier; edited by Patrick H. Carmichael.
p. cm.
Includes bibliographical references and index.
ISBN 0-7619-8964-1 (cloth : alk. paper)
1. Nazca culture. 2. Nazca Lines Site (Peru). 3. Indian pottery—Peru. 4. Peru—Antiquities.
I. Collier, Donald, 1911–1995 II. Carmichael, Patrick H.
III. Title.
F3429.1.N3K76 1998
985'.27—dc21 97-21229
CIP

98 99 00 01 02 03 04 9 8 7 6 5 4 3 2 1

Printed in the United States of America

*Design and Production:* Gordon Chun Design, Berkeley, California
*Editorial Management:* Jennifer Collier
*Copyediting:* Deborah Schoenholz

Illustrations in this volume provided courtesy of The Field Museum, Chicago, Illinois.

Color photographs are by John Weinstein, Photography Department, The Field Museum.

Back cover photo provided courtesy of the Bancroft Library.

W. D. Strong's map, figure 68, reproduced by permission of the Society for American Archaeology, from *American Antiquity*, vol. 22, no. 4, 1957.

# TABLE OF CONTENTS

## EDITOR'S ACKNOWLEDGMENTS

I wish to thank The Field Museum for the travel grants that allowed me to return to the collections and prepare this book. Special thanks go to my colleagues in Anthropology, Collections, Photography, Illustration, and The Field Museum Press for their assistance and patience over the years.

I wish to express deep gratitude to Donald Collier for his encouragement, generous hospitality, and continuous support during this endeavor.

The Department of Archaeology, University of Calgary, made a singular contribution in providing clerical and material support. Elizabeth Carmichael deserves special credit for giving up many evenings and weekends to transfer the original draft onto a word processor.

PATRICK H. CARMICHAEL
Department of Archaeology
University of Calgary

# LIST OF TABLES AND ILLUSTRATIONS

## TABLES



## ILLUSTRATIONS

*Abbreviations*

MAP Museo de Arqueología Peruana (Magdalena)
EH Early Horizon
EIP Early Intermediate Period
(N3) Nazca stylistic phase 3, Berkeley seriation
MH Middle Horizon
LIP Late Intermediate Period

The Field Museum of Natural History photo negative numbers appear in square brackets [ ], while object accession numbers and Kroeber's pottery seriation appear in parentheses ( ).

*Figures*

*Plates*

# ABOUT THE AUTHORS

ALFRED LEWIS KROEBER (1876–1960) was one of the great anthropologists of his time. His prolific and innovative work was central in shaping the field of anthropology, and was foundational to the emergence of New World archaeology as a scientific discipline. Kroeber taught at the University of California at Berkeley from 1901–1941, where he founded what is now the university's Hearst Museum of Anthropology, and for many years he was chair of the anthropology department and director of the museum. His many areas of research included the archaeology and ethnology of California, and in 1925 the Bureau of American Ethnology published his classic *Handbook of the Indians of California.* To the end of his life, he never ceased to be an active scholar, serving as a visiting professor at Columbia, Harvard, Yale, Brandeis, and Chicago after retirement, as well as continuing to be a prominent emeritus faculty member at Berkeley.

Kroeber was a pioneer in using systematically compiled archaeological evidence to construct cultural chronologies. In 1915 he began a typological seriation of Zuni ceramics, and in the early 1920s applied this technique to Max Uhle's Peruvian collections, which were housed at Berkeley. In 1925, having established a cultural chronology which would remain definitive in Peruvian archaeology for many years, he began to work in Peru, where he initiated an important collaborative relationship with the prominent Peruvian archaeologist Julio C. Tello.

The Field Museum of Natural History in Chicago was a crucial institutional pole for Kroeber's fieldwork. By 1903 he was already making ethnographic collections for The Field Museum, and in 1925 he was awarded financial support to conduct the First Marshall Field Archaeological Expedition to Peru. Thus began a prolific relationship with the museum, whose holdings in Peruvian archaeology nearly doubled as a result of excavations in the Lima, Cañete, and Nazca Valleys. The year 1926 saw the Second Marshall Field Expedition to Peru, again directed by Kroeber, as well as Kroeber's appointment as a research associate at The Field Museum. The publication of the present book finally completes the set of reports deriving from these expeditions.

Upon Kroeber's death, Donald Collier observed in an obituary that his passing marked the end of an era in American anthropology, for Kroeber was intellectually at home in all of the now more segregated fields of archaeology, ethnology, linguistics, and folklore.

DONALD COLLIER (1911–1995) was Curator of Middle and South American Archaeology and Ethnology at The Field Museum, where he also served as Chief Curator of Anthropology between 1964 and 1970. His monographs reported archaeological research in Ecuador and Peru, as well as the Pacific Northwest, and his study *Cultural Chronology and Change* (1955) was undertaken as part of the Virú Valley Project, a major interdisciplinary research program carried out on the North Coast of Peru. *Indians before Columbus* (1947, with Paul Martin and George Quimby) was for many years a basic reference on the archaeology of North America, and he wrote numerous articles on archaeology, American Indians, museology, exhibits, radiocarbon dating, and related topics. Collier designed a series of innovative permanent exhibits at The Field Museum, and his exhibition catalogs include *Indian Art of the Americas* (1959) and *Ancient Ecuador* (1975, with Donald Lathrap and Helen Chandra). As a lecturer in anthropology at the University of Chicago between 1950 and 1970, he helped to organize and teach one of the first museology courses for anthropologists, and later in his career he was centrally involved in efforts to develop computer catalogs for museum anthropology collections. He was a founding trustee of the Council on Museum Anthropology.

PATRICK H. CARMICHAEL is a Research Associate with the Institute of Andean Studies, Berkeley, and Adjunct Assistant Professor in the Department of Archaeology at the University of Calgary. Since 1979 he has participated in studies of Inca and pre-Inca cultures in the central and northern Peruvian Andes and the desert south coast. His contributions to Nasca studies include original research on mortuary patterns, marine resource exploitation, ceramic technology, and iconographic analysis.

KATHARINA J. SCHREIBER is a Professor of Anthropology, and currently chair of the department of anthropology, at the University of California at Santa Barbara. Her initial work in Peru was carried out between 1974 and 1982 in Ayacucho, where she studied the Wari Empire (AD 750–1000), its architecture, and its political and economic control of provincial regions. This research resulted in her book, *Wari Imperialism in Middle Horizon Peru.* In 1984 she turned her interests to Nasca and undertook a study of prehistoric irrigation; her forthcoming book on the subject, *Los Puquios de Nasca: Paleotecnologia Hidraúlica de la Costa Sur Peruana*, will be published in Lima. She also initiated a series of systematic regional surveys of the southern valleys of the Nasca drainage, locating and recording more than 600 archaeological sites to date. As a consequence of that work, she has been able to relocate most of the sites studied by Kroeber in 1926.

# PREFACE

*Patrick H. Carmichael* (1993)

PREPARATION OF THIS VOLUME WAS WELL ADVANCED in 1960 but ceased with Alfred Kroeber's death in October of that year. I never knew Alfred Kroeber, although in the course of editing this work I have felt close to him, especially while sorting through his hand-written field notes and correspondence to fill gaps and answer queries penciled along margins in his hand. Donald Collier first introduced me to the manuscript in 1986 when I was a graduate student. With a travel grant from The Field Museum and enthusiastic support from Robert Feldman and Donald Collier, I was able to spend several months in Chicago studying the collections described in this book. At that time and during subsequent visits, Collier graciously extended every assistance and invited me to edit the manuscript for publication. I reassembled the earlier drafts and illustrations, answered questions penciled on the originals, completed and organized the figures, checked metric and statistical data, completed the pottery descriptions from Collier's notes, and undertook the final editing, a process that continued over several years.

Donald Collier's immense contributions to this work are recorded in Kroeber's Introduction. Collier's career at The Field Museum spanned half a century. He served as Curator of South American Archaeology and Ethnology (1941–1964), Chief Curator in the Department of Anthropology (1964–1970), and Curator of Middle and South American Archaeology and Ethnology (1971–1976). During this time he mounted many exhibitions and contributed numerous scholarly articles to American archaeology, ethnology, and museology. He continued his distinguished career at the museum as Curator Emeritus until his retirement to California in 1991.

In the division of labor between the authors, Kroeber wrote the narrative account and overall interpretations, while Collier provided most of the description and analysis of specimens.

### EDITORIAL COMMENT

Editorial changes have been kept to a minimum to ensure that the current text remains faithful to the original. There has been no attempt to update or reinterpret the flow of discussion. Historical accuracy is best served by letting the record stand as Kroeber left it. Publishing this volume in its original form also ensures continuity with Kroeber's earlier Field Museum reports on Peruvian archaeology, allowing the current work to be used in the same manner.

Editorial additions to the original text have been placed in square brackets, [ ]. For the most part these consist of notations providing additional detail, such as the biological age and sex of skeletal remains. Notations within round brackets, ( ), are in the original. Where Kroeber was unsure about a particular description, location, interpretation, and so forth, he used the convention "(sic)" to indicate his uncertainty.

Throughout this volume, Kroeber often refers to himself in the third person. For example, in Chapter 3 he writes, "The measurements of the structures are taken from Kroeber's notebook . . .," and, "The discrepancy is not helped by Kroeber's data. . . ." These are Kroeber's words, and not the commentary of a second party.

Following the convention of his time Kroeber consistently spelled Nazca with a "z." In recent years it has become common practice to differentiate the river, town, and geographical region of that name from the archaeological culture by spelling the former with a "z" and the latter with an "s"—the Nasca culture. Here, and probably for the last time, the original "z" spelling is maintained to preserve historical flavor.

Grave and pottery descriptions are often in point form, for Kroeber was transcribing directly from his notes. I have not set these accounts into full sentence structure in order to avoid inadvertently altering the nuance or meaning of a passage. The descriptions are generally clear, and in instances where questions or ambiguities arise it is best to let the record stand rather than impose potentially erroneous interpretations.

Notations in the original draft indicate that Kroeber had intended to write additional chapters on vessel shapes, slip colors, and pigments and a comparison of his results with those of Duncan Strong, John Rowe, and Lawrence Dawson. Unfortunately, these were never realized. If in some parts of this text the reader receives the impression of being provided with information leading to a larger conclusion, yet finds none, it is for this reason. There are missing chapters. The text therefore ends abruptly without formal conclusions. This is vexing but is best left as is, for I do not propose to second guess Alfred Kroeber. However, the data presented are important in their own right and should stimulate future researchers to follow Kroeber's lead. As one reviewer put it, "It is the data orientation of Kroeber that has led to his immortality. Interpretations are often fad-biases. They come and go. But the field data live on forever."

## VOLUME ORGANIZATION

Kroeber's Introduction describes the range of materials he encountered and the rationale leading to his focus on pottery. His review of field work and attempts to chronologically order the Nasca ceramic sequence up to 1960 provide important historical background to the study. Chapter 1 gives a fascinating account of field work and conditions in 1926 as Kroeber recounts an archaeological expedition of that era. The Nasca region and Kroeber's site locations are described in Chapter 2. Additional information on individual sites is found under the respective headings in Chapter 3.

The excavations described in Chapter 3 are central to this volume. The accounts provide the context upon which all subsequent interpretations rest. Sites and their internal features are discussed in the order in which they were encountered. The reader is here alerted to the great range of materials found in the graves, all identified by museum accession numbers, and the potential for future research on aspects of this remarkable collection.

Chapter 4 provides a rare descriptive account of Nasca architectural features (see Architecture, below). This chapter concludes the field work section; the remaining chapters deal primarily with ceramic analysis.

Chapter 5 is essential for understanding the organization, descriptions, and deliberations in Chapters 6 through 13, and serves as an introduction to the ceramic analysis.

Up to Chapter 4, findings are dealt with in sequence, but from Chapter 6 onward the pottery is treated by stylistic phase. All of the gravelots from a given phase are considered together, irrespective of their original locale. However, the pottery from each grave is discussed as a unit and site origin is noted, so that provenience is not lost but subordinated to stylistic comparison.

Discussion of Kroeber's earliest Nasca material, phase *A0*, is left for Chapter 12 because findings were limited and attain more significance by contrast with phases *A1* through *Y2*. Although the 1926 expedition was primarily oriented toward Nasca cultural remains, Kroeber and his assistant William Schenck also encountered post-Nasca material corresponding to the Middle Horizon, Late Intermediate, and Late Horizon periods in modern terminology. These findings are summarized in Chapter 13.

## HISTORICAL OVERVIEW

The material presented in this study constitutes the largest documented collection of Nasca mortuary goods in existence. No collection of this nature and size has ever been published in such detail. In the following chapters, the reader will find individual descriptions of over 350 ceramic vessels, and accession numbers for nonceramic artifacts are given throughout to guide researchers toward future study material.

Among the many contributions offered here are Kroeber's observations on Nasca sites and archaeological features in 1926. These provide a reference by which to measure the amount of destruction that has taken place since, and his descriptions of Nazca Lines and filtration galleries constitute some of the earliest recordings of these phenomena.

This volume also represents Kroeber's final thoughts on Nasca pottery—a subject that occupied him throughout much of his career. Introduced to Nasca studies by Max Uhle in the early years of this century, Kroeber published Uhle's collection from the Ica Valley with Duncan Strong in 1924 and Uhle's collection from Nazca with Anna Gayton in 1927. The latter, written in 1925–1926 (prior to his Nazca field work), constitutes the first serious attempt to seriate Nasca pottery. In 1925, Kroeber worked in several valleys on the central and northern Peruvian coast and made a short reconnaissance down to Nazca. At that time he determined to spend the entire 1926 field season in Nazca.

Kroeber's first two field seasons in Peru were remarkably productive. In later years he devoted much of his Andean writing to documenting the 1925 findings (Kroeber 1926, 1930, 1937, and 1954). However, aside from collaborating with Lila O'Neale on Nasca textiles (O'Neale and Kroeber 1930; O'Neale 1936, 1937) and some discussion in his overview of Peruvian archaeology (Kroeber 1944), he did not return to the 1926 Nazca data until the 1950s.

In 1953, before embarking on the current volume, Kroeber began revising the 1927 seriation to address weaknesses and ambiguities and to provide a more solid framework for the work at hand (Kroeber 1956). The 1956 seriation was partially successful; here it is taken further.

The late 1950s were exciting times in Nasca studies. Duncan Strong's Columbia team and John Rowe's Berkeley crew had returned from new surveys and excavations in the Nazca region, and Lawrence Dawson was completing a new Nasca seriation at Berkeley. It was in this context of renewed interest and new finds that Kroeber began to write the current volume, his last contribution to Nasca studies.

## SITE LOCATIONS

The descriptions of site locations given in Chapters 2 and 3, Table 1, and Figure 8 are not as precise as modern researchers would prefer, for Kroeber was working without the benefit of government maps and air photos. However, Kroeber's sites were relocated during Katharina Schreiber's recent surveys and, together with a new map, are listed in her overview at the end of this volume.

As to the accuracy of features shown in the numerous site sketch maps, I can verify that I have undertaken field inspections of the great site of Cahuachi following Kroeber's maps (Figs. 61, 66, 67, and 69) and encountered no difficulty identifying his locations, including the important subsite of Cahuachi A. I have no doubt that his other maps are as accurate.

## FIELD METHODOLOGY

The field methods employed by the 1926 expedition were remarkably thorough for the era; indeed, such standards were not applied in the region again until the 1950s. Precise measurements were recorded in the metric system and, for the most part, the entire contents of the graves were preserved. These included potsherds, scraps of cloth, hair bundles, and an array of oddments considered incidental and abandoned by Kroeber's contemporaries. Records and collections thus provide a complete document of each interment, which has led to several unexpected revelations, such as the interconnection of graves through articulating sherds and the contribution of human-hair artifacts by several individuals to a single burial.

Kroeber's concern with complete tomb contents stemmed from his conviction that gravelots were essentially units of contemporaneity: in effect, that all of the objects in a grave were likely the property of one person or family and that all were probably produced within a generation and therefore in use at one time. Grave goods, especially painted ceramic vessels, thus provided the key to a chronology based on stylistic variation through time. Few would argue with this approach today, although the principle, while known, had little currency in American archaeology in 1926.

Kroeber was also ahead of his contemporaries in the use of stratigraphy. At Huayurí (Chapter 3), he initiated a test excavation in 50-cm levels through refuse in an attempt to discern ceramic changes at different depths. The results were negative; the method exceptional for the era. This effort marked the first systematic use of stratigraphic excavation in Peruvian archaeology. Later, at Ocongalla West B, Kroeber carefully recorded a series of Nasca burials encountered below pure strata of later materials (Figs. 44, 46). The significance of these stratigraphic separations are discussed (and underlined) in the text as they were in the original field notes. Although standard practice today, the principles and applications of stratigraphy were largely unrecognized in 1926.

William Schenck supervised many of the excavations and deserves equal credit for thorough recording. Schenck's earlier work in California archaeology is recognized as the most detailed and comprehensive of his generation. To the great credit of both Kroeber and Schenck, the work presented in this study is as valuable and applicable today as it was in 1926.

## GRAVES AND "GRAVES"

One idiosyncratic procedure employed throughout the 1926 field season requires mention at the outset. The term "grave" was applied to all excavations regardless of whether or not a human interment was encountered. We find, for example, that at Majoro Chico A, Grave 10 contained fragments of a ceramic antara only, Grave 11 a trophy head, Grave 19 a cookpot, and Grave 22 a camelid skeleton. In these instances, there was no grave shaft or human burial. Such finds were probably dedicatory offerings within a cemetery context. Conversely, on occasion some graves were actually large, meandering excavations that encountered two or three separate interments, such as Majoro Chico A, Graves 7 and 14, and Agua Santa, Grave 1. In these cases I have distinguished the separate interments from each grave in the text as, for example, Grave 14A, 14B, and 14C. A few lots purchased from looters were also given grave numbers, such as Agua Santa, Graves 14, 15, and 16.

## AGING AND SEXING OF SKELETAL REMAINS

The 1926 expedition recovered human remains from many of the excavated graves. These now include 117 entries in the museum's catalogue, each entry representing from one to a dozen or more elements from an individual. However, some remains were so fragile that they could not be recovered and had to be left *in situ*.

Aging and sexing of skeletal remains was undertaken in the field by Kroeber and Schenck, including those of individuals not recovered. Some of their field observations, as given in Chapter 3, were very precise; others were brief, such as "an old woman." The age and sex of the interments are important for accurate reconstructions of Nasca mortuary customs, social differentiation, and the circulation of goods (artifact types) within Nasca society. Thus where skeletal remains are not available for reexamination, how much faith may we place in the original field observations?

In 1986, physical anthropologist Lyle Konigsberg completed a general inventory of the museum's skeletal collections, including those recovered by Kroeber and Schenck. This was done without reference to the original reports. Konigsberg's age and sex determinations for the Nasca material agree in virtually all instances with the original field assessments; hence, we may have faith in observations on other skeletal remains that were not kept. Additional remarks from Konigsberg's inventory regarding age and sex have been added to the text of Chapter 3 where applicable.

**ARCHITECTURE**

Very little has been published on the ancient architecture and construction methods of the Nazca region. Chapter 4 makes a singular contribution to Nasca studies with its detailed discussion of adobe shapes and dimensions and wall construction methods at several sites. Valuable information is also provided in the site descriptions of Chapter 3. In this chapter, the reader will find descriptions of Nasca mounds at Ocongalla Zero and Soisongo A and terrace construction at Cahuachi (discussed near the beginning and end of the Cahuachi section in Chapter 3). Post-Nasca structures are also noted, such as the reed-wall enclosures at Ocongalla Zero, the stone walls at Majoro Chico A, and the palisade described in the introduction to Ocongalla West A and B. Descriptions of Paredones and La Estaquería, although brief, are notable for their time.

**NASCA LINES AND FILTRATION GALLERIES**

The Nazca Lines are perhaps the most widely known and enigmatic features of the south coast. They have kept and will continue to keep popular writers and scientific investigators preoccupied for a long time. Kroeber made no special study of these features, but he noted their presence and described and illustrated several. This record, published here for the first time, must be counted among the earliest recordings and duly noted in future histories. His photographs and illustrations are perhaps the earliest; some of his illustrations are shown in Figures 5–6, 9–10.

Kroeber's observations on Nazca Lines appear in Chapter 3, at the sites of La Calera and Aja B, where he describes the *caminos del Inca*, or "ray roads," and suggests that they may have been used for religious processions or games. Also under La Calera, he describes a wide, straight line running from Ocucaje to Santa Cruz, effectively connecting Ica with the Río Grande drainage.

Filtration galleries, another subject of much debate, are mentioned for the Taruga area in Chapter 3. Here, Kroeber refers to *puquios*, but he is clearly describing *ojos*, or the vertical shafts that punctuate the underground galleries. He recounts the claim that in Taruga twenty-eight had been located and cleaned in 1925, while some eighty more were said to exist in the Las Trancas region. The references are again brief but of historical note.

**THE NASCA POTTERY SEQUENCE**

This publication presents Kroeber's final assessment of the Nasca pottery sequence, a subject that continued to interest him for over forty years. His 1927 seriation with Anna Gayton was not widely adopted, nor was his 1956 reevaluation. The reader may judge the extent to which the current analysis improves on these earlier studies.

This manuscript contains references to several researchers' Nasca seriation systems, all of which use alphabetical denotation for their categories. However, categories such as "Nazca A" may or may not mean the same thing in other systems as in Alfred Kroeber's. In order to facilitate the reader's quicker comprehension, we have always and only presented Kroeber's seriation categories in italics.

The system used by most Peruvianists today is the similiary seriation developed by Lawrence Dawson under John Rowe's supervision at the University of California, Berkeley, in the 1950s. Dawson was refining his seriation, which identifies nine stylistic phases, at the same time Kroeber was preparing the current report, and the two men interacted and compared notes frequently. There was undoubtedly an atmosphere of friendly competition at this time and perhaps some urgency to publish or delay and await the other's results. Although Dawson's system is widely used today and Kroeber's is seldom mentioned, it is ironic that after so many years, Kroeber is still the first to present his final results with the publication of this volume; Dawson's seriation still has not been published in its entirety. Kroeber remains the only author to attempt a full description of the entire Nasca stylistic sequence.

Kroeber had no special argument with Dawson's approach; however, he continued to favor the methods of his original study in the 1920s, which entailed a quantitative stylistic analysis based on *shape*, *color*, and *design*. As illustrated in the current work, major emphasis is placed on shape, color, and quantitative distributions. Design or motif is also taken into account but in partial and subordinate terms. Kroeber recognized the utility of design-feature analysis but chose to stand by his earlier statement: "The identification, classification, and validation of painted design features is at least equally important, but done systematically it will be a long job, and I leave it in other hands" (Kroeber 1956, 340).

In this volume Kroeber defines seven Nasca stylistic phases, labeled *A0*, *A1*, *A2*, *B1*, *B2*, *Y1*, *Y2*. At first glance this appears to parallel Dawson's phases 1–9, and there is a temptation to reconcile the two schemes. In fact, there are many similarities, and had Kroeber lived longer, there may have been a merger eventually. But in his absence it would be presumptuous to attempt such a union, for there remain as many points of disagreement. We find, for example, that some vessels classified by Kroeber as phase *A1* and *A2* and many of his *B2* pieces are all phase 5 in Dawson's Berkeley Seriation, while other *A1* vessels correspond to Dawson's phase 3 and some *B2* pots with his phase 7. The two schemes are not directly convertible. However, in spite of disagreements each system supports the other in demonstrating that the Nazca style is amenable to division into a series of stylistic subphases, and these provide a degree of chronological control seldom achieved in archaeology.

Kroeber's sequence is presented in the text as he intended, without annotation, to stand on its own merits. Phase *A0* is considered in Chapter 12. Phase *A1* is discussed more in relation to *A2* in Chapter 7, and phase *B1* and *B2* characteristics are defined in Chapter 8. The later phases, *Y1* and *Y2*, are treated in Chapter 10.

For ease of comparison I have classified the illustrated Nasca vessels according to Dawson's Berkeley Seriation in the figure captions, that is, (N3), or Nazca stylistic phase 3, Berkeley Seriation (see List of Illustrations).

### Editorial Introduction to the Ceramic Descriptions: Methods and Abbreviations

In following the pottery descriptions given in Chapters 6 through 12, it is important for the reader to bear in mind that these sections were drafted shortly after the appearance of Kroeber's 1956 monograph, *Toward Definition of the Nazca Style*, which served as a point of departure for the current work. In these accounts, Kroeber naturally assumes the reader is familiar with this earlier work and, in the context of 1960, it would have been redundant to repeat his methods and deliberations of 1956. A close reading of the current text therefore requires some familiarity with the 1956 monograph. This introductory note provides a few points of clarification for those less familiar with Kroeber's earlier work.

I could find no record of the abbreviations and vessel shape categories used in the pottery descriptions among the many documents preserved at The Field Museum. Presumably they had not been drafted at the time of Kroeber's death. Notations in the original manuscript indicate that Kroeber had intended to devote an entire chapter to the subject of vessel shapes and another to colors and pigments. Unfortunately, these were never realized. The shape charts in Chapter 5, Figures 90 and 91, are based on an earlier, partial draft that I completed from Kroeber's 1956 work and references in this text. Kroeber discusses Nasca *Y* shapes in Chapter 10. In treating vessel shapes, Kroeber proceeds directly from his 1956 work, and many of the forms identified here correspond to his earlier categories (Kroeber 1956, 377–381). However, there are several changes from the 1956 classification. The definitions of shapes *A* and *B* have been modified, shape *G* was eliminated but *GG* retained, and *F* was included as a distinct shape. I have added shapes *Ba–d* and *Ea* because they appear visually dissimilar from *B* and *E*.

The reader should also be aware that Kroeber sometimes used design location to define his shape categories. For example, the primary difference between plates (*A*) and bowls (*B*) is that plates have painted designs on their interiors while bowls are painted on their exteriors.

There are no examples of shapes *I1* or *Y2* among the current materials. They were defined in 1956 and are included in Figure 90 to complete the numerical sequences. The 1956 monograph describes several subtypes for some shapes that are represented here by a single letter, for example *C* and *V*. As these varieties play no special part in the current text, they have not been included in the shape chart.

Abbreviations used in the pottery descriptions are as follows:

METRICS

H – height
D – diameter
H/D – height/diameter percentage ratio

The height/diameter percentage ratio was introduced by Kroeber as a useful means of characterizing the various pottery shapes. It is determined by dividing maximum vessel height by maximum diameter and multiplying by 100. The resulting figure is then rounded to the nearest whole number.

COLOR ABBREVIATIONS

B – black
C – cream
F – flesh
G – gray
O – orange
V – violet (sometimes a dark reddish purple)

W – white
Y – yellow
LBr – light brown
DBr – dark brown
LR – light red
DR – dark red

## SUBSEQUENT RESEARCH ON THIS COLLECTION

There has been comparatively little research on this remarkable collection since 1960, a situation that this publication may rectify, for the research potential remains enormous. Two studies that relied in part on Kroeber's findings deserve brief mention.

Donald Proulx (1968) used twenty of Kroeber's gravelots in his definitive stylistic analysis of phase 3 and 4 ceramics (Berkeley Seriation). The Kroeber specimens are not treated individually in the text but form an important component in the larger sample, which included hundreds of vessels from Ica and Nazca. Kroeber's gravelots are listed in Proulx's Appendix 3, where Proulx also classifies the vessels according to shape and his refined seriation of phases 3A, 3B, 3C, 3D and 4.

The burials described in this volume also formed the core data set for my study of Nasca burial customs and society (Carmichael 1988). I used ninety-nine of Kroeber's tombs in my total sample of 213 burials. Kroeber's material is not treated separately within the larger sample, but frequent references are made to specific finds throughout. Kroeber's graves are listed by phase (Berkeley Seriation) in Appendix 1 of the study.

### Analysis of Human Hair Artifacts

Kroeber found artifacts manufactured from human hair in some well preserved burials. These objects consist of hair bundles, braids, wigs, and twine and are preserved at The Field Museum today. The presence of several hair objects in a single burial provided an opportunity to determine through forensic analysis whether such objects were manufactured from the hair of one individual (the deceased) or whether various individuals were represented (contributed grave goods), thus providing a means of testing the following propositions: a) that all grave goods belonged to the deceased; b) that grave goods were contributed by members of the funeral party.

The samples from Soisongo A, Grave 1 and Cahuachi A, Graves 12 and 13 indicate that several different persons contributed the hair artifacts to each of these burials. The Cahuachi burials are particularly interesting. Graves 12 and 13 were located side-by-side in a line of burials. Braid fragments in Grave 12 matched with a hair bundle in Grave 13, suggesting that one person contributed to both tombs. Also, a hair bundle in Grave 12 matched the hair of one of the deceased in Grave 13, indicating that Grave 12 preceded Grave 13 in time. Some of the graves in this line of interments were also interconnected by articulating sherds and matching pottery vessels, as noted in Kroeber's discussion. These findings strongly suggest that the burials at Cahuachi A represent a family or lineage cemetery.

Grave 18 at Cantayo presents a different situation. In my opinion this grave encountered an offering cache above a child burial. The two events may or may not be related. Forensic analysis of hair artifacts in the offering cache indicates they were all manufactured from the hair of one individual but not the child interred below (the hair strands are too thick and coarse, and the total amount of hair is too abundant for an infant). The customs surrounding human burials and offering caches evidently varied (Carmichael et al., n.d.).

### Stable Isotope Analysis and Nasca Diet

Stable isotope analysis is one of the most direct means of evaluating prehistoric diet. The relative contributions of all food groups are recorded as carbon, nitrogen, and sulfur isotope values in human bone, hair, and soft tissue. The large number of Nasca remains recovered by Kroeber provide an excellent sample for isotope analysis because the collection is well documented and includes desiccated soft tissue and hair in addition to skeletal elements.

In 1989, an isotope study was initiated to determine the relative contribution of maritime resources to the Nasca diet, for while the Nasca are best known from the inland areas studied by Kroeber, the proximity of the ocean allows the potential of significant marine input. A total of sixty-eight samples of human bone, hair, and skin from several of Kroeber's sites were analyzed for carbon, nitrogen, and sulfur isotope ratios. The samples included male and female individuals of differing status from the entire span of the Early Intermediate Period (EIP) in addition to five samples from the Middle Horizon (MH) and one from the Late Intermediate Period (LIP). For the most part, bone samples taken from the skeletal collection consisted of small rib fragments, but where these were not available the distal end of a minor element was removed and, in a few instances, a circular plug was extracted from large elements.

Isotope results from the EIP sample were uniform and were paralleled by the more-limited MH sample. The contribution from marine resources was less than 10 percent throughout the EIP, while approximately 50 percent of bone carbon was ultimately derived from maize. The lone LIP sample was somewhat more enriched from both marine foods and maize. It was concluded that while marine resources have tremendous food potential, they played no special role in the agrarian-based Nasca dietary economy (Kennedy and Carmichael 1991).

### PROPER USE OF THIS VOLUME AS A RESEARCH GUIDE

This volume provides a great amount of detailed information on a variety of topics, but the reader should be aware that complete information on a given subject (whether a site, a burial, or a particular vessel) is seldom presented in one place and may be spread over two or three chapters. This is not as cumbersome as it may at first appear. The report follows a logical, orderly method of presentation, and the thorough researcher will have no difficulty cross-referencing data.

The key to understanding cross-referenced information is found in the numerous chapter, section, and subsection headings in the Table of Contents. If, for example, the reader is interested in a particular site and its architectural configurations, the appropriate sections will be found in the introduction to each site in Chapter 3 and among the details of wall construction and adobes in Chapter 4, where the sites are again listed under subheadings.

To understand the context and pottery associations of a particular grave, the researcher should be familiar with local site conditions (extent of looting, etc.) given in the site introductions in Chapter 3; the account of the excavation, also in Chapter 3; and the pottery descriptions given in a later chapter as well as the vessel illustrations. To facilitate cross-referencing, I have listed the appropriate pottery chapter and illustration numbers with the ceramic contents of each grave discussed in Chapter 3. Additional information on graves and levels of confidence in the associations is often provided with the ceramic descriptions. Researchers more interested in the tombs than the pottery should still consult the pottery chapters. Conversely, those interested more in the pottery should also review the excavation accounts for clues to associations and disturbance factors. Reliance on the figures alone for gravelot associations can lead to erroneous conclusions, for some of the gravelots are mixed, as clearly indicated in the text.

The importance of cross-checking data in separate chapters is demonstrated by Ocongalla Zero, Grave 3. The vessels from this grave are illustrated in Figures 286–290. In Dawson's Berkeley Seriation, these pots correspond to phases 5 and 6. Kroeber ultimately classifies them all as *B2* in Chapter 9, although he is troubled by features on a couple of the vessels that he feels are earlier. The problem is readily resolved in the Chapter 3 account of the excavation where it is evident that this grave was a large excavation that encountered two or possibly three separate burial events. Similarly, the excavation of Grave 18 at Cantayo Cax, which contained a child and a large urn full of oddities, is presented in a brief, straightforward fashion in Chapter 3, but further discussion in Chapter 12 reveals Kroeber's well-founded doubts about the validity of the child and urn association. In another example, Grave 9 at Ocongalla West B is also summarily described in Chapter 3, but in Chapter 9, where the pottery is discussed, a wealth of additional information on the exact placement of each item in the tomb is also provided.

Used carefully, this report provides a tremendous amount of information, and where questions arise in one chapter they are frequently answered in another. A careful perusal of the Table of Contents will provide all necessary direction for cross-checking data and alert the reader to the full potential of this volume.

### REFERENCES

Carmichael, P. H. 1988. Nasca mortuary customs: Death and ancient society on the south coast of Peru. Ph.D. diss., University of Calgary. Microfilms International (1990), no. 8918465:1–587. Ann Arbor, Michigan.

Carmichael, P. H., B. K. Kennedy and J. L. Lacapra. n.d. Unbraiding the past: A forensic examination of Nasca hair artifacts. Manuscript.

Kennedy, B. K. and P. H. Carmichael. 1991. The role of marine resources in Nasca diet. Paper presented at the 31st Annual Meeting of the Institute for Andean Studies, Berkeley.

Proulx, D. A. 1968. *Local Differences and Time Differences in Nasca Pottery.* University of California Publications in Anthropology, vol. 5, 1–48.

# INTRODUCTION *Alfred L. Kroeber* (1960)

This monograph is the joint production of Alfred Kroeber and Donald Collier on archaeological explorations and excavated discoveries made in the Nazca Valley in south-central Peru in 1926 by Kroeber and William Schenck. Both authors are on the staff of The Field Museum. Kroeber, retired from the University of California, has been Research Associate in American Archaeology in the museum since 1925, and Collier Curator of South American Archaeology and Ethnology since 1941. Both authors have explored repeatedly in Peru.

There has been a division of labor in the preparation of the monograph, sharpened by geographical separation of residence. Kroeber collected and catalogued the material, mainly designated those [items] to be photographed, wrote the first draft of the text, and supervised most of the drawings, largely based on sketches made by him in the field. Collier assembled, measured, and described in detail on cards the objects selected, supervised their photographing, answered questions and made corrections, and assisted with revisions, a process that continued reciprocally until the text was fully agreed upon by both authors.

Because Nazca ruins and structures are modest in comparison with the fine ceramics and textiles contained in Nazca cemeteries, more stress was laid by the 1926 expedition on grave contents and the interrelations of these as intact units than on settlements and buildings. Most of the graves are simply sunk deep into the sandy soil of a plain or gentle slope and give no surface indication of their presence unless neighboring graves have been opened by treasure or pot hunters.

For this reason, the sites themselves, and even the cemeteries, can be described rather briefly, and our main attention will be devoted to the description, classification, and interpretation of the grave furnishings recovered. Among these, ceramics are outstanding. Nazca textiles are equally impressive but are preserved only in special cases. There is not enough rain in Nazca to reach them, even through the centuries, but some groundwater from the rivers and ditches does penetrate to most cemeteries, which tend to lie just outside and barely above the cultivation. As a result, many graves and even cemeteries, especially of the earlier periods on which the expedition's interest was concentrated, contain no cloth at all: it has long since rotted away. The principal significant find of textiles was made only at the very end of the expedition's sojourn, in and about a series of early Nazca *A* graves at Cahuachi, the most downstream site explored, but also high terraced and well drained. These cloths and embroideries have been described by Lila O'Neale (1937). The textiles found here and there elsewhere in the valley will ultimately be of considerable importance, even when fragmentary, because of their attribution to specific phases of Nazca culture history by their association within graves with the more numerous pottery objects, nearly all of which have their place in the developmental scheme of the Nazca culture as it is being gradually determined in the present and other monographs. We therefore in general only call attention to the presence of such non-Cahuachi textiles; their full significance will emerge after this monograph when they, with their datings, are compared with other phase-dated cloth samples from the region.

More or less the same holds for most other artifacts, many of which decay in contact with moisture about as rapidly as textiles. Their preservation thus depends on accidents of immediate situation and is spotty. Artifacts like baskets, pyrographed gourd vessels, atlatls, clubs, and other wooden objects will also come into their full significance on ultimate comparison with like objects from the area, when their association with definite stages in the pottery series will help build up likenesses, distinctions, classifications, and datings for whole classes of objects.

Objects of metal form an exception, because metals, with one exception, seem to have reached Nazca late in its native history. The exception is beaten-out placer gold, which occurs sparingly in the *A*, *B*, and *Y* stages of the Nazca (pre-Tiahuanacoid) culture. The Expedition encountered only two small pieces of sheet gold, one of them found by Dr. Julio C. Tello's assistants, which, by the terms of the permit from the Peruvian government, went to the National Museum of Peru. These circumstances will explain why the present monograph is so heavily centered on ceramics.

It may be added that there is a considerable element of luck even in the preservation of pottery vessels. Thus the pottery of cemeteries Cahuachi A and Aja B is nearly identical in style and phase. Yet the former produced many whole vessels and much cloth, the latter very few intact pots and not a scrap of cloth. The Aja cemetery was barely above the cultivation and in the wide mouth of a side arroyo, which possibly did not flow as a visible stream but once a century. Even pottery is affected by such intermittent but repeated moisture: it softens, absorbs salts, then these crystallize until the weight of the soil breaks the vessel into small pieces. These can be soaked, dried, and often put together again in the museum well enough for their type and even design to be visible; but they mostly suffer somewhat in color, texture, or completeness. Cahuachi A pottery came from a hilltop and was dug out much more often complete, clean, and brilliant.

When these collections were made in 1926, the Nazca culture had been long known for its remarkable ceramics, of which sizable collections had been brought to Chicago, New York, Lima, London, Paris, Berlin, and elsewhere—but none with exact data as to provenience or associations. Scientifically, the culture was first examined in its habitat by Max Uhle, in Ica Valley in 1901 and in the Nazca (Río Grande) drainage in 1905, on expeditions for the University of California. While Uhle announced his discoveries and discussed their significance, he never completed a systematic description of what he found. Eduard Seler in 1923, drawing on the large but dataless collections in Germany and employing his almost preternatural skill in interpreting symbolic and decorative visual representations, analyzed more than 400 painted Nazca pottery designs, with a soundness of judgment that makes nearly all of them seem convincing today. But he treated the style as one large unit, did not try to associate differences of patterns with differences of phase, and, as in most of his Mexican work, simply ignored the time factor. His monograph (Seler 1923), with its 430 excellent drawings, is still one of the largest printed storehouses on Nazca culture ceramics.

Meanwhile, the effort to unravel such an internal chronology had begun in California, where Uhle's full Nazca-style collections, catalogues, and many notes were accessible to Kroeber, Strong, and Gayton. The two former published in 1924 a summary with illustrations of what Uhle had discovered about the Nazca culture (then still called Proto-Nazca) in Ica Valley; and in 1927 Gayton and Kroeber issued a more fully illustrated report on Uhle's collections from Nazca Valley itself. They were forced to substitute for the almost complete lack of excavatory material in the Nazca Valley data, an endeavor to analyze out substyles or phases using the internal evidence afforded by correlation of vessel shapes with painted designs. This resulted in setting up four successive phases or stages: *A*, *AB* (or *X*), *B*, and a decadent *Y*. Tello, at about the same time, inverted the sequence, calling the *B* phase pre-Nazca, and the *A*, Nazca; but he did not elaborate or press this view.

The Gayton-Kroeber scheme was too summary to account for all the facts, so that some Peruvianists stood aloof from it, whereas others used it because there was no other general interpretation. In 1956 there finally appeared *Toward Definition of the Nazca Style*, a review by Kroeber, stimulated in part by his reacquaintance with what he had dug up with Schenck in Nazca Valley in 1926, and in the process of beginning the present monograph. He also drew upon thirty additional years of contact with Peruvian material in museums and publications. This monograph revised the classification of Nazca ceramic shapes, dealt with additional designs, used frequency counts without correlations, and altered the 1927 scheme by resolving stage X into substages of an A–B–Y continuum.

Meanwhile Lawrence Dawson had stylistically seriated the Uhle collections from Nazca in Berkeley, and subsequently several thousand more pottery pieces elsewhere in the United States and Peru into nine phases, beginning with Paracas Necropolis, of which numbers 4 and 5 may be contemporaneous but all others are successive, according to a summary by Rowe (1956, 138, 147). Dawson's full report is awaited with expectancy.

The determination directly by stratigraphy was finally made by Strong in 1952–1953, in association with Stigler, Lilien, and Sonin, on which achievement a fairly full advance report of forty-eight pages has appeared (Strong 1957). Kroeber and Schenck in 1926 had not been blind to stratigraphic possibility, but they were looking for lucky breaks presented by natural agencies or previous treasure hunting. Strong, following up his previous successes in central and northern Peru, depended on massive and deep penetration into refuse in large, important sites. This he accomplished at Nazca primarily at Cahuachi in a series of "cuts," or trenches. In addition, the Columbia expedition surveyed eighty-one sites in the Ica-Río Grande area and did some excavating at fifteen of them. They also opened nine Late Paracas graves at Ocucaje, though none of Proto-Nazca or Early Nazca (the latter a sort of incipient Nazca *A*), six Middle Nazca (our Nazca *A*), and nineteen Late Nazca (our Nazca *B*) graves at Cahuachi, an unknown number of Huaca del Loro-type (Nazca *Y*) graves at Huaca del Loro and at Cahuachi burial area 4, and one Coastal Tiahuanacoid tomb at Ocucaje in the Ica drainage. It is evident that while the phase separations fall somewhat differently in detail and nomenclature, the Columbia results and ours conform well.

Strong and his associates had access to most of our photographs—all that had been made when they published—as we now have the advantage of Strong's preliminary memoir. These have been the principal grapplings with the Nazca problem to date.

Inasmuch as the expedition was primarily directed toward the Nazca culture (including Nazca *Y*), its post-Nazca results come out somewhat scattered. Upon consideration, it has seemed to us likely to be most productive in the end for us to report these Late results only in outline, so that students specializing in Tiahuanacoid and later periods will know what objects and data there are available at The Field Museum still awaiting larger integration.

**CHAPTER 1**

# *History and Itinerary of the Expedition*

IN 1924, DR. BERTHOLD LAUFER, AS HEAD CURATOR of Anthropology, and Director D. C. Davies planned the Captain Marshall Field Archaeological Expedition to Peru with A. L. Kroeber.

The first installment of this expedition was carried out in the first half of 1925. Kroeber went alone and secured his equipment, other than a museum camera, in Lima, including a second-hand model-T Ford car, one of the first motor vehicles to be used in archaeological exploration in Peru (Fig. 1). He put himself at the disposal of Dr. Julio C. Tello, director of the (then) Museo Nacional de Arqueología, who was outgoingly cooperative, demonstrated sites, and secured for the expedition the services of three loyal Indians from Huarochirí. With these three workmen, and without adjutant or assistant, Kroeber, after some preliminary trials, excavated at Marques at the mouth of the Chillón, at Maranga-Aramburú in the valley of Lima, and in Cañete Valley. He also visited parts of the northern coast. The results of most of these studies have been published (Kroeber 1926, 1930, 1937, and 1954).

With excavations at Cañete well under way in the spring of 1925, Kroeber left his diggings and workmen in charge of one of Tello's assistants, Sr. Hurtado—this work becoming a joint undertaking with the National Museum of Peru, which shared in the collections—in order to make a brief reconnaissance of Chincha, Pisco, Ica, and especially Nazca as a basis for future operations. Nazca was surveyed for several days from Paredones down to La Estaquería, with retrieval of surface materials.

After returning to the United States and Chicago in the summer of 1925, Kroeber discussed with Laufer continuance of this exploration, with efforts to be centered at Nazca and directed particularly to the origins and early development of that remarkable culture. It was agreed that the second trip should be made with larger means, on a larger scale, and that Kroeber should be accompanied by his associate William Egbert Schenck, a man of maturity with several years of excavatory experience in California archaeology.

A second objective was to be an endeavor to discover *in situ* the remains of a type of rich embroideries—then vaguely attributed to Pisco or Ica—of which a few splendid examples had begun occasionally to appear in collections or dealers' hands and even in Europe. Near Pisco,

FIGURE 1. *Alfred Kroeber (right) on Peruvian expedition, 1925 [49732]*

in 1925, Kroeber had been given by a *huaquero* a few scraps from such a mantle, with imprecise indications that they came from the arid and uninhabited Paracas peninsula. This was indeed true; and Dr. Tello received similar information, with the result that he was able to discover Paracas—both Cavernas and Necropolis—for his native country, as indeed was fitting, within the same year of 1925.

Nevertheless, exploration of the Nazca culture remained unimpaired as an objective, and Director D. C. Davies received authorization and funds for a second trip from Captain Marshall Field, president of the museum.

On completion of the academic year at the University of California in May of 1926, Kroeber and Schenck, both accompanied by their wives, repaired to Chicago, where Kroeber remained a week, occupied both with planning arrangements with Dr. Laufer for the impending second expedition and attending to the inevitable problems that had come up regarding the restoration, cataloging, exhibition, and publication of the 1925 collections. Another full week was occupied in New York with outfitting, which was required because they planned to live in camp in Nazca Valley close to the excavation sites and yet far enough from irrigated cultivation and settlements to minimize the risk of malaria.

On June 11, the expedition sailed on board one of the four "Santa" passenger ships of the Grace Line, through the Panama Canal, of course, landing at Callao on the morning of June 23. On June 21, while the ship

FIGURE 2. *Expedition workgang at Majoro Chico A [53976]*

discharged cargo at Salaverry, most of a day was available in the valley in which Trujillo is situated for visits to the gigantic Moche pyramid and to the largest city of ancient Peru, Chanchán.

In Lima, headquarters were at the Hotel Plaza directly behind the cathedral. Dr. Tello was as cooperative as the year before, and on July 18, Kroeber was able to write Director Davies in Chicago that the necessary official permit, with favorable terms, had been obtained through the Ministry of Education. This was a short interval as such procedures went in 1926.

About four nights were spent in Huancayo in the interior, reached from Lima by railroad over the nearly 15,000-foot-high pass across the continental watershed, here formed by the first or coastal range of the Andes. In the highlands, archaeological conditions and remains are notably different from those on the coast, which Kroeber had previously experienced, and they were carefully observed. Most striking was a supergigantic pseudopyramid visible from Huancayo, which proved to be a natural trapezoidal mountain face set off by a ravine on each side from which small ditches had been led across the exposed front, giving the effect from the valley of a pyramid in several steps. There were no terraces to speak of, nor any ancient sherds or remains; but enough vegetation followed the horizontal ditches to give the effect of a step pyramid many hundreds of feet high. Local tradition ascribed the seemingly monumental undertaking to the influence of a priest in late Colonial times.

Huancayo's market day fell on Sunday and drew attendance not only from the immediate valley but adjacent ones, with characteristic local styles of weaving. A collection of ponchos, caps, bags, and other textiles were acquired for shipment back to Chicago as first fruits before the expedition had set a spade in the ground.

With a governmental permit in sight, the expedition on July 16 bought a Ford truck and a Ford passenger touring car with Ruckstell axle geared to extra power in sand and heavy going. The higher Ruckstell speed, actually intermediate, proved extremely convenient in ordinary travel, Peruvian roads in 1926 being wholly unsurfaced except for cobbling of city streets. Even the north-south road that was later to become the Pan-American Highway was dirt, and often sand.

Through Dr. Tello, a native of Huarochirí, word was sent to the three mountain Indians from the province who had done Kroeber's digging for him on the 1925 expedition. The most mature of the three could not come, but Pedro Macavilca and Pablo Torres reported at Lima and brought with them a *primo*, or first cousin, of Pedro's, Pablo Pomajulcu (called by the expedition by his family name to avoid confusion) who proved to be exceptionally deft with his fingers in salvaging and retrieving broken vessels in deep graves, and was often sent in for the final stage of grave excavations mainly dug by local labor. Pedro was an unusually adaptable archaeological worker, and Torres, who had formerly been drafted into the Peruvian army, was not only thoroughly steady but proved to be a competent cook, both in 1925 and when the 1926 expedition's work force began to shrink. These three mountain Indians formed the permanent core of the fluctuating digging crew employed by the expedition and were engaged in advance for the Nazca trip, from the day of leaving Lima until return to it; which dates proved to be July 18 and October 16. The prevailing rate for day labor on the coast at that time was two *soles*. On account of their experience, character, and reliability and being away from their homes, the engagement of three Huarochírians was agreed upon at three soles a day, the same paid in the field to *caporales*, or foremen.

Aristide Palacios was engaged as chauffeur—skilled labor—at four soles, and a burly Argentinian, Antonio Nolli (soon nicknamed Firpo), drove the truck until he was superseded, after a time at Nazca, by Fabio Lopez.

When the expedition's general permit was received July 18, an error was discovered in the driving licenses that had to be corrected, and the actual start from Lima by the two cars was made on July 20. That first night out, the personnel stayed in the Gran Hotel at Cañete; the next night it slept in the open among sand dunes and the third night in the clean little town of Pisco, after which a local brandy and a famous punch are named. The next morning was spent visiting Tello's exploration of the year before on the Paracas peninsula—or at least Necropolis, whence the fine mantles. There was as yet no custodian and no guide, so the expedition did not find the Cavernas site. The Necropolis had begun to fill with sand in the part-year interval, but the walls still showed, and there were sherds and debris of which samples were taken.

Then the party pushed inland into the desert of pure sand and bare rock stretching between Pisco and Ica for 60 kilometers, with many ruts of tires in the same general direction but no firm road. In the stretches of soft sand, tires were deflated from 50 pounds to 8 pounds, to be pumped up again when rock was reached. The car and the truck stuck and had to be pushed in different spots, and by dark they had got separated a mile or two even though heading for the same low place on the horizon that marked the little pass by which ruts and railroad entered Ica Valley. The Ford Agency in Ica had been telegraphed to expect two cars that day, and when none had appeared by dark, the agent sent two pilot cars out into the open desert that communicated by turning lights on and off. By midnight, the passenger car had been guided to the buffet of the Hotel Mossoni in Ica. The truck arrived an hour or two later, having dumped part of its load on the desert sand overnight.

The sixth day, the two cars drove southward down in the inland Ica Valley to the oasis of Ocucaje, from where, leaving the Ica River, they struck almost due eastward across a level, boulder-strewn desert of sand to the oasis and hacienda of Huayurí on the Río La Chimba [Santa Cruz], which flows due south, the northwesternmost of the many arroyos and rivers that together form the fan-like Río Grande area. The route to Huayurí followed a crow's-flight Inca highway—perhaps before that a pre-Inca road—marked by boulders stood up along its two edges. The ruts and donkey caravan trails wobbled from running between the markers to outside them: when the going got too tough in the sand, a car or a lead animal tried shifting to a parallel course.

At Huayurí, the Yorkshire manager of the Peruvian cotton hacienda, lonely for company and English speech, made the expedition welcome for two nights and led them to a Late Period ancient settlement a few kilometers upstream, which was prospected. A stratigraphic section cut was made, as described in Chapter 3.

An eighth day brought the party, now heading southeastward, across the Grande-Palpa-Vizca and the Ingenio affluents—dry or trickling—and to the town of Nazca. Here the party stopped only for road directions and to locate a Chinese-run general store and the one butcher shop that three days a week slaughtered a steer at daybreak and was sold out by 9 o'clock in the morning. They then pushed on some kilometers on the road down along the Nazca River on its southern side, arranging to take daily water in small barrels from the pump well at Pangaraví hacienda. They unloaded before dark on July 26, in a flat cove of sand reaching back into the bare-rock first foothills, a few hundred yards from the road to Lomas port and south (later improved into a stretch of the Pan-American Highway). Here, sheltered from south and east wind and drafts, permanent camp was set up, which remained the expedition's Nazca base except for its last ten days. The camp and the road were in bare (sandy) pampa; beyond was a varying strip of *huarangual*—scrubby brush outside the irrigated cultivation but with roots penetrating to seepages of groundwater. Beyond that was the cultivation of haciendas Majoro Chico and La Huayrona; beyond that, to the north, lay the bed of the Nazca River (Figs. 3–6). Looking out westward from the camp into the distance, one saw the isolated peak Criterión. At the end of a little point or low ridge of rock that partly sheltered the tents, beds, and fires from view of the Lomas road, a bit of quarrying had been done to get limestone for burning lime; whence the name of the spot: La Calera, the "limery."

After a day or two used in setting up camp, recruiting additional labor, and making personal and business connections, the first graves were dug into about July 29, on nearby Ocongalla hacienda at a spot later designated as Ocongalla Zero. Much of Kroeber's time went into prospecting; Schenck supervised the digging and kept most of the records.

From August 6 to 20, excavations were conducted on Hacienda Majoro Chico, at the warm invitation of the

FIGURE 3. *La Calera camp, looking west [53989]*

FIGURE 4. *La Calera men's camp with Pablo Torres [53966]*

FIGURE 5. *La Calera, view southwest from hill behind camp. Note lines on desert surface [53977]*

FIGURE 6. *View northwest from hill behind La Calera toward hills at Majoro Chico in the cultivation [53951]*

proprietor, Señor Fracchia, who with his Señora was in residence at the time and extended pleasant hospitality. By this time the digging crew averaged eight workers.

Before conclusion of the Majoro Chico diggings, on about August 15, Kroeber left Schenck in charge and drove with his wife and Mme. Fracchia to the latter's seaside home at Lomas. There, a day or two later, the Kroebers took the northbound steamer of the Peruvian National Line to Callao and Lima, from where Mrs. Kroeber sailed by Grace Line to New York on August 26, returning to California. Kroeber started from Lima on August 29 in Tello's car, with Tello and Sr. Mejía Xesspe, to return to Nazca, which they reached September 1.

Schenck had meanwhile excavated at five sites: on Majoro Chico, at La Huayrona (one day, eight men), and at Agua Santa; and, returning to Ocongalla, he opened Site West A and was engaged at West B, with some 350 or more specimens catalogued by Kroeber's return. The detailed story is recounted in Chapter 3, "Excavations."

Soon after Kroeber's return, operations were shifted farther downriver to Soisongo. Here The Field Museum expedition and Tello's National Museum group worked cooperatively at five cemeteries, each party finding, opening, and retaining its own graves; no graves were split. The sketch map covering the five graveyards (Fig. 47) was entered in his notebook by Kroeber on September 7.

On completion of the digging at Soisongo, Schenck severed his connection with the expedition and withdrew, first to Ica and Lake Matachina, then to Lima. From this point on all records including the field catalogue, are in Kroeber's handwriting.

Tello remained, and, his inclinations being upstreamward, it was he who found the Aja A and B sites, which were dug and exhausted in a few days, by September 25. After that his urging led across to the south side of the Nazca River once more, upstream of Nazca City, at Cantayo, where very rich cemeteries had previously been plundered, but intact graves remained amid the spoilage. These included the little site Cantayo Cax, which contained probably the oldest Nazca *A* remains (*Ao?*) found by the expedition, though under unfortunately disturbed and complex conditions.

Drs. Tello and Mejía remained at the expedition camp through September. On October 2, Tello and Kroeber visited Taruga. Immediately thereafter the National Museum party returned to Lima. Kroeber, now alone except for his three mountain Indians and four local workmen, broke up the La Calera camp and established a new temporary one for a final week of work 20 km downriver at Cahuachi South, with his tent pitched on the flat top of one of the terraces shown in Figure 66. It was here that the only Paracas wind, a driving sandstorm from the south characteristic of the area, was encountered during the expedition. The tent had to be struck and weighted down with stones. The workmen burrowed under it or found shelter elsewhere; Kroeber crawled into the expedition's largest packing case that had brought provisions and equipment and had been carefully saved for transport of specimens on the impending return to Lima.

This final stay at Cahuachi proved very productive. A series of wholly unrifled tombs interlocked by matching pieces of specimens of Nazca *A1* period were opened, and more textiles in good condition were recovered than in all the previous months of the expedition, owing to the graves on the high terraces having never been reached by groundwater. A total of 250 objects were secured at Cahuachi.

October 11 was a final day of reconnaissance to Poroma, an Inca outpost on the southernmost tributary of the Nazca drainage.

The next day the local workmen were paid off, the Ford truck loaded with specimens, and a driver engaged for its trip to Lima. It also carried two of the Huarochirí Indian workers, the third accompanying Kroeber in the passenger car; one rarely traveled any distance alone by automobile in Peru in 1926. With overnight stops at Ica and Chincha, Kroeber reached Lima on October 16, and the Nazca part of the expedition was over.

The next morning was accumulated-pay day for the three faithful Indians. About two weeks of packing and shipping, of completion and copying of catalogues and accounts followed. Places like Nazca were at that period extremely short of wooden boxes or even cardboard containers. A trickle of miscellaneous cases was irregularly obtainable by purchase from the general merchandise stores, but the main reliance had to be on the light wooden cases built in the United States to hold two 5-gallon cans of gasoline. These, as well as the cans, were in great demand and furnished a considerable extra profit—some said the main profit—on the sale of gasoline. Fortunately, most ancient objects found at Nazca were of a size to stow in these containers. With packing material, they would protect for truck haulage nearly all pottery vessels except an occasional large coarseware jar; and skeletons were split after all bones had been marked with their number, six to eight skulls filling one box, a series of long bones another.

Of course, for steamer and rail shipment, heavy packing cases were needed. Profiting by the experience of the preceding year, not only were these built at a box factory in Lima, but the cases were ordered of a size to contain snugly so many units, eight or twelve, of the gasoline boxes, which were then stowed inside as they had been packed in camp.

There was also a truck to be sold and, ultimately, a passenger car.

With these matters and completion and copying of catalogues and accounts, a fortnight was taken up; but there remained the month of November, which had been reserved for a longer exploration of the northern coast than had been possible in 1925, although once again without excavation.

There was as yet no passable road extending very far along the coast north from Lima such as the Pan-American Highway was to provide later; but a car was necessary for free movement in the northern territory, which was more heavily settled and had more roads than the intervening coast. It was, however, possible to ship the expedition's passenger Ford from Lima to the northern provinces as deckload on a coastwise freighter and then follow in person by passenger boat. On November 2, Kroeber bought return passage to New York, using the first part of his ticket for the stretch to Salaverry, the landing port for Trujillo, metropolis of the northern coast. The Ford had started on its way blocked down under a tarpaulin on its freighter. It arrived duly and was transferred from the freighter to one of the great open launches that lightered for all freight between ship and shore. And there a longshoremen's strike left it, again white under its tarpaulin, bobbing with every wave that lifted the undecked lighter at anchor some hundreds of yards off shore, until the strike was settled after ten days. Kroeber meanwhile began the first drafting of parts of the present report, and in between times traced a recently discovered fresco painting in an open-air chamber of the Huaca de la Luna adjacent to the great sun pyramid near Moche, a matter of minutes' distance by trolley or taxi from his hotel in Trujillo.

With the car finally landed, he telegraphed Tello, who was to be his companion in the north coast exploration, and Tello promptly arrived by steamer, along with his museum chauffeur to handle the car. A couple of days were spent at the bewildering courts of Chanchán of the Gran Chimú, the largest city of ancient Peru; and on November 17 they drove northward to Chicama Valley, where Rafael Larco, the younger at Chiclín, had just begun what was to become the great Larco family museum of Peruvian archaeology. Thence the route went on to Pacasmayo, the road sometimes consisting of the ocean beach at low tide, and to the Jaquetepeque Valley; thence by an Inca road through a desert stretch to Sana and on to Chiclayo, which became headquarters, with trips on to Lambayeque, the former provincial capital, and to the striking ruin of Purgatorio on the Leche River, Kroeber's northernmost in Peru. The pyramids, ruins, and cemeteries examined on this trip have been reported (Kroeber 1930).

Tello separated at Pimentel, the port for Chiclayo, to return, as he had come, by steamer. Kroeber drove back to Trujillo by December 1, made a last-minute favorable sale of the Ford, and reembarked at Salaverry, again by Grace Line, for New York on December 4. That afternoon he confirmed by radio the sale of the truck in Lima through the Ford Agency, and the business affairs of the 1926 expedition were wound up. The collections from Nazca had been loaded on the ship that carried Kroeber to the northern coast a month before. The trip home was eventless and restful, and Kroeber reached New York on December 14, Chicago on December 19, and California by Christmas.

**CHAPTER 2**

# *Areas and Sites*

THE ICA RIVER HAS NO TRIBUTARIES OF IMPORTANCE once it comes down out of the mountains, whereas the Río Grande is a system of nine or ten confluent streams, each with some cultivation along it and bearing a name of its own. The Ica runs a southerly course. The first two Río Grande confluents also run south, but thereafter, as one proceeds southward, each successive stream flows somewhat more to the southwest, west, and finally to the northwest, until they have all united. Only when all the branches have joined, for the final 40 km or so, does this combined stream run southerly again, nearly parallel to the lower Ica, whereupon the two enter the sea less than 25 km apart (Fig. 7). By contrast, at the 500 m contour the Ica and the southernmost affluent (Tunga) of the Río Grande are about 168 km apart. Airline distance between Ica and Nazca cities is around 125 km.

The total run-off of the several Río Grande confluents varies in proportion to how far up in the Andes their sources lie and how large their catchment basins are. How far down they generally carry water is largely a function of how much fails to be drawn off for irrigation above, and this again depends on the width of the irrigable bottom of the valleys above. In time, much of the infiltration above seeps back into the stream bed. Thus the Nazca River usually runs a fair-sized, clear stream through sand at Cahuachi even in the dry winter, while on its way through the upstream haciendas above and below the town of Nazca it presents a dry, cobbly stream bed or a mere half-stagnant trickle.

We do not know whether there exist comparative run-off figures for the several Río Grande tributaries, but the Nazca River itself, especially after it has received the Aja, seems to be bordered by the greatest area under cultivation, and this may mean that its total flow is the greatest. That is probably why the single town of the drainage, the city of Nazca, stands by it.

Apart from the differing shape of their drainage basins, the Ica and the Río Grande systems are alike in several respects compared with almost all other Peruvian rivers; they very rarely carry water to the sea, and while there are ancient sites most of the way down, these become sparser and fewer in the lower courses.

The main areas of cultivation and population thus lie inland on both stream systems, at an elevation of 300–500 m. The cities of Ica and Nazca are both around 55 km by air from the nearest point on the coast and about 90 km each following their streams to their mouths. The elevations are given as 439 meters above sea level (m.a.s.l.) for Ica and 598 m.a.s.l. for Nazca. Both towns are too far inland to be reached by fog and are noted for their high summer temperatures. They lie far too low to be reckoned as of the Ceja, or "eyebrow," of Cordillera, let alone as of the main Andes themselves, and they are no nearer to having rainfall than other south Peruvian river valleys.

The peculiarities of the Ica and Río Grande Valleys seem owing primarily to their being separated from the sea by an ancient, low, westernmost fold of the Andes, represented by remnants like Criteríon mountain southwest of Nazca, the Tablaza de Ica near the coast, the Paracas peninsula, and the nearer of the Guano Islands.

The expedition's mapping and measuring were attended by frustrations. There were no military air maps in 1926, or, if there were any, they remained unsuspected; Tello did not know them. Speedometers at

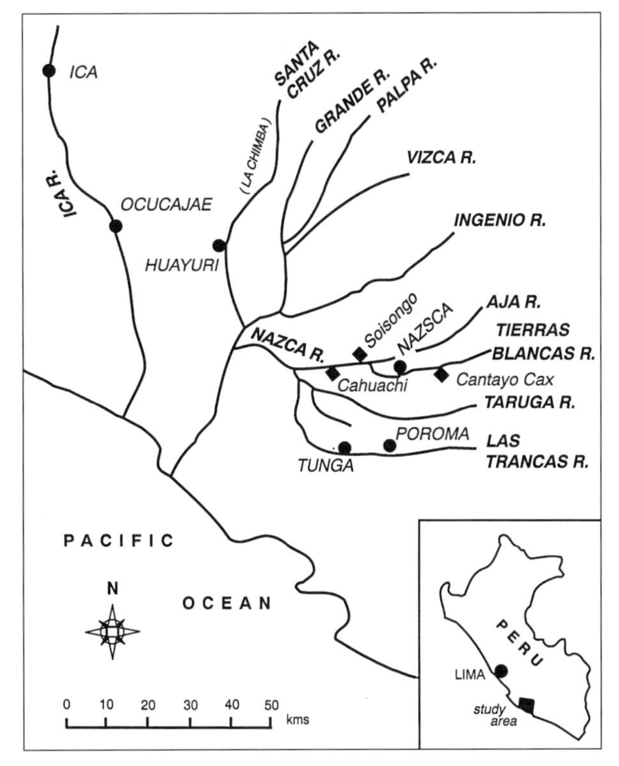


FIGURE 7. *South coast of Peru showing major rivers and locations*

that time were not standard equipment of Ford cars, and the Lima agency was reluctant to sell them because around 1926 it seemed the practice for the American manufacturers to ship their defectives to Peru. Kroeber and Schenck nevertheless persisted and eventually obtained one; however, the instrument broke down before Nazca was reached. Consequently all distances between streams and between places and properties on the same stream were estimates made on traversal, supplemented by occasional statements by residents in terms of leagues. Independently, Kroeber compiled a schematic map of Nazca Valley (with the river taken as straight) that is reproduced in Figure 8, and Schenck produced a list of distances shown in Table 1. To the latter we have added some figures derived from Uhle's 1905 catalogue statements in leagues, which we multiplied by 5 to convert to kilometers, and several based on measures of Strong's 1957 maps, whose scale is 1.2 km per millimeter. The relative distances in our Figure 8 have been converted into absolute ones by assuming a scale of 5.2 mm of the original drawing as equaling 1 km.

The figures in the several columns of Table 1 agree tolerably for archaeological identification. Kroeber's only criticism of the Schenck column of distances is that the gap between Huayrona, 3 km from Nazca City, and Majoro Chico, 7 km, is unduly large, however, the 7 may be a misreading of 4, which the Uhle and Strong figures for Majoro Grande and Ocongalla seem indirectly to confirm. From Soisongo down the properties all seem to extend across the narrowed valley, that is, to lie both north and south of the river, so that discrepancies of side do not mean much. For Las Cañas, Cahuachi, and La Estaquería the important grave fields lie mainly on the south side, whereas the hacienda house and most the cultivation are on the north.

The dotted line in Figure 8 is an attempt to suggest the extent of the cultivation. Locally, the stream that flows past the town of Nazca is often called the Tierras Blancas until its union with the Aja, and it is the Nazca only from there down to its junction with the Río Grande; although Nazca is understood also if used for its upper course.

The folded-in outline map in Strong's monograph is extremely useful for the many archaeological features it shows in the area of the Nazca culture. It must be used with one caution: the lengths of the rivers. Some of these are cut off at arbitrary points upstream without indication of the fact. There is also a draftsman's error: Sites 74–77, Huayurí I–IV, have been transposed from the northernmost tributary of the Río Grande system, the (La) Chimba [Santa Cruz], to the southernmost, the Tunga. The four sites lie near where La Chimba is crossed by the Pan-American Highway. The famous Paracas sites Cerro Colorado and Necropolis lie about above the top of the S in the entry PARACAS.

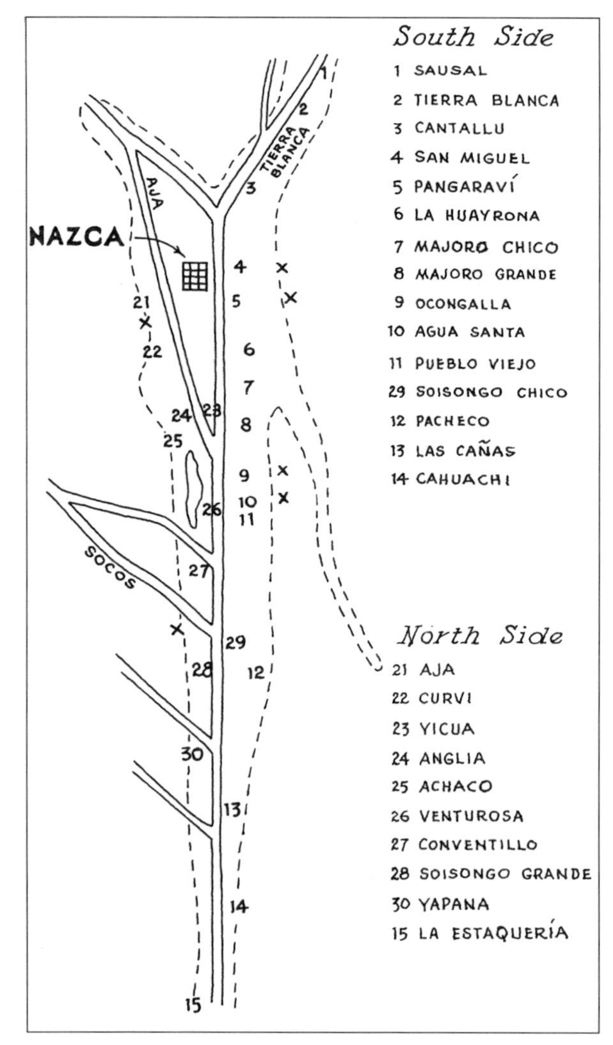


FIGURE 8. *Site locations in the Nazca area*

TABLE 1

**DISTANCES IN THE NAZCA VALLEY**

| HACIENDA | FROM NAZCA SCHENK KM | ON RIVER | SIDE | UHLE 1905 | STRONG MAP | FIG. 8 |
|---|---|---|---|---|---|---|
| Tierra Blanca | 4 upstream | T. Blancas | S | | | 3.5 |
| Cantayo A–F | 3 upstream | T. Blancas | S | | | |
| L–M | 2 upstream | T. Blancas | S | | | |
| Paredones | opposite | T. Blancas | S | | | |
| Aja | 1 downstream | Aja | N | | | |
| Pangaraví | 2 downstream | T. Blancas | S | | | |
| La Huayrona | 3 downstream | T. Blancas | S | | | 2.5 |
| Majoro Chico | 7 downstream | T. Blancas | S | | | 3.5 |
| Majoro Grande | 8 downstream | T. Blancas | S | 4 | | |
| Ocongalla | 9 downstream | Nazca | S | 7–8 | 7 | 6 |
| Agua Santa | 10 downstream | Nazca | S | | | 7 |
| Pueblo Viejo | 11 downstream | Nazca | S | | | |
| Pacheco | 12 downstream | Nazca | S | | | |
| Soisongo | 14 downstream | Nazca | N | 12–13 | 10 | 12.5 |
| Yapana | 17 downstream | Nazca | N | | | |
| Las Cañas | 18 downstream | Nazca | S | 17–18 | | 17 |
| Cahuachi | 20 downstream | Nazca | S | 20–22 | 18 | 20 |
| La Estaquería | 25 downstream | Nazca | S | | 24 | 23 |
| Tambo de Perro | | | | | 34 | |

CHAPTER 3

# *Excavations*

## LA CHIMBA [SANTA CRUZ] AND HUAYURÍ

SINCE COLONIAL AND PROBABLY PRE-SPANISH TIMES, the principal road across the desert from the Ica to the Río Grande drainages left the former at the oasis of Ocucaje and struck somewhat south of east, straight for where the largest cultivation on La Chimba River now lies in the Hacienda Huayurí. Over much of the intervening 40–45 km, the 1926 road followed an Inca road, which is discussed briefly below in connection with the ceremonial paths at La Calera.

The expedition spent two nights at Huayurí, thanks to the courtesy of its English superintendent. It examined a townlike settlement of Late Ica age at the mouth of the first *quebrada*, or "embayment," entering La Chimba from the east above Huayurí. A cleft in bedrock filled with rubbish was excavated in five 50-cm cuts down to the base at 250 cm, all decorated sherds being sorted out and counted. All were from 3-color ware and therefore Late Ica (now renamed Tajaraca); not a single fragment showed a fourth color, which would presumably have made it Middle Ica (Chulpaca). The salvage from the five levels now reposes in the Field Museum as accession numbers 170380–84.

The variety of oddments expected on the surface of a settlement and from test pits were encountered and are preserved as 170385–402. They are not described here because the post-Nazca- or Late- or Ica-period recoveries of the expedition being somewhat scattered (owing to the search being oriented toward the Nazca culture), they can be interpreted more significantly in context with studies of the Late Period such as Dorothy Menzel and others are engaged upon.

We mention specifically only four small lots of sherds that were either all black or incised or both, because black and incised ware is a characteristic of what Strong (1957) renamed Proto-Nazca and what we here tentatively designate as Nazca *Ao*. There is, however, another black and sometimes incised ware in Late Chincha and Late Ica, and even in Middle Ica (see Kroeber and Strong 1924, 104, 106, and pl. 35f, 36b, and 38j). The four lots here in question, 170394–98, were adjudged Late Ica in type on the spot. We have reexamined them in 1957 against the possibility of their containing a Nazca *Ao* fragment or two: the finding is negative; everything found here by the expedition was Late, or even Colonial. Such was a large, plain, reddish potsherd (170394) incised with writing in bold, flowing letters, including the date 1669.

Behind the Huayurí hacienda house some 150 m is a flat with ruins and remains (170403–4) which are Colonial as well as Late Native. They include a small piece of sheet copper.

About 0.4 km below the hacienda house, still on the left (E) bank of La Chimba, the expedition reconnoitered among former diggings and their refuse on a flat that had included graves. The sherds went back from Late to Middle Ica and Nazca period (170405–7).

## TIERRAS BLANCAS, AJA, AND NAZCA RIVERS

### La Calera

La Calera, "the limepit" or limestone quarry, is a rather flat-bottomed quebrada, or embayment in the rocky hills, inside the northeast point of which (where the quarry is situated) the expedition's camp was pitched [near Pangaraví, see Fig. 8]. There is visible evidence that at times water ran through this area. There are Nazca sherds in the washes, around the edges of the flat part of the quebrada, and especially near the opposite northwest point or promontory (Fig. 9). The sherds are fresh, with clean edges, not rolled or carried far; most of them look as if they had been covered superficially and washed out recently. Ten trial holes and two trenches, however, yielded only one sherd (probably 10 cm deep) and two small cylindrical bones (100 cm down). The fair abundance of sherds on the surface (often several fragments from the same vessel close together) and the good condition of most are unexplained.

There are a half-dozen caminos del Inca, or "ray roads," in the quebrada, mostly running out from near the southwest point; several more between rocky points in the quebrada next northeast of La Calera (Fig. 10); and about eleven radiating out from an islandlike rocky knoll 3–4 m high situated northeast of the northeast point of La Calera (Fig. 9, also see Aja B). These roads stretch across the open pampa, at most running a little up the lowest slopes of the hills. One end regularly points to a knoll, hill, promontory, pass, or other landmark (Fig. 5); the other end may do the same or lose itself in the plain. The roads are 3–4 m wide and are made

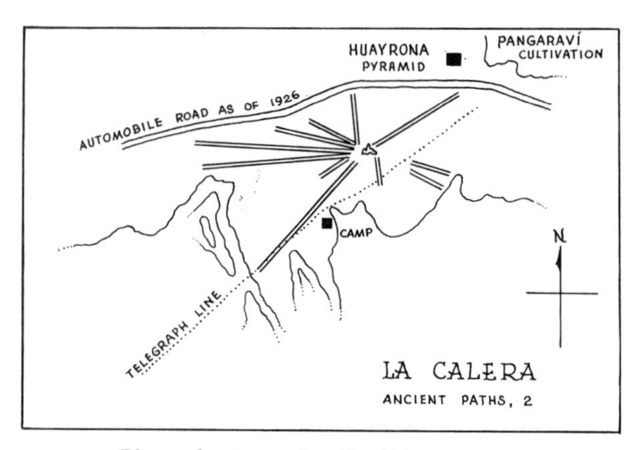


FIGURE 9. *Plan 2 of ancient paths at La Calera*

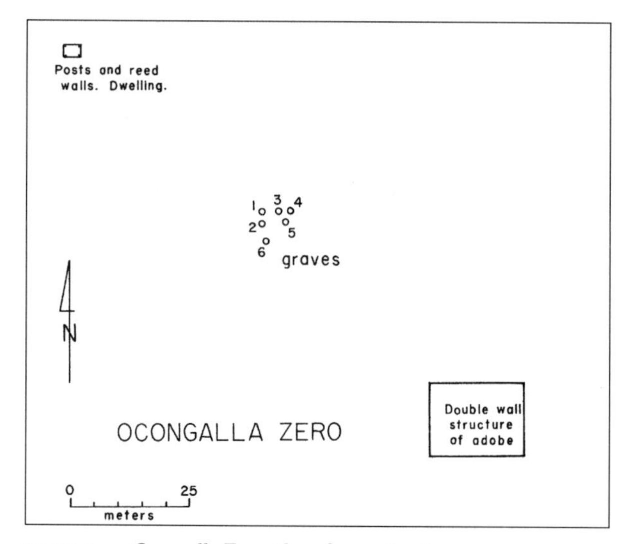


FIGURE 12. *Ocongalla Zero, plan of grave locations*

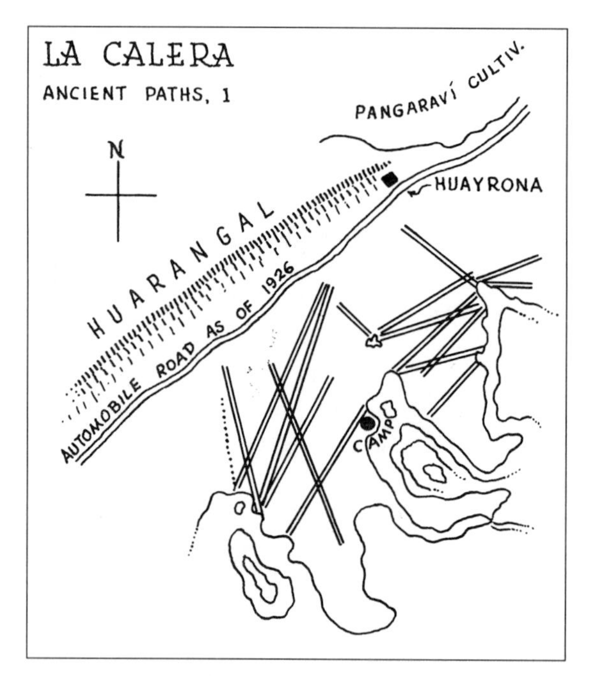


FIGURE 10. *Plan 1 of ancient paths at La Calera*

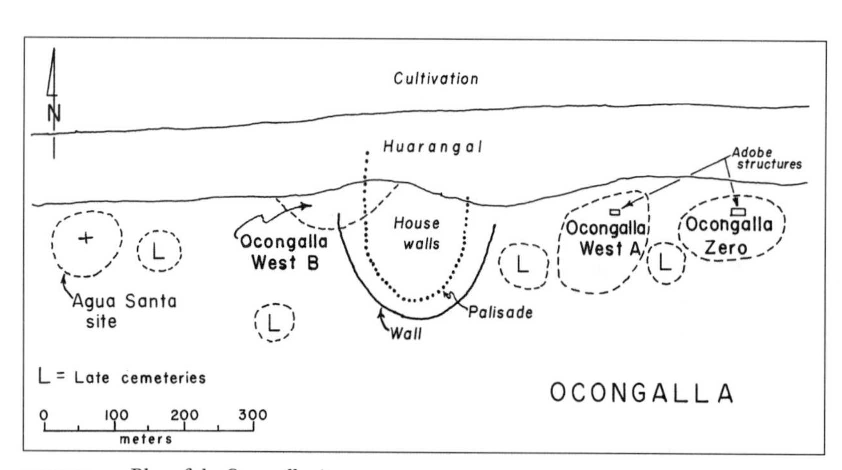


FIGURE 11. *Plan of the Ocongalla sites*

merely by removing all larger stones from the surface. They make excellent motorways over the pampa, where not subsequently dissected by washes, but are generally not so used because they lead nowhere. Purpose: religious processions or games?

A much wider road leads east-southeast from near Ocucaje over the Pampa de Huayarí for miles before the descent to the Huayurí (La Chimba) River. It has been utilized as a motor road—but unsuccessfully, because the pampa is sand and stones mixed and it cuts into folds, so that there are more ruts parallel to the road than in it. This road is absolutely straight, ca. 10 m wide, and has the removed boulders laid along the edge. It looks as if constructed for motor traffic, especially as the telegraph lines (of 1926) follow it part way, but it is attributed to the Incas. It may really be a pre-Spanish road, since it is the shortest cross-desert connection between the Ica and Río Grande drainages.

Figures 9 and 10 show two not wholly concordant sketch maps of these straight, radiating smoothings on the pampa at La Calera. (The two drawings accord better if one disregards the compass sign of Figure 9 and tilts the left side of the sketch up so that the automobile road more nearly parallels that of Figure 10.) The first sketch shows the crisscrossing of the paths and their direction from and to promontories; the second shows all the paths emanating from one rock outcrop in the flat pampa.

Several of these ray roads are also visible in Figure 7, photographed from above the camp site, looking southwest, with huarangual, or scrubby brush, which borders the cultivation downstream, showing at the right. The exposure is defaced by two light streaks extending up into the sky at right angles, but four or five of the roads are visible on the smooth floor of the embayment. One of them can be seen headed directly across it to the promontory at the end of a ridge running down from the peak opposite.

### Ocongalla Zero

The expedition excavated on Ocongalla hacienda, at a site later named Zero to distinguish it from Ocongalla A and B (Fig. 11), with five workmen for five days. If, after 50–60 cm of digging, loose soil was not encountered, experience indicated that there was no grave.

No plan of Ocongalla seems to have been preserved, though a sketch is referred to. Figure 12 is derived from the statements in Schenck's field notes. All graves and practically all loose sherds left about by previous excavators were Nazca *B*. This expedition's graves proved to be the same. The following is the grave record:

**GRAVE 1.** At 225 cm deep through stream boulders, gravel and sand, with slight traces of pottery, reed stalks, and decayed wood, lay the skeleton with a Nazca *B* bowl (170409: Fig. 284; Chap. 9) beside its left foot. Skeleton lying or fallen on left side, head to south of west, semiflexed, legs apart; excavation hole too small to permit total exposure. Probably an old woman. Skull frontally flattened and intact but fragile (170408). No tomb walls; no cloth.

**GRAVE 2.** About 3 m south of Grave 1. Same type, except that two irregular hand-formed adobes were encountered at about 150 cm. The workmen pointed out two "walls," but they were at different levels and apparently were only naturally deposited boulders. Skeleton at 225 cm, head east, with a Nazca *B* vase nearby (170410: Fig. 285; Chap. 9). Adult of 40+, bones not recovered.

**GRAVE 3.** About 4.5 m east of Grave 1. At 60–80 cm were two broken Nazca *B* vessels (170411–12: Figs. 286–287; Chap. 9) above and in close association with a fire-blackened globular pot, diameter (D) 130 cm, height (H) 25 cm, with two handles and a lip 9 cm high with a top diameter of about 12 cm—pot broken and dimensions approximate. In the pot was the body of a very young infant wrapped in ordinary white cotton cloth (170413). With the pot were two canes about 1 x 25 cm. The baby's bones were in fair preservation.

At 180 cm were found a Nazca *B* flaring bowl and a face jar (170414–15: Figs. 288–289; Chap. 9), near the center of the tomb. Both had previously been broken, for two pieces of 170414 were found at the south and north edges of the tomb well (Fig. 13). Also at 180 cm but at the northwest edge were five sets of gourd vessels, too fragile to preserve, each set consisting of two half-gourds, one in the other, placed upside down.

At the west side of the tomb in a niche beyond the tomb wall, about 180–200 cm deep, was the skeleton of an old person (170417), with bones intact but fragile, hair on skull and this somewhat flattened frontally. The body inclined considerably to the left but apparently was originally in squatting posture facing west, that is, away from the grave shaft. Part of a plain, rough jar, estimated H 350 mm, D 320 mm, was broken over the knees. Near the right pelvis, 190 cm deep, was bowl 170416 (Fig. 290; Chap. 9).

"Tomb" here equals the hole as dug by us, about 150 cm in diameter. On east edge was an adobe wall about 80 cm long. Other parts of the hole were like the surrounding area but possibly more sandy, that is, looser.

**GRAVE 4.** About 1.8 m east of the adobe wall of Grave 3 was the center of Grave 4, the most elaborate thus far.

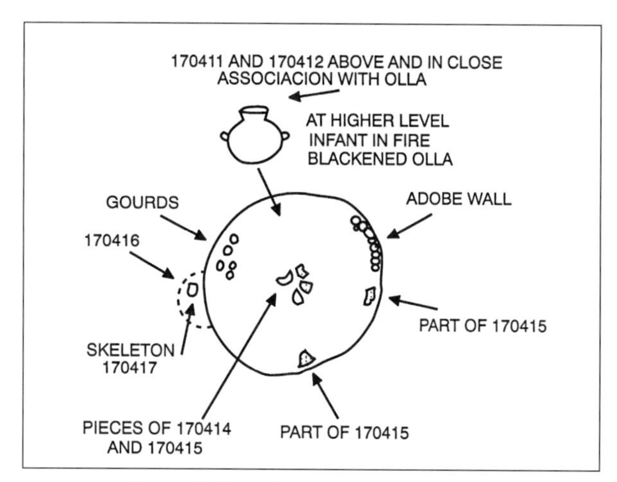


FIGURE 13. *Ocongalla Zero, Grave 3, overview*

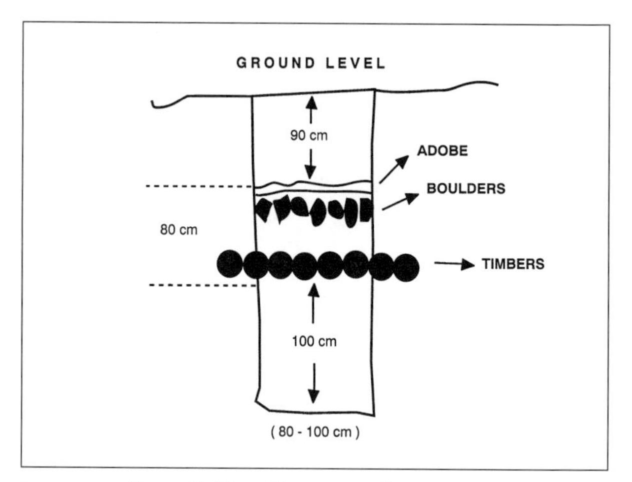


FIGURE 14. *Ocongalla Zero, Grave 4, profile*

It consisted of roughly circular hole, ca. 80–100 cm in diameter, in natural gravel and sand, unlined, perhaps paved at the bottom with boulders. It was covered over by eight natural timbers, above them a layer of larger boulders, then a layer of adobes. From bottom of tomb to underside of timbers: 100 cm; the timbers, boulders, and adobe: 80 cm thick; from the top of this roof to ground level: 90 cm; total depth: 270 cm (Fig. 14).

The majority of the timbers had been burned off at the ends, but some were hewn. The tomb was about one-third full of fine sand, some of which had probably sifted in. Covered by this sand was a skeleton [adult female, age 35+] that apparently had been seated facing west but inclined to right. The skull (170420) was upside down, chin to southeast, bones intact but more fragile than those of Grave 3. At right and left ca. 40 cm were a pair of matching cylindrical jars (170418–19: see Fig. 291; Chap. 9). Both had been repaired before burial. A wooden implement (170421) was found at 80 cm (Fig. 15).

The relation of the adobe wall between Graves 3 and 4 to both is uncertain. It was not actually in contact with Grave 4.

**GRAVE 5.** About 6 m east by a little south of Grave 1. At 80 cm a skeleton 170422 [adult male] was encountered, on its back, head to south. Right leg bones apparently missing, traces of cloth near center of body. Bones very fragile, but deformed skull intact.

**GRAVE 6.** About 5.4 m south of Grave 1: a prepared tomb like Grave 4. To top of roof: 100 cm down; roof 45 cm thick, of five timbers somewhat heavier than in Grave 4, laid north-south (in Grave 3 E–W). Well 90–120 cm across and 165 cm deep from underside of roof to bottom, that is, total from bottom to surface 310 cm. Timbers burned to length. At 290 cm a face jar was intact (170423: Fig. 292; Chap. 9). Bones in very rotten condition. Thick salt deposits encrusted two boulders in this grave, as observed also in Grave 4, and in test pits.

**ADOBE STRUCTURE.** About 50 m southeast of Grave 1, at top of slope, was a structure of adobes consisting of exterior and interior walls, measuring 20 m x 15 m. It was about 150 cm higher toward its center. A trench run across near the center revealed three layers of old cornstalks about 30 cm apart, some Nazca-type sherds, a half-gourd, mussel shells, and miscellaneous debris—all in small quantities. The trench was dug only to the level of surrounding plain—about 150 cm at deepest point. Bottom of interior walls at northeast side was not reached. Adobes mostly irregularly hand shaped.

**DWELLINGS.** To the west of the principal burial area, on lower slopes of terrace (i.e., nearer cultivation), several remains of reed structures were noted. These consisted of the ends, 8–15 cm long, of reeds vertically placed and charred to the ground level. Some were saved as 170426. The line of one lot, about 50 m northwest of Grave 1, could be traced as a rectangular enclosure of 3 m x 2.5 m. The area within was excavated for 50 cm. It had not been disturbed, as evidenced by fireplaces. Posts about 40 cm long had been placed about 30 cm from the corners; two of these were cataloged as 170425. All were burned at the top end, three at the lower; one hewn below was of "willow." The reeds were well preserved, and in one corner the cord used for binding them was still in place (170426). All sherds were saved and showed four or five types of vessels, designated 170424 (Fig. 16). Also obtained were a skewer-like wooden artifact (170427), a few mussel-shell fragments, corn cobs, pallar beans, "llama" dung and bones, a half gourd, much ash, some cotton cloth (170428), and part of a crystal (170429).

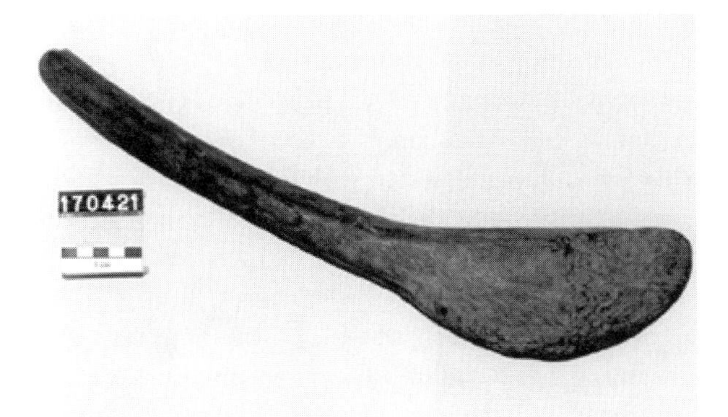


FIGURE 15. *Wooden artifact (170421) found in upper grave shaft, Ocongalla Zero, Grave 4*

FIGURE 16. *Sherds (170424) from reed-wall enclosure, Ocongalla Zero*

**Majoro Chico**

At Majoro Chico the expedition included a strip of land mainly uncultivated, perhaps 200 m wide and 600 m long, belonging in 1926 to Señor Oropezas, and stretching along the cultivated area from the side road leading from the Nazca-Lomas road, south of Nazca River on the pampa, to the hacienda of Señor E. Fracchia on the west (and N) and eastward to a group of small granite knobs or hills. The land is highest on its north, immediately adjacent to the cultivation. There was a scattered growth of *huarango* trees over the entire plot and a strip of straggling cotton on the south. The general location is shown in Figure 8.

Within this area considerable excavation had been done by huaqueros. The principal burial concentrations revealed by the expedition's work are designated Sites A to E. Their relative position is shown in Figure 17. They are discussed in the order of their exploration. Work at Majoro continued for thirteen working days, August 6–20, Sundays excepted, generally with a crew of eight (Fig. 4).

*Majoro Chico Site B*

Site B was adjacent to the road into the Hacienda Fracchia of Majoro Grande and about 130 m south of the cultivated area. It was marked principally by a knoll about 1 m high. Ten or fifteen graves had been excavated south and east of this knoll, as well as a large grave in its top. All surface sherds were Late type. White and pink cotton cloth and an undeformed skull were also on the surface. The graves opened were also Late or Ica style.

**GRAVE 1.** About 4 m from the fence to the west, on the north slope of a knoll about 1–1.5 m high by 20 m in diameter, in the top of which a large grave had been excavated. Just below the surface one large rectangular adobe partially covered a mass of cloth, cordage, cotton,

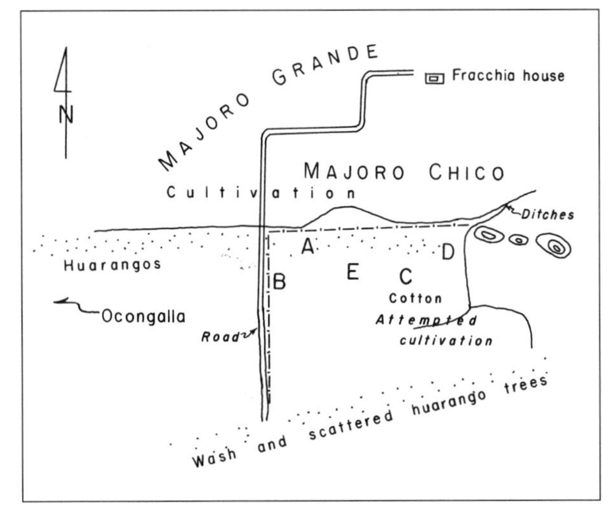


FIGURE 17. *Plan of Majoro Chico site divisions*

hair, and so forth, but no bones. Below and somewhat to the east was a portion of a large red jar. At 75 cm on southwest side of the hole, a small fire-blackened cooking pot ca. 20 cm x 20 cm (170452) was recovered intact. Immediately below this, at 85 cm, was a flat red bowl with design (170433: Fig. 409; Chap. 13) in three pieces. At about the same level but in the northwest section of the grave was the partial skeleton of an infant wrapped in cotton and cotton cloth, bones in fair condition. At 90 cm were some ten irregular, rather small, hand-shaped adobes roughly arranged so as to more-or-less cover an area about 110 cm in diameter. (If these adobes were actually hand shaped in a Late grave, they must have been Nazca ones reused.) They appeared to cover a well-like grave dug through sand and gravel to a total depth of 190 cm below the present surface. In this grave (not counting the infant) were the bones of probably four individuals, much confused and extending from 80 cm to 190 cm down. Only one skull was identified, 170434 [adult male]. This was undeformed, intact, hair preserved, with red paint covering the forehead and bits of cloth on the face, depth about 120 cm. Sherds of two or three small Ica style vessels were recovered from the same depth (170435). Sherd 170436 seemed to bear an ownership mark [a crude X incised after firing]. At the bottom of the grave at 190 cm was a heavy red bowl (170437: Fig. 408).

**GRAVE 2.** This lay 2 m southeast of Grave 1, measuring center to center. Again just under the surface there lay a large mass of white cotton cloth, cordage, and bound tresses of hair (170438). In this mass was a spindle of espinosa spine with whorl in place (170439). At 70 cm there were adobes as in Grave 1 and below these a well about the same as Grave 1, but only 140 cm total depth. Below the adobes at 100 cm was a mass of unspun cotton containing the undeformed skulls and principal bones of two adults [170440, male?; 170441, female]. Some of the cotton had been wrapped and tied about the limbs and probably other portions of the bodies. The position of the bodies was obscure but apparently one skull was toward the southeast, the other northwest. The cotton mass and bones extended to about 115 cm. Amid the cotton cloth near the center of body 170440 was a strip of tapestry with highland style design (170442). Several types of weaves were represented in the cotton cloth (170443–44). From 115 cm there came also a plain red bowl containing ears of corn (170445) and a gourd with a square hole cut in one side and equipped with a carrying string. Just below the main bodies was a small mummy bundle containing a young child's body and consisting of an outer wrapping of cotton cloth and two inner layers of unspun cotton bound with string.

**GRAVE 3.** About 1.25 m east by south of Grave 2. No adobes or well. At 40 cm, the top of the mummy of a child [age 2–5 years], seated with face to west (170446), wrapped with cotton cloth and unspun cotton. The skin still covered the ribs, the head was covered with a helmetlike cap of cotton with cloth cover, face open. On lap of child, 70 cm deep, was a Late (Ica) bowl (170447) containing bones and fur of a guinea pig, ears of corn, and a small roll of brown cotton cloth. Bottom of grave 100 cm.

## *Majoro Chico Site A*

Site A constitutes the northwestern portion of Majoro Chico. It extended about 80 m south of the cultivation for about 100 m east of the road. From a cut in this road, it seems that the site extends continuously to west of the road. Huaqueros had done considerable damage, particularly near the adobe structure south and east of the graves. Few bones lay on the surface, and little cloth—less than in the much smaller Site B—but many sherds were visible.

As at Ocongalla Zero there were not only graves but an adobe structure and dwellings. The graves are best oriented by reference to the walls, so these will be described first.

### Structure of Low Adobe Walls

About 70 m east of the side road and 60 m south of cultivation, at the top of the slight slope from the cultivation, was a structure or series of adobe walls (Figs. 18–20). These walls had been covered from 15 cm to 150 cm deep by sand and gravel and more-or-less refuse and had also been much disturbed by grave excavations near them. The overburden carried a considerable number of Nazca sherds, and decorated fragments from five spots were collected (170560–64).

The structure consisted of a number of more-or-less connected walls setting off an incomplete quadrangle that in its west portion had then filled in (i.e., of itself, by wind action) until higher than both the surrounding ground level and the walls. All walls found were traced to an end. Sometimes this was very definite; at other times the excavation of a tomb by huaqueros had interrupted a wall's course, and no indication could be found of its continuance. The walls found are shown in Figure 22.

The walls seem to vary in height; in places they were 150 cm, in others not over 50 cm. This may have been because they followed an originally uneven ground

FIGURE 18. *Majoro Chico A, north wall of adobe structure [53980]*

FIGURE 19. *Majoro Chico A, southwest corner of wall construction [53961]*

FIGURE 20. *Majoro Chico A, ends of adobes embedded in mud mortar, detail of grave or chamber wall, north side of adobe structure [53972]*

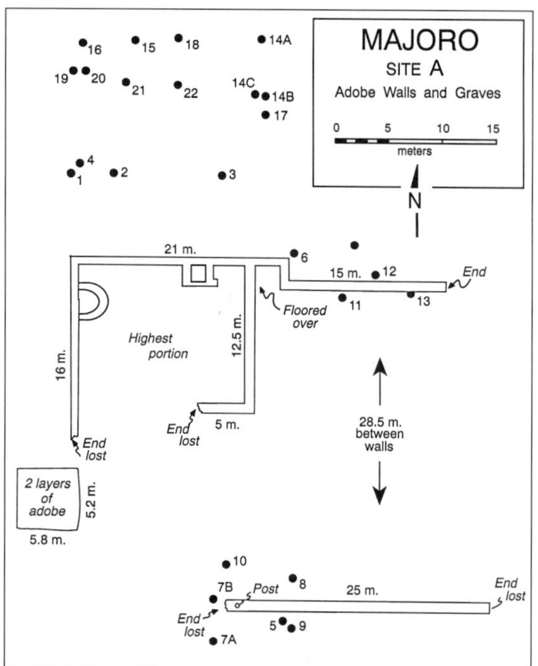


FIGURE 22. *Majoro Chico A, plan of adobe walls and graves*

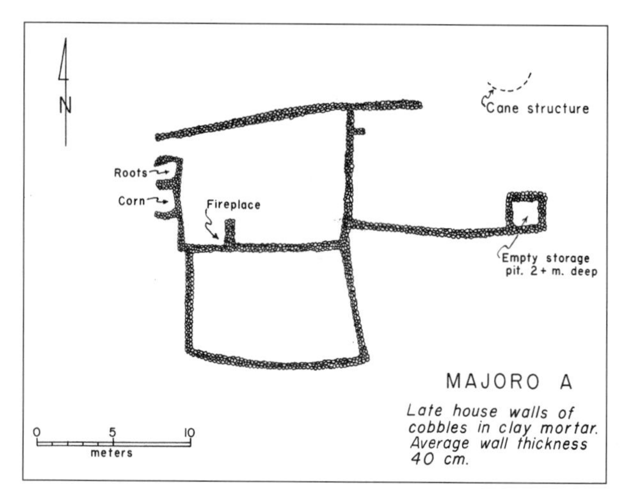


FIGURE 23. *Majoro Chico A, plan of Late house walls*

surface, although the top of the wall by no means maintains an even level. The extent of continuous wall, the existence of sherds and refuse, and the presence of a fire line in the region of Grave 1 at about the level of the bottom of the walls all seem to point to the walls having originally been constructed above ground; the accumulation around and over them has taken place since.

The space between the west and middle wall had obviously been filled in by man. There are layers of corn stalks, camelid bones (always called *guanaco* by our workmen), guanaco (?) dung, sherds, miscellaneous refuse, and heaps of adobes tumbled in no regular order. In this section a large grave had formerly been dug out by one of our workmen. Inside the north wall and against it was a square chamber with solid walls (Fig. 20) that had also been dug out and may have been a tomb. A similar chamber but smaller and rounded was on the inside of the west wall near its north end. Graves occurred near all walls, but the walls do not seem to have formed part of such graves. Moreover, it seems probable that any straight line drawn through the area would show a number of graves close to it. In places, as at the bend in the north wall, a space inside the wall had been covered over with an adobe layer 5–7 cm thick. This could have been a floor or the roof of a grave, although we were not able to discover any tomb. Sherd lots 170564 (Fig. 24) from under this undisturbed adobe floor and 170565 from under an undisturbed portion of the south wall seem certainly to be older than the wall. Some of the graves, such as 13, may have been older than the wall.

The walls were mostly of rather large hand-shaped adobes of half-spool (half-cylinder), wedge, and tooth (conical) shape set in adobe mortar, generally vertically (on end). The adobes are discussed in Chapter 4. The width of the walls averaged about 65 cm.

Immediately adjacent to the south end of the west wall was an independent rectangular area floored over with two thicknesses of adobes laid horizontally. In this rectangle a huarango tree had grown and died, and a large grave had been excavated. It seems probable that this rectangle was an elaborate tomb, which suggests that the other walls were also connected with burials rather than residence. Another evidence pointing the same way was the small amount of ash found.

On the other hand, what appear to have been house walls existed in the vicinity and will now be described.

### Majoro A Houses

Toward the west end of Site A, at its highest part, lines formed by walls of boulders and adobe mortar could be followed on the surface, and a number of them were cleared (Fig. 23). They were from 15 cm to 150 cm high and covered to about that depth by wind-blown sand, small boulders, and so forth. In places the sand was very fine. The boulders had perhaps been part of the structure. Sherds were plentiful, and the decorated ones in the vicinity of the walls (170577, 170560) show a majority of Late (Ica) type (Figs. 26–27).

The arrangement of these walls is puzzling owing to the lack of doors on one hand and the lack of connection between some walls on the other. Possibly this was because the walls were simply foundations for an upper-construction of reeds, when the doors would be in the reeds. In such a case, entire sides of the houses may have been open or closed in only by reed construction. Stumps of reeds in place at the northeast corner bear out this theory.

During the excavation we noted fireplaces and accumulations of material such as would be expected in living quarters, for example, pockets of maize (170573), balls of unworked wool, a pile of snail shells (170576), material for sizing cloth (170570), skeins of thread (170569), spindles and whorls (170567–68), and so forth. In the southeast corner was a deep, lined pit, probably for food storage, since at the northwest corner were two pits not so well constructed, one of which contained probably a half bushel of dried roots and the other a quantity of maize.

The material found and the fact that these walls are not deeply covered seem to point to their being Late. However, surface indication of walls could be detected eastward toward the adobe structure. Also, graves dug north of the adobe structure disclosed portions of irregular walls apparently not part of the tombs. These walls were of adobes of the same types as used in the adobe structure, viz., Nazca shapes.

Possibly these last irregular walls to the north were those of ordinary dwellings of Nazca time; the adobe structure was a Nazca dwelling of better class, and the house walls sketched in Figure 23 were those of Late period. Graves lay very close to the first two classes of adobe walls, but not to the boulder and reed walls of the residence compound. The locations of graves in the following descriptions are charted in Figure 22.

### Majoro A Graves

**GRAVE 1.** This lay at the high point of the river terrace, about 50 m south from the cultivation, 70 m east of the hacienda road, and 8 m north of the northwest corner of the north wall of the adobe structure described. At 75 cm, skeleton 170450 [adult female, age 27–35], on face, extended, right arm doubled in with hand near chest, left thrown above head. Traces of cotton cloth; no other artifacts; no indication of tomb. Lower jaw lay above body and skull and 40 cm east of undeformed skull. A layer of ash and charcoal was noted both north and south of skeleton 20 cm higher and may have extended across above it. [The catalogue states that three sherds, 170451, were found above this grave, but their depth below the surface was not recorded and the excavators apparently did not associate them with the burial. These sherds are from Ica-style cumbrous bowls.]

**GRAVE 2.** 4 m east of Grave 1 in same type of soil. At 180 cm, a large plain red jar, 50 cm D (top) by 40 cm deep, inverted, under which was the skeleton of an old woman—accession number 170452 was assigned to the vessel and bones both. No artifacts aside from a sherd in the jar [appears to be Nazca *Y* or later]. Bones fragile, skull undeformed. Body apparently flexed, set humped in a shallow hole, and the jar placed upside down over body facing west. Bottom of body 240 cm deep.

**GRAVE 3.** 10.5 m east of Grave 1 in same type of soil, with Nasca and Ica sherds and refuse. At 200 cm, fragments of a jar, similar to that in Grave 2, with some of the bones of a foot and scraps of brown cloth. None of the fragmentary finds were saved.

**GRAVE 4.** 1.5 m northeast of Grave 1. Part of the body was under half-spool and tooth-shaped adobes, 160 cm deep to top of vertebrae, 100 cm below a definite fire line. The headless body, 170454 [adult female, age 19–20], was in sitting posture with knees flexed but spread apart, arms between lower legs and thighs, facing north. A thin red jar (170456: Fig. 28a) was inverted over top of the spine. The fireplace [fire line?] was above and around the adobes that lay over the body. Some adobes had been burned red by fire, and much ash and charcoal were present. No cloth or other artifacts. [Sherd lot 170455, found just above the body, is shown in Figure 29.]

These first four graves lay in an east-west line north of the north wall of the adobe structure and seem all of Late period, subsequent to the Nazca phase of the structure's walls. We turn now to several graves near the opposite south wall of the same structure, which were Nazca, not Late like the foregoing.

**GRAVE 5.** 5.5 m east of the west end of the south adobe wall and 1 m outside (S) of this wall of the adobe structure. There was a well-like hole, about 125 cm in diameter, in sand and gravel, no roof, no lining, no paved bottom. At 180–200 cm was the body of a very old person, seated at east side of grave facing west. Skull broken. Body bones very much dried out but in fair condition (170457). Considerable cotton cloth (170458) of a fine and a coarse weave about body. Pacae leaves also about body, and a few corn cobs near it. At feet, an intact face pitcher (170461: Fig. 367 [Pl. 29]; Chap. 11). Near left side were the major fragments of an undecorated flat

FIGURE 24. *Sherds (170564) from below undisturbed floor of adobe structure, Majoro Chico A*

FIGURE 25. *Sherds (170466) found in grave shaft, Majoro Chico A, Grave 6*

FIGURE 26. *Sherds (170577) from Late house structure in 23*

FIGURE 27. *Sherds (170560) from Late house structure in 23*

FIGURE 28a. (170456, interior) *Majoro Chico A, Grave 4*

FIGURE 28b. (170456, exterior) *Majoro Chico A, Grave 4*

bowl (170459: Fig. 368), and the fragments of half of another (170460).

**GRAVE 6.** This grave lay just outside a jog in the middle of the north wall of the adobe structure (Fig. 22), about 6 m south and 7 m east of Grave 3. It was immediately adjacent to a corner in the adobe wall but apparently this wall was not a part of the tomb. Sandy and gravelly soil. At 140 cm was a bundle of maize stalks that had been stood upright in the southwest part of the grave. To the north were several canes. Between were a considerable portion of the backbone and a number of ribs of a llama or guanaco bound with human hair and cloth of at least three kinds (170462) and some pacae leaves. (Hair and cloth were noted above the bodies at Site B also.) Below, at 160 cm, were a number of adobes—large irregular, hand-shaped. At 200 cm, near center of grave, was a lower jaw in good condition (170463). A bundle of *caña brava*, apparently tied together at the base, stood on the northwest side of the grave, and behind these at 2.25 m was a frontally deformed skull (also 170463), which had a small hole in the forehead and its base missing, that is, a trophy head [adult male]. The eyes and upper jaw showed traces of a covering of copper (*sic*?). A little south and east of skull was a large upright intact plain jar (not saved, too fragile), filled with sand, canes, pacae leaves. Pieces of a similar jar had been found in the soil above. From 240 cm to 260 cm, in north side of grave, portion of a skeleton, 170464 [adult male, age 50+], wrapped in cloth of several kinds (170465), similar to 170462. No ribs or vertebrae found. Probably 170463 and 170464 belonged together. Sherds from 160–250 cm were saved as 170466 (Fig. 25). The deformed trophy-head puts this grave into the Nasca period. Five of the textiles (170462–65) are shown in O'Neale (1937), plates 36, 38, 57, and 67.

**GRAVE 7[A].** With this grave we are away from the north wall and back at the south one, near Grave 5. It lay 2 m south of S adobe wall and 1 m west of its west end, 6–7 m west of Grave 5. At 100 cm deep, in sand and gravel, on SW side, a handled cookpot, intact except for lip (170467: Fig. 323; Chap. 10), containing an interesting lot of feathers, nets, spindles of thread, balls of thread, comb, and several bits of fine weaving (170468).

Following the loose soil, the workmen developed a much larger hole to the north (Fig. 22). In the north part of this larger hole, at 150 cm to the top of its skull, was the body of an adult [male: Grave 7B], in sitting posture facing west (170469). Much hair on skull, bones in fair condition. Since the artifacts just described [7A] and this body were 3 m apart and at different depths, any connection between them seems doubtful, though our workers were emphatic in their belief that they were associated. The skull was frontally deformed; it had been wrapped with pinkish gauze, and a coarser cloth had been wrapped around the body.

Immediately below this body, at 250 cm to top of the skull, was the body of a second adult (170470), a very old person, bones intact but very fragile, in a squatting posture, facing west. At least two kinds of cloth had been about the body. In front of it and to its right were three bowls, upright and containing corn cobs, and so forth (170471–3: Figs. 324–326; Chap. 10), one mended with holes and gummy materials. To the left and in front was a strap-handled bottlelike jar (170474: Fig. 327). Between this and the bowls were guanaco bones. This is a phase *Y1* grave.

**GRAVE 8.** 2 m north of (inside) the south adobe wall, 6.5 m east of its west end and about abreast (N of) Graves 5 and 9. At about 130 cm down in the southeast part of grave were sherds from two vessels (170475/

FIGURE 29. *Sherds (170455) from just above interment, Majoro Chico A, Grave 4*

170477: Figs. 334 and 331; Chap. 10) and some bits of cloth (170476). At 120 cm, in southwest part by edge of grave wall, were four vessels close together, all upside down, one mended, another half imbedded in a chunk of clay (170479–82: Figs. 328–329 [Pl. 25]; 332–333). [Several sherds, numbered 170478, representing Nazca *A* and *B* were recovered from 150 to 230 cm.] From the surface to 175 cm down, the grave had a diameter of 2–2.4 m. Thence to 240 cm down the diameter was about 1.5 m, and it was partially lined with adobes, large, wedge-shaped, handmade, set on end. At 230 cm down was a flat red bowl (170483). Also at 230 cm, northeast, was a very old [female] person with bits of skin and hair and cotton cloth adhering (170484), facing W, squatting. Bones wrapped in badly disintegrated cloth of several varieties, some of it as in Grave 6. Skull normal. On the other side of this body was a flat bowl (170485: Fig. 330) similar to 170483. A little deeper, at about 240 cm, but above the recognizable floor of the same tomb, were the heavily deformed skull and at least principal bones of another [adult] individual (170486). This body was on the northwest side of the tomb, the bones confused, the skull apparently resting on the legs. This intricate grave seems also *Y1*. Several textile fragments, numbered 170476 a–f, are shown by O'Neale (1937) in her plates 41–42, 53, and 65, though misattributed to the preceding Grave 7. As O'Neale's monograph deals with "Early" Nazca, cloth from a *Y1* grave ought strictly not have been included. Both errors are not O'Neale's but in the data furnished by Kroeber.

**GRAVE 9.** 1 m east and 0.5 m south of Grave 5. At 80 cm was a child's frontally flattened skull (170487), milk dentition erupted [age 3–5 years]. Skull and body enveloped in cloth, seated facing south but head turned to face west. Part of old cookpot below was not saved, nor was the cloth.

**GRAVE 10.** 3 m north of west end of south wall at the side of an old excavation. At 40 cm, major parts of a Pan's pipe (170488: Fig. 30), but no burial was found.

With Graves 11–13 we return to the vicinity of the east end of the long north wall.

**GRAVE 11.** 5.5 m east and 2.5 m south of Grave 6, alongside and just south of the wall. At 25 cm was a trophy head (170489) with carrying string [adult male], part of scalp, and some covering over right eye. No evidence of a body and no other artifacts.

**GRAVE 12.** 8.5 m east and 1 m south of Grave 6, just north of the long north wall. At 80 cm, a plain, fire-blackened pot, 30 cm high by 25 in diameter, with side handles, which contained the skeleton of a child [age 2–3 years] wrapped with cotton cloth. The skull (170490) was deformed. In the pot with the child were also a number of corn ears tied up in a cloth (170491). This grave as dug out by us was about 1.5 m in diameter. The body was found in the extreme north part. The south part looked out through the wall. However it seems improbable that the wall would have been cut through and such a large hole dug for the burial of the pot in a position that would neither have required the cut nor the large hole.

**GRAVE 13.** 12 m east of Grave 6 and just south of wall. This grave had been previously robbed, as only part of the roof, some corn, cañas bravas, and a few odd bones were found. The roof consisted of a thin layer of adobe, a number of small poles, some of which were hewn, and a lot of pacae leaves. This roof probably extended a little way under the wall, but the evidence as to which was older was not conclusive. It was about 1 m from the top of the wall to the roof and about 1 more from roof to bottom of grave. No body and no artifacts.

Graves 14–22 were found some 14–20 m north of the west half of the north wall of the enclosure, farther from it than Graves 1–4 and in two alignments. These were Nazca period interments, and mostly Nazca *A*.

**GRAVE 14[A].** 12 m north and 4 m east of Grave 3. At about 100 cm, a fire line (*sic*) of considerable extent. As much the same line appeared at about the same depth in Graves 1–4, this may have been the surface at the time of occupation. Below the fire line, sand and gravel with a few sherds. At 300 cm, the body of a child. It was disturbed and confused by the diggers and was not saved. With it was a pinkish shell bead with part of the cord on which it had been strung (170492); also a vessel that since was stolen.

**GRAVE 14[B].** Following the apparently loose soil, we dug a large hole until, 5 m south of the first body, was a second, 170493 [adult female, age 20–21], 120 cm deep, and just above the extensive fire line, therefore probably from a different phase. This one was flexed, more-or-less wrapped in cloth, on its right side, head to east, facing north. The skull was undeformed.

**GRAVE 14[C].** At about 300 cm, near center of the hole dug, were two pieces of wood fashioned to length but broken and very rotten. At 375 cm northeast was a body too fragile and broken to save, facing southwest in sitting posture, flexed. About 50 cm in front of this body were two bowls, a miniature plate painted with a guanaco head design (170494: Fig. 178; Chap. 6), and another, broken, which was retrieved only in part because of a cave-in of the excavation (170495: Fig. 179; Chap. 6). Sherds were collected at several levels (170496–8).

**GRAVE 15.** 12 m north of Grave 3 and 8 m west. At 100 cm was a "roof" of four small huarango poles burned to length (i.e., not cut). Below this, the grave was 90 cm in diameter. At 300 cm deep was an adult [male] body with much-deformed skull (170499), huddled, facing southwest. In front, at 310 cm, two bowls, one containing a mussel shell (170500–1: Figs. 208–209 [Pl. 11]; Chap. 7).

**GRAVE 16.** 5 m west of Grave 15. At 50 cm, a roof of five large huarango poles burned to length, with many pecay leaves. Grave well about 100 cm in diameter. At 150 cm deep, at northwest, the body of an infant in a cooking pot with a bowl (170504: Fig. 235; Chap. 8) and mussel shell outside but in touch with the pot. At 200 cm, about in center of tomb, a skeleton too badly deteriorated to save, skull undeformed but position not determinable. Traces of cloth on bones. Near body, three vessels (170505–7: Figs. 232–234; Chap. 8).

**GRAVE 17.** 1 m south of second body [B] of Grave 14 (170493). Just below the fire line mentioned, at 150 cm, was a roof of cañas brava (Fig. 21). At 350 cm were twelve vessels (170509–16: See Figs. 199–201, 203 [Pl. 9]; Chap. 6 and Figs. 204–205; Chap 7). The associated body, southeast of these vessels, apparently in east part of grave, was 380 cm deep, the bones very rotten, too broken to save. Near the head was a thin sheet of gold (original number 157, Peruvian government) stamped with a monster head and with four small holes for attachment. [Kroeber's field notebook indicates that this gold artifact was trapezoidal in shape, being 160 mm wide at the base and 125 mm wide at the top, with sides 130 mm in length.] To the SW of the body were three more vessels (170517–19: Fig. 202, Chap. 6 and Figs. 206–207, Chap. 7). Most of the fifteen vessels were intact when discovered but cracked, hence several were recovered broken.

FIGURE 30. *Section of antara (170488), Majoro Chico A, Grave 10*

**GRAVE 18.** 20 m north of the north adobe wall and 11 east of its northwest corner. At 150 cm was a roof of six rather small huarango poles burned to length. Below this roof, the grave was about 100 cm in diameter through sandy soil, less gravel than usual. At 300 cm was a group of fourteen vessels near the body of an adult [female with deformed skull] in east part of grave, with a pathological tooth but the bones badly deteriorated, and the skeleton was confused by our workmen in removing vessels, most of them pairs (170522–35, 170540: see Figs. 163–174; Chap. 6).

**GRAVE 19.** 9 m north of Grave 1. At 20 cm down was a black cookpot, 60 cm by 45 cm, with conical bottom, cloth over its opening, and held down by a boulder. The pot was empty; it did not even contain sand as usual. No burial was found.

**GRAVE 20.** 9 m north of Grave 1 and 1 m east. At 50 cm was the top of a row (sic: layer?) of adobes set vertically, more-or-less covering the grave, which was about 1 m in diameter, in more soil and less sand and gravel than usual. At 250 cm were two bodies, one on right, other on left, both with head to north. Bones in bad condition; neither skull could be recovered. One was the body of an old person, one of a child. On level with skull and arranged around southwest side of grave were three vessels and a shell spoon (170536–9: see Figs. 175–177; Chap. 6).

**GRAVE 21.** 8 m north and 5 m east of Grave 1. At 75 cm, a couple of huarango poles. Below, hole 1 m in diameter through much gravel. At 250 cm, a body, apparently in sitting posture, in northeast part, facing southwest. Bones too rotten and broken for recovery. No artifacts.

**GRAVE 22.** 5 m east of grave 21. At 100 cm was a llama (guanaco?), practically entire.

### *Majoro Chico Site E*

Kroeber's record of field work at Majoro Chico east has not been located. The catalogue lists recoveries from two Majoro east locations.

**GRAVE 1.** 170541–53, 400 cm deep. [Sherds and nine vessels were recovered. The pottery is shown in Figures 369–377 and described in Chapter 11, where Kroeber says of the grave, "Every vessel in it was broken, and the bones in such shape that none were saved."]

**GRAVE 2.** 80 cm deep, sherds (170554) [test pit?].

## La Huayrona

La Huayrona is about 3 km from Nazca on the Lomas road. The site worked is partly on the southeast corner of Hacienda Pangaravi (Fig. 10), but mostly on Huayrona, and is marked by a small knoll north of a cavelike formation in the hills to the south. At Huayrona begins a wash that in its westward course swings considerably south of the Nazca Valley cultivation (see schematic map, Fig. 9) and is marked by a scattered growth of huarangos. The site itself is very little above the level of cultivation and within 10 m of the southernmost irrigation ditch.

A north-south fence about 50 m east of the knoll divides the Huayrona site into two parts. In the west part, huaqueros had excavated graves, some of which must have been large and deep, with a roof consisting of a layer of vertically set adobes of the irregular, hand-formed type. Surface sherds were mostly Nazca. In the east part, the sherds were of Late type, there were more bones and some coarse cloth, and the graves appear to have been shallower (Fig. 32). The surface sherds from both sections of Huayrona unfortunately got mixed (170593) before the difference was realized.

We worked at Huayrona one day (August 21) with eight men. A number of prospect holes in the west section met with no success. All graves dug were in the east section and were mostly either poor or of Late type.

**GRAVE 1.** About 60 m east of the north-south fence and 15 m south of the irrigation ditch. At 40 cm the mummy bundle of an infant, upright, facing southwest, bound in cloth held around the head with a sling (170578).

Some 50 cm northeast of this was a more confused bundle consisting of a child's bones in rough cloth. Under this, at 80 cm, was one large huarango pole, or log, and more-or-less below this a grave about 1 m in diameter. At 200 cm was a skeleton [adult female] with deformed head and one pathological leg bone (170579), hair on head, a wad of cotton in mouth. There were bits of cloth on the bones, two sticks across the lap, and two more (170580) at sides, apparently bracing body in upright position, in flexed sitting posture, facing west. In front of body were four vessels (170581–84: see Figs. 378–380; Chap. 11).

**GRAVE 2.** 26 m south of Grave 1. At 30 cm deep, in gravel, were the bones of a child of about 6, wrapped in coarse cotton cloth. Nothing else.

**GRAVE 3.** 14 m south of Grave 1. At 150 cm, in a very definite well 90 cm in diameter, was a decorated bowl (170586: Fig. 407; Chap. 13) which contained corn and some cotton rope. No burial was found.

**GRAVE 4.** 18 m east and 12 m south of Grave 1. At 25 cm, in sand, the body of an adult woman on right side, head toward northwest, cloth band (170587) around head. Right leg flexed, left bent only at knee, hair over face. Guinea pig at chest, arms at sides. Bones in good condition, but only the undeformed skull was collected (170588). Some sherds were under this body (170589: Fig. 31).

**GRAVE 5.** 12 m east and 4 m north of Grave 1. At 25 cm, a mummy bundle of a child, seated, flexed, hands on knees, face to northwest. Wrapped in coarse cloth garments, cotton over head, face, and around body under garments. Limbs wrapped separately. Nothing else.

**GRAVE 6.** 17 m east of Grave 4. At 100 cm deep, in sand and gravel, a quantity of cotton cloth and cordage, among which was a gourd containing a guinea pig, a sling (170590), and a thorn spindle with whorl and leather (170591).

**GRAVE 7.** 3 m north and 3 m east of Grave 1. At 25 cm, in soil, slings and cordage (170592), and immediately below them bones wrapped in coarse cloth. Position obscure; woman(?); no head. Half gourd with undetermined contents was set with the bones.

FIGURE 31. *Bowl (170589) from beneath interment, La Huayrona, Grave 4*

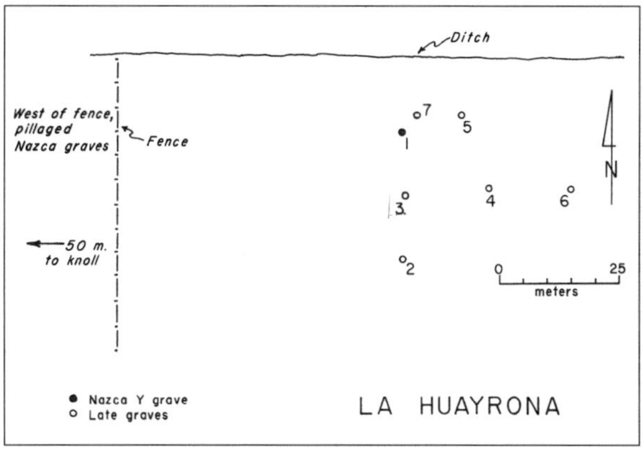

FIGURE 32. *La Huayrona, plan of grave locations*

## Paredones

This site is on the hills almost due south of Nazca. The hills come close to the cultivated area, leaving practically no pampa between. The main ruins are of large molded adobes built on the rocks in fort style, but rubble walls of mixed rock and adobe are also present (Fig. 33). Buildings stretch for some distance both east and west (Figs. 34–36). The site has been so much exploited by huaqueros that it was not deemed worthwhile to work it.

In local opinion, this is an Inca ruin. A great many sherds are on the surface and are largely of Late type, though not particularly in Inca style. A small lot collected (170595) appears typical. In his brief 1925 reconnaissance, Kroeber saw huaqueros digging out a grave east of the ruin, in which were the fragments of a jar painted with disarticulated human elements, which he purchased. The piece is described below, under post-*Y* (170150: Fig. 362; Chap. 10).

## Agua Santa

Agua Santa lies about 1 km west of Ocongalla in the same type of situation, where the road from the Hacienda Agua Santa comes out onto the pampa (Fig. 11). This road divides the site into two parts, which our work showed to be quite different in period.

The east portion was flatter, and some of the graves dug here (numbers 1,3,4, and 5) appeared to be of Late Period; others were Nasca *Y* and Nazca *B:* numbers 6–13. Grave locations are shown in Figure 37.

The west part was a slight knoll perhaps 100 m in diameter at the top. This had been so thoroughly dug up that it was difficult to find an undisturbed spot large enough for a grave. Most of the sherds here were Nazca. The proportion was even larger than shown in our surface collection (170652–3) since this contains sherds from the east part as well. Hand-formed adobes, sticks used in grave roofs, a few undeformed skulls, some cloth, and a number of large pots were observed from old diggings. The best pieces from this site were bought from a *peon* living by the site, who said they were from three graves in the west or Nasca portion, considered by the expedition as Graves 14, 15, and 16.

We worked here two days with eight men (August 23–24). A great many barren trial pits were sunk, and it appeared improbable that much more material existed at the site.

**GRAVE 1[A].** At the top of the slope just east of the road into Hacienda Agua Santa, 100 cm deep in sand and gravel, was the body of an old woman wrapped in cotton and cloth and tied with alpaca rope (170605), flexed, facing west. At her feet were two Late Period vessels (170606–7: Figs. 410–411; Chap. 13), one of them containing a guinea pig. A small cloth bag (170608) was tied at the back of her neck. The skull was undeformed. At 150 cm were two more vessels (170609–10: see Fig. 381; Chap. 11) in terminal *Y* style, evidently from an earlier interment [Grave 1B].

About 3 m south of this grave was dug up the body of a llama, apparently prematurely born and wrapped in cloth and bound with a sling like a human.

**GRAVE 2.** About 70 m west and 30 m north of Grave 1. At 150 cm, in sand, two skulls touching each other. One broken, upside down, face to south, the other with face to northwest; the first perhaps slightly flattened frontally, the other undeformed. With them were two vessels (170612–3: Figs. 412–413; Chap. 13) and several sherds

FIGURE 33. *Paredones, detail of stone wall construction [53957]*

FIGURE 34. *Paredones, view east up valley, with summit of ruins in foreground [53990]*

FIGURE 35. *Paredones (foreground), view east from summit toward lower Cantayo cemeteries [53953]*

FIGURE 36. *View west (downstream) from Paredones over Pangaravi and Majoro [53952]*

(170611). At about 100 cm was found the lower jaw of the first skull. This grave was some distance west of Graves 1, 3, 4, and 5, which lay close together.

**GRAVE 3.** 1.5 m west of Grave 1. Same type as Grave 1. Body of youthful person facing northeast at 50 cm deep. Two long detached braids of hair in lap (170614: Fig. 38a). Skull undeformed.

**GRAVE 4.** 5 m east of Grave 1. At 100 cm, in sand, the body of an adult woman, the undeformed head (170615) and body bound in cloth, a sling (170616) around the head, and tied to sling was a bag containing coca (?) leaves. The mouth was very full of coca leaves. Hair dressed in roll across back of head, body seated facing west, hands on chest, and "bound about (with ?) ears of corn and cotton." Elbows held out from body by a cane about 80 cm long passing through hands across chest under cloth. In front of her was the body of a very young child wrapped in cloth, tied with a sling, also a bowl (170618: Fig. 414; Chap. 13) in front of body. A wooden implement (170619) was in the grave at 50 cm. This grave as dug by us was about 80 cm in diameter, but both north and south walls showed indications of there having been other bodies.

**GRAVE 5.** 10 m south of Grave 4. Just under surface of ground, a mass of cloth, hair, and cordage; also sherds. Below was a layer of small branches. At 50 cm was the top of the head of the body of an old woman arranged as in Grave 4. Under right arm, 80 cm deep, a bowl (170620: Fig. 415; Chap. 13) containing a guinea pig. Under left arm, skull of another body (a younger woman) arranged immediately alongside (S) of the first, but slightly lower.

In the area covered by Graves 1, 3, 4, and 5 there were apparently many similar, shallow, and poor Late burials.

**GRAVE 6.** 35 m east of Grave 2 but nearer to it than to Graves 1, 3, 4, or 5. At 40 cm was a layer of five small cut-to-length poles and some canes bound together, also many pacae leaves. Under this was a very large jar with top broken, maximum D 85 cm, H 95 cm. In this was a body [adult female], much disarranged, with two kinds of cloth about bones, the skull frontally flattened (170621), 100 cm deep. Plain sherds, parts of adobes also in jar.

**GRAVE 7.** About 0.3 m east (outside to outside) from Grave 6 was a much smaller jar, D 45 cm, H 50 cm, intact. This contained the body of a young person with wisdom teeth not erupted, with hair on frontally flattened skull but skull broken. A few sherds (170622: Fig. 39) were in jar with body.

**GRAVE 8.** 20 m east and 10 m south of Grave 6. At 40 cm, in sand, fire-blackened pot with flaring lip about 30 cm high by 35 m in diameter; covered over with cloth and stone slab. In this the body of a very young infant wrapped in cotton and badly rotted cloth.

**GRAVE 9.** 18 m east and 4 m south of Grave 2. At 20 cm, some textile fragments (170625). At 40 cm, in much disturbed soil, the disarranged body of an adult. The frontally flattened skull (170623) was between the leg bones and all were wrapped in a piece of net cloth (170624). The lower jaw lay 40 cm to the north. Skull on right side facing southeast. Near the body were three vessels (170626–8: see Fig. 416; Chap. 13); fragments of several more (170629); a white bowl filled with hard adobe (170630: Fig. 417); and a small pencil-like wooden artifact (170631). A necklace of cordage with shell pendants (170632) was near the skull.

Grave 9 was doubtfully of Nasca *Y* phase; Graves 10, 11, 12, and 15 were Nasca *B*.

**GRAVE 10.** 10 m east of Grave 6. At 100 cm deep, in 90 cm D hole in gravel, was a skeleton [adult, female?] with frontally flattened skull (170633), facing southwest. Near the body were three vessels (170634–6: Figs. 293–295; Chap. 9) and three small balls of cotton yarn with a thin wooden weaving implement exhibiting incised designs (170637). [The wooden artifact is illustrated in Figure 40. It is 14.8 cm in length, 5 cm wide, and 3 mm thick. The surfaces are very smooth. There are two end panels pyroengraved on each side. Bits of cloth and yarn adhere to the surfaces, obscuring the pyroengraved designs; however, they all appear similar to the panel illustrated in Figure 40.]

**GRAVE 11.** 12 m west of Grave 8. At 30 cm, a large fire-blackened pot containing the body of a young child; also a jar (170639: Fig. 296; Chap. 9).

**GRAVE 12.** 12 m south of Grave 6. At 20 cm were adult leg bones in good condition, skin still over one knee; two vessels in fragments (170640–1: Figs. 297–298; Chap. 9);

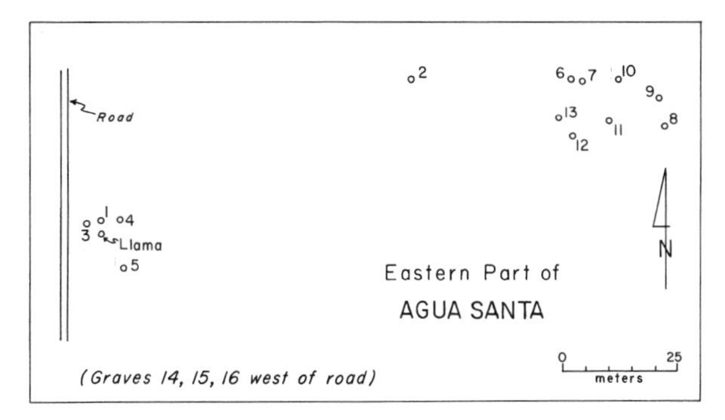


FIGURE 37. *Agua Santa, plan of grave locations*

llama or guanaco bones; and part of an infant skeleton—all more-or-less confused (possibly a reburial or discards from a previous excavation).

**GRAVE 13.** 8 m south and 3 m west of Grave 6. At 100 cm were the bones of a child wrapped in coarse cotton cloth; nothing with them.

**GRAVE 14.** Material from this and Graves 15 and 16 was bought from a peon living adjacent to the site, and the data are his. Grave 14 was shallow and without *barbacoa* roof; it contained a jar (170642: Fig. 299; Chap. 9).

**GRAVE 15.** Four vessels (170643–6: Figs. 300–303; Chap. 9).

**GRAVE 16.** Four pieces (170647–50: Figs. 212 [Pl. 12]–215; Chap. 7), the last a miniature double-spout.

### Ocongalla West

Ocongalla Zero, where the expedition began its active operations, has already been described. It was on Sr. Enrique Fracchia's invitation that work was switched to Majoro Chico. About August 24, excavations were resumed at Ocongalla, a short distance downstream from the former site.

Most of the strip of pampa bordering on the south of the huarangual and cultivation between Haciendas Ocongalla and Agua Santa was used as a burial ground. More than half of the east part of this strip is known locally as Ocongalla (i.e., belongs to it), hence we used the suffixes West A and West B to distinguish certain areas from Ocongalla Zero proper, where the expedition had worked previously (Fig. 11).

About halfway between Ocongalla and Agua Santa there are remains of a Late settlement (Fig. 11). There is a semicircular row of low, wind-blown hummocks whose approximate diameter is the edge of the huarangual. Around the outside slope of these hummocks is a row of stumps of large huarango limbs or pacae poles so regular and complete as to leave no doubt of having been planted

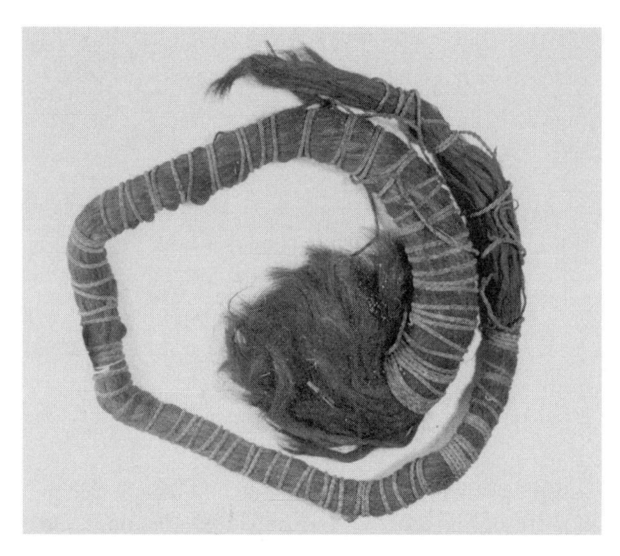

FIGURE 38a. *Agua Santa, Grave 3, hair braid (170614)*

FIGURE 38b. *Cahuachi Aj, Grave 12, hair braid (171255)*

FIGURE 39. *Sherds (170622) from inside burial jar, Agua Santa, Grave 7*

(Fig. 41). The space between the east and west sides of the semicircle of stumps is about 150 m, but the stumps extend into the huarangual and may have formerly encircled a larger area. About 35 m outside the palisade and parallel to it is an enclosing wall, mostly of boulders but in places of rectangular adobes. Inside the wall and palisade are remains of houses. The hummocks may be attributed to wind drifting sand behind the palisade, although in that case the hummocks would be expected on both the lee sides of the stumps instead of always outside them.

We dug out some of those limbs and found that they had originally been planted somewhat less than 1 m deep and that, since their erection, over 1 m of refuse and sand had accumulated, so that they now stand over 2 m deep (Fig. 42). The portions originally below ground differ in condition from the upper portions. There were also smaller poles between the larger trunks and limbs (see Grave 7, Ocongalla West A).

Within the walled area sherds are abundant and practically all Late. No Nazca sherds or burials were found within the walled area except in the northwest corner which formed part of Ocongalla West B (see below).

## *Ocongalla West A*

A Late graveyard stretched from just east of the east enclosing palisade and wall for about 100 m east. Still farther east there is a Nazca cemetery, our Ocongalla West A, which reaches nearly to Ocongalla Zero. There is also another Late burial ground in this vicinity, but so far as we could see the Late and the Nazca cemeteries do

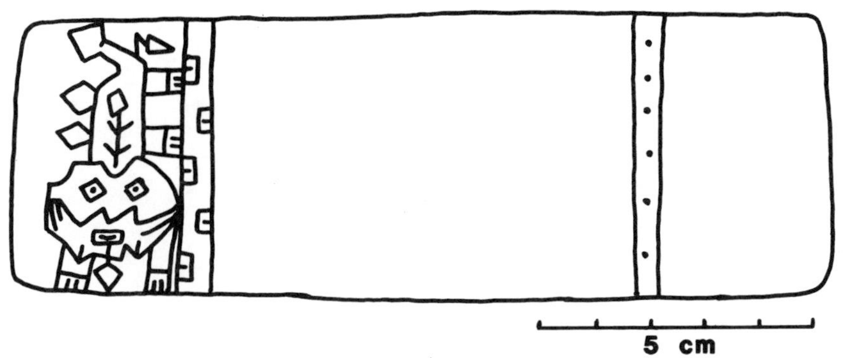


FIGURE 40. *Pyroengraved wooden artifact (170637), Agua Santa, Grave 10*

not overlap; certainly not to any considerable extent. At any rate, about 200 m west of the adobe structure of Ocongalla Zero was another structure, perhaps more definitely pyramidal in form (sic), which we took as the marker for Site Ocongalla West A (Fig. 43). Both areas had been much worked by huaqueros, who had dug out many graves some 3 m to 4 m deep and as much in diameter. In one case observed, a single layer of boulders and hand-formed adobes constituted a roof, like a floor, only a little below the present surface, and 2 m below this was another roof of large huarango sticks, below which was the grave. A considerable number of trial pits sunk by us in the Ocongalla West A vicinity were fruitless.

FIGURE 41. *Ocongalla West B, looking across edge of pampa and cultivation to ridges north of valley. Palisade in foreground [53954]*

**GRAVE 1.** Adjacent to north face of the West A "pyramid" and just east of a north-south buttress wall, at 200 cm, was a partial skeleton in coarse cloth. Thrown up during our excavation, though apparently not part of this burial, was a fragment of a skull (170654) that may have been a trophy head [adult frontal bone with small, circular hole between orbits].

**GRAVE 2.** 1 m west of the wall of Grave 1 but on the other side of the buttress wall, at 100 cm, was a roof of cane. At 200 cm was a much disintegrated skeleton with traces of an elaborate textile in colors. Near the bones lay some presumed coloring material (170655).

**GRAVE 3.** 0.5 m west and 1.5 m south of Grave 2, under the 1-m-high west wall of the pyramid. At 100 cm below the bottom of this wall, directly under it, were portions of a fire-blackened pot inverted over a frontally flattened skull (170656). The [adult female] body sat in almost pure sand on the north side of the tomb, skull on (its) left side with face to west. Bones in fair condition. Slight traces of cloth.

**GRAVE 4.** At some distance, about 30 m west of Grave 1. At 60 cm, a layer of cane and pacae leaves; under this a thin layer of adobe; under this, five huarangos about

FIGURE 42. *Ocongalla West B, palisade in area in which several graves were opened [53973]*

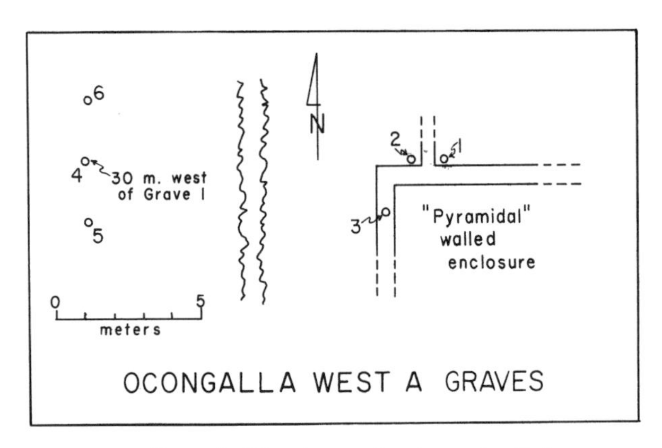


FIGURE 43. *Ocongalla West A, grave locations and walled structure*

FIGURE 44. *Ocongalla West B, excavation profile showing upper Ica layer and clean layer above Nazca graves [53960]*

18 cm in diameter, some cut and some burned to length. Under these, a number of small huarango poles tied together in the center. Below this, a pit 50 cm in diameter through gravel. At 140 cm, a skull of a child [age 20–36 months], frontally flattened. Near the body, a bowl (170657: Fig. 180; Chap. 6) containing squash seeds. Traces of cloth. There was a tarlike material on some of the bones (170658).

**GRAVE 5.** 2 m south of Grave 4. At 20 cm (in field notes; catalogue says 70 cm), in very gravelly soil, were five pottery vessels (170659–63: Figs. 181–185; Chap. 6). The body was that of a child, seated, facing southwest, the bones very fragile. In the upper part of the grave (this suggests 70 cm as the total depth) was a joint of cane containing thread (170664). [The field notes state that bowls 170660–61 had gourd vessels inside them, and bits of cloth adhered to the outside of gourd or bowl, 170660.]

**GRAVE 6.** 2 m north of Grave 4. At 20 cm were a net-like cloth in colors (170665: shown in O'Neale 1937, pl. 37i), some coarse cloth, and a child's embroidered garment (170668) with an infant's bones in these textiles; also the fragments of a bowl and a jar (170667–8: see Fig. 216; Chap. 7). The grave (proper) was below, in gravel and sand, 200 cm deep, the body of an adult with bones much broken and the skull deformed. Nothing from the 200-cm level seemed worth saving. The objects with the child at 20 cm must have represented a secondary burial, if not, a reinterment. But the two vessels seem Nazca *A*.

## *Ocongalla West B*

The northwest corner of the walled and palisaded enclosure of Late Period overlapped part of a Nazca burial ground (Fig. 11). Here several deep graves had been excavated by huaqueros; one under a huarango tree must have been 4 m deep in very heavy gravel. Near it, a large tree had grown over a wall of hand-formed adobes. By the palisade, one old excavation passed through 60–80 cm of refuse with Ica ware sherds, then 60–80 cm of sand and gravel to a roof of huarango poles. Below this the grave extended about 100 cm deeper, and a few sherds seemed to indicate a Nazca burial. [Stratigraphy is shown in Figure 44.]

The following represent the expedition's operations here, which include several graves showing *stratification*.

**GRAVE 1.** About 20 m west of northwest segment of the palisade and 15 m south of fence. After 20 cm through sand and 100 cm in sandy soil, in a well about 60 cm square, at 120 cm, there were six vessels (170671–6: see Figs. 335–338; Chap. 10) in Nazca *(B-Y)* style; the bones of an infant wrapped in coarse cloth and in white net cotton cloth (170677), and in this a sealed joint of cane (170678). A detail of textile 170677b is shown in O'Neale (1937), plate 67. Properly, of course, cloth from a *B-Y* grave should not have been included in an Early Nazca monograph; compare comment on Majoro Chico Site A, Grave 8.

**GRAVE 2.** 20 m west of Grave 1. Just under present ground surface was the slightly deformed skull of a body, flexed and seated facing northwest. Coarse cloth around ribs and arms; part of old cookpot over head. Bones in very poor condition. Nothing was saved.

**GRAVE 3.** Contained a *stratification*, immediately outside the huarango palisade. To the west there were about

FIGURE 45. *Ocongalla West B, Grave 3, wooden artifact (170681) found in upper grave shaft*

100 cm of undisturbed soil, containing a number of sherds, all Late (170679). Below this were no such sherds. At 220 cm there was a roof consisting of a number of large boulders arranged over a large coarse pot with a broken-out mouth, the boulders being surmounted by a dome-like layer of adobe about 80 cm in diameter. Between 100 cm and 220 cm we found a number of Nazca sherds (170680), but no more Late ones. A wooden implement (170681) was found above the roof at 130 cm (Fig. 45). The middle bottom of the pot was about 300 cm deep. In it were traces of many disintegrated bones and seven Nazca *B* vessels (170682–8: see Figs. 222 [Pl. 14]–227; Chap. 8).

**GRAVE 4.** 1 m south of Grave 2. At 100 cm was set a large upright piece of huarango. Under this, at 180 cm, were at least five vessels in fragments (170689–92: see Figs. 228–231; Chap. 8) arranged in a circle east of two large hand-formed adobes. No bones were found in this grave, which was dug to over 3 m. The pottery is Nazca *B*.

**GRAVE 5.** *Stratified*, 2 m south of Grave 3 and of similar type. The 100 cm of topsand carried Ica sherds. The top of the roof came at 200 cm. This consisted of adobe with boulders set in it and was about 40 cm thick by 150 cm in diameter. This sealed over a large red pot, 50 cm high, which was about half full of sand, along with two large boulders and fine traces of bones. There was nothing else.

**GRAVE 6.** 0.8 m southwest of Grave 2. At 100 cm, through gravel, was a much-broken pot over the bones of an adult. The skull was broken, the bones confused and fragile. To southwest of skull (probably in front of it) was a plain red bowl (170698: Fig. 394; Chap. 12), which was set in a larger plain red bowl (170697), broken. A mussel-shell spoon (170699) lay in the first bowl. There were additional bowls (170693–6: Figs. 392–393, 395–396; Chap. 12), apparently nested one in another and with mussel-shell spoons.

Graves 2, 4, and 6 were quite close together but apparently independent. About 1.5 m south of Grave 4 was a pot similar to that in Grave 6, near the surface and empty. And 1 m northeast of this was a similar pot, also near the surface, and containing the badly broken bones of a child.

**GRAVE 7.** *Stratified*, 3 m southeast of Grave 6, partly under the palisade and also partially under a layer of large thin rectangular adobes just under the present surface. Figure 46 gives the plan and section. Below was an undisturbed stratum, 80–120 cm thick, of refuse—corn stalks, sherds, sand, and so forth. No Nazca sherds were found in this stratum, those identifiable being Ica. Next came a stratum of sand and gravel of about the same thickness. Then, at about 200 cm, a roof of five or more fairly large poles so much decayed that two of them had given way and allowed the tomb below to be filled in with sand and gravel. Also helping to constitute the roof were a number of small, irregular adobes with boulders and adobe mortar. The grave below was about 1 m in diameter and 160 cm deep below the roof, or 390 cm below the present surface, and dug through heavy gravel. Near the bottom were some very-much-disintegrated bones, apparently in the northeast part of the grave, facing southwest. At the sides were seven vessels with Nazca *B* decoration (170700–06: see Figs. 239–243; Chap. 9). A few sherds (170707) collected below the tomb roof were also Nazca.

**GRAVE 8.** *Stratified*, 8 m south of Grave 7. Like 7, this grave was partly under but mostly just east of the palisade. There was an undisturbed top stratum of 80 cm of Ica type refuse; then 100 cm of sand and gravel with little

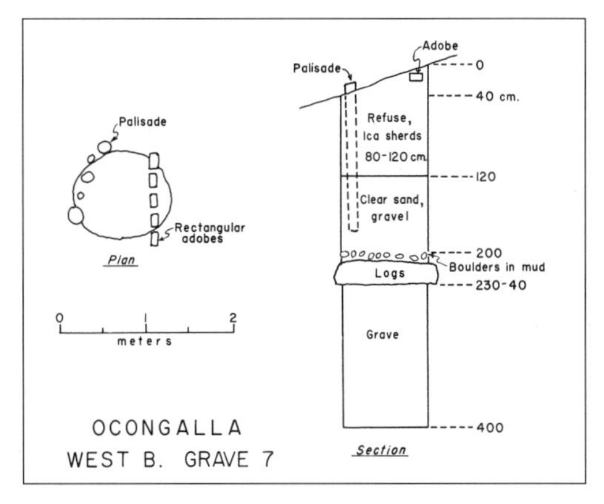


FIGURE 46. *Ocongalla West B, Grave 7, profile*

or no refuse. Then came the roof: first a thin layer of adobe; below this, a layer of small huarango or pacae poles about 2 m long, mostly burned to length; below this, canes laid side-by-side and tied together. Near the center of the roof were vertical canes that may have been set as a marker. Beneath the roof was a well about 110 cm in diameter, sunk through heavy gravel, which apparently was as empty as when left by the original diggers, since a painted goblet (170708: Fig. 244; Chap. 9) was found practically uncovered. The skeleton of a child had gone to dust except for the lower jaw. The bones and jar were 360 cm deep. It seems certain that about a meter of soil accumulated over this grave after it was made. Such graves cannot be detected until most of the undisturbed top layer has been removed.

**GRAVE 9.** *Stratified*, 1 m south and a little east of Grave 7, hence more definitely under the palisade. This grave was an almost exact counterpart of Grave 7 except that its total depth was 400 cm and it contained ten or eleven vessels (170709–19: see Figs. 245–253; Chap. 9) near the bottom of the grave, at 380–400 cm. At 400 cm. there were also a number of stone objects that include two beads, a pendant, and stained stones (170719–22). [The locations and groupings of the artifacts in this grave are given with the pottery descriptions in Chapter 9.]

**GRAVE 10.** *Stratified*, 1.5 m south and a little west of Grave 9 and similar in type to it. At 300 cm had been a rotten roof that had given way so that portions of poles and hand-formed adobes were found below. The soil there was definitely damp, as in Graves 7 and 9. At 500 cm there were eighteen pieces of pottery (170723–40: see Figs. 254–267; Chap. 9). The well of this grave was entirely filled with sand and gravel, not partially empty. Small fragments of badly disintegrated bones were noted, but not enough for determination. The total depth of the grave was about 550 cm.

**GRAVE 11.** Transitional *B-Y*, *stratified*, 7 m south of Grave 10 and immediately east of the palisade. Same type of overburden as in Grave 10. At 300 cm was a wooden implement [deaccessioned] and some sherds (170742). There was no roof. At 330 cm were the bones (170743) of an adult [female, age 35+ years], without skull, in squatting posture in northeast part of grave, facing southwest. Around the bones were traces of four kinds of cloth: netlike brown, coarse brown, fine blue net, and a pinkish net of which some could be saved (170744). There was a layer of pacay leaves and rushes (or bark?) under the bones. Beneath the pelvis were three bowls (170745–7: Figs. 339, 345–346; Chap. 10), 350 cm deep, containing traces of corn and other materials. In southwest part of grave, on bones of the feet, at 340 cm, were three more vessels (170748–50: Figs. 341 [Pl. 27]–342, 348; Chap. 10). There were also four other vessels at about the same depth (170751–54: see Figs. 340 [Pl. 26], 343–344; Chap. 10).

**GRAVE 12.** Nazca *B*, *stratified*, 2.5 m north and 2 m east of Grave 11. Top stratum as in Graves 10 and 11. At 170 cm were found two sherds (170782), one of blackware and the other incised and colored (i.e., presumably Paracas Cavernas). Just below these, at about 175 cm, was a roof of poles covered with boulders and adobe mortar. The poles were unusually large, up to 30 cm in diameter and 3.5 m long. Not all of them were uncovered, and the total number in the roof is not known. The ends seen were burned. Below them was an entirely independent second roof of the same type, the direction of the poles in this running at an angle of about 20 degrees to the first. This second layer was quite intact after removal of a portion of the first or upper. Below it was a well-like grave about 160 cm in diameter and apparently as empty as when left by its makers. Here, at 500 cm, (250 cm below the top of the second or lower roof), was the skeleton (170781) of an adult [female, age 35+ years] with deformed skull. The bones were very soft and were recovered only in part. They were only partially covered (by sand?). The body was on the north side of the grave, apparently in squatting posture facing southwest. With this body were twenty-six vessels, practically all intact when discovered (170755–80: see Figs. 268 [Pl. 21]–281; Chap. 9). This was the largest number of vessels in any grave opened to date and the highest proportion of intact ones. Of the twenty-six vessels, sixteen came in eight pairs of twins or duplicates, four others formed a set of "quadruplets."

### Pueblo Viejo

This site has much the same type of situation as Agua Santa, although the descent from the pampa to cultivation is greater and more precipitous. The site was inspected and some surface sherds (170796) collected. There were two graveyards. One was typical Nazca. In the other were an unusual number of skulls thrown out by huaqueros—over fifty, all undeformed. Sherds and cloth also suggested that this was a Late burying ground. The burial areas at Pueblo Viejo seemed so small and so worked over that we decided not to dig there.

## Soisongo

Soisongo Grande is, other than Aja, the one property on the north side of the river in which the expedition excavated. It lies about 15 km below Nazca, opposite Pacheco on which the Tiahuanacoid type of ware was found by Olson and Tello. [Julio C. Tello excavated at Pacheco in 1927, and Ronald L. Olson, on behalf of the American Museum of Natural History, New York, in 1930.] It is also more-or-less opposite Soisongo Chico. Soisongo extends upriver to Majoro Chico on whose south as well as north it abuts. Downriver from it lies Yapana.

The cemeteries noted at Soisongo were on the flat, gravelly first terrace back (N) of the cultivation. A few hundred meters behind (N) of the scarp of the first terrace rises the front of a second terrace. The first terrace is irregularly dotted with huarango trees, especially near its upstream end and along its south rim close to the cultivation. Just beyond the upriver end, the usually dry Río Socos comes in. According to some, this is only the easternmost of three mouths of the Socos, two others entering the Nazca above and below Yapana, but according to some, these two lower mouths are separate quebradas or have separate names.

The cemeteries explored by the expedition at Soisongo extend somewhat less than 1 km downstream (W) from the mouth of the Socos to a small point in the terrace scarp, and the burials opened were all within the first 100 m or so in from the scarp. Kroeber, Schenck, and Tello recognized five principal cemeteries, which were designated, in order from west to east, as Soisongo B, A, C, D, and E. Their general situation is shown in Figure 47, reproduced from a sketch drawn by Kroeber on September 11. Sites B, A, and C, are shown in Figures 48–50. No graves were opened at Sites D or E. Nasca styles *A*, *B*, and *Y* were all represented at Soisongo, but *Y* most heavily.

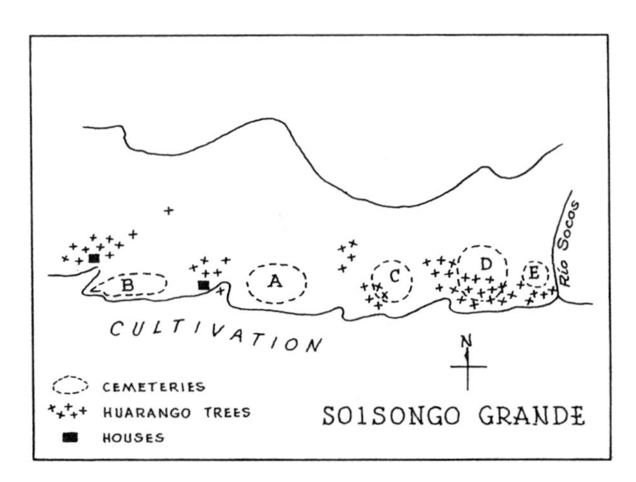


FIGURE 47. *Cemeteries A–E at Soisongo Grande*

There is a conflict of record over the first graves opened by the expedition at Soisongo, owing perhaps to the fact that not only had Kroeber returned to Nazca but that Tello and his assistants were now excavating cooperatively alongside the Marshall Field Expedition. The site plans were penciled by Kroeber in his field notebook (1), and he furnished inked copies of two of these to Schenck for inclusion in his grave-by-grave record, where they are still preserved as pages 32A and 34 of Schenck's typed field notes. Schenck also was still entering the catalogue, which reads:

Location A, Grave 1, 170797
  Grave 2, 170798–9
  surface, 170800–02
Location B, Grave 4, 170803

In his field notes, Schenck also describes Graves 1 and 2 as at site A in accord with his catalogue, and Graves 4–11 at Site B.

On the other hand, between Grave 8 and Grave 9 at B, there is in the field notes an inserted sheet, page 32B, which deals first with Soisongo B. This page of the record is a combination of Schenck's own records and data taken by him from Kroeber's notebook and differs from his own statements as they are summarized above. Thus he says, "Site A contains two small pyramidal structures, but not a single intact grave was found." The measurements of the structures are taken from Kroeber's notebook, which does not mention intact graves at Soisongo A, and the statement indeed contradicts what Schenck had already said on his page 32 and in the catalogue, 170797–802.

The discrepancy is not helped by Kroeber's data, which are silent on graves at A, showing only the pyramidal structures, and which at B show the positions of Graves 1, 2, 3, 4, and 11 and of two unnumbered graves but nothing on Graves 5–10. From C on there are no discrepancies.

As best the record can be restored today, it runs like this. The Marshall Field Expedition's crew and Tello's smaller Peruvian Museum crew dug at Soisongo simultaneously but of course in different graves and partly at different sites. Schenck kept record only of the expedition's work; Kroeber tried to keep track of both parties, but did not get complete records. He failed to enter the two expedition graves in his plan of A, he did not complete his plan at B, he did not begin to describe or sketch grave finds until B, Grave 11 and C, Grave 1. The result was some duplication and some omission of record for a few graves at Sites A and B.

We shall now present the record as it stands, though in part rearranged and as usual slightly condensed.

### *Soisongo A*

Site A contains the two small pyramidal structures X and Y as shown in Figure 48, but this plan does not show the two graves excavated there.

The smaller pyramid, or Mound X, in the center of the grave field, was cut into (by us) from the north face to its middle. It is an 8-m-sq. mass bounded by an adobe wall averaging 1 m or more in height and filled mainly with gravel (taken from an excavation just E), together with layers of maize straw. The wall was built of wedge-shaped adobes set on their base ends, as described and illustrated in Chapter 4.

The larger rectangular Mound Y, about 60 m north-east of X, outside the grave area, is 20 m east-west by 12 m north-south, plus an 8-x-6-m annex extending out from the north half of the west end of the main rectangle. H ca. 1.5 m. This heap was not excavated, but the rectilinear shape, plus an adjacent depression from which the material was taken, show its artificial nature.

The expedition opened two graves at Soisongo A.

**GRAVE 1.** 30 m north and 5 east of "Pyramid" X. This must have been near the north edge of Site A. At 50 cm down was a roof of five rather short poles burned to length. There were no boulders or adobes in the roof. At 100 cm was the deformed skull (170797) of a middle-aged woman, seated facing southwest, with most of the skin still on the bones, some bones still joined, hair on head. Coarse cloth about shoulders and lower limbs.

[Specimen 170797 includes a mass of hair, among which a wig of human hair has been identified. The hair on the wig is attached to a narrow band of twined hair that, presumably, was wrapped around the head. The wig hair and the hair mass in which it was found were derived from different individuals. See Hair Analysis under Subsequent Research in the editor's Preface.]

**GRAVE 2.** 8 m east and 2 m north of Grave 1. At 50 cm, in small hard-packed gravel, were traces of a badly rotted floor (*sic*—roof) of poles with boulders on them. Below, in fine gravel, was an oblong grave about 1 m x 1.5 m. At 150 cm, traces of an adult skeleton, head in north part of the grave. Near the left foot were two vessels, a rectanguloid bowl and an angled goblet (170798–9: Figs. 349–350; Chap. 10), both characteristic of latest *B* or early *Y* phase and described in Chapter 10.

### *Soisongo B*

Site B was less than 100 m west of Site A by Schenck's notes, nearly 150 m by Kroeber's Figure 47. According to both, the site was about 75 m long east-west, half as broad, back in from the rim of the terrace.

In the plan of Soisongo B (Fig. 49), graves plotted in 1926 are shown by hollow squares; but hollow circles represent graves entered on the plan in 1957 from inter-grave distances and directions mentioned in Schenck's field notes. The black square on the right evidently represents a peon's hut (as in Fig. 47), not an ancient structure as in the plan of Soisongo A.

At the southwest end of the site Dr. Tello excavated two Nazca *Y* graves, his 1 and 3, both with shallow log roofs. Just south of Grave 3 was the small Grave 2, of a child under a jar with two Nazca (i.e., pre-Nazca *Y?*) bowls, the base of Grave 2 being on a level with the roof logs of Grave 3 and almost in contact with them, suggesting but not quite proving Grave 2 as being subsequent to Grave 3. (Thus Schenck's notes; Kroeber entered the three graves on his map but no information on their contents.)

Soisongo B Graves 4–11 were excavated by the expedition and were described both in Schenck's field notes and in the catalogue.

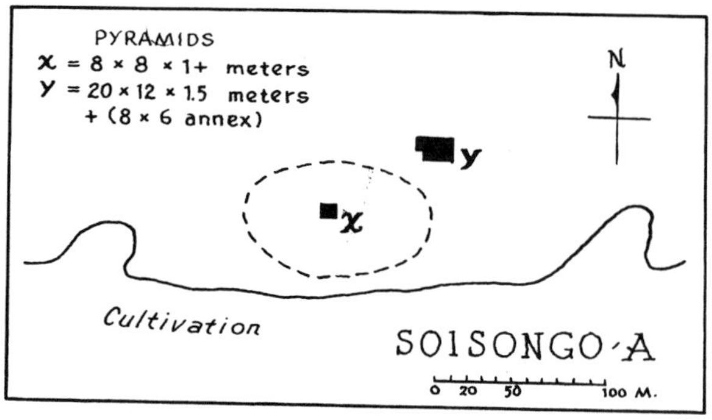

FIGURE 48. *Ancient structures at Soisongo A*

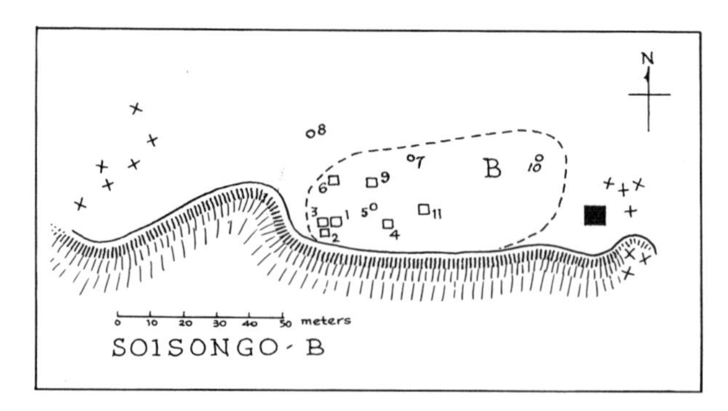


FIGURE 49. *Soisongo B, plan of grave locations*

**GRAVE 4.** In the south part of Site B close to the rim of the terrace (Fig. 49). At 40 cm was an inverted commonware red jar without handles with seven semicircles incised around circumference (170803: Fig. 397; Chap. 13). It had held food. About 50 cm west of this was a large jar with side handles, upright and full of sand, gravel, and soil; it was not collected. No burial was found.

**GRAVE 5.** 6 m west and 6 m north of Grave 4. At 20 cm the top of the undeformed skull (170806) of an adult seated facing south was encountered. The skin was intact to such an extent that practically all bones were in place and the body could be lifted intact from the grave. A coarse cloth around the shoulders, a half gourd near the body, and the skin and bones of a guinea pig were not saved; a sling was saved (170805). There were Nazca sherds (170804) in the soil around the body. (The shallowness, preservation, grave contents, and undeformed skull all suggest a quite Late intrusive burial in grave soil containing sherds of the earlier period.)

**GRAVE 6.** 10 m north and 17 m west of Grave 5. At 70 cm was a roof of boulders and badly rotted poles that could not be removed intact. Below there was a rectangular pit in fine gravelly soil; at 190 cm, the body, facing south, seated between two large semicylindrical adobes (as props?). The skull was not deformed [or only slightly deformed], hair still on the head; the bones (170807) in fair condition [adult female age 35+ years] but very dry; traces of coarse cloth and cordage. An inside-painted bowl (170808: Fig. 398; Chap. 13) was near the body.

**GRAVE 7.** 18 m north and 12 m east of Grave 5. At only 10 cm under the surface there was a child's undeformed skull, facing east; the body was bound in cotton and coarse cloth with two slings. At the right side of body was an inside rim-painted bowl (170809: Fig. 399; Chap. 13).

**GRAVE 8.** 30 m west and 5 m north of Grave 7. This would have been outside Site B as shown in Figure 49. Just under the surface was a child's body (with undeformed skull), bound in coarse cotton cloth, with two slings and nothing else. Not saved.

**GRAVE 9.** 5 m north of Grave 5. At 90 cm was a roof of boulders set in (a cake of) adobe on top of six huarango poles burned to length. Below was fine gravelly soil. The grave contained two bodies. At 270 cm was an old person with deformed skull [170810, male age 50+ years] seated in the west part of the grave, facing south. There were traces of cloth. South of this body [in the SW part of the grave], at 280 cm, were two bowls (170811–12: Figs. 363–364). [Vessel 170811 contained corn.] In the northeast part of grave was a young person [age 8–10 years], also with deformed skull (170813), at 280 cm deep, facing up *(sic)*. This skull also faced south. Both bodies had apparently been seated side-by-side in north part of grave. Under each was a handled face pitcher, that under the first body being considerably larger (170814–15: Figs. 365–366; Chap. 11). (These *FPY* pitchers are characteristic of *Y2* phase.)

**GRAVE 10.** At the northeast limit of Site B. At only 3 cm was a bowl (170816: Fig. 400; Chap. 13) with traces of an infant burial.

**GRAVE 11.** 13 m east of Grave 5 and 1 m south, near the center of Site B. At 30 cm was a plain bowl (170817), very similar in shape and size to 170816 (Fig. 400) in Grave 10, but with black slip only on interior and exterior, and with some carbon adhering to the exterior. Two wooden implements (170818–19) were also found at the same level as bowl 170817. [Artifact 170818 is a cylindrical digging-stick, 57 cm long by 3–5 cm in diameter, with a fire-hardened point. The opposite end is broken (as noted in the original field catalogue), and the now-missing 170819 may have been part of 170818.] At 80 cm came a roof of eight huarangos laid east-west. At 180 cm was exposed the deformed head of a mummy (170820) facing southwest [male, age 50+ years], whose feet were at 240 cm. By the left side stood a three-handled, swollen-mouthed, crude whitish jar (170821), the only vessel (Fig. 186: Chap. 6). The mummy was clothed (but not stuffed) and it held together until it was moved. Over shoulders and body, outside, was a pink cloth (170822); inside, another (170823, embroidered designs of 170823d are shown in Fig. 51), and a wool belt (170824); wound around the head, turbanlike, three times, was a yellowish cloth with yellow feathers attached (170825). (The jar suggests Nazca *A;* the textiles are described in Chapter 6.)

### *Soisongo C*

Soisongo C lies between A and D. It was a smallish cemetery less exploited than A and B, studded with Nazca *A*, *B*, and *Y* graves plus intrusive later burials.

The sketch map (Fig. 50), notes on adobes (Chap. 4), and notes on specimens, including Tello's, are from Kroeber; Schenck continued his catalogue of specimens destined for Chicago and his field notes, though the latter are partly based on Kroeber's notebooks. What follows is these field notes, somewhat reduced, especially as regards specimens.

**GRAVE 1.** Near the northwest (N) end of Cemetery C as found previously dug up (Fig. 50). There was no roof; total depth, 190 cm. Body apparently seated, fallen over, skull broken. There were three angled goblets and two

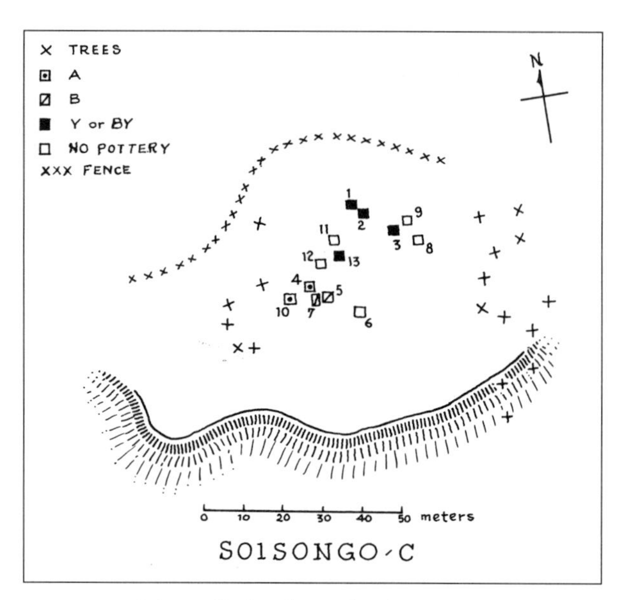


FIGURE 50. *Soisongo C, plan of grave locations*

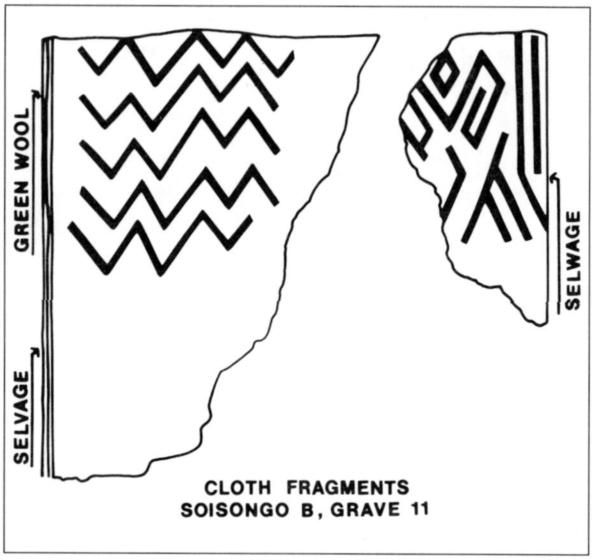

CLOTH FRAGMENTS
SOISONGO B, GRAVE 11
GREEN WOOL
SELVAGE
SELWAGE

FIGURE 51. *Embroidered textile designs (170823d), Soisongo B, Grave 11*

jars of late *B* or *B-Y* phase (170826–30: Figs. 351 [Pl. 28]–355; Chap. 10).

**GRAVE 2.** 3 m southeast of Grave 1. At 80 cm, top of a large reddish jar (170831: Fig. 356; Chap. 10) with convex mouth and black-and-white E design (cf. Grave 13 below), set over body of a child or young adolescent [age 14–20 years], around whose head (170832) a tapestry band (170833) was wound twice. Bottom of body at 125 cm. On the side toward Grave 1, a little higher than the body in Grave 2, was a fire-blackened cookpot with wide-flaring mouth, two-handled, 40 cm in diameter, 50 cm high, which was not saved.

**GRAVE 3.** 8 m southeast of Grave 2, had at 80 cm the usual stick roof. At 190 cm, the frontally flattened skull (170834) of a young adult (no wisdom teeth), probably male, facing east. At foot of body, at 225 cm, a bowl of unique shape (170835: Fig. 357; Chap. 10).

**GRAVE 4.** Dug by Tello for the Museo Nacional de Arqueología. Roof sticks at 50 cm. Underneath, a "well" 80 cm in diameter, through gravel down to 240 cm. Fairly dry, but skeleton much decomposed; no teeth, only skull fragments, most bones very light; two femoral fragments, though hollow, were heavy, and edges seemed anciently fractured. Three vessels: a figure-and-spout jar of a fisherman with net (Museo de Arqueología Peruana, MAP number 30/39); a low bowl with vertical walls, s-shaped sling design (30/40); slightly deeper bowl, also with sling design (30/41). This Grave 4 lies 22 m southwest of Grave 1 and is datum for the following:

**GRAVE 5.** About 5 m southeast of Grave 4 and 2 m southeast of Grave 7. At 90 cm, top of a huarango roof. Then a *caja*, or well, about 120 cm in diameter, through gravel, to 300 cm. Skeleton (170836) badly decomposed and broken; jaw fragments indicate an old person. Five vessels around the skeleton of Nazca *B* type (170837–41: Figs. 304–308; Chap. 9).

**GRAVE 6.** 400 cm deep, containing Nazca sherds (170842: Fig. 52) and a layer of burned straw and sticks, to hard gravel at bottom. No bones or vessels. An adobe wall on east side, about 100–200 cm down. The adobes are described in Chapter 4.

**GRAVE 7.** (Tello's first, numbered 1; our Grave 7) Between Graves 4 and 5, nearer 5. Roof sticks at 40 cm, the 80-cm well below lined with boulders set in mud. At 160 cm, the decayed skull and skeleton, and a pair of small-waisted goblets (MAP 30/37–38), probably of Nazca *B* phase. A child's skull, undeformed, was said to have been in the upper part of the tomb. The excavation was not followed through by Kroeber.

**GRAVE 8.** 5 m southeast of Grave 3. Depth, 150 cm to skull. Roof present, depth not noted. No vessels. Seated skeleton (170843) facing southeast, in good condition, probably of a young adult male, all molars erupted, some wear to bite. Skull frontally flattened. Phase within Nazca Period not determinable.

**GRAVE 9.** 4 m northeast of Grave 3. No roof, no vessels found. At probably about 120 cm, a frontally much-shortened skull (170844), probably of an old woman, some hair left, face downward. Bones fragile but mostly intact. A new workman caved this tomb in as being useless, without orders. Again, it was evidently Nazca, but nothing can be said as to phase.

**GRAVE 10.** 4 m southwest of Grave 4. At 50 cm, several pieces of a large, crude, three-handled, wavy-line-striped jar (170845: Fig. 187; Chap. 6), covering a plain red, conical-bottomed, wide-mouthed, two-handled jar 40 cm high (170846: Fig. 188; Chap. 6). This contained a child's skeleton; the skull seemed deformed but fell apart at touch. The red jar was otherwise empty and was set on a few large fire-blackened sherds. Nothing was found deeper.

**GRAVE 11.** 8 m southwest of Grave 1, ca. 8 m northeast of Grave 12. Roof of ten small, chopped-off pacae sticks, sloping from north to south from 60 cm to 120 cm. On these lay, at 60 cm, face up, a crude stone head (170847): only a nose is definitely recognizable (Fig. 53). Frontally flattened adult skull [female, age 35+ years], about as broad as long, (170848) at 150 cm; total depth of grave, 200 cm. Body faced west. No vessels.

**GRAVE 12.** 8 m southwest of Grave 11, 6 m northeast of Grave 4. Six burnt-end huarango logs sloping from 70 cm depth at west to 120 cm at east. At 150 cm, skull, facing south; skeleton down to ca. 180 cm. Skull was of an aged person, perhaps slightly deformed, hair left on it; too fragile to keep. All bones light and brittle, imperfect, but seemed fairly fresh. Only the mandible seemed worth preserving (170848). No vessels were found; the style of grave is Nazca.

**GRAVE 13.** (Tello's) 3 m east of Grave 12. Mud layer *(torta)* over stones at 70 cm, bottom of east-west roof logs at 100 cm, below that 100 cm of air space to about 10 cm of sand, total depth of tomb 210 cm. The tomb was square with slightly rounded corners, 120 cm x 120 cm, cut through the gravelly soil and lined with a mud plaster. Body facing south, fallen apart, knees spread widely, backbone half fallen to right, skull toppled backward so that the base was up. The hair was 20 cm long, carefully combed, including some narrow plaits or tresses. There were four vessels (MAP 30/42–45?), which were sketched by Kroeber (Figs. 358–361: Chap. 10). One of them is a tall mouthed jar with a capital-E, or winged-dish, design found by the expedition only on one other vessel, from Grave 2 in this same Soisongo C cemetery. The vessels were terminal Nazca *B* or incipient *Y*.

Only Nazca graves were found at Soisongo C. Of these, two are *A;* two are *B;* four are terminal *B* or incipient *Y;* and five are Nazca in type of tomb and frontal flattening of skull, but absence of artifacts prevents their assignment to a phase.

FIGURE 52. *Sherds (170842), Soisongo C, Grave 6*

FIGURE 53. *Stone head (170847), height 26.3 cm, Grave 11, Soisongo C*

On the surface at Soisongo C were found two dark unpainted sherds with line incision—in the Nazca area a sign of possible pre-Nazca-*A* origin. One was found by Mejía and is presumably now at Magdalena in Peru (Fig. 391; Chap. 12); the other is 170851 in Chicago [a plain body sherd with segments of three incised lines].

### *Soisongo D and E*

These two grave fields had been much exploited by 1926. There were some deep tombs with large roof poles. In E, a huarango stump 80 cm across was seen in a grave. There were *A*, *B*, and *Y* phase sherds. The expedition opened one grave at D that, however, yielded only a skeleton, 170853 [age 12–16 years, slightly deformed skull].

After Soisongo, field notes, sketches of sites or specimens, and catalogue are all Kroeber's. During most of this later period he was accompanied by Tello and Mejía; but the work at Cahuachi was done single handedly.

## Aja

Aja is a hacienda whose headquarters stand at the foot of Cerro San Luis, a pyramidal foothill about 1 km northwest of Nazca, across the Aja River, which here is flowing nearly parallel to the Nazca, into which it enters some kilometers to the west. From San Luis hill westward there extends a stony quebrada, about 1 km wide across its mouth where it meets the cultivation and nearly 2 km long back to the foot of the *cerros.* This quebrada runs southerly (actually nearly SW), and the edge of cultivation runs east-west. Aja hacienda lies at the east end of the quebrada mouth, Curvi just beyond to the west. There are at least three sites in the lower margin of the quebrada, just above the cultivated lands of Aja. They were designated by Dr. Tello.

Aja C is near the middle of the quebrada. It is a Late site, had been looted, and was not excavated.

Aja A is next in order west, about 350 m short of the west edge of the quebrada and close to the cultivation. It is also Late and is briefly described below.

Aja B is farthest downriver, about 150 m from the west edge of the quebrada. This was diagnosed as a site of Nazca *A* culture and excavated.

### *Aja B*

This is a small, pure-site, Nazca *A* cemetery (Fig. 54) at the south (or SW) foot of a rocky knoll 12–15 m high, 100 m back in from the cultivation or huarangual. There are ancient roads raying out from this knoll, especially on the north side, like those in and near La Calera. The soil

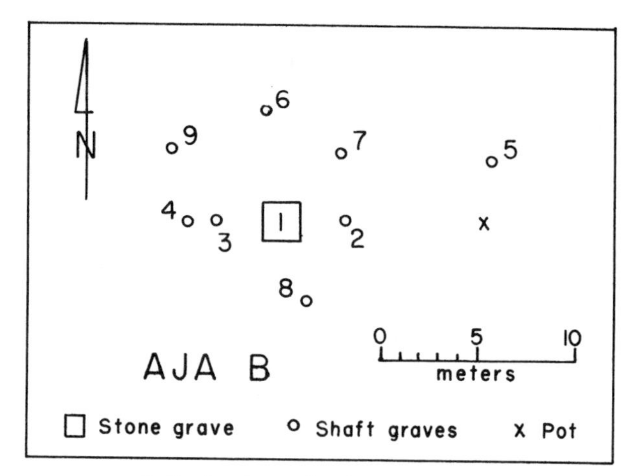


FIGURE 54. *Aja B, plan of grave locations*

is variable layers of broken stone and sand; grave soil is mostly a mixture of both. Grave roofs are near the surface. Very few adobes were seen about the cemetery, and those friable. All the skulls found were partially flattened, and some long *(cabeza larga)* instead of broad *(chata).* The pottery was early Nazca *A* throughout.

**GRAVE 1.** (Fig. 54) Excavated when the site was first explored by Dr. Tello but was apparently the only one previously exploited. It was the central grave of the cemetery and serves as a datum point for the others. It was completely stone lined, 2 m square, and was clear to a depth of 2 m: there had been some refill.

**GRAVE 2.** 2 m east of Grave 1, opened by Tello. There were 30 cm of fine rock and earth; then a torta (cake) of mud and stones, and on the southwest some adobes and a vertical cane; then came the roof of four canes; under this a layer of canes and pacae leaves; below these the chamber, ovoid, 1 m in diameter, cut into the gravelly soil. The skeleton much broken, the skull deformed, senile, looking to northeast. One double-spout and six open bowls (MAP 30/52–58) were found here. The vessels are described in Chapter 6, and four are sketched in Figures 157–160. (Mejía's notes mention "un monton de adobes odontiformes" above the roof.)

**GRAVE 3.** 2 m west of Grave 1, total depth 240 cm (Kroeber's notes; Mejía's said 300 cm). Roof of more-or-less carbonized sticks, 30 cm down, covered with stones and 20 cm of mud torta. Chamber unlined, not quite 200 cm deep, 130 cm across east-west, 100 cm north-south. A huarango root had grown below the roof through the chamber. Only minute fragments of bones were recovered; these lay at east end of chamber (the body presumably facing W); the pottery in rows at west. Nine vessels, viz., one double-spout, two crude small pots, and six bowls (170891–99: see Figs. 136, 148–150, and 152; Chap. 6).

**GRAVE 4.** 0.6 m west of Grave 3, total depth 160 cm. Roof of four huarangos laid east-west, at 30 cm down, canes north-south below them, mud and stones above. Chamber 1 m in diameter. Skull deformed, long; bones very fragile. Thirteen vessels (MAP 30/70–75), of which one was a double-spout and most of the others low bowls. The pots are described in Chapter 6, and two are sketched in Figures 161–162.

**GRAVE 5.** 7 m south of Grave 2. Huarango roof north-south, at 40 cm, broken; chamber 120 cm diameter, 150 cm deep below roof. Bottom damp. No bones recoverable; only fragments of one double-spout and perhaps other vessels (170900).

**GRAVE 6.** 4 m north of Grave 1. Roof at 90 cm; total depth 240; bottom humid; no bones recoverable. Ten vessels, all broken except one (170901): one double-spout, one crude small pot, eight low bowls (170901–10: see Figs. 133, 135, 138–140, 143–145, and 153; Chap. 6).

**GRAVE 7.** 2 m southeast of Grave 6. At 40 cm, canes with three wooden sticks among them formed the roof; three vessels at 100 cm (*sic*, possibly head jar only); total depth 160 cm. Skeleton (170922) in good condition [adult male] but lacking head, the place of which was taken by a face or head jar with turban (170924: Fig. 154; Chap. 6). Two other vessels: a plate and a bowl (170925–26: Figs. 137, 151; Chap. 6). There were also some hair braids (170923).

**GRAVE 8.** 3 m south of east edge of Grave 1, total depth 130 cm. A trophy-head burial at 110 cm. Skull deformed and long like that of Grave 4, large male, occipital and basal portions had been removed, perforation in frontal (170912). Removed intact but broken up on first handling, being covered with salt crystals and much decayed. It was covered by the upper portion of a three-handled, vertical-striped jar (170911: Fig. 155; Chap. 6). In the excavation was found a polished blackware sherd with one incision (170913). Probing in the vicinity of the grave failed to reveal a body.

**GRAVE 9.** 5 m northwest of Grave 1, total depth 260 cm. The roof was of a few thin sticks, carbonized, which, being regarded as roots, were taken out piecemeal. Probably above the roof were two wedge-shaped (Tello's "odontiform") adobes, very soft. Bottom of tomb damp; only small fragments of bones, none of skull, no teeth. The ossuary fragments were north of (the actual) east side of the chamber; the body therefore probably faced west. The vessels (170914–19: Figs. 134, 141–142, 146–147, and 156; Chap. 6) were all badly broken and on account of oncoming darkness could not be segregated with certainty. They include at least four bowls, probably several others, and one small crude pot (170919); no trace of a double-spout.

Eight m east of Grave 1, at 150 cm, was found the top (opening) of a large jar containing cooked sweet potatoes; otherwise empty. Jar removed [no record, apparently not saved], no burial below.

Many trial holes were sunk in vain. The little cemetery seemed exhausted. All graves lay within 7–10 m of the central and elaborate stone-lined Grave 1 in an area of barely 200 sq. m. The consistency of the special qualities of the site is evident: shallow roofs; little or no adobe; skulls tend to long deformation; pottery mostly open bowls, with often a double-spout or unpainted cookpot or jar per grave; colors somber; and designs often not outlined.

Sherds 170890, from a trial excavation at Aja B (location not recorded), are described in Chapter 12 under "Various *Ao* Sherds and Fragments" and are shown in Figures 388–389.

### *Aja A*

This site lay between B and C. There was a flat, clean space, 35 m east-west, ca. 28 m north-south, bordered on west, north, and south by a wall consisting of two rows of two courses of wedge-shaped, hand-made adobes, 30–40 cm long, thicker than high, set with edges toward wall surface. These suggested Nazca culture; but except for two small sherds (170944), everything else at the site was clearly Late. The wedge-shaped adobes may have been reused. Using modern techniques, test pits would have been sunk through the Late level to look for an underlying earlier one.

At a slight rise just south of the open end of the Aja A plaza, near the south end of the east wall, was a large hole, 9 m in diameter, 2 m deep, the edges raised above the plain, evidently an old huaquero excavation. West and south of it were other large circular holes, and smaller ones between, with bones and grave refuse around them. The north and east peripheries of the largest hole yielded six skulls (170928–33), eight vessels (170934–36, 170938–42), and cloth fragments (170947–49), all evidently thrown out and covered with soil from deeper in the hole by treasure hunters. Almost all of this was Late material—four of the six skulls, for instance, were occipitally flattened only. In one of the dumps was a rectangular adobe, 40 x 25 x 15 cm.

**GRAVE 1.** At the inner slope of the big hole, just below the rim at SE. At only 20 cm, a little roof of canes, and just below this a bundled [adult] mummy (170927), seated, broader than high, facing northwest; some stuffing of cotton, red cloth headcover, belt or shoulder band with coca bag and tassel at back, and so forth; and a feather-ornamented gourd (170937).

#### Curvi

This hacienda is in the next embayment downstream from Aja, viz., on the north side of the Aja River, downstream from Nazca, a little upstream from Achaco. Directly behind the house (ca. 200 m away) on a narrow sandy shelf between the cultivation and the hills were a refuse heap (E), a cemetery, and a small stone town (W), the latter mostly running up the side of the hill. Many sherds were Ica type, and all were Late; the town, in size of rooms, stone construction, and terracing up the hill, was similar to La Chimba upstream from Huayurí. No excavations were made.

#### Cantayo

Until Soisongo, the expedition's operations had crept slowly down the Nazca River. The presence of Dr. Tello, born a highlander, reversed the trend: Aja is abreast of Nazca pueblo and Cantayo upstream from it.

Cantayo, sometimes spelled "Cantallu," is one of the larger haciendas in the Nazca Valley. It is on the south side of the Río Tierras Blancas or main Nazca, upstream from the city of Nazca. The properties thereabouts are, in order upstream: San Miguel (at Paredones), Cajuca (graveyard of present-day Nazca), Cantayo, Tierra Blanca, and Sausal. The cultivation (which includes sugar cane as well as cotton) faces several quebradas or *ensenadas* (embayments), two of which run far back as canyons, evidently heading on Cerro Blanco itself. Down these water runs at times. The flood plain or alluvial slope is wide and stony.

Drs. Tello and Mejía Xesspe divided the ancient cemetery frontage of Cantayo into Parts I (upstream) and II (downstream), further making the upstream Part I consist of areas A, B, C, D, E, and F, the last four separated from one another by little dry gullies (Fig. 55). Then there follows, downstream, ca. 0.5 km of rocky cerros. Then Part II commences, beginning at the end of the wagon road with an Inca cemetery on an ancient river terrace; and next, downstream, a lower terrace or plain, with ancient cemeteries nearly continuous down to Paredones. About the middle of this Part II, halfway between the Inca site on the terrace and the Cajuca graveyard, two of these lower cemeteries were given the designations M (upstream) and L (downstream) (Fig. 56).

Sites M and L have been much exploited (as of 1926), upstream C through F somewhat less so and mostly in spots; A and B were not excavated by the expedition. Sites C through F are about opposite the Cantayo *fábrica*, or mill; they are continuous.

##### *Lower Cantayo Site L*

Site L, whose situation is shown in Figure 56, is a cemetery with great excavated Nazca tombs in rows, with roofs of large logs (up to 2 m long) extending north-south. To the southwest is a mound (to the right of circle L in Figure 56), running east-west, with two large excavated graves at its west, and space for possibly two more at the east, these Nazca *Y* or later. They might be called Cantayo K, and are not properly part of L. Site L, 30–60 m outside the cultivation, is more-or-less bounded on the east by a north-south wall.

Three excavations were made in L. Of these, Grave 1 was east of the middle against a north-south wall and in a grave area, as indicated by its position in north-south and east-west rows of exploited graves. Excavations 2 and 3 were outside the area, although adjacent to the same north-south wall, respectively 7 m and 10 m east of Grave 1.

**GRAVE 1.** No roof. Top of [adult] body 215 cm deep, curled, lying (fallen?) on left side, well preserved, face to northeast head deformed (170950). Nothing with it. Upright cone-wedge-shaped adobes in this grave.

**EXCAVATION 2.** Only refuse found. A crosswall of six courses of cone-wedge adobes, averaging about 35 x 27 x 18 cm.

**EXCAVATION 3.** More refuse, including Nazca sherds, one cut into a disk; also, at 50 cm, *pallar* (or *ava*?) beans, and another of *huayava*(?) fruits, evidently deposits (170951–4).

##### *Lower Cantayo Site M*

Cantayo M is perhaps 100 m east of L, about same distance from cultivation, but larger. Five graves were opened (Fig. 57).

**GRAVE 1.** About 10 m south of cultivation. At 60 cm lay the top of a large, dark-gray coarse water-storage jar, mouth broken. Inside the jar was a baby skeleton, two molars erupted, skull definitely deformed; also a red 2-handled low jar or olla (170980: Fig. 220; Chap. 7). At 70 cm, beside the water jar, to the SW, was a Nazca *B* bulbous vase (170981: Fig. 221; Chap. 7).

**GRAVE 2.** 50 m south-southwest of Grave 1. At 90 cm, a roof of logs, with pacay leaves in the cracks and cane underneath. A branching huarango log had its thin ends chopped off, whereas other huarangos and a heavy pacae

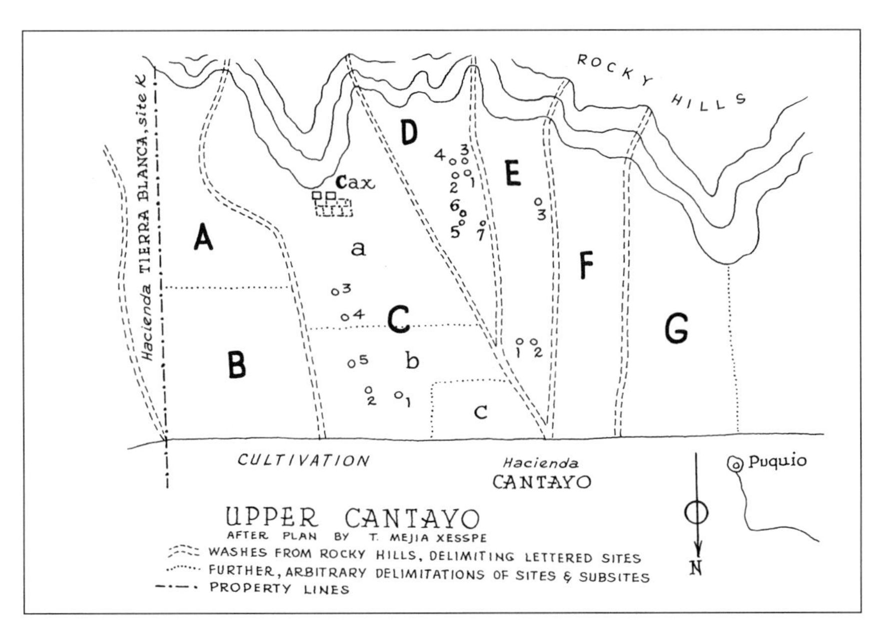


FIGURE 55. *Upper Cantayo sites*

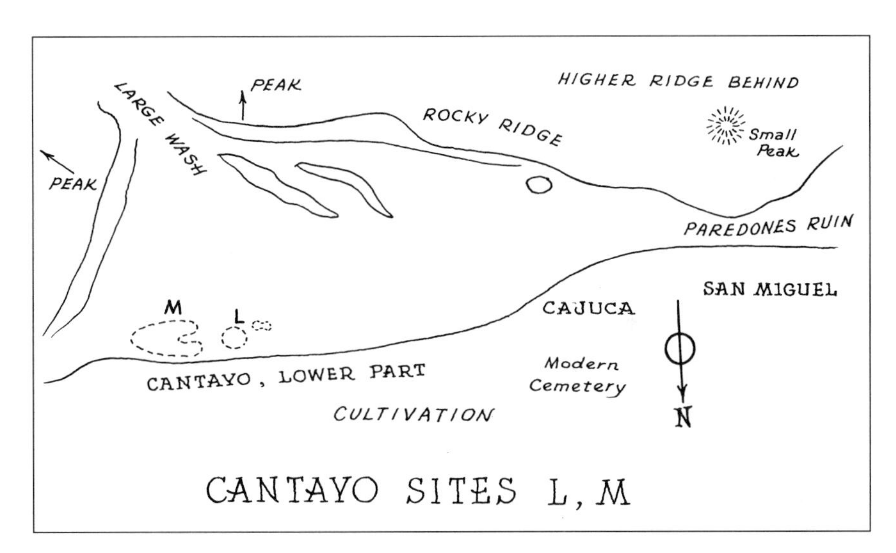


FIGURE 56. *Cantayo sites L and M*

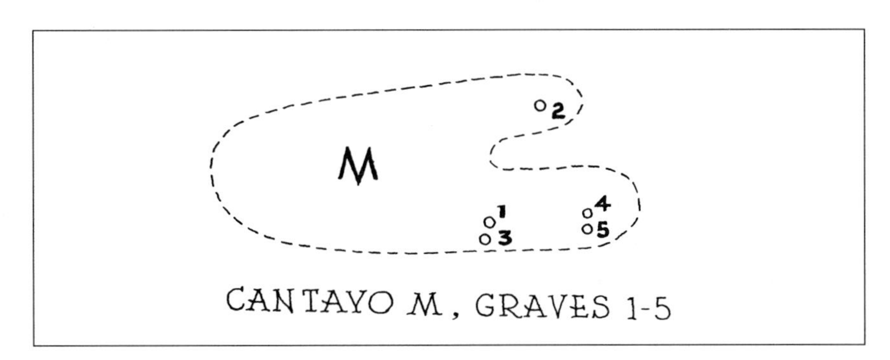


FIGURE 57. *Lower Cantayo M, plan of grave locations*

log were burned off, showing that size of the timber determined whether fire or a tool was used for cutting it. Above the middle of the roof, an upright cane rose to within 25 cm of the surface. Total depth 240 cm. Skull (170982), deformed, of a large adult, fallen face down, apparently had looked over knees to west since its hair was on the east side. Bones in good condition. Against north side of head was a large bulbous vase (170983: Fig. 309; Chap. 9), at the feet a small-mouthed jar (170984: Fig. 310; Chap. 9). This was a Nazca *B* grave.

**GRAVE 3.** 7 m north of Grave 1. At 50 cm, an infant [age 1–2 years], skull heavily deformed, with cloth fragments and pallar beans (170985–7).

**GRAVE 4.** Empty, 30 m west of Grave 1. Roof of four sticks at 30 cm. Between them, two completely broken pots with designs of diamonds and trophy heads (170988–89: see Fig. 210; Chap. 7). At 70 cm to the south, on sticks, lay a mass of volcanic ash nearly the size of an adobe (170990: see Appendix). Nothing under the roof but soil; no sign of bones.

**GRAVE 5.** 3 m north of Grave 4, was also false. There was a roof of north-south sticks 30 cm down. On this lay half a ring-shaped, stone club head (170964). Below was nothing except two logs.

**GRAVE 6.** 7 m north of Grave 5. It is not shown in Figure 57 but lay at the edge of the graveyard. Below a log roof was a seated skeleton, the head at about 70 cm down, facing northeast. At or under its feet, at 110 cm, was a southeast-facing skull without body. Both skulls were friable and fell apart; they were little or not at all deformed. No artifacts whatever.

## *Upper Cantayo Sections E and D*

In Upper Cantayo (Fig. 55), Tello and Kroeber numbered the graves in one joint series but, for the most part, were too occupied to transcribe field notes from one another.

Section E at Upper Cantayo yielded three graves, opened by the Peruvian party. These show as 1–3 in Figure 55. The only expedition material possibly associable to east is 171018–20, three vessels that appear to have been actually from a grave in either east or D, but the local workmen, having worked out of sight, misrepresented the spot as on the surface. (There may have been an adjacent grave that they were concealing for themselves later). The three vessels are shown in Figures 192–194 and described in Chapter 6.

Section D held four graves close together, 1–4, that were excavated by Tello and Mejía; Graves 5–7, somewhat downhill, excavated by Kroeber.

**GRAVE 5.** No roof, well 90 cm deep. Skull (171004) little deformed [age 14–20 years]. Three bowls (171005–7); one plain white, one small with red and black stripes, one with eye or diamond design (Figs. 217–219; Chap. 7).

**GRAVE 6.** 2.5 m south of Grave 5. No roof, 40 cm to top of large inverted jar, 90 cm to two vessels (171011–12: see Fig. 189 [Pl. 5]; Chap. 6) beside it, 140 cm to feet of [adult male] skeleton (171013) under jar. When the jar was lifted, the deformed skull lay exposed, facing west, body on soil. The large jar was 40 cm in diameter, 35 cm high, partly preserved, without handles, bottom rounded and conical, plain red, coarseware 6–7 mm thick.

**GRAVE 7.** 7 m west of Grave 5. No roof, 90 cm to top of deformed [adult] skull (171014), facing northwest. No vessels.

## *Upper Cantayo Sections Ca and Cb*

These two subsites, Ca and Cb, are treated together because they are separated only by an arbitrary line and form part of the same gentle slope. Cax is the part of Ca higher up, at the foot of a rocky point, and is a natural subdivision. It also has an adobe structure and will be treated separately.

**GRAVE Cb-1.** Excavated by Dr. Tello.

**GRAVE Cb-2.** 10 m east of Cb-1. A trophy-head burial in an enormous jar or bowl (171010), 100 cm high and ca. 120 cm in diameter, which broke in removal. The engraved rim (original number 649 for Tello; rubbing taken) was 70 cm down. In it, on the west, some 30 cm from bottom, a trophy head (171008), looking north, frontal perforated, remnants of black cord in hole, no hair, bone in good condition, foramen enlarged a little, a

FIGURE 58. *Incised gourd fragments, Cantayo Cb, Grave 2*

half-healed irregular hole (trepanation?) in left side of frontal [age 14–20 years]. Mandible separate, in east part of bowl. Inside skull, a black wool or hair band fragment, and guinea-pig hair and skull. Scattered in the bowl, which of course was filled with soil, were some Nazca sherds, braided string, a piece of limestone (171009: see Appendix), and a fragment of incised gourd (171034: Fig. 58).

**GRAVE Ca-3.** About 100 m (NNW) from the large tombs at subsite Cax, half as much southeast from Cb-2. Three bodies within a radius of 1.5 m; 40 cm, 50 cm, and 30 cm respectively down to their skulls; no roof. Bodies fairly fresh, and all artifacts Late in style. Body 1 young adult (170993), squatting posture but laid nearly flat on back, facing west to northwest; sling, tapestry headband, gypsum (?), yucca root (170994–97). Body 2 adult [male] (170998), squatting upright, arms crossed over stomach, wrapped in plain cloth, half sitting on a plate with rectangular three-color design inside four times repeated on rim (171002: Fig. 403; Chap. 13); sling, wool rope, animal skin pouch, small calabash (171099–101). Body 3 bundled baby, seated or stood upright; small calabash (171003).

**GRAVE Ca-4.** Excavated by Dr. Tello.

**GRAVE Cb-5.** Definitely between Graves 2 and 4 by Kroeber's plan, but his notes place it with equal definiteness 10 m west of Grave 1, which would be near the boundary of subsections Cb and Cc. At 40 cm, three east-west huarango logs; below these, six north-south; just below these, three "bodies," heads 80 cm, feet 130. Bodies 1 and 2 at east side of grave, facing west, second body behind first, both with skulls slightly deformed; seated. Body 1 (171023), male [age 50+ years], in fragments of white cloth; body 2 (171025), naked [male, age 50+ years]. Body 3 (171020) at south side of grave, facing north at the front left of body 1, proved to be a dummy made of four sticks ca. 50 cm long and a huarango-wood shovel, a cotton head with corncob nose, human hair spread flowing all around, over this a pink cloth pressed and wound around "head," about this a thin ribbon of red and blue wool (171029), at rear of top of head a bunch of yellow feathers (also 171029). The "mummy" was lashed with reed rope and was taken for real until lifted out; it was padded out with pacay leaves. In front of it (near the left foot) were three vessels: an unhandled jar (171026: Fig. 404; Chap. 13), an incurved bowl (171027: Fig. 405), and a flat bowl (171028: Fig. 406; Chap. 13) with Andean-influenced late Nazca designs (Coastal Tiahuanacoid, Huari). The expedition found almost nothing else as highland-derived as was this grave.

**GRAVE Ca-21.** Opened in Kroeber's absence. Mejía declared it was not a grave. The workmen reported there was no body but presented an [adult] leg (171017) with a badly healed fracture. Of vessels, 171015 is a cumbrous bowl with W-Y-R-B rim design on buff background; 171016, heavily fragmented, was described and cataloged at the time as a large bowl with a white overpainted design, but it mended into two incomplete spherical jars evidently representing skulls, wholly unlike anything Nazca or Ica, and showing rather North Peruvian influence. As the grave association is unreliable, the pottery must be used with caution in comparisons. The vessels are shown in Figures 401–402 and described in Chapter 13.

### *Upper Cantayo Structure Cax*

A rocky point comes out from the south cerro to project north or northwest into the upper part of area Ca. Below the cerro are a series of large adobe walls and tombs in rows, thoroughly rifled and with more labor than huaqueros usually spend, suggesting that the yield was productive. South of the southeast-most of these empty chambers, that is, toward the very foot of the rocky point, was made the excavation Cax (Fig. 59), which did not yield one important grave, as had been hoped, but several subsidiary or partial burials, Graves 11–18, and much refuse. The cluster of walls suggested a low pyramid, and Kroeber continued several days with a sense that part of the complex might be earlier than anything he had yet encountered in Nazca. The structure was complex and had been much worked over, so that nothing decisive eventuated. With a larger crew, assistance, and more time remaining, it would have called for a large, systematic, and deep excavation.

North of wall A (on the map, Fig. 59) was an excavated tomb chamber filled in by the expedition with soil and refuse taken from south of A and B, and from J, the areas chiefly excavated. Letters A, B, C, D, E, J, K, L, and M in Figure 59 indicate adobe walls (see Fig. 60 for construction details and Chap. 4 on adobes). Their lengths are: A, 4.2 m; B, 5.4 m; D and E, 1.5 m; J, 4 m; and C, 8 m. The numbers 11 through 18 indicate burials. Locations W, X, and Z are points at which loose objects were found.

**GRAVE 11.** Under 170-cm-high buried adobe wall D, total depth 240 cm from surface. Baby (171032), in a black-gray wide-lipped two-handled water jar (171031: Fig. 382; Chap. 12), a striped cotton cloth (171033) overhead. This cloth is shown in O'Neale (1937), plates 37g, 64c.

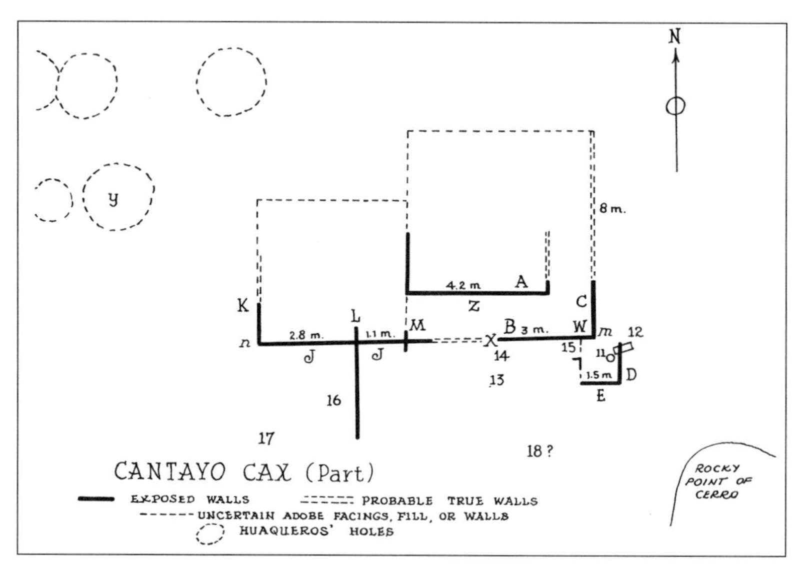


FIGURE 59. *Cantayo Cax, plan of grave locations and walls*

**GRAVE 12.** Just northeast of Grave 11, under the north end of wall D. There was a roof of canes laid northeast-southwest, and of pacae leaves. [It appears that this "roof" was not separate from the jar below it, as the original field notes continue "or rather, cover to jar".] Below was a large jar set on its mouth, the bottom broken out, covered by canes. Inside was a child's body [age 2–3 years], dried out, skin and hair preserved (171048); the legs were spread like a frog's, the body and head had fallen flat; it had apparently faced west; the skull deformed. There was a guinea pig with it. No pottery other than container.

Above the roof of Grave 12 were several sherds (171046), among which was one plain black, another patterned (stylus-burnished) black, (characteristic of Strong's Proto-Nazca, as of 1957). These sherds are discussed in Chapter 12 and shown in Figure 387.

**GRAVE 13.** North end of its barbacoa 210 cm south of south face of wall B; this roof lay 110 cm higher than base of wall B and was 160 cm below the surface; its south end was deeper, since the ground sloped downward from south to north. The barbacoa roof consisted of five north-south sticks. At 70 cm below roof was a cake of clay 40 cm diameter; below this, a bed of pacae leaves; then a dozen canes laid east-west, covering the mouth (30 cm diameter) of a jar. This jar had its bottom broken and displaced by soil pressure; maximum D 90 cm, estimated H 100 cm, distance from lip to sand in bottom of jar 70 cm; the ware was micaceous, 8 mm thick (171053: Fig. 383; Chap. 12). Inside was a seated [adult male] skeleton (171052), facing west, skull frontally deformed but longish, distance from its sacrum to top to roof 180 cm, to surface 340 cm or more. Under the hip was a wad of coarse brown voile cloth (171055); on head and down one side of face a red crocheted fringe (171054), shown in O'Neale (1937), plates 55b, 65e, and 65f. No pottery besides the burial jar.

**GRAVE 14.** Against south face of wall B, 75 cm above its base, 200 cm deep. Skeleton [of adult female] on left (sic) side, facing east, head south, feet against wall B. (If it faced east with its head S, it must have lain on its right side; if on left, would have faced W.) Tissues fresh, skull undeformed (171041). No artifacts.

**GRAVE 15.** Similar burial, with hips near wall B, east of Grave 14, 100 cm above base of wall, 150 cm from corner BC. Body to southwest, skull looking upward, broken; some deformation. No artifacts except some white cloth with patterned border (171050) from near Grave 13 or 15; this cloth has been illustrated in O'Neale (1937), plate 57d.

**GRAVE 16.** 340 cm south of wall J, 200 cm deep. Child's skeleton, no skull found; on and in bed of pacay leaves, covered by part of a jar. Some cloth used to wrap or tie body. A broken pot, handled, just to north.

**GRAVE 17.** 370 cm south of corner N (or JK), 170 cm deep. Child trophy head (171058). Deformed skull, lacking basal and occipital bones, present from mandible to lambda, fairly fresh, skin on top, tissues remaining in postpalatal area; perforation low in frontal, without cord; dentition of milk and permanent teeth, twenty-four in all [age 8–9 years]. On head, bordered cloth 20 cm square (171059: shown in O'Neale 1937, pl. 43a, 43c), from nose to back end of skull; on this, cotton. Head bedded on pacae leaves with a mass of wool cords to which tied three metatarsals; also small double-barreled, bird-shaped pottery whistle (171064: Fig. 385; Chap. 12). By side, small flat blackware bowl with food remnants, covered with piece of a plain jar (171066: Fig. 384; Chap. 12).

**GRAVE 18.** Located only approximately (under Mejía's direction), but south of wall B, southwest of wall E, 180 cm deep to jar, 260 cm to child's skeleton. Deformed skull (171067), permanent incisors replacing milk teeth [age 6–8 years]; with two small gourds. Jar (171068), globular, two handles, fire-blackened, 40 cm diameter (Fig. 386; Chap. 12). It contained three parcels or ornaments and trinkets, viz.: 171069a–b, quill necklace, gourd; 171070a–m, hair wig, felted human hair sack, skeins of wool and cotton cord, necklaces of seeds, husks, crustacean legs, beetle wings, quills, and so forth; 171071a–f, crocheted fringe, feather-covered leather, gourd, double cane whistle, stone knife with case, and so forth (the textiles are shown in O'Neale 1937, pl. 34d, 37a, 61e, 62 c–d, 63c, 66b–c, and 68g). The jar and its contents are discussed again in Chapter 12. [In Chapter 12, Kroeber questions the association of the child with the jar, and Carmichael agrees that the two should be treated separately.]

Except Graves 14 and 15, which were without artifacts and therefore undeterminable, all the burials are Nazca; and several indications—deformation, blackware, hair wigs, and felting—point to Nazca *A1* as it occurs at Aja B and at Cahuachi A, or to an even earlier phase. All the burials were either in jars, or of children, or were heads, or headless, or showed two or more of these features.

Specifically, the eight burials ranged between 170 cm and 260 cm deep; three were of adults, five of children. Of the latter, one was a trophy head, another decapitated, four were in or under jars, one had a cache-containing jar above the body. Six burials were accompanied by cloth, two seemingly without it; but five wholly lacked pottery vessels (other than the large burial jar), one had an empty jar nearby, one a filled jar above, and only one was accompanied by a bowl, a pottery whistle, and a jar fragment as offerings.

The relative abundance of cloth may be attributed to the dryness of the burials, resulting from the use of jars, elevation of the burials well above cultivation, and position at a rocky hill. However, the striking near-absence of pottery (other than interment jars) cannot, of course, be attributed to aridity or position and, unless it is an accident of small numbers, must be a trait characteristic of a cultural period.

FIGURE 60. *Cantayo Cax, adobe walls and "braided" straw fill. Probe shown is 90 cm long [53997]*

It therefore seems worth listing the principal objects found outside Graves 11–18 but around and near them. Some of these objects may have been deposited before the graves were made, or intruded later; but any of them may be, and some probably are, contemporary with the graves.

| | |
|---|---|
| 171035 | Sherds; from between walls A and B. |
| 171036 | Broken bowl (Figs. 211a–211b; Chap. 7); wall A at Z. |
| 171037 | Corn ears; under broken rock lower than and between bases of A and B. |
| 171038 | Yucca roots and pallar beans; between A and B. |
| 171039 | Dove and parrot feathers, guinea pig, net cloth; between A and B. |
| 171040 | Foreshaft of dart; above base of wall D, on side toward C. |
| 171042 | Small wooden implement or needle. |
| 171043 | Heavy sherds from angle BC (W) or ED. |
| 171044 | Two heavy sherds and a pallar bean (see Appendix); trench south of wall J. |
| 171049 | Embroidered cloth border; 100 cm deep, south of wall B, near corner BC (O'Neale 1937, pl. 57b). |
| 171056 | Sherds from fill south of walls B and J. |
| 171057 | Wisp of cotton on stick; south of wall J. |

## Cahuachi

Below Soisongo are Yapana and Las Cañas; below these, Cahuachi, a long hacienda, the valley here having narrowed to a fraction of a kilometer. Next below is La Estaquería, and after an interval, Tambo de Perro, the

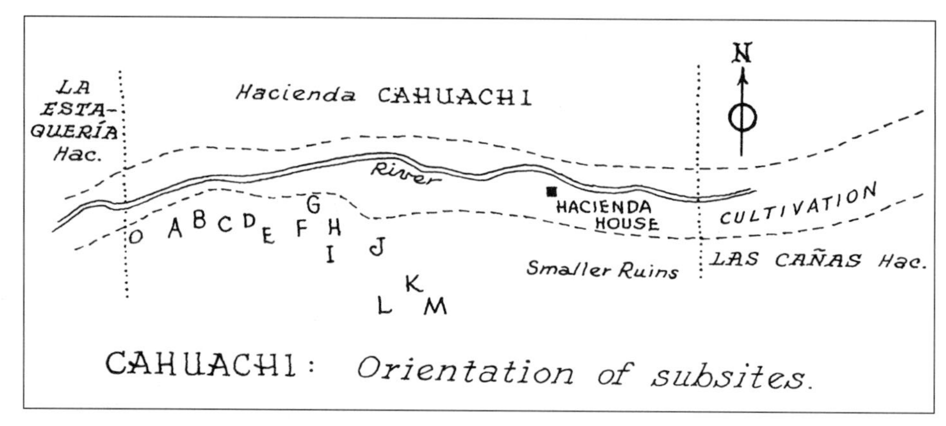


FIGURE 61. *Cahuachi, location of Subsites A–M*

FIGURE 62. *Cahuachi, Terrace K, view from west [54013]*

FIGURE 63. *Cahuachi, Terrace K, showing gash in east face of summit [53999]*

FIGURE 64. *Cahuachi, central part of Terrace L, view from east [54004]*

FIGURE 65. *Cahuachi, Section Eb, niches and underground walls of plastered adobe [54001]*

last hacienda on the Nazca River, which the expedition did not visit. After having run dry above, the Nazca River begins to flow again at Las Cañas, from infiltrations into its bed, and flows through Cahuachi and, in normal years, through La Estaquería, in a narrow bed. The arid sides of the valley are close to cultivation, and the first river terrace is usually followed by several others above it.

The north side has several well exploited sites on the edge of high terraces, apparently of Nazca *A* phase. These the expedition called Cahuachi North and did not explore (Strong did, however, in 1952–1953).

On the south side there are not only cemeteries but a series of artificial terracings or, possibly in part, natural river terraces developed and faced with adobe walls. These extend more-or-less the whole length of the hacienda. Those upstream from the hacienda house for 0.5 km or more and those downstream from it for nearly 1 km were not explored. Those worked by the expedition are in the last kilometer downstream from the large five- (or six-) step pyramidal hill K (Figs. 62–63) and L (Fig. 64) and M behind it, set well back from the river. From Terrace K, similar hills and terraces stretch westward on downstream through the alphabet to B and A. Location B is a pyramid a little less high and large than Terrace K. The overall grouping of these terraced hills is shown summarily in Figure 61.

Beyond Location A to the west a draw or wash enters the river from the south after flowing behind most of the M-A series of pyramids or terraces. Downstream from the mouth of this wash is a cemetery in the plain and running up the next hill, which is unterraced and juts into the cultivation near the Cahuachi and Estaquería boundary. This cemetery, Location O, seems largely Nazca *B;* from A up to K and L the opened sites are almost wholly Nazca *A*. At any rate, Nazca *A* prevails both in surface sherds and in graves, though a few Nazca *B* sherds were found. There are also Nazca *Y* and Late grave sites, but they are localized and generally not associated with the terracing.

Excepting the Late Ica and Inca ruins of stone and squared adobes at Paredones and Curvi and the log pillar temple or structure at La Estaquería, (Kroeber 1944, pl. 9–10), Cahuachi South is the one site in the Nazca Valley where there can be said to be systematic constructions. There is a pyramid similar in style, although not very large, southwest of the main wooden "Stonehenge," which Kroeber called Estaquería A. Also, the large adobe walled tombs in which the expedition dug at Cantayo Cax, as already described, are somewhat reminiscent. At both these two places, as at Cahuachi, Nazca *A* is the dominant type. The terracings at Cahuachi have crumbled and rounded with time and at first seem natural; but adobe is often evident, sometimes even to the separate bricks, and can regularly be encountered where lines are straight and terraces level (Figs. 62–64). Advantage was taken by the Nazca builders to a great extent of natural lines and contours, as unworked hills farther back show, and the labor expended was certainly only a minute fraction of that which would have been needed to actually rear the piles from cultivation level. Still, a large amount of labor went into the levelings, facings, and walls between, many of which extend underground as chambers or as now-unexplained lengths of wall, all of handmade adobes (Fig. 65).

Intact tombs were opened in area E, Section d, near the cultivation, and listed as E, Graves 1 and 2; in the terraced hill A and in various sections, Graves A 1–15; and in O, west of A, Graves 16 and 17. However, the placing of these graves will be clearer after a somewhat more detailed description.

Figures 66 and 67 show hills (or Terraces) A through J, and then K, L, and M on a larger scale than the orienting Figure 61, as they were sketched into a notebook by Kroeber.

Figure 68 is redrawn from Strong's (1957) figure 4, which is based on an air map and reversed north to south. The thin lines represent contour levels; the heavier black lines are wall constructions as traced by Strong. The Arabic numbers indicate Strong's cuts dug to find stratification; BA1 and BA2 are his burial areas, and GrT stands for Great Temple. So far, everything in Strong's map is somewhat simplified to allow for reduction to our smaller format. On this, we have entered the heavy capitals A through M as identified by Kroeber from his own sketch maps reproduced in Figure 61. Of course, no hill, terrace, contour, or wall was drawn exactly true in Kroeber's free-hand sketching, but all salient features as he saw them identify indubitably on Strong's true map. The topographic relations of the explorations of 1926 and of 1952 are therefore fortunately clear, and they are close. The difference between the two enterprises was that Strong's was primarily directed toward stratigraphy, operated with a larger labor force for a longer time, and dug very much deeper.

In addition to the foregoing plots, Figure 69 reproduces a larger-scale sketch by Kroeber of Terrace A, where he made his principal Cahuachi grave finds. The legend probably suffices to explain the diagram, except that it is necessary to distinguish the plain Arabic figures, which denote estimated meter heights above the river,

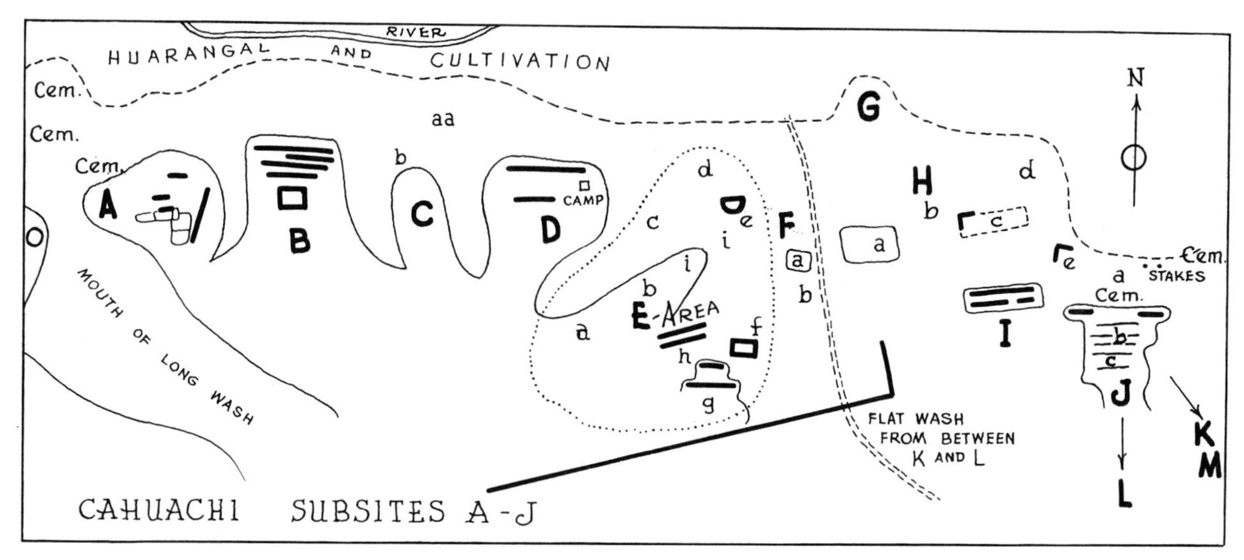


FIGURE 66. *Cahuachi, location of Subsites A–J*

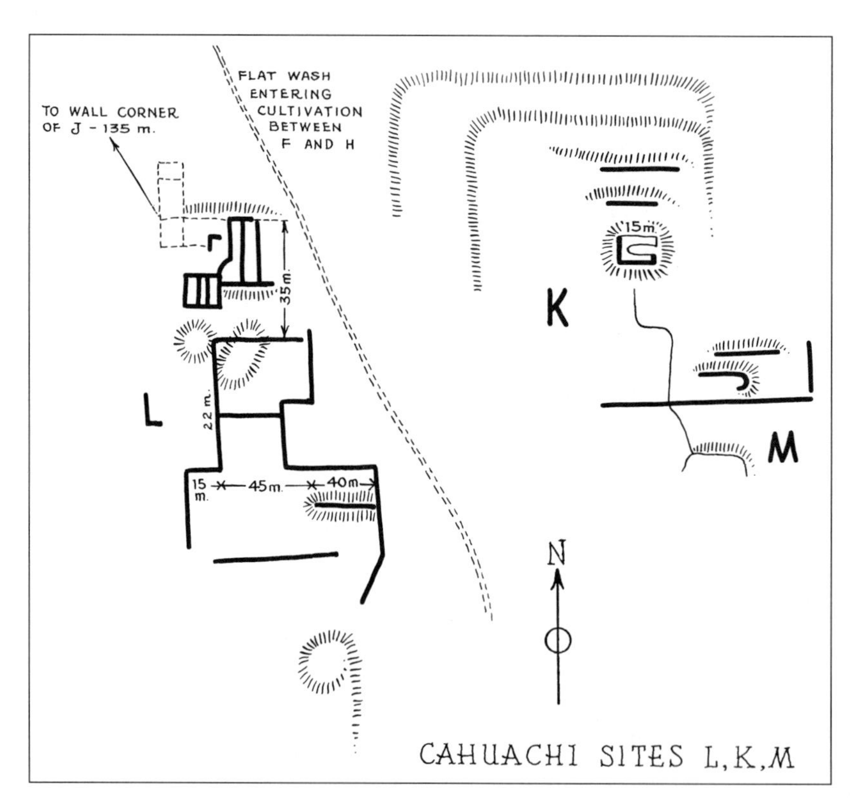


FIGURE 67. *Cahuachi, location of Subsites L–M*

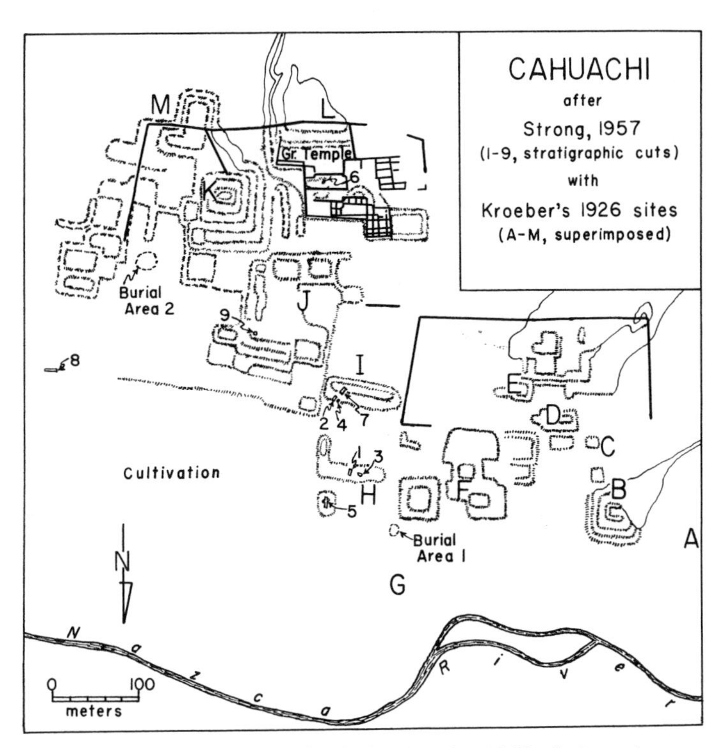


FIGURE 68. *Cahuachi Mounds, after Strong (1957), with Kroeber's 1926 designations*

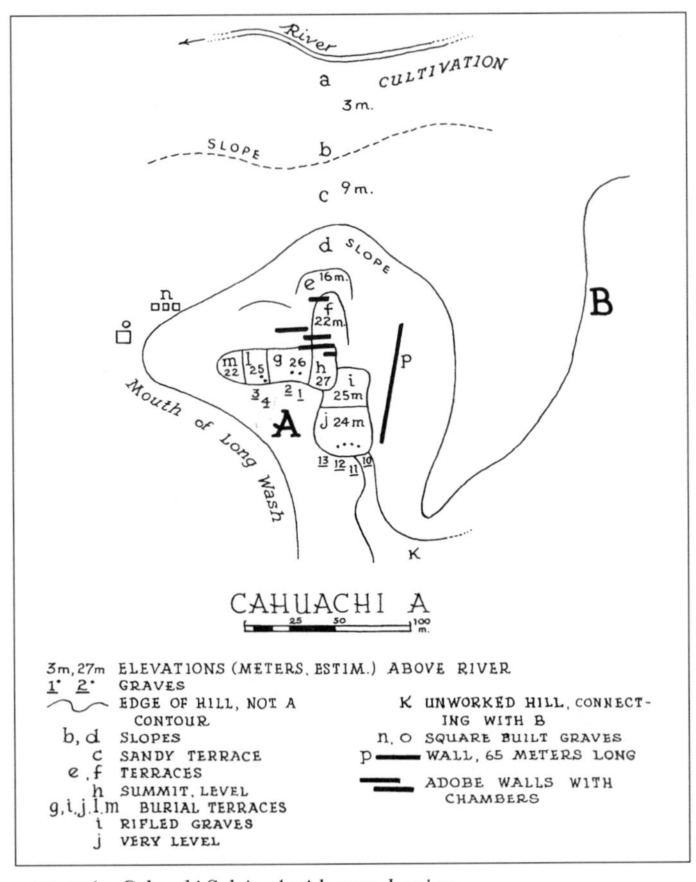


FIGURE 69. *Cahuachi Subsite A with grave locations*

from the underlined Arabic figures, which are for graves as numbered. Space crowding has made it necessary to set these grave numbers at a little distance from the dot representing the grave's position. Thus, the level area g is marked as 26 m above the river, or about 1 m lower than the adjacent summit, H 27. In the area g, two intact graves were discovered, as shown by the pair of dots; but their number designations, 1 and 2, have had to be drawn outside the g area; and similarly for Graves 3, 4 and 10, 11, 12, and 13. An approximate scale is furnished by the wall p, 65 m long. This indicates the level area g as being about 25 m wide from east to west, and j about 33 m wide.

## *Cahuachi Location A*

**GRAVE Ag-1.** (171292–99, 171328) One roof stick at 25 cm, then east-west canes; two small canes upright at east edge. In the roof, a man-shaped jar with fox-skin headband. Total depth of grave 170 cm. Roof apparently fallen in; fragments of six or more bowls and plates (171292–7) scattered pretty well down to bottom of grave. Fragments of cloth; purple paint (171299; see Appendix). No skull or part of one; [adult] skeleton (171075) partly in place, but one tibia to north of rest and one forearm high above this, pointing up. No adobes. The pottery is shown in Figures 92, 108, 116, 121, and 126 (Pl. 8)–127, and described in Chapter 6.

**GRAVE Ag-2.** (171300–01) Disturbed tomb 4 m west of Ag-1. Long-deformed [adult] skull at 40–50 cm on left side, looking northwest, some hair left, three forearm bones, one clavicle, nothing else of skeleton. Fragments of several vessels (171301a–b: Figs. 100, 109; Chap. 6).

**GRAVE OR CACHE Al-3.** 25 m west of Ag-1. At 50 cm, top of a three-handled striped jar with small hole in bottom; empty (171302: Fig. 128; Chap. 6).

**GRAVE Al-4.** (171303–06) 3 m northeast of Al-3. Roof of north-south canes at 40–80 cm below sloping surface; total depth 110 cm more, viz. about 170 cm. Body intact (171303), including skin but headless, probably faced southwest; windpipe or esophagus showed in throat region. Right hand on right knee, left hand inside thigh around right waist. A much-folded cloth laid around middle and legs as a rope, with one knot. Enveloping the whole cadaver was a white cloth 280 cm x 180 cm. Some fragments of semi-veil cloth. (The textiles are shown in O'Neale 1937, pl. 36b, 37j.) Northeast of body, an intact double-spout (171304: Fig. 124; Chap. 6). In grave soil, several sherds, including one pitted and painted. [The mummified remains (171303) were of a female, age 25+ years. A reexamination at The Field Museum by physical anthropologist Lyle Konigsberg and pathologist Robert Pickering determined that the head had been removed after the body had become mummified.]

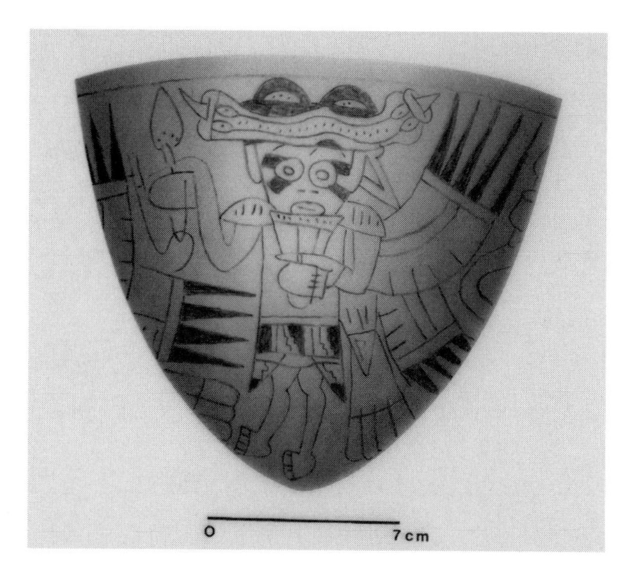


FIGURE 70. *Pyroengraved gourd (171322), Cahuachi Al, Grave 6*

**GRAVE Al-5.** (171307–321, 171341) 7 m northeast of Al-3. Four east-west huarango logs, then canes; partly fallen in. [Adult male] body not under roof but to north and northwest, 160 cm from sloping surface to bottom of body (171307). Usual drawn-up posture, but on belly, face down, head to southwest, left arm behind back. Fine decorated cloth "frozen" on to skull; two cloths over shoulders, both with crocheted fringe and one with embroideries; two plaid and one striped cloth; fragments of crocheting and embroideries, including designs of faces; middle part of a sling; hatchet-shaped object of braid, string, and feathers [171313: fan handle of braided vegetable fiber, feathers attached to form fan]. Single-spout bird-form jar [now missing]; three bowls; two small cookpots of crude micaceous ware. The vessels are described in Chapter 6 and shown in Figures 111, 114, 120, and 130–131. (The textiles are pictured in O'Neale 1937, pl. 36c, 34e, 37h, 48d, 61d, 61h–j, 62, 66d, 67a, 67c, 67e, 67g, and 68a.)

**GRAVE OR CACHE Al-6.** (171322) 5 m south of Al-5. Parts of a broken pot and an incised gourd (Fig. 70). Probably Nazca *A*.

**GRAVE OR CACHE Ag-7.** (171323–27). Only 15 cm deep. In south part of Terrace g (in Figure 69), in area free of burials. A nest of two flat wads of hair, white quartz pebble, pallar beans (171326–27; see Appendix), two canes, and fragments of Pan's pipe (171324: Fig. 132; Chap. 6).

**GRAVE OR CACHE Al-8.** 10 m southwest of Al-5. A coarse red jar with two handles and flaring mouth; H 50 cm, D 40 cm, of neck 15 cm, of lip 30 cm. Abandoned.

**GRAVE OR CACHE Ag-9.** (171185–86) 4 m west of Ag-1. At 15 cm, nest of three trophy heads side-by-side, looking southeast and somewhat up. Nothing with them. Child's head, with milk dentition, went to pieces; young woman's head, no wisdom teeth, hole in frontal, foramen magnum enlarged; middle-aged male's teeth show wear, perforations the same as last. All three had jaws and occiputs.

**GRAVE Aj-10.** (171187–229) Near southeast corner of level Aj. Roof, at 70 cm, of one stick and canes under it, all east-west, had collapsed under weight of four wedge-form or bread-form adobes laid on it and had broken the vessels and disarranged the [adult male] skeleton (171187); thus the mandible was at the bottom of the smooth grave well, 210 cm deep, the skull being only 140–150 cm down. Most of the cloths were at the bottom. The skull was deformed; cotton had been used to stuff out the mummy's clothing. Artifacts: double-spout jar; broken modeled double-spout, of which one piece was found in grave Aj-11; twelve or more plates and bowls; ca. fifteen textiles, plain, embroidered, crocheted, some in good condition; a wicker basket (171211: Fig. 71); a "cradle" of canes; hoof-shaped bone haft (171205: Fig. 72); dart shaft fragments; ornaments of shell, shrimp claws, feathers, and so forth. The pottery is described in Chapter 6 and shown in Figures 93, 95–96, 98–99, 101–102, 106–107, 112–113, 122, 125, and 129. (The textiles are shown in O'Neale 1937, pl. 32–33, 38a, 38c–d, 39b, 39d, 40b, 43e, 44b, 45d, 47, 49–52, 58–59, 60b, 60h, 61a–c, 62a, 67b, and 68d.)

**GRAVE Aj-11.** (171230–39) 1.5 m west of Aj-10. Same construction, depth, and roof. There was no skeleton or skull, only some [adult] metatarsal bones [left and right represented]. This was, however, a true interment, as shown by its containing a sherd (171233) of a jar the rest of which was found in Grave 10 (171189) and several sherds (171232) of a bowl of which the remainder was in Aj-12 (171244). Other pottery: one plate bowl (171231: Fig. 97 [Pl. 1]; Chap. 6), some sherds. Other contents: three textile fragments, three maize ears, and a parrot mummy (171239: Fig. 73; see Appendix). (The textiles are pictured in O'Neale 1937, pl. 35b–c, 46d–f.)

**GRAVE Aj-12.** (171240–58) 2 m west of Aj-11. Smaller well, depth to top of skull 150 cm, roof of quite small sticks. Skull deformed [adult male]. Tissues partly remaining on body (cf. arm 171241). This grave interlocked with Aj-10 and Aj-11 through specimens 171189 and 171233, 171232 and 171244, as stated. One double-spout, two bowls (171242–44: Figs. 103, 115, and 123; Chap. 6). No cloth, but tassels and narrow bands. Masses

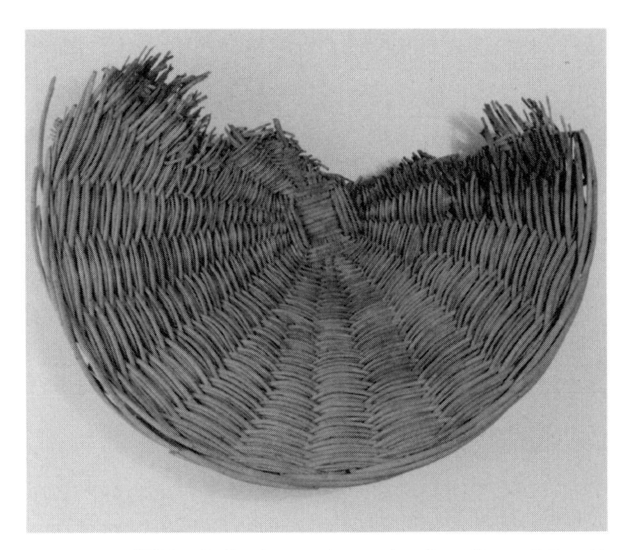

FIGURE 71. *Wicker basket (171211), exterior view of base, Cahuachi Aj, Grave 10*

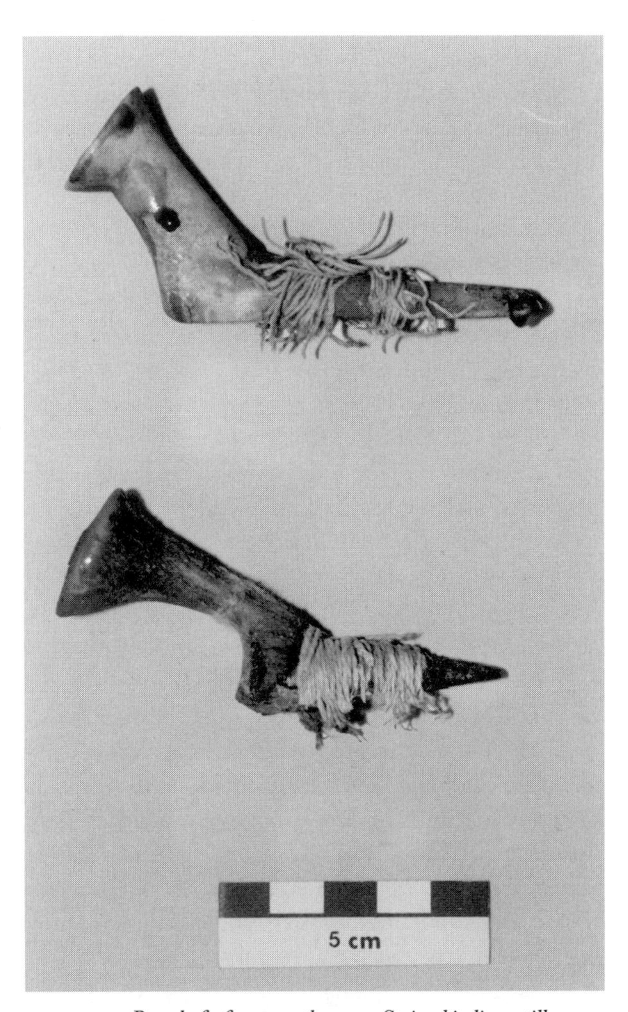


FIGURE 72. *Bone hafts for spear-throwers. String bindings still present: (171205) Cahuachi A, Grave 10; (171249) Cahuachi A, Grave 12*

FIGURE 73. *Parrot mummy (171239), wrapped in cloth, Cahuachi A, Grave 11 (see Appendix)*

of human hair with fringe cords and with sling of braided basketry (hair braid 171255 is shown in Fig. 38b). Hoof-shaped haft (171249: Fig. 72); fragments of spear-throwers and darts; cloth containing obsidian core and flakes, llama metatarsal bones, haft, spoon, and so forth (171248: Fig. 74; see Appendix).

[Forensic analysis of samples from five human-hair objects in this grave found that none were consistent with having originated from the same source. See Hair Analysis under Subsequent Research in the Preface.]

**GRAVE Aj-13.** (171259–91) 1 m west of Aj-12, in line with Aj-10–12, near edge of platform Aj. Cane roof at 60 cm. Three bodies, all cloth wrapped (see Fig. 75): body 1 (A) at 100 cm [adult male], body 2 (B) at 140 cm [adult male], body 3 (C) at 130 cm [male, age 20–21 years]. Body 1 looked east, body 2 facing it west or southwest, body 3 (to south of both) also southwest. Some soft tissues still adhered to the bones of body 1 (171261). (The garments have been pictured in O'Neale 1937, pl. 34b–c, 37d–f, 56, 60a, and 60c.) There were loose bones above the bodies. The usual double-spout was lacking; about nine plates or bowls, mostly broken, some very similar to those in Aj-10–12. The ceramics are described in Chapter 6 and shown in Figures 94, 104–105 (Pl. 3), 110, and 117–119. Bodies 1 and 2 wore a red garment; body 3 also had an embroidered garment. Besides plain, striped, and plaid cloth fragments, the grave contained cords for shoulder stuffing, human hair rope around body 3, masses of narrow turban bands, string, wads of hair, slings with center of braided fiber, tassels, a drum stick(?), cane darts or spindles(?), sweet potatoes (171290; see Appendix), peanuts, and so forth.

[Four samples from hair objects in Grave 13 and a hair sample from body 1 were submitted for forensic analysis. It was concluded that none of these samples was consistent with having originated from the same source. See Hair Analysis under Subsequent Research in the Preface.]

**GRAVE Aj-14.** About 15 m north of Aj-10. Skeleton of a child of ca. 8 years, with flat deformed skull and fragments of plain cloth. Skull 30 cm deep.

**GRAVE Aj-15.** (171329–30) 2 m north of Aj-14. At 40 cm, lower part of jar covered with a cloth and sherds, containing a wrapped baby whose medial incisors were only just erupting. At its leg was a fiber pad, possibly for deforming the skull; also a little cloth pillow or mattress. Probably Nazca *A*.

**SURFACE AND MISCELLANEOUS.** At An of Figure 69, at the northwest foot of hill A, were three rectangular adobe tombs. From south side of the west one, a trophy head had been taken by Kroeber in his scouting visit of 1925. This year, five more were secured (171096–100) close by, ca. 40 cm deep, lining the tomb, as it were; all deformed and without occiput [171096: adult male; 171097: adult; 171098: adult; 171099: adult; 171100: age 3–7 years]. The three tombs also yielded red maize (171102) and a wool tapestry of Epigonal type (171101), which should determine the phase in the total absence of pottery. Location An lies at the foot of pyramid A, not part of it, and its material is not necessarily of the same age as the Nazca *A1* material from the top of Location A.

The much-dug-over platforms Ag and Al yielded a long deformed skull, fragments of four Nazca *A* vessels, and numerous textile fragments, much as they had yielded in 1925 (171103–118).

Platform Aj yielded, from two graves previously dug by huaqueros just east of Aj-10 and in line with Aj-10–13, or from their vicinity, several specimens (171332–34), all conforming to the rest of Terrace A.

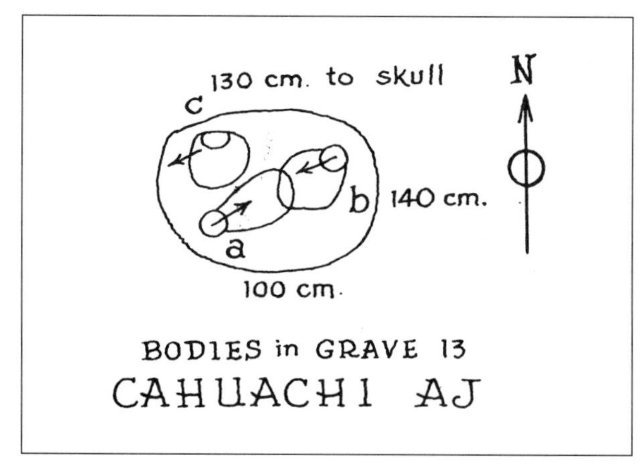


FIGURE 75. *Placement of interments in Cahuachi A, Grave 13*

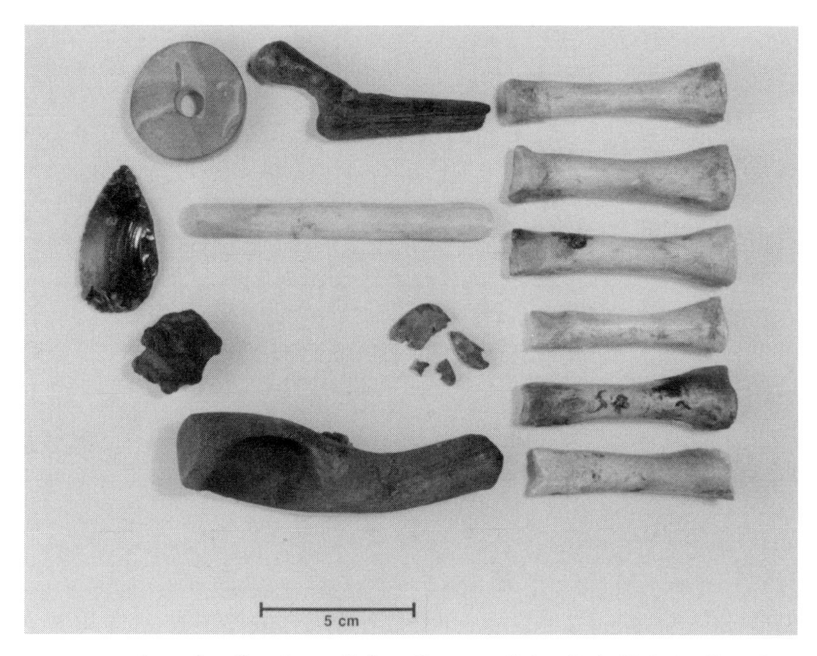


FIGURE 74. *Assorted artifacts (171248) from Grave 12, Cahuachi A. Clockwise: llama foot bones; copper fragments; wooden spoon; ball of resin; obsidian point; perforated stone disk; smooth splinter of long-bone; wooden haft for spear-thrower (top)*

### *Cahuachi Locations B, C, and D*

Location B (Fig. 66) is the largest and most regular pyramid in the west half of the series explored, but it seems sterile. Location C is a promontory between two short gullies and seems natural, without modification, but it has well-worked cemeteries at its foot. Location D has a straight front and flat top and shows sherds but no cemetery. Samples from these three locations are 171119–22, 171160.

### *Cahuachi Location E*

Location E (Fig. 66) includes not only a promontory but an area around and before it and is rich in exploited graves and surface remains, but several days' search failed to yield intact graves of importance. In the flat, at Ed, were found two graves, either Nazca or Nazca *Y*-Tiahuanacoid; there was no pottery.

**GRAVE Ed-1.** (171132–33) Baby, brown cloth with colored rectangles in stripes (171132), copper disk (171133). This is the only copper found by the expedition except a few pieces in clear Late association.

**GRAVE Ed-2.** (171135–39) 5 m south of Ed-1. Total depth 250 cm. Skeleton somewhat scattered, skull slightly deformed [171135: adult male]. A trophy head without occiput [171136: adult female]; several pieces of cloth. Apparently the grave had been disturbed.

Surface collections from Ea-i include Nazca *A* and *B* sherds, cloth, and plant remains: 171124–30, 171134, 171151–59, 171161–62, 171176–84, 171331, and 171336–39.

### *Cahuachi Location G*

Location G (Fig. 66) was at the edge of the cultivation, into which it projected. There was a limestone or hardpan formation—*caliche*—into which about a dozen holes had been sunk, 1 or more m in diameter, 60–80 cm deep, probably graves, all excavated. In and around these pits were found some interesting beads of stone and shell, spindle whorls, cloth fragments, a long-deformed skull, and Nazca *A* and *B* sherds (171140–50, 171163), mostly from one pit.

### *Cahuachi Locations I, J, K, and L*

These four (Fig. 66) are all large terraces but seemed rather sterile on the surface except for a cemetery in front of J. Surface gatherings of sherds indicated mostly Nazca *A* (171172–75, one number for each terrace). (Strong's seven stratigraphic cuts, some of which penetrated down well beyond Nazca *A* level, were in H, I, and L; his Burial Areas 1 and 2 were in H and K; and his Great Temple was in L. See Fig. 68.).

FIGURE 76. *La Estaquería, main structure, view from the south [53978]*

### *Cahuachi Location O*

Site O, shown in Figures 66 and 69 across the wash, is about 100 m west of the northwest foot of Location A (An), and outside the series of foregoing terraces, near the Estaquería boundary line. It has the layout and appearance of sites upstream rather than at Cahuachi.

**GRAVE O-16.** (171342–45) Roof; total depth 200 cm, [adult] skull, deformed, longish; faced west. Cookpot with handles, bowl, plate. The vessels are shown in Figures 190–191 and described in Chapter 6.

**GRAVE O-17.** (171346) 6 m west of O-16. At 50 cm, a large jar covered with another and containing a skeleton [adult male], a cookpot, and a fox skin. Skull longish, deformed. Phase not determined. [The skull was the only object saved.]

### *Terracing at Cahuachi*

The number of terraces in the various platforms and pyramids (see Figs. 61, 66, and 67) is as follows (½ denotes an extra terrace not extending across the whole front of the structure):

| | | | |
|---|---|---|---|
| A | 3 | Ha | 2 ? |
| B | 4½ | Hb | 2 ? |
| C | – | I | 2 |
| D | 2½ | J | 4½ |
| Eg | 2 | K | 5½ |
| Eh | 2 | L | 4 |
| Fa | 1 ? | M | 3 |

Location L in addition to four terraces, also has a nearly level front area with adobe walls (Fig. 64). It is the largest in area; Location K is highest (Figs. 62–63). Areas B, J, K, and L are the largest in mass and in amount of construction. (These field notes of 1926 generally concur with Strong's later findings.)

## La Estaquería

This hacienda is so named from the "stakes" or *algorrobo* posts, formerly projecting from graves and standing in alignments in a famous Stonehenge-like temple or ruin of logs and stakes south of the river, about 0.5 km below the hacienda house. A roughly measured survey of this structure and its outworks was made to scale, which was published by Kroeber in 1944; a view of the site and a detail of wall construction are given in Figures 76 and 77, other views are provided in the 1944 publication. Some trial diggings were attempted. Two negative facts emerged from the digging: the structure is not true Nazca, nor is it Late Ica or Inca. Not a single Late sherd or other characteristic was observed. There are Nazca remains near the structure, but they are not actually associated with it. The ware fragments found are difficult to place, but tend to Nazca *Y* or Tiahuanacoid; the adobes are hand-formed (not mold-made) semi-cylindrical, often concave or quite flat, suggesting the same style or period (surface collections 170870–72, 171379–84).

Southwest of the main log structure is A, an adobe terrace or pyramid like those of Cahuachi and with similar remains, prevailingly Nazca *A* (surface collections 170866–69).

## Taruga

Kroeber and Tello drove twice to the streams south of the Nazca River in reconnaissance and secured some specimens, both by purchase and by picking up what huaqueros had discarded.

Taruga is the stream next south of the Nazca, flowing in part from Cerro Blanco and in part past its south side. The divide between the two rivers becomes low about

Majoro and a little farther west was easily crossed by motor car in 1926. There is little water in the Taruga. Hacienda Taruga is situated where the narrow valley begins to spread out; below, the dry stream bed seems to divide.

**PUQUIOS.** It was said that twenty-eight puquios had been located and cleaned out in the past year (1925) on Hacienda Taruga, upstream from it. They are wells 4–6 m deep, log lined, connected by tunnels through which a boy can crawl, stone-lined, and roofed. The tunnels connect the wells into one flow of water. At first, two lines of wells converge; then, below, the tunnel is replaced by a deep open ditch. The series of these puquios lies higher than the river, to its north, at the base of the cerro on that side; the area is overgrown with trees and brush. The wells are from 10 or 15 m to 100 m apart. There may be more that they have not found. Las Trancas, beyond, is said to have a system of eighty of these, long in use.

**RUIN.** Below Taruga hacienda at the foot of the north cerro, just above the cultivation where the valley has already spread out, is an extensive stone ruin, the walls still stretching ca. 0.5 km and reaching up the rocky hills. This ruin is of Late type, like Curvi and La Chimba; and the sherds of Late Ica.

**SITE.** In the cultivation, ca. 1 km downstream from the hacienda, is a low sandy knoll surrounded by algorrobos. Here is a cemetery, also some adobe walls. The downstream end of the cemetery seems Late: the upstream is clearly Nazca. The graves are in very soft sand. A lot of pottery from here was bought, probably all from one site on which the owner's house stood. Most of the lot was retained by Tello for Peru; numbers 171076–95 came to Chicago (Figs. 319–322; Chap. 9). They were roughly classified as Nazca *B*, except 171091–95 as Nazca *Y*.

### Las Trancas

Las Trancas is the stream next south of the Taruga, which unites with this shortly before flowing into the Nazca-Río Grande. It seems to head farther up than the Taruga and to carry more water, and it has a more deeply cut bed. Haciendas are: Las Trancas, farthest up (above it the valley is still narrow); Copara, formerly and now again one property with Las Trancas (the river is sometimes called Copara); Poroma, a small town where the Nazca-Lomas road (of 1926) crossed the river; Corralones, a brushy *monte* or *chacra* where there was said to be much old ware still; and Tunga, far downstream, from which much fine Nazca *B* came and comes, of which eight vases and jars were purchased (171348–55: Figs. 311–318; Chap. 9).

FIGURE 77. *La Estaquería, detail of wall construction in adobe and stone, in excavation near foot of Terrace A [53956]*

At Trancas hacienda there are a few cemeteries on the north side of the fertile narrow valley, and a long series on the south side, scattered from just above the cultivation to well up the slope, which is considerable; they are said to extend upstream and downstream. They seemed only partly exploited in 1926. Mostly they are full Nazca; but some are Nazca *Y*, with very large adobe-lined tombs. Kroeber picked up here an embroidered shirt and four textile fragments (171072–73), all apparently Nazca *Y*. This is the area in which Henrich Ubbelohde-Doering later excavated as well as, in 1952, Strong, who renamed the Nazca *Y* culture Huaca del Loro after his type site.

### Poroma

All sites at Poroma on the Trancas seem Inca or local Late Ica. Material purchased is the same (171368–77). Most of it is said to have come from the south side of river. On the north side, Site A, downstream 0.5 km from the settlement, is Late Ica (171356–67). Site B, 1 km upstream, is also Late Ica. In Grave 1 of this was a seated mummy, bundled, with thin gold and silver in mouth; secured were a metal-headed bone lime-stirrer from in its hair (171358), together with Late cloth, slings, and so forth (171359a–j); also small wooden figures of a couple in coitus and a spoon, the two tied together (171378). Surface finds (171360–67) from Site B are of same type; skulls unshaped, or somewhat flattened occipitally only. The pottery is the local type of Late Ica, including blackware, and one *aryballos* pattern fragment; a shirt (171377) is of Inca patterning. Four bowls purchased at Poroma are described in Chapter 13 and shown in Figures 418–421.

CHAPTER 4

# Adobe Bricks and Wall Construction

## ADOBES AT OCONGALLA

THERE IS A FIELD NOTEBOOK RECORD BY KROEBER ON adobes at what is merely listed as Ocongalla (1926, notebook 2, 31). It was most probably at Ocongalla West B, a Nazca *B* site where the expedition excavated longest, last, and with most results from the three subsites. The position of the data in the notebook—after Aja, Cantayo, and Majoro—also suggests that the record, like that for Majoro, was entered on a supplementary visit to the site after digging there had been finished.

At any rate, Figure 78 shows what was noted. The vertical line of the right end of the main diagram is the end of a wall; at the left is an inner corner. It is clear from this and the cross-section that what is depicted is not a solid little pyramid but a two-adobes-thick wall seven or more courses high, which may have come out from a block structure or have been a rectangular enclosure.

The following measurements were made of particular adobes in this wall, and then from a tomb in our excavations. It is evident that the adobes are conical, or odontiform (Tello), but roughly so, two diameters of the base sometimes differing by 3 or 4 cm. In two out of ten adobes one base diameter even exceeded the height, in one it equaled it.

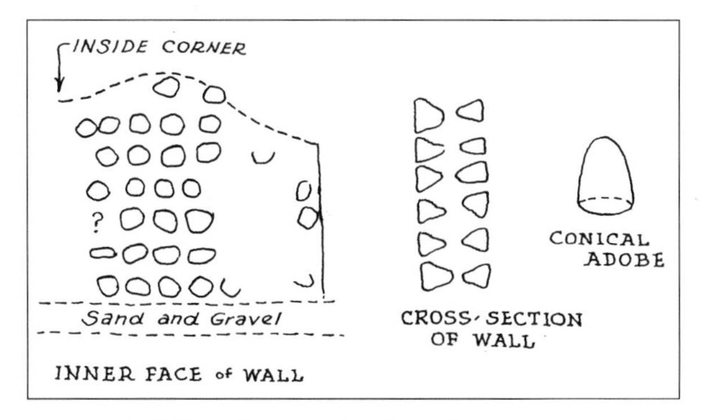


FIGURE 78. *Adobe wall construction, Ocongalla*

**ADOBES IN WALL OF FIGURE 78** *(measurements in cm)*

| HEIGHT | MAX. D | MIN. D | REMARKS |
|---|---|---|---|
| 22 | 20 | 19 | Rounded point |
| 19 | 22 | 19 | Sharp point |
| 18 | 21 | 18 | Wedge point |
| 17 | 17 | 15 | Rounded point |
| 23 | 17 | 17 | Irreg. tapered round, cone frustum |
| 23 | 18 | 14 | Near cylindrical |
| 19 | 15 | 15 | Cylindrical |
| 23 | 15 | 15 | Near cylindrical |
| 21 | 17 | 15 | Blunt point |
| 20 | 15 | 14 | Very blunt point |
| 20.5 | 18 | 16 | Mean |

**ADOBES FROM A TOMB** *(measurements in cm)*

| HEIGHT | MAX. D | MIN. D | REMARKS |
|---|---|---|---|
| 21 | 18 | 17 | Round-topped rather than conical |
| 24 | 21 | 17 | Cone frustum |
| 20 | 17 | 15 | Taper very slight |
| 21 | 16 | 14 | Rounded top, middle gently concave |
| 20 | 17 | 16 | Blunt cone, rounded |
| 21 | 18 | 16 | Mean |

In spite of the variation of individual adobes, the mean proportions of the two samples are almost identical.

Whatever the subsite was, the adobes are of Nazca Period and, of course, hand made. The Ocongalla West A graves were Nazca *A*, Ocongalla Zero and West B both mainly Nazca *B*.

## ADOBES AT MAJORO CHICO A

For Majoro Chico A, the principal Majoro subsite, there are photographs, observations, and measurements of adobes. The graves excavated here included five of phase *A*, one of *B*, and three of *Y1* and *Y2*. The adobes are thus again certainly from the Nazca culture, most likely from Nazca *A*, and they will be seen to be very similar to the adobes just described from Ocongalla. Figure 79 is a photograph of a Majoro Chico A adobe (top D 12.5 cm, basal D 15.5 cm).

FIGURE 79. *Adobe from Majoro Chico A (170565)*

In the northwest corner of Majoro A, outside of and northwest of the portion plotted in Figure 22, a rectangular area was enclosed by walls of stream cobbles set in clay. There were no graves in the enclosure, but there was some refuse, suggesting that this might have been the foundation of dwellings. The associated remains were Late in period. Nearby was a road (Fig. 17) that had cut through Ica-type refuse. Figure 19 shows this area.

To the southeast of these cobble walls was a rectangular construction of low walls consisting of two tiers of conical Nazca-type adobes. Figure 18 shows part of the north wall. Adjoining this north wall inside (probably about the middle of its length, as visible in Fig. 18) was a square recess, which upon clearing showed on its north face elliptoconical adobes laid on one of their flatter sides and with their smooth bases toward the exposed wall surface (Fig. 20). The spacing and amount of mud mortar is characteristic and supports our drawings of Nazca adobe construction. Adobes rarely touched one another in the wall. Near an elliptical niche inside the west wall (Fig. 22), the wall seemed to be of solid packed clay *(tapia).*

To the southwest of the larger enclosure was a smaller rectangle construed at the time as a burial platform, consisting of two layers of adobes, which will be discussed in a moment. At this terrace a grave was excavated through which a tree root had grown.

South of the larger enclosure was a separate east-west wall (at bottom of Fig. 22) whose adobes were also noted.

The following sketches, measures, and observations were made on the adobes and construction of the main rectangle, the smaller one to its southwest, and the free wall to the south, as located in Figure 22.

The west wall of the main enclosure, about the middle of its length, had wedgelike adobes, stood on end, their narrow side toward the wall. Two are shown in Figure 80 (the bases below). Of these, adobe a measured 36 x 28 x 21 cm, with its top rounded and slightly flattened; it seemed to have been built up of four layers. Adobe b measured 29 x 25 x 19 cm and had a quite flat base, the top being a well-rounded edge.

Figure 81 shows another portion of this west wall in which adobes were variably stood or laid, with a few smaller lumpy ones, or stones, included near the top.

On the north wall of the main structure, adobe shapes were similar but they were mostly laid flat, with bases at the wall surface. Here are some dimensions, height from base to point being given first.

| | HEIGHT | MAX. D | MIN. D *(cm)* |
|---|---|---|---|
| | 30 | 26 | 15 |
| | 31 | 22 | 17 |
| | 33 | 26 | 18 |
| | 26 | 30 | 18 |
| | 27 | 23 | 16 |
| MEAN: | 29 | 25 | 17 |

The bases here were genuinely flat, in a 3:2 ellipse, the tops rounded but brought to somewhat of an edge. The taller ones often showed striations parallel to the base as if they had been manufactured by piling about four lumps of clay on one another.

Toward the east end of the north wall there was a square recess, the south face of which had three courses of adobes set on end; the cross-wall facing east had at least four courses laid horizontally, bases toward the wall surface, tops inward. These adobes showed quite yellow against the dark clay mortar in which they lay (Fig. 20).

Figure 82 shows a sample of the east wall of the main enclosure. It appears that the wall was begun, as well as being finished on top, by setting wedge shaped adobes on end. In the middle course, the adobes were smaller and chunky; or if large and wedge shaped, they were laid lengthwise. There were four or five courses and two tiers in the wall. The spacing shows that there was far more mortar than bricks in this wall. Dimensions of four measured adobes:

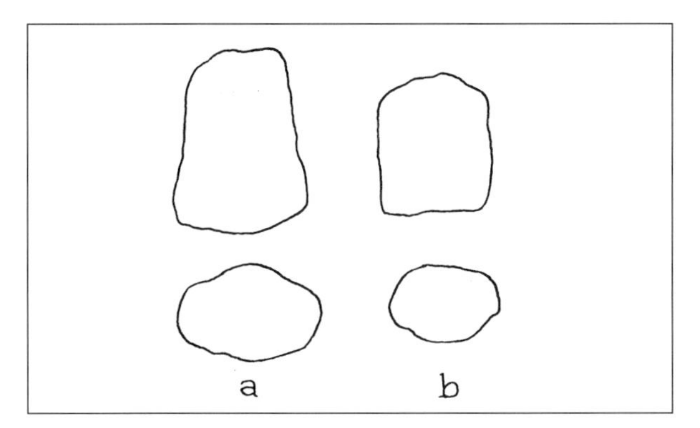


FIGURE 80. *Adobe profiles (bases at bottom), Majoro Chico A, west wall of main enclosure*

| | Height | Max. D | Min. D *(cm)* |
|---|---|---|---|
| | 24 | 19 | 15 |
| | 26 | 26 | 18 |
| | 28 | 24 | 18 |
| | 30 | 25 | 18 |
| Mean: | 27 | 23.5 | 17 |

We come now to the small platform southwest of the main enclosure. This consisted of a pavement of a double layer of adobes, seven of which (a–g) are shown in Figure 83. The first four are from the north edge of the platform, laid flat, with their bases to the edge; the last three are from 0.5 m in from the edge. It will be noted how irregular overall these adobes are as compared with those from the large enclosure; even the bases are really elliptical only sometimes, and the profiles mostly show local concavities somewhere. The largest, a, showed traces of its composite building up; g has finger marks, and also d, five of them, from a right hand considerably smaller than Kroeber's—as expected for a Peruvian Indian compared with a Caucasian of North European descent. The sizes are:

| | Height | Max. D | Min. D *(cm)* |
|---|---|---|---|
| a | 25 | 19 | 14 |
| b | 19 | 17 | 14 |
| c | 22 | 18 | 15 |
| d | 23 | 16 | 15 |
| e | 21 | 16 | 14 |
| f | 20 | 17 | 16 |
| g | 21 | 15 | 15 |
| Mean: | 22 | 19 | 15 |

This is the first time we have encountered adobes that differed markedly within a construction, and in all three dimensions. Possibly it is because these lumps were from a pavement instead of a wall.

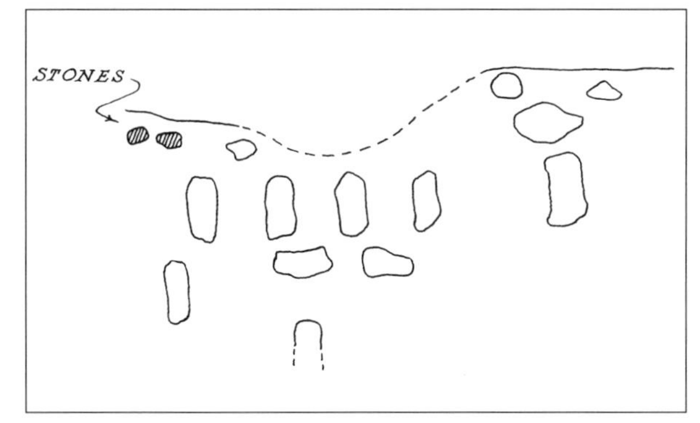


FIGURE 81. *Adobe wall construction, Majoro Chico A, west wall of main enclosure*

The free wall to the south in Figure 22 was only one course of adobes high, wedge shaped and stood on end crosswise, in two tiers, as shown in Figure 84 in cross-section about one-third of the way from the west end and in top view near the west end. At the cross-section, the wall rested on a mixed layer of sherds, straw, and gravel; the draftsman has neatly sifted these out into three separate layers, but the aggregate thickness is about right. At the stake there was a hole (grave entrance?) under the wall. Some adobe dimensions:

| | H | Max. D | Min. D *(cm)* |
|---|---|---|---|
| | 32 | 26 | ... |
| | 36 | 28 | ... |
| | 30 | 29 | 20 |
| | 22 | 25 | 19 |
| Mean: | 30 | 27 | (19.5) |

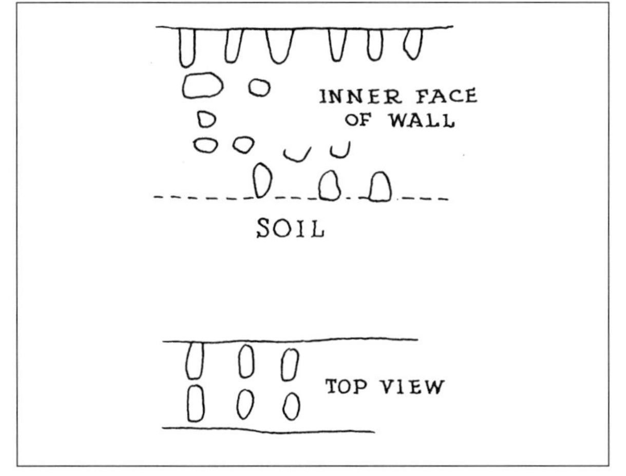


FIGURE 82. *Adobe wall construction, Majoro Chico A, east wall of main enclosure*

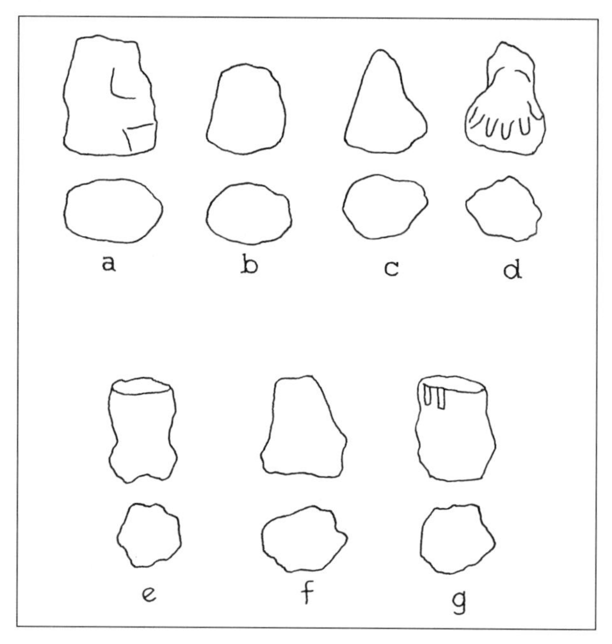


FIGURE 83. *Adobe profiles (bases at bottom), Majoro Chico A, platform southwest of main enclosure*

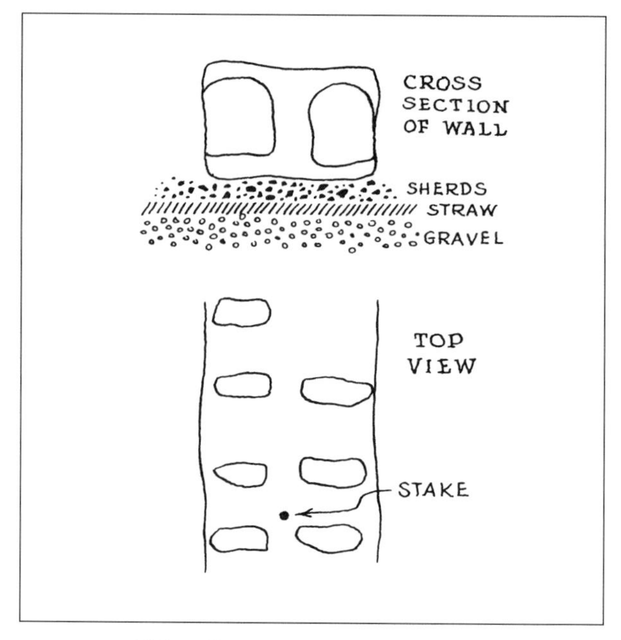


FIGURE 84. *Adobe wall construction, Majoro Chico A, wall south of main enclosure*

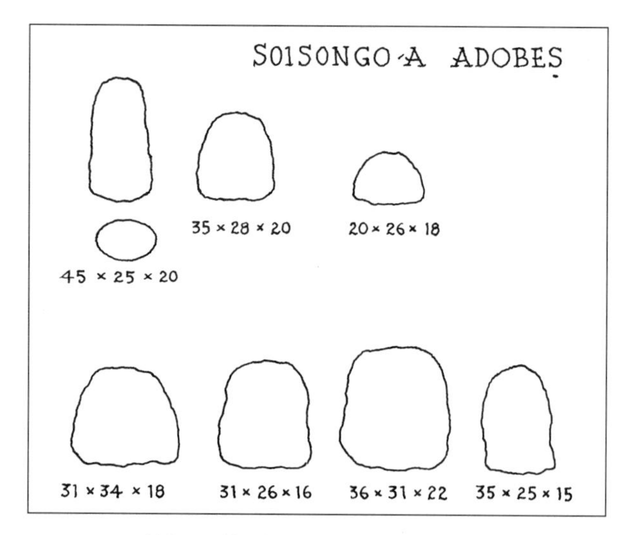


FIGURE 85. *Adobe profiles, Soisongo A, "pyramid," north wall*

FIGURE 86. *Adobe profiles, Soisongo A, from a looted grave*

The average space between adobes in the same course was around 20 cm; Figure 84, top view, perhaps exaggerates but not unduly, allowing for taper upward. All in all, there must have been twice as much clay mortar as dried clay adobes in this piece of wall.

To conclude our section on Majoro, we add in Figure 21 a view of Grave 17 at Majoro Chico A, one of a pair at the east end of the north row of graves excavated by the expedition. This is the grave at the bottom of which, at 380 cm down, a sheet of pressed gold was found along with Nazca *A2* pottery vessels. Behind and above the workman's head can be seen canes from the roof of the tomb chamber; on a level with his shoulder to the right is the end of a small log from the roof.

## ADOBES AT SOISONGO A AND C

On Site A at Soisongo stood a little block pyramid, about 8 m x 8 m square and 1+ m high. This was built of wedge-shaped, hand-formed adobes stood on end. Tello would have called them odontiformes. Their flat bases were elliptical with the ratio of their diameters varying from 5:4 to nearly 2:1. In the series of seven from the north wall shown in Figure 85, the long diameter of the base exceeds the short diameter, on the average, by 40 percent. The height is even more variable, exceeding the long diameter of the base in the same seven adobes by 20, 10, 7, 5, 5, –3, and –6 cm. It will be seen from the drawing that the top of each adobe came to a rounded edge rather than a point, as viewed from the side. This top edge would have been steeper and narrower on an end view (along longer axis of base) but still an edge more than a peak. It was the narrower side of each adobe that was on the outer side of the wall. They were well spaced, 25–30 cm in the clear between them, as against 16–22 cm of their own width. Since they tapered upward, the volume of mud mortar or filling between the bricks must have been around double the aggregate volume of the bricks.

Each of these seven adobes examined had been built up by superimposing cakes of layers of mud, which then dried together. The number of such cakes composing an adobe seemed to be from three to seven.

Some 25 m north of the pyramid was an exploited grave, part of whose log roof was still *in situ*, and above this a bit of adobe construction. In Figure 86 are shown two adobes that lay on their longest flat side. Above is their profile as viewed from above; below, as viewed from the side. It is clear that these adobes were laid, but those in the pyramid face were stood. The volume is very much less (19 x 16 x 11 cm and 18 x 14 x 10 cm), no doubt because they were laid on a wooden roof: 3300 cubic cm and 2500 cubic cm (if parallelepipedal) as against 9000 cubic cm for the smallest brick measured from the pyramid and 22000 cubic cm for the largest. (Actual volumes of the irregular adobes were probably around half of the figures mentioned.)

At Soisongo C, nine adobes from the wall of Grave 6 (from which unfortunately nothing was obtained) were measured (see below). They average in size rather similar to those from the Soisongo A grave but are rounder than any other consistent lot of Nazca Period adobes examined. They all had one flat side, on which they were laid. This may seem self-evident, but is not so. Irregular hand-formed adobes of this rather small size might without difficulty be made wholly within two hands and then be laid directly onto their wall. Two of these nine adobes are shown in Figure 87, first as seen from the side lying on their flat base, and then as seen from above. The dimensions of these nine Soisongo C adobes are:

| | Length | Width | Height *(cm)* |
|---|---|---|---|
| | 18 | 15 | 14 |
| | 20 | 14 | 13 |
| | 19 | 15 | 13 |
| | 17 | 14 | 12 |
| | 18 | 17 | 14 |
| | 18 | 12 | 12 |
| | 14 | 13 | 16 peaked |
| | 18 | 16 | 13 |
| | 20 | 12 | 10 |
| Mean: | 18 | 14 | 13 |

The parallelepipedal volumes run from about 2400 cubic cm to 4200 cubic cm.

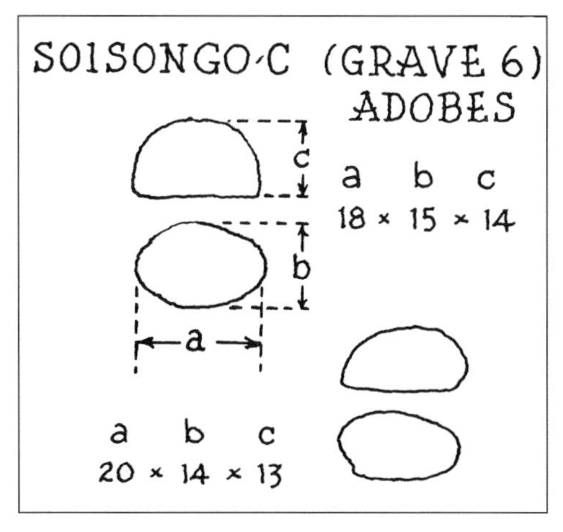


FIGURE 87. *Adobe profiles, Soisongo C, Grave 6*

## ADOBES AT AJA A

The small cemetery at Aja B, which yielded a pure Nazca *A1* set of graves, had little construction and no adobes were measured. Site Aja A had been ransacked, especially a large crater 2 m deep and 9 m across that must have contained a cluster of fairly rich Late tombs, to judge by the litter and refuse still strewn about in 1926. Just inside the perimeter of the crater, however, at only 20 cm depth, was encountered a small roof of canes, under which was seated a broad mummy pack of a gray-haired person with bags, cloths, cotton pads, wool rope, and red twine on fingers and toes (170927a–n), all plainly of Late Period.

This set of Late burials, and remains of a similar one some meters west of it, were south of a quite level space, cleared of stones, some 30 m or more square, enclosed by a low wall on its west, north, and east but open to the south, where the Late graves lay. There was nothing to show whether the wall and the graves were synchronous or not.

It is, however, clear that the adobes of the walls at Aja A are much more regular and uniform than the adobes of most Nazca period associations here described. They are rounded wedges with a blunt edge, curving two ways, opposite the flat bottom. These bottoms were set on fine gravel to dry, as shown by embedded gravel only there. The elliptical bases have their axes in about a 4:3 ratio. The height averages a little less than the width (short axis of base), though some individual adobes are higher than wide. The wedges are rounded all over so as to exclude any planes or edges, except for the base. The surface of the adobes is striated with marks of fingers drawn from bottom upward. These striations are most marked in the larger bricks, such as prevailed in the lower of the two courses of the wall. The dimensions of the upper-course adobes averaged about five-sixths those of the lower, which would make their volume and weight little more than half as much.

The walls were perhaps only two courses high and were two adobes thick, these being set on their bases with their long axes across the wall, so that their ends showed when the wall surface was cleared; the wedge side, of course, was regularly up. They were set much more closely and regularly than the adobes in walls of unquestionable Nazca Period construction at Ocongalla, Majoro, and Cantayo Cax. In fact, in the bottom course the adobes almost touched endwise and sidewise. While there was perhaps as much mortar as formed adobes, the proportion of mortar was definitely less than in the walls examined elsewhere. The chunks of mortar between adobes were almost as hard as these—they got their drying in the wall and not in previous exposure to the sun. The adobes themselves, however, seemed somewhat less hard than the general run in Nazca Valley.

The three walls at Aja A may of course antedate the nearby Late graves. They may have been built in a late phase of the Nazca culture when adobes were more nearly uniformized in shape and size than at first. On the other hand, it is also just possible that hand-formed adobes continued to be made in post-Nazca Late times in the Río Grande drainage, perhaps even until the Inca conquest. Unfortunately, the 1926 expedition made no observations on this point; but the work of Rowe and his associates has probably accumulated the knowledge by now.

These are the measurements made at Aja A in 1926:

| | LENGTH | WIDTH | HEIGHT *(cm)* | |
|---|---|---|---|---|
| East wall, | 40 | 28 | 23 | |
| lower course | 40 | 32 | 28 | |
| | 38 | 22 | 25 | |
| | 37 | 30 | 20 | |
| MEAN: | 39 | 28 | 24 | |
| East wall, | 31 | 22 | 20 | |
| upper course | 27 | 19 | 17 | 2 layers |
| | 36 | 24 | 23 | |
| | 35 | 23 | 23 | |
| | 32 | 27 | 22 | |
| MEAN: | 32 | 23 | 21 | |
| North wall, | 30 | 24 | 26 | |
| upper course | 31 | 22 | 16 | |
| | 35 | 26 | 22 | |
| | 37 | 21 | 26 | |
| | 38 | 26 | 25 | |
| MEAN: | 34 | 24 | 23 | |

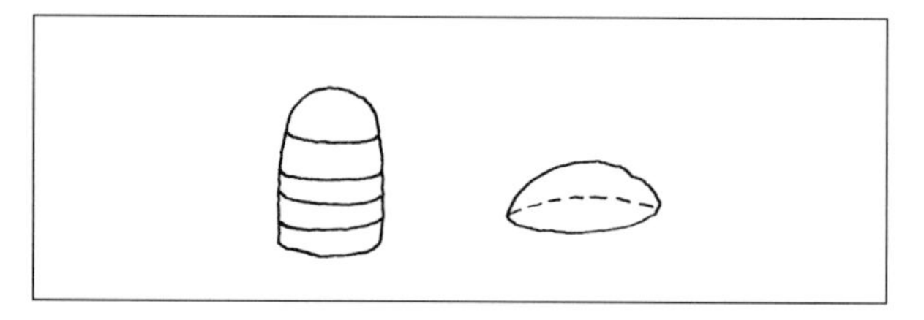

FIGURE 88. *Adobe forms at Cantayo Cax, wall B, point X*

## ADOBES AT CANTAYO CAX

At Cantayo Cax, at point x in wall B in Figure 59, which was of early construction (more probably *Ao* than *A1* in phase), several adobes were measured. They had ellipsoid bases but varied in height and structure. The following measurements are in centimeters:

| LENGTH | WIDTH | HEIGHT | LAYERS |
|---|---|---|---|
| 22 | 18 | 36 | 5 |
| 22 | 15 | 38 | 5 |
| 19 | 15 | 10 | 1 |
| 19 | 11 | 11 | 1 |

The high adobes here, which stood in the wall, were built up of five layers or cakes, the first four rather flat, the topmost domed considerably higher. The low adobes were less in height than in length and width and were not composite but made of a single cake or layer of mud. They were also somewhat smaller in base (Fig. 88).

The parallelepipedal volumes of the two sizes would be in the ratio of 12:15,000 cubic cm and 2:3,000 cubic cm. The two appear to have been laid in the same construction.

At point y in Cax (Fig. 59) similar adobes were seen, but of two to four superimposed cakes (measurements in cm).

| LENGTH | WIDTH | HEIGHT | LAYERS |
|---|---|---|---|
| 19 | 14 | 32 | 4 |
| 20 | 15 | 30 | 4 |
| 18 | 13 | 29 | 2(+?) |
| 15 | 12 | 30 | 2(+?) |

These measures of individual adobes perhaps give an undue impression of their uniformity. Figure 89 will correct such an impression. It is a reproduction of a drawing made of the inside corner formed by walls D and east at Cax (also see Fig. 60).

These walls were 70 cm thick and consisted of two tiers of adobes between which there was fill of clods, mortar, and occasional stones. At the left (N) end of wall D it was finished with four adobes all the way across. It is the inner face of D and of E, as they showed when cleared, that is illustrated by the drawing.

It is evident that virtually all adobes were stood on a base, though some were lower than long or broad; that the variation in height was great and even greater in volume; and that in spite of this variation there was some endeavor to maintain setting in courses.

We add the vertical and horizontal dimensions (in cm) visible in certain bricks as they stood or lay in the walls, the individual bricks being identifiable by their inscribed numbers in Figure 89. The + beside an adobe number

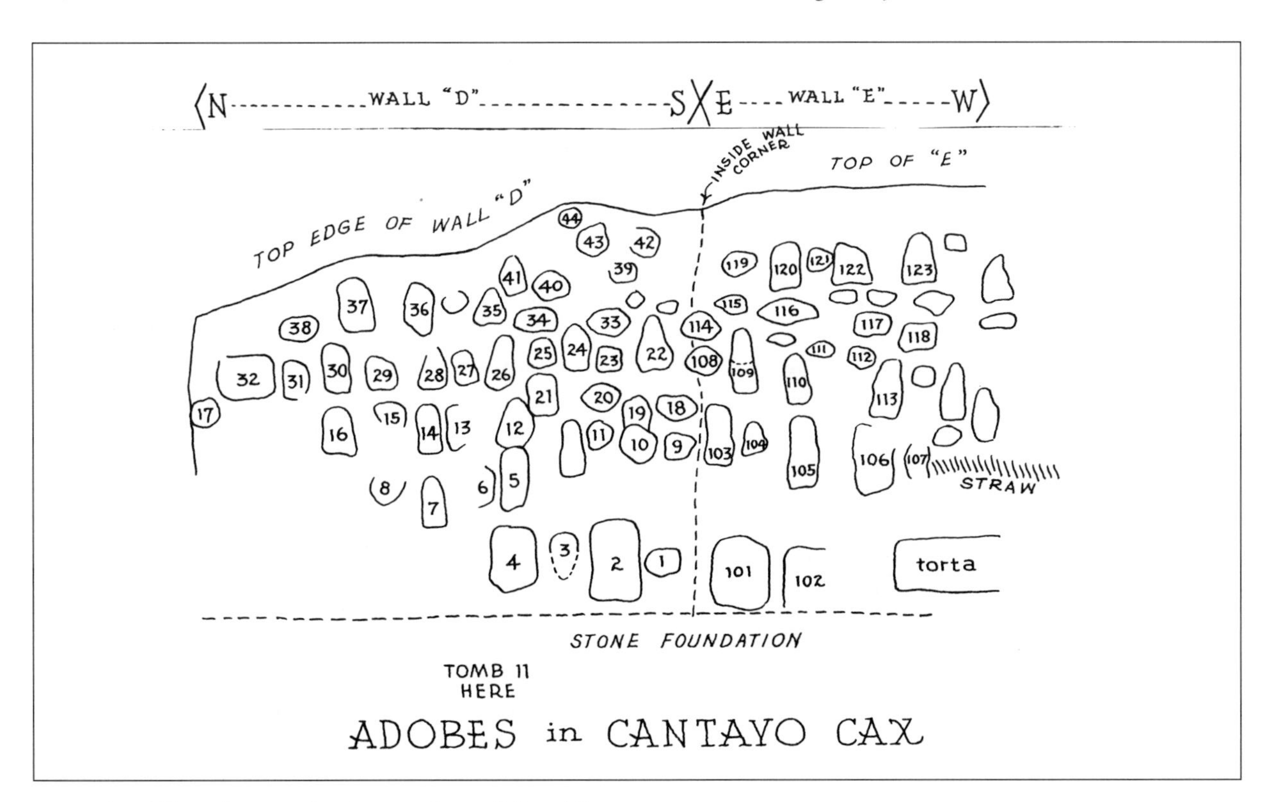


FIGURE 89. *Adobe wall construction, Cantayo Cax, walls D and E*

indicates it is lying, oval end of base to wall face; * means it is erect, broad side to wall face; unaccompanied numbers are erect, edge to wall face.

**WALL D**

| ADOBE NO. | VERT. | HORIZ. *(cm)* |
|---|---|---|
| *2 | 33 | 19 |
| *4 | 27 | 22 |
| 5 | 24 | 11 |
| 12 | 23 | 13 |
| 16 | 24 | 13 |
| 10,19 | 28 | 13 |
| +20 | 17 | 19 |
| 22 | 29 | 15 |
| +33 | 14 | 17 |
| +34 | 15 | 19 |
| 37 | 26 | 14 |
| +40 | 15 | 16 |
| 41 | 20 | 13 |

**WALL E**

| ADOBE NO. | VERT. | HORIZ. *(cm)* |
|---|---|---|
| *101 | 25 | 20 |
| *102 | 29 | 19 |
| 103 | 27 | 12 |
| 109 | 34 | 15 |
| 113 | 26 | 12 |
| +116 | 16 | 26 |
| +117 | 16 | 19 |
| +118 | 15 | 18 |
| 123 | 25 | 15 |

## ADOBES AT CAHUACHI

At Cahuachi, four adobes were measured from one piece of retaining wall (with rubbish behind it) at the north edge of the summit of Sector A, among rifled tombs. This is probably one of the walls bounding Subsection h (see Fig. 69) on the side toward the river.

| | LENGTH | WIDTH | HEIGHT *(cm)* |
|---|---|---|---|
| | 37 | 22 | 20 low rounded |
| | 35 | 20 | 27 side-flattened cylinder |
| | 38 | 21 | 30 |
| | 25 | 20 | 18 almost rectangular |
| MEAN: | 34 | 21 | 24 |

The sample is small, but suggests greater height than breadth. The association with early Nazca, *A1*, is pretty reliable.

The following observations are from Cahuachi E, Sectors Ee and Ed, below the main terrace (Fig. 66):

**CAHUACHI EE:** set on end, very wedgy

| LENGTH | WIDTH | HEIGHT *(cm)* |
|---|---|---|
| 31 | 18 | 40 |
| 34 | 15 | 35 |
| 30 | 15 | 36 |

These are notable for being narrow and high.

**CAHUACHI ED:** wedges

| LENGTH | WIDTH | HEIGHT *(cm)* |
|---|---|---|
| 29 | 18 | 28 |
| 27 | 15 | 32 |

These are similar to the preceding from Ee, but less high.

**CAHUACHI EE:** laid, wiped, concave, half spool

| LENGTH | WIDTH | HEIGHT *(cm)* |
|---|---|---|
| 40 | 25 | 15 |
| 37 | 25 | 16 |

These, on the contrary, are low and long. The shape is that of a longitudinally split cylinder expanding toward its ends, the split serving as a base for the adobe to lie on. This semispool shape was observed elsewhere at Cahuachi.

## SUMMARY

Of the measured adobes, the earliest are probably those from Cantayo Cax, with Cahuachi A next, those from Aja A latest, and the remainder uncertain. There appears to have been a slow progress toward increased uniformity. However, the variety within the period of Nazca culture is very great. There is usually one flat side, serving as base. Beyond that there is little uniformity. We have cones, wedges, cylinders, and half cylinders, none standardized, plus shapeless or haphazard pieces. But a fairly regular building up of circular pads or layers into a dome-ended rude cylinder does occur. Only it never long remains either prevalent or closely adhered to. All this irregularity was possible because, in most Nazca Period construction, formed adobes constitute only about a third of the wall volumes, the rest being mortar inserted in gobs or chunks, no doubt by hand also. There is no indication that rectangular or parallelepipedal shapes were made at any phase of the Nazca culture.

CHAPTER 5

# *Succession of Phases in Nazca Culture*

## METHOD OF PRESENTATION

So far we have followed the sequences of travel and exploration in our account. We come now to the descriptive presentation of the materials obtained, and it seems more profitable to depart from the order of excavations in favor of classing together all objects, especially ceramics, of each style and phase in turn, irrespective of the locality and time at which they were retrieved. In this way similar and related objects and their illustrations will reinforce one another by collocation and help to give a clearer impression of the particular form taken by the Nazca culture in each of its successive phases of development. Within this general framework of successive phases in successive chapters, localities are kept separate (with an exception noted below), and graves within localities also, in order that the total record may remain intact and any errors in our judgments of what belongs together stylistically and in period will be susceptible to check from the accompanying data on site and grave association. The record of physical association in one grave, of objects belonging to one person or owned in one family, and with that the contemporaneity of the objects, is probably the most important scholarly information attaching to the collection of specimens.

An exception is made in the first two accounts in this chapter on Nazca phase *A1* as represented at the two sites of Cahuachi A and Aja B. These were both small sites, less than an acre in extent, although rich in grave goods and these manifestly unitary in style, with the graves interlinked by pieces broken apart to be interred in two or more graves. On the other hand, the style involved and its principal forms and strands are better depicted by treating together first all its plates, then successively the bowls, double-spouts, jars, and figure vessels. The grave proveniences are not obliterated in these two special presentations but are subordinated to stylistic relations.

In this way we shall present in their time order the expedition's recoveries from phases *A1*, *A2*, *B1*, *B2*, *Y1*, and *Y2*. This succession is based on Kroeber's 1956 classification of the Nazca style into temporal divisions *A*, *B*, and *Y*, in place of the 1927 classification by Gayton and Kroeber into *A*, *AB (X)*, *B*, and *Y*; but with only partial discrimination here between early and late *A*, early and late *B*. In the present work we have wherever possible taken the additional step of setting up criteria for distinguishing *1* and *2*, that is, earlier and later *A*, *B*, and *Y*. Most objects and graves seemed to slip easily into one of the six pigeonholes provided, although some remained ambiguous and are designated by us as "transitional" or "probably" so and so.

Three of our six classes *A1*–*Y2* proved to be represented by two or three times as many objects as their counterparts: *A1* pieces outnumber *A2*, and *Y1* the *Y2*, but *B2* outnumbers *B1*. This may mean that we set the stylistically defining limits of our phases in an arbitrarily uneven way, or that some phases were more productive or lasted longer than others. This problem can obviously be considered more fruitfully after all of the material has been presented, and we shall therefore return to it then.

Another difference, although a less-accentuated one, can be more summarily disposed of. The expedition excavated more phase *A* than phase *B* objects, and more *B* than *Y*. It is natural to be aesthetically more interested in the great manifestations of a culture than in its declining ones. This would favor *A* and *B* over *Y*. And it is perhaps expected, or at least legitimate, to be intellectually more intrigued by the origins of a culture, or (with luck) in its antecedents, than in its smooth maturation and fulfillment. This would account for the numerical preponderance of *A* over *B*. In any event, Kroeber was conscious in 1926 of having set as a special goal of the expedition the earliest variety of Nazca culture that it might be possible to discover. But it takes time to learn local field conditions, and it was not until the last third of the expedition's stay at Nazca that the unbroken arrays of Nazca *A1* graves were found at the "pure" sites of Aja B and Cahuachi A; indeed, the latter was worked only in the last ten days of digging.

The possibility of finding a precursor of the Nazca *A1* phase was faced consciously from the beginning in 1926. It was discussed with Dr. Julio Tello. Here and there would be a symptom: a strange design, an incised or all-black sherd. Nothing coherent or systematic eventuated, however, until just before the final move to Cahuachi, a series of half a dozen unusual graves were discovered in the three-fourths plundered maze of walls constituting the subpyramidal structure Cax at upper Cantayo. Unfortunately, these graves contained almost no aesthetically decorated pottery—only a large utilitarian jar or pot

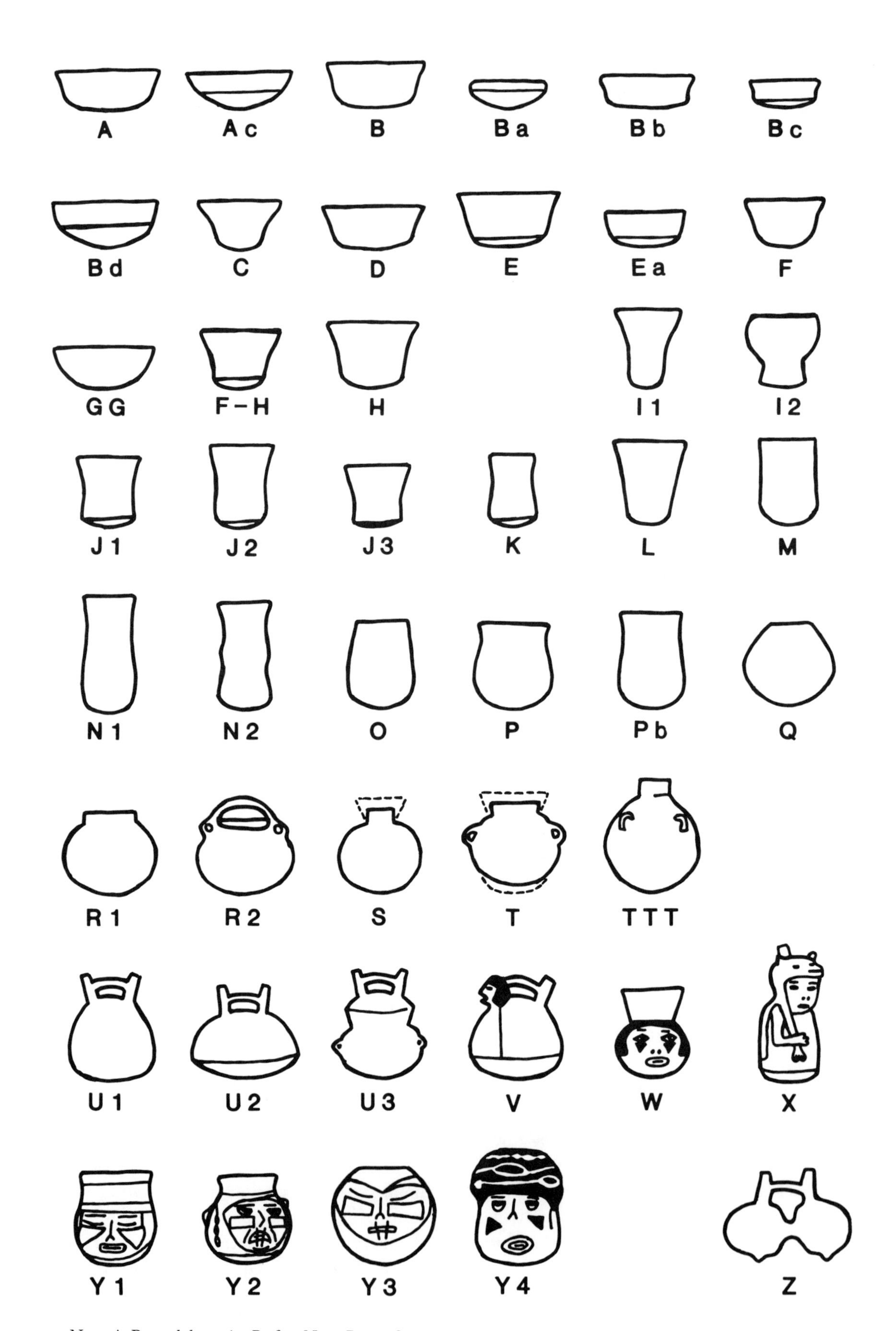


FIGURE 90. *Nazca* A–B *vessel shapes (see Preface: Nasca Pottery Sequence)*

apiece, mostly broken and used as body covers. There was in these same graves a variety of nonceramic oddments. Materials comparable to these were rare in the other sites explored by the expedition, largely because they were situated where groundwater at times penetrated into the deep graves and destroyed nearly all perishable materials. Cahuachi A alone was consistently well drained like Cantayo Cax, and its graves also yielded textiles, feathers, and perishable objects. But, alas, the graves remaining from the huaquero plunderers at Cax—or at least those discovered by the expedition—were of children or poor people, with mainly scraps or trivia or bits instead of wealth accompanying their persons.

It seems almost certain that the seven or eight graves at Cax, and possibly two or three elsewhere, represent the pre-*A1* or *Ao* phase of the Nazca cultures—what Strong has discovered more of *in situ* and has renamed Proto-Nazca. But the 1926 expedition's sample of the *Ao* culture is pitifully small. To begin our total description with this meager sample would be almost meaningless; it only attains some significance, largely by contrast, after the Nazca culture as a whole, from *A1* to *Y2*, has been presented. So at this point we depart from the chronological sequence: our brief account of earliest phase *Ao* follows that of latest *Y2*.

After that, we return to sequence but hardly to seriation, and everything recovered from periods subsequent to *Y2* is presented in the Late or post-Nazca culture chapter. This was obtained as a by-product of the search to learn more about the Nazca style as a totality, and the data secured were rather random for systematic interpretation. If a Late grave was struck, effort was made to preserve its contents and data; but then work was mostly moved to another spot that might yield something older.

## NASCA *A* AND *B* SHAPE SUMMARY

[The reader should consult the Preface, The Nasca Pottery Sequence before proceeding to the ceramic analysis.]

**FIGURE 90: NAZCA *A–B* VESSEL SHAPES**

|  |  |
|---|---|
| *A* | plate painted top and bottom |
| *Ac* | interior-painted plate |
| *B* | outside-painted bowl |
| *Ba–c* | low bowls |
| *C* | flaring-sided bowl |
| *D* | flat-bottom flaring bowl |
| *E* | outside-painted bowl |
| *Ea* | medium-height bowl |
| *F* | high bowl |
| *GG* | hemispherical bowl |
| *F–H* | bowl |
| *H* | high flaring bowl |
| *I1* | angled goblet |
| *I2* | angled goblet |
| *J1* | waisted goblet |
| *J2* | waisted goblet |
| *J3* | waisted goblet |
| *K* | double-convex goblet |
| *L* | conical goblet |
| *M* | tapering vase |
| *N1* | cylindrical vase |
| *N2* | cylindrical vase with bulging sides |
| *O* | bulbous-convex vase |
| *P* | bulbous-concave vase |
| *Pb* | bulbous-concave vase |
| *Q* | lipless jar |
| *R1* | wide-mouthed spherical jar |
| *R2* | wide-mouthed spherical jar with lugs and handle |
| *S* | small-mouthed spherical jar |
| *T* | two-handled jar |
| *TTT* | three-handled jar |
| *U1* | double-spout jar, ox-heart shape |
| *U2* | double-spout jar, lenticular shape |
| *U3* | double-spout jar, capped-jar shape |
| *V* | head-and-spount jar |
| *W* | flaring-rim head jar |
| *X* | figure jar |
| *Y1* | face jar |
| *Y2* | modified wide-mouthed jar with three faces |
| *Y3* | trophy-head jar |
| *Y4* | head jar |
| *Z* | miscellaneous shapes |

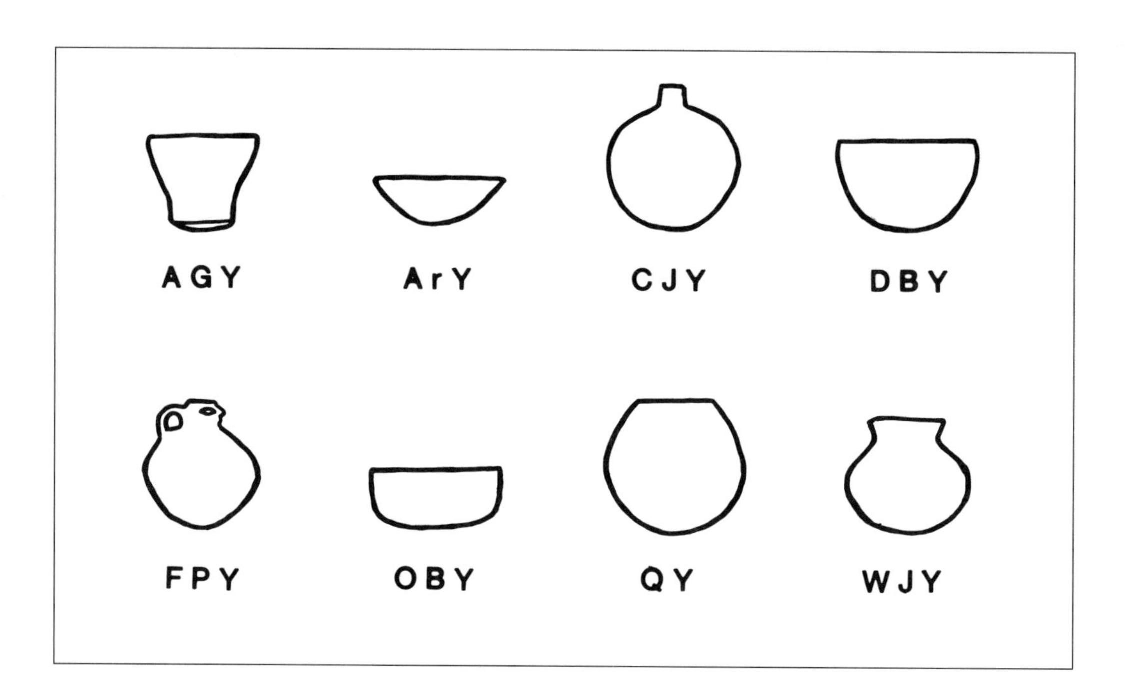


**FIGURE 91: NAZCA *Y* VESSEL SHAPES**

| | |
|---|---|
| *AGY* | angled goblet |
| *ArY* | plate |
| *CJY* | cylindrical-collared jar |
| *DBY* | deep bowl |
| *FPY* | strap-handled face pitcher |
| *OBY* | oblong rectangular bowl |
| *QY* | incurved jar |
| *WJY* | wide-mouthed jar |

CHAPTER 6

# Pottery of Phase A1

## CAHUACHI A: PHASE *A1*

IN DESCRIBING THE POTTERY OF CAHUACHI SITE A, we lump together all the graves excavated there. This procedure seems justifiable because the fifteen graves were all sunk into the top of the same pyramidal knoll; because their contents looked as if they dated from one moment of stylistic development; and because the graves, even in separate subareas such as Aj and Ag, were tied together by neatly fitting fragments of the same vessel occurring, several times, in different graves. The whole little assembly was perhaps interred within one generation.

By treatment of the fifteen graves together, descriptions of plates, of bowls, of double-spouts, and so forth are brought together instead of being scattered among the several graves. If, on the other hand, the associations within a particular grave ever become of importance, the several pieces that were within it are easily reassembled, through mention of the grave number in each description.

It is the present Cahuachi A site that furnished nearly all of the Nazca *A* textiles that the late Lila O'Neale described (1937).

### Interior-Painted Plates of Shape *Ac*

The following sequence of vessels is arranged by design themes. [See the Preface under Methods and Abbreviations for colors and measurements.]

**FIGURE 92, 171294 (N3).** Grave 1 in Ag (see Fig. 69). A fragment of a duplicate of mate of this plate was in Grave Aj-10, 171197. Hummingbird and flower design on DR background. Colors: W eye; Y tail stripe, flower; LR; DR; V (grayish), head, proximal wing, and tail; and B. Outlines B. Rim with fourteen pairs of radiating B lines. Outside rim washed LR, edge to shoulder. D 159 mm, H 45 mm, H/D 28%.

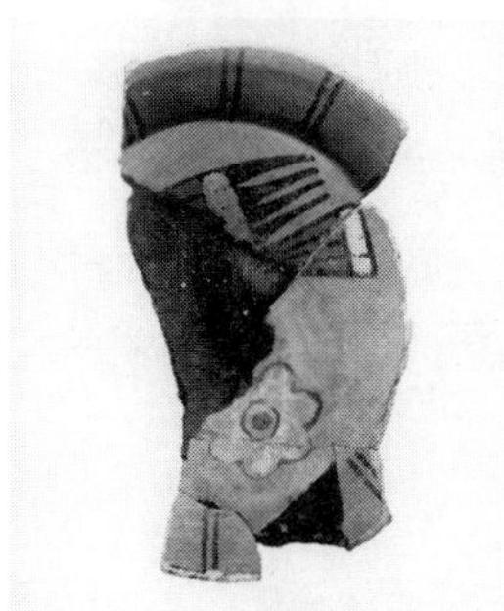

**FIGURE 93, 171197 (N3).** Grave 10 in Aj. Broken duplicate of Figure 92, 171294. Inside background, outside wash, B pairs of rim lines, and colors are all the same as in Figure 92, except W lacking because eye is missing in this incomplete duplicate. D 159 mm, H ca. 45 mm, H/D ca. 28%.

**FIGURE 94, 171275 (N3).** Grave 13 in Aj. Two hummingbirds facing head to tail on LR background. Colors: W; LR; DR; DBr head, proximal wing, and tail; and B. Outlines B. Rim carries sixteen pairs of radial W lines. Lip edge B. D 190 mm, H 56 mm, H/D 29%.

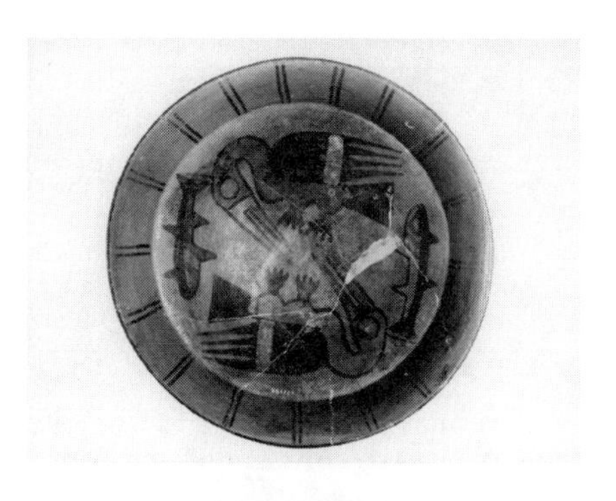

**FIGURE 95, 171195 (N3).** Grave 10 in Aj. Paired birds, probably pelicans, with smaller fish on LR background. Colors: W eyes, wing stripes, gills, and fish-tail stripe; LR on one bird body, beak of other; DR converse, also one fish belly; G proximal wings, one fish belly; B bird feet, tails, wing tips, and fish backs; also DBr on exterior only, rim to shoulder. Outlines B. Rim with seventeen pairs of B radial bands. D 235 mm, H 76 mm, H/D 32%.

**FIGURE 96, 171202 (N3).** Includes sherds from lot 171198–9, Grave 10 in Aj. S-looped fish (or cetacean: teeth, blow hole?) and human face outlined in B on W (cream) background. Fish back DBr (purplish); belly LBr; separated by DR line (the only use except on rim); LBr stripe at tail tip; mouth and eye W; and teeth and human face, B outline. Rim DR without bars, same on underside (exterior), but separated by a B line at lip edge. Colors thus are five: W, DR, LBr, DBr, and B. D 284 mm, H 83 mm, H/D 29%.

**FIGURE 97, 171231 (N3); PLATE 1.** Grave 11 in Aj. S-looped fish on creamish W background. Rim plain DR, exterior (underside) rim LR, separated by B line at lip edge. Outlines B. Fish back B, belly LR (verging on orange), separated by DR stripe plus B line, mouth DR, and tail stripe LR. Total colors four: W, LR, DR, and B, applied with clean, sure, flowing stroke. D 245 mm, H 72 mm, H/D 29%.

**FIGURE 98, 171190 (N3).** Grave 10 in Aj. A small, crudely made and poorly painted plate. Pair of fish, heads pointing in reverse but belly to back (not belly to belly), on W background extending over rim as well as panel. Underside unslipped. Colors three: W mouth, eye, and central stripe; LR bellies; and B backs and outlines. Rim has ten triplets of radial B lines; lip edge B. D 125 mm, H 41 mm, H/D 33%.

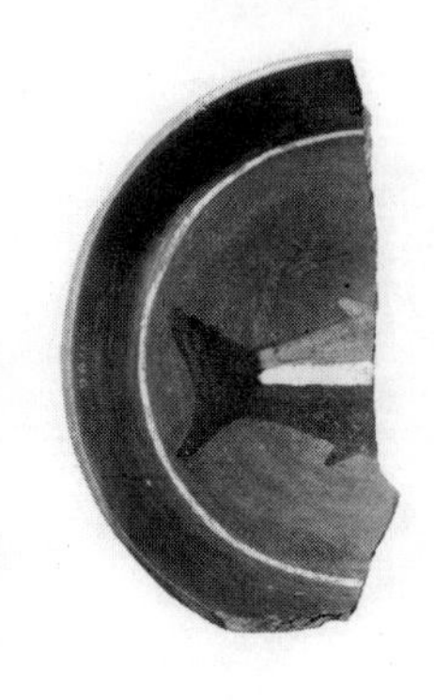

**FIGURE 99, 171196 (N3).** Grave 10 in Aj. Half of a smallish plate. Tail end of fish on DR background, plain rim being LR both inside and outside, with W line on lip edge. A line of W separates panel and rim. Outlining is faint or lacking. Fish back and tail, B; belly DR, mostly rubbed off; lateral stripe W. Total colors four: W, LR, DR, and B, of which LR occurs only on plain inside rim. D ca. 160 mm, H 49 mm, H/D 31%

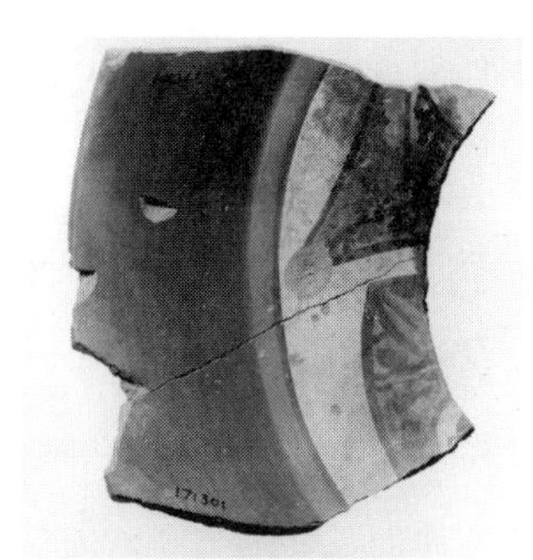

**FIGURE 100, 171301A (N3).** Grave 2 in Ag. Fragments of a large plate. Large curled fish, parts of mouth, eye, and tail end remaining, on W background. Rim plain DR (also DR on underside), separated from W panel by a LR stripe bordered by two B lines. Fish mouth LR, eye W with B center, head below mouth DR, upper head dark G with B mottling, proximal tail the same, and distal tail LR. Outlines B. Total colors five: W, LR, DR, G, and B. D ca. 300 mm, H± 120 mm, H/D 40±%.

**FIGURE 101, 171202B (N3).** Includes sherds from 171200, Grave 10 in Aj. Four bean-shaped seeds or fruits connected by B lines on W background. Plain rim LR, inside and outside, with B line at lip edge. Outlines B. Beans alternately LR and purplish DR. Total colors four: W, LR, DR, and B. D 216 mm, H 70 mm, H/D 37%.

**FIGURE 102, 171202C (N3).** Grave 10 in Aj. Single large flower on B background in panel, plain rim DR (same on underside), B line on lip edge. Outlines W, two W lines separate panel and rim. Flower tendrils or stamens are W, petals probably were DR, center probably G. Total colors four: W, DR, G?, and B. D 205 mm, H 64 mm, H/D 31%.

### Outside-Painted Bowls of Shapes *B, E,* and *F*

The order of presentation of these bowls is not by shape but by subject represented in the painted design—birds, fish, fruit, and inanimate objects. There are thirteen *B*-shape bowls, three *E*, two *B* or *E*, and one *F*.

**FIGURE 103, 171244 (N3).** Grave 12 in Aj. Shape *B*. Five left-facing birds on W background; top band and bottom DR, interior also slipped DR, lip edge B. Outlines B. Colors six or seven: W, LR, DR, LBr, F, G, and B; possibly flesh is thinner application of LBr. The birds vary only in their lower bodies: the one central in Figure 103 has this LBr, the next behind G, third DR, fourth flesh, last (tail shows) DR. They are alike in W eye, beak, and wing stripe; G head, proximal wing, and main part of tail; LR throat, tail end stripe; DR beak base; and B wing tips, feet. The execution is somewhat stiff but precise. D 190 mm, H 85 mm, H/D 45%.

**FIGURE 104, 171270 (N3).** Grave 13 in Aj. Shape *B*. Four identical right-facing birds, probably condors, or *gallinazos*, on LR background. Bottom stripe below lip DR, interior also DR; lip edge B line. Outlines B. Colors five: W, LR, DR, G, and B, distributed W eye, beak, collar, and wing stripe; LR lower collar, upper wing stripe; DR does not occur in figures; G head and neck; and B pupil of eye, body, feet, circular tail, and wing tips. Execution firm. D 212 mm, H 95 mm, H/D 45%.

**FIGURE 105, 171271 (N3); PLATE 3.** Grave 13 in Aj. Shape *B*. This is an identical duplicate (except in one small spot of coloring) of the following Figure 106, 171192 from Grave 10. Four identical right-facing birds on W background, base DR, inside also DR, with B stripe on and below lip edge. Outlines B. Bird figures have W beak, eye, crescent above, shoulder, wing body (cut by three wavy B lines), and base of tail; also upper part of feet (not closed in) can be seen as W; LR throat; DR head; B pupil, wing border, stripes, feathers, body, toes, tail, and short line or comma in W base of tail. Colors four: W, LR, DR, and B. Execution firm. D 212 mm, H 84 mm, H/D 40%.

**FIGURE 106, 171192 (N3).** Grave 10 in Aj. Shape *B*. This is as identical as the potter could make it to the preceding in size, pattern, and coloring. The one difference discerned is that the small comma in the tail base of the birds is DR instead of B as in Figure 105 (Pl. 13). (This slight difference, being constant, shows that the painter did not complete the whole of a bird figure before beginning on the next one, but evidently blocked out all four, then filled them in with color around the vessel.) Dimensions are the same as in 171271.

We have reproduced 171192 as well as 171271 in Figures 105 and 106 in order to convey the minor differences that escaped the painter. In the present figure the top of the head starts in front of the throat area, but in Figure 105, from on top of it. The feet are shorter and closed in the present rendition. The following bird's beak is farther from the central one's tail and the central one's beak is raised higher toward its predecessor's tail, in the present illustration. But these are all very small points in the face of the astonishingly successful general similarity, which must have been executed free-hand.

The wider significance of these near-duplicates is that they render it morally certain that two particular bowls in separate graves were painted and probably modeled by one person.

**FIGURE 107, 171193 (N3).** Grave 10 in Aj. Shape *B*. Four left-facing birds on LR background. Bottom Br (grayish chocolate); interior slipped the same; and rim a B stripe with W line bordering it below. Outlines B. The birds are in four colors: W eye, "eyebrow horn," wing stripe, and tail tip; DR (purplish red) beak, throat, and body; G crown of head, proximal wing, and tail; B pupil, feet, wing tips. Add to these LR background and Br bottom and interior, so there are six colors in all. D 185 mm, H 80 mm, H/D 43%.

**FIGURE 108, 171297 (N3).** Grave 1 in Ag. Shape *B*. Five sharp-beaked birds with droop tail on W background, a B stripe above to rim. Outlines B. The bird in center of view has DBr head, proximal wing, and tail; LBr throat, proximal wing stripe; and G lower body (DR and LR replace some of these colors in the four other birds). W eye, distal tail stripe; B pupil, feet, and wing feathers. Seven colors in all. The whole inside is painted LR. D 175 mm, H 75 mm, H/D 43%.

**FIGURE 109, 171301-B (N3).** Grave 2 in Ag. Two sherds from bowls, painted with birds.

*Upper:* right-facing birds, B outlined on LR background, DR border stripe at rim (with W line at bottom), and B lip edge. Head and body W with B stippling; wing shoulder B with W stippling; beak DR; patches on upper and lower beak and wing, LBr; eye, wing stripe, DR; pupil, wing tips, B; five colors in all. Another fragment, not photographed, indicates that all the birds on the bowl repeated these colors. (D of original bowl estimated 200 mm, H 75 mm, H/D 38%.)

*Lower:* left-facing birds on DR background panel, which is enclosed between W line-bordered B stripes above and below. B outlines. Beak, eye, distal wing stripe, and tail stripe, W; head, tail, and wing, G; throat and wing stripe, LR; body, base of beak, DR; and pupil, wing tips, B. Five colors in all. So far as the same parts appear in the two fragmentary birds, their coloring is the same. (D originally estimated 195 mm, H 78 mm, H/D +40%.)

**FIGURE 110, 171273 (N3).** Grave 13 in Aj. Shape *F*. The background is DR, outlined above and below by a W line, above which is a B rim stripe and below a B bottom. Vertical W lines divide the background into eight panels. Each panel contains a crudely painted (no outlining) bird with right-facing beak but body, wings, tail, and long legs disposed vertically and bilaterally symmetrical. Head, body, wings, and tail are B; eye, collar, and tail edging, solid W; and beak and legs, flesh color, which is a separate pigment. Thus the birds are executed in three colors: F, B, and W; DR is limited to the background and slip on inside of bowl. D 157 mm, H 91 mm, H/D 58%.

**FIGURE 111, 171318 (N3).** Grave 5 in Al. Shape *B*. The design is two-tiered, the upper with B, the lower with W background. The lip edge is B; the inside is slipped LR. Designs are not outlined.

*Upper tier:* nine fish, back and tail G; belly and head W; and eye, mouth, gills, and dividing lateral line all B. An upper and a lower W line frame this tier.

*Lower tier:* B vertical lines divide circumference into twenty W panels. Each of these contain a solid semicircle alternately B and DR. Overpainted(?) on each of these are seven to ten short white erect lines of varying length, each rising to a point, somewhat like grass. A B stripe borders this tier above and below. Colors: in lower tier W, B, and DR only; in upper W, B, and G; LR as interior slip only, LR on exterior bottom. D 165 mm, H 56 mm, H/D 34%.

**FIGURE 112, 171191 (N3); PLATE 4.** Grave 10 in Aj. Shape *B*. Colors: only W, B in design, LR only on bottom and inner side. Background of design W, bordered below by a B line and above by a B stripe up to lip and divided (originally into ca. 16–18) panels by vertical B lines. Each panel contains the B head-up figure of an ant (head, thorax, abdomen) or spider (eight legs) with W (overpainted?) eyes (hollow circles) and mouth (hollow oval). Original D ca. 160 mm, H ca. 80 mm, H/D ±50%.

**FIGURE 113, 171194 (N3).** Grave 10 in Aj. Shape *B* or *E*. Two-tiered design arrangement, upper on a W background, lower on DBr, separated by DR stripe that is bordered by a B and a W line. The bottom as well as the interior are slipped LR. There are strictly no bounding lines. In the upper tier the design is formed by B lines on W background, showing a double band of overlapping, round-ended figures with face(?) of three dots. There are about fourteen of these in each band. Lower tier has eleven W seven-point stars (probably) overpainted on the DBr background, each in a panel made by LBr (orangish) vertical lines. Colors: upper tier W, B; lower W, LBr, and DBr; dividing stripe W, DR, and B; bottom and interior, LR. This makes six colors, of which, however, LR and DR occur only outside the design, LBr only as dividers, and DBr only as background. The total effect is close to a B and W one. D 165 mm, H 69 mm, H/D 42%.

**FIGURE 114, 171316 (N3).** Grave 5 in Al. Shape *B*, approaching *E*. The background is W, divided by B lines into nine panels, each containing a pair of down-pointing solid color triangles, the space between which is marked by seven lines and two dots into what may be a lizard or reptile head or a human figure. In alternate panels the triangles are purplish DR, their bordering outlines and the figure between in B; in the next panels, solid B with DR lines. A stripe at the rim is DR, with actual lip B. Bottom, also interior, LR. This makes a total of four colors, only three in the design. D 160 mm, H 55 mm, H/D 34%.

**FIGURE 115, 171243 (N3).** Grave 12 in Aj. Shape *B*. W background, B dividers making eight panels, each containing an unoutlined (capsicum? see Seler 1923, figs. 387–395) pod or fruit, alternately B and DR. This balancing of B and DR is as in Figure 114, 171316. Stripe at rim is B and includes actual lip edge. Design colors three: W, DR, and B; to which LR is added as slip of interior; exterior bottom is unslipped flesh color. D 216 mm, H 87 mm, H/D 40%.

**FIGURE 116, 171296 (N3).** Grave 1 in Ag. Shape *B*. Varicolored fruits of a type apparently not shown by Seler (1923), heart shape with central circular spot and curved stem, on cream-tinted W background, in panels made by vertical B lines. Each fruit is outlined in B; the spot is also B and so are three transverse lines; and there is a (cream) W scalloped line across fruit between spot and stem. The shield-shaped body of the fruit varies in color as follows, so far as sherds remain: DR, LBr, F, G, probably DR, G, Y, LBr, and G. There may have been twelve fruits in the intact vessel. The rim stripe is DR with two B line borders. Interior, DR. Total colors seven: W, F, Y, DR, LBr, G, B. Original D ca. 180 mm, H 60 mm, H/D ±33%.

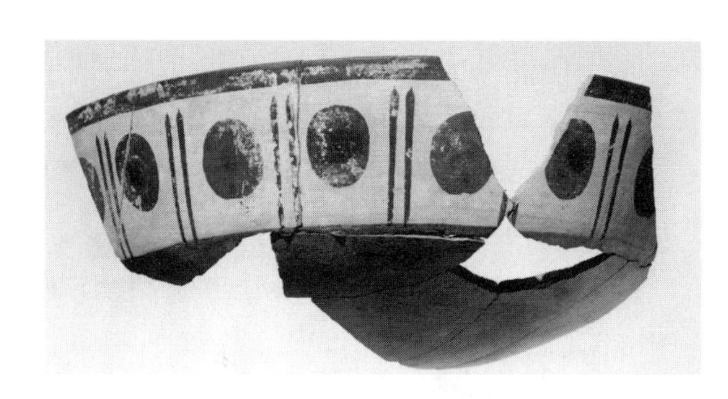

**FIGURE 117, 171274 (N3).** Grave 13 in Aj, containing parts of two identical bowls. Shape *B*. Background W, separated by pairs of B vertical lines into panels, each containing a solid oval, alternately B and DR. The rim stripe is B. Exterior bottom is unslipped flesh color; interior slip, LR. Colors: W, DR, B in design plus LR inside. Original D ca. 180 mm, H 64 mm, H/D ±36%.

**FIGURE 118, 171272 (N3).** Grave 13 in Aj. Shape *E*. Background B, bordered by W line below, against LR base and bottom. No outlining. Design, slings, seven in number, overlapping, not paneled. Sling cord and body are W, finger loop LBr, rhombus body has central LBr wavy stripe and two DR ones. Interior LR slip. Colors: W, LBr, DR, B, and outside design, LR. D 150 mm, H 77 mm, H/D 51%.

**FIGURE 119, 171278 (N3).** Grave 13 in Aj. Shape *B*. Background LR, bordered by W lines above and below and divided by W verticals into twelve panels, each containing a B trophy head with overpainted W mouth and eye and reserved(?) LR headband(?). There is no outlining. The rim stripe is DR with B lip edge, bottom DR. Interior also DR. Colors: W, LR, DR, and B. D 166 mm, H 69 mm, H/D 42%.

**FIGURE 120, 171317 (N3).** Grave 5 in Al. Shape *E*. Background B in upper half of bowl but otherwise DR; the outlining is W (or cream). Rim stripe B, bottom painted DR, interior LR. Three-step design element, descending to right, complementing a rectangle with the B background. The color sequence in the elements remaining is DR, G, LR, DR, G, DR, LR, and G. It will be seen that while the three design colors appear to come about equally often, there is no rigid repetition of a fixed order. The total number of elements was +18. Colors: W, LR, DR, G, and B. D 150 mm, H 59 mm, H/D 39%.

**FIGURE 121, 171293 (N3).** Grave 1 in Ag. Shape *E*. Background LR, outlining in (cream) W. The bottom (separated off by a W line) and rim stripe B. Lip and interior LR. Design, six crude pendant "step-frets" (although the fret portion is merely a vertical bar), in the color order B, DBr, LR, LBr, DR, and DDR (nearly B, and truncated for lack of space). The background and elements complement each other, but the six elements are wholly outlined in W, whereas the six B background step-frets are open at one spot to the B rim stripe. One erect step-fret is LR instead of B, distinguishable from its pendant complement only by a white dividing line. Paint is applied thickly and carelessly in this piece, the firing is uneven, and the workmanship in every way sloppy. D 162 mm, H 84 mm, H/D 52%.

## Double-Spout Jars, Shapes *U1* and *Z*

**FIGURE 122, 171188 (N3); PLATE 6.** Grave 10 in Aj. Double-spout ox-heart shape *U1*. Background LR, outlines B, spouts B, base LR (seems lighter than body background), base separated off by W line and DR stripe. Design element, full-face trophy heads, total thirteen, in two tiers plus two close to spouts. One (lower left in Fig. 122) is replaced by profile head. Color sequence of heads is LR, DR, and G. Hair, headband, eye pupil and edge, mouth slit and outline, all B; eyes and lips, W. Spout openings polished without slip or paint. Colors: W, LR, DR, G, and B. The bottom is unslipped buff. D 155 mm, H of body 155 mm, H/D 100%; H of spouts 205 mm, H/D 132%.

**FIGURE 123, 171242 (N3).** Grave 12 in Aj. Double-spout, shape *U1*, body nearly spherical. Background LR, outlines B, spouts B, base unslipped, separated from body by W line and B stripe. Design, right-facing flying bird (pelican?) carrying fish—one on each side of pot. The bird is shown in Figure 123, has head, body, and wing DR; throat pouch orange-red, also one wing stripe; beak, rump, and tail, G; feet, wing feathers, B; and W eye, top of head, throat edge, wing stripe, and two outer-edge tail feathers. Fish colors W and orange-red. On opposite side, same design with a few color variations, namely, head and wing, G; tail orange; position of orange and W wing stripes reversed; position of orange and W portions of fish reversed. Six colors: W, LR, orange-red (different from LR, more orange), DR, G, and B. Orange-red (vermilion) is not a Nazca color; could its occurrence here be a mixture of Y and DR? D 170 mm, H of body 141 mm, H/D 83%; H of spouts 184 mm, H/D 108%.

**FIGURE 124, 171304 (N3).** Grave 4 in Aj. Double-spout, ox-heart shape *U1*. Background W, outlines in B. Spouts LR, stripe below panel LR; base unpainted LR. Left-facing crested bird filling panels on opposite sides of spout bridge. Colors: crest of head and neck, wing shoulder, tail, G with wavy transverse B lines; beak, body, DR; throat an orange-tan flesh color; eye, distal wing stripe, tail stripe, W; proximal wing stripe and spot on shoulder, LR; eye pupil, feet, wing feathers, and stripes in colored areas B. Bird on opposite side, same color arrangement. Total six colors: W, F, LR, DR, G, and B. D 147 mm, H of body 135 mm, H/D 92%; H of spout 184 mm, H/D 125%.

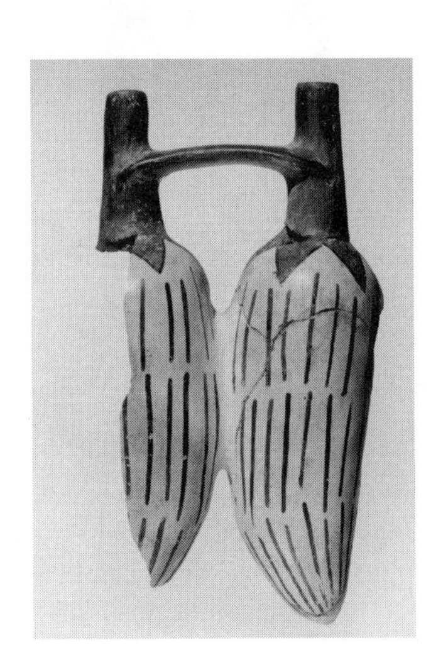

**FIGURE 125, 171189 (N3); PLATE 7.** Grave 10 in Aj. Shape *Z*, double-spout on double vessel modeled to represent two fruits (pepinos?). Background W. Spouts and contiguous star calyx, DR, the latter with B outlining. Three tiers of longitudinal lines on the fruits are alternately DR and B. Colors: W, DR, and B only. H to top of spout, 180 mm. One sherd fitting this incomplete piece was found in Grave 11 (171233).

## Figure Vases, Shape *X*

**FIGURE 126, 171292 (N3); PLATE 8.** Grave 1 in Ag. Shape *X*, human-figure vase, seated man, wearing animal headdress, probably fox. There are seven colors: W, C, F, LR, DR, G, B. The cream and flesh are much alike, but both differentiate from W even in the photograph: compare W eyes and teeth of fox with its flesh face, and man's W fingernails with cream forelegs of the animal. The three trapezoidal pendants are also flesh. The man's face is LR, his lips DR; his hands, arms, and shoulder are DR, his body G. His fingers are divided by B lines, but his arms are not thus separated from the G body, nor his W nails from the body. The fox's hind legs and tail, hanging down the man's back, are also cream. The painting is precise and, in spite of the static posture, spirited. D 135 mm, H to lip opening 268 mm, H/D 199%.

**FIGURE 127, 171295 (N3).** Similar shape-*X* piece from the same Grave 1, but head was broken off at neck. The background, namely an enveloping cloak, is W, the outlining B, the bottom of the vessel unpainted; and the base of the body is G (its row of bars at top perhaps meant to indicate W fringe of cloak). The arms are DR, so is the collar and one of the two fruits, and the squares on shoulder sleeves alternate between DR and B. The least-used color is LR, only in the club head in right hand. The fingernails are W and contrast with the cream of the sheaf of stalks and fruit in left hand. However, the W s-ornaments on the collar, which are not outlined and therefore merely overpainted on the DR collar, are less purely W than the outlined fingernails or even the W cloak background, and therefore suggest that no separate pigment was used to produce a cream effect, rather, the painting was done thin W over a color. This conjecture as to technique will need verification from examination of other pieces or chemical analysis of the pigments. D of body 156 mm, H to neck break 204 mm.

## Three-Handled Jars, Shape *TTT*

**FIGURE 128, 171302 (N3).** Grave 3 in Ac, shape *TTT*, three-handled jar with constricting cambered mouth. The reddish-buff paste is rough, and, as regularly in this shape, unslipped, except so far as a W background around the neck and three W stripes down each panel of the body might be considered a slip. On this W, and nowhere else, DR and B are applied in approximate balance as follows: on neck, top and bottom border of W band, DR; stripes on fruits DR; outline of fruits, B; on vertical W stripes, side outlining, B; the long wavy bands break in the middle, the upper and lower halves being alternately B and DR. This is a large vessel, about 320 mm in D, 470 in H. Compare Kroeber and Strong (1924), plate 28i, Uhle's find from Ocucaje, and Strong (1957), figure 12b, 12d "Cahuachi Broad-Line Red, White, Black". The ware in the present piece is thick: 8 mm at shoulder, 7 at neck, tapering to 3 mm at lip.

**FIGURE 129, 171202D (N3).** Grave 10 in Aj. Fragment of a large jar with flaring rim broken off; possibly part of another *TTT* shape jar with somewhat different painting from last. The maximum width of the fragment is 135 mm; the thickness, around 6 mm.

The paint looks thin because the porosity of the unpolished surface absorbed the pigment. Broad (5–6 mm) lines or stripes radiate down from the neck, leaving spreading panels between them. Alternate panels are empty of design but painted over LR. The in-between panels are filled with complementary three-step blocks, one B and W, the next LR and DR, then B and W, and so forth. One cannot properly talk of background, nor are the steps outlined.

## Unslipped Utility Vessels

**FIGURE 130, 171319 (N3).** Grave 5 in Al. Wide-mouthed, two-handled, unslipped cookpot, ancestor of later shapes *R*, *S*, and *T*. Compare also the following piece, Kroeber and Strong (1924), plates 28f, 29d and Kroeber (1956), pages 348–351, 379. The paste of 171319 is dark brown, rough, and 4–5 mm thick. On each side of the cambered collar between the handles is a modeled (bird?) face: punctuate eyes and mouth, slightly protruding nose or beak, also six or seven rudely scratched diagonal lines on each side of nose. The only painting is of faint LR stripes running vertically from lip to shoulder on each side. Only one stripe on the right of Figure 130 is barely perceptible; the porous paste evidently sucked in most of the thin wash of pigment. D of body 130 mm, H 123 mm, H/D 95%; maximum D across handles 152 mm, D across outer edge of mouth 79 mm, H/D 63%, making this definitely wide-mouthed (*R* = >50%, *S* <50%); minimum exterior D of neck 86 mm, slightly greater than mouth. H of cambered collar 22 mm, being 17% of total H; maximum aperture in handles 9 mm.

**FIGURE 131, 171320 (N3).** Also from Grave 5 in Al. Similar rough, two-handled, collared cookpot, but wholly without paint or incision. The paste is reddish brown, 5 mm thick. D body 105 mm, H 80 mm, H/D 76%; maximum D including handles 106 mm. D mouth (outside edge) 73 mm, being 70% of body D; minimum D neck 63 mm, or 60% of body D. H of collar 13 mm, or 16% of body H.

Of the two comparable unpainted pieces from Ica Valley, Kroeber and Strong (1924), plate 28f from Ocucaje F is also cambered, two-handled, and incised; pl. 29d from Ocucaje A is ovoid in body and one-handled, with cambered collar, incised eyes, and protruding beak.

## Pan's Pipes

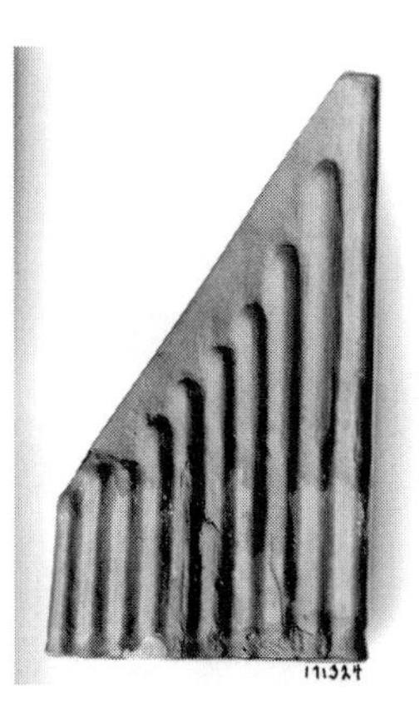

**FIGURE 132, 171324 (N3).** Grave 7 in Ag. Pan's pipe, ten-tubed, 134 mm wide, DR polished. The figure shows the piece as restored for museum exhibition; the added lower two-thirds of length appearing darker in the photograph. A whole Pan's pipe from Grave 4 of Ocucaje B in Ica Valley is shown in Kroeber and Strong (1924), plate 29a. This is also DR polished but carries a W stripe down the middle with five DR foot or paw prints on it.

## AJA B: PHASE *A1*

We consider next another pure *A1* site, a very small one, Aja B, north of the Aja tributary of the Nazca (Tierras Blancas) River, flowing nearly parallel to the latter. This little cemetery lay at the south or southwest foot of a rocky knoll some 12–15 m high, about 100 m back (N) from the cultivation, 150 m from the right (W) edge of a side quebrada. Some cleared roads radiated from this knoll. Sites Aja A and C lie in the same side quebrada but a few hundred meters farther upstream along the Aja River. They were Late, and we are not concerned with them here. All three sites lay back of the cultivation of Aja hacienda. The Aja hacienda house is near the east end of the same quebrada, at the foot of a pyramidal foothill called Cerro San Luis; it is only about 1 km from the town of Nazca, to the northwest. The three Aja sites were discovered by Tello, and he began excavating Site B with his crew. The Field party then joined his, each keeping for its museum the contents of the graves excavated by it. Graves 2 and 4 thus went to Lima and are presumably now at Magdalena; Graves 3, 5, 6, 7, 8, and 9 belong to Chicago. Grave 1, which was the largest, stone-lined, and central grave in Cemetery B, had been looted before our arrival. Kroeber made sketches of pottery vessels and designs from Graves 2 and 4, which are shown redrawn in Figures 157–162.

The whole Site B contained only nine graves that we could find (see Fig. 54), measured merely 18 m x 12 m, and is obviously all from one moment of style development. Moreover, there was one case of grave intercrossing, sherds forming part of 170917 in Grave 9 being found with 170909 in Grave 6 and having a duplicate vessel, 170905, in Grave 6. We therefore do not hesitate to describe the ceramics of the site as a unit, as in the case of Cahuachi A, classified in the presentation by shape instead of grave source. The one departure is that we have arranged the Aja bowls in the order of their height, whereas the Cahuachi bowls are grouped by design.

## Center-Painted Plates of Shape *Ac*

**FIGURE 133, 170905 (N2/3).** Grave 6. Paired fish with a third smaller one. Background of center panel W stippled with LR. Design colors W, LR, and B; outlining in B; rim LR, also LR underneath, but the lip edge is B. The design colors are evident from the figure, except that the bellies and distal part of tails are LR and that the small fish's belly is like the background, W stippled with LR. H 64 mm, D 208 mm, H/D 31%.

**FIGURE 134, 170917 (N2/3).** Grave 9. In spite of some difference in general appearance because of paint wear, this plate is the mate of 170905 of Grave 6, already shown in Figure 133. The colors W, LR, and B are the same, and so is the design except that the supplementary small fish is reversed, having its B back toward the center instead of the rim of the plate. Dimensions are also the same.

**FIGURE 135, 170907 (N2/3).** Grave 6. Long fish, looped head to tail. Background, panel, and rim, DR; under rim also DR, but lip edge B; outlining in B. Fish: back B, central stripe G, belly LR. There are seventeen B radial single lines across rim. H 62 mm, D 230 mm, H/D 27%.

**FIGURE 136, 170895 (N2/3).** Grave 3. Paired fish, opposite-facing. Background LR, which also covers the back of the plate; the design colors are W, LBr, and B; outlining in B. The fishes have B eye pupil, gill stripes, tail, and back; W eye; in one the central body stripe is W and the belly LBr, in the other the W and LBr are reversed. There are ten pairs of radial bars on the rim, alternate pairs being B and W. H 57 mm, D 188 mm, D/H 30%. 170896 of Grave 3 is the exact mate of 170895.

**FIGURE 137, 170926 (N3).** Grave 7. Colors four: W, LR, DR, and B. Design, a six-pointed star, W-bordered B, on DR background, in B rim. The circular center of the star is LR, bordered by DR and W. The photograph shows numerous radiating marks of burnishing or polishing on the DR background. The unpainted upper outside bears similar marks or lines, proceeding from left to right as the vessel is viewed in profile. This burnishing is reminiscent of burnishing imparted to blackware of phase *Ao* vessels (cf. sherd 171046 from Grave 13 of Cantayo Cax). H 63 mm, D 179 mm, H/D 35%.

## Plate with Painted Interior and Exterior, Shape *A*

**FIGURES 138a–b, 170909 (N2).** Interior and exterior of 170909, painted nearly alike on the two sides. The vessel, from Grave 6, is also unusual in that the rim carries a design: four jagged snakes(?) issuing from the top and bottom of the central head to gradually cross each other. The lower side (Fig. 138b) shows better this rather complicated and not-very-skillful arrangement.

The background is W, to which LR, DR, G, and B are applied; outlining in B. The face is LR, the ears DR, the mouth DR, the teeth B and W. The forehead (hair?) is B. The snakes issuing from the right side of the forehead and left side of the jaw are G, the complementary ones respectively DR and LR. A black line swelling into knots goes down the middle of each snake's body. The G snakes have LR heads, the DR body has a G head, and the LR one has a DR head. H 72 mm, D 218 mm, H/D 33%.

## Hemispherical Bowl, Shape *GG*

**FIGURE 139, 170906 (N2).** Grave 6. Strictly, the bowl is a segment nearer a third than a half of a sphere. It is close in shape to the negatively painted bowl from Ocucaje A shown in plate 29f of Kroeber and Strong (1924). In the center of the bottom is a short bump, evidently representing the broken-off stem of a calabash or gourd. Inside at the center are radiating ridges, which confirm the imitative representation. The W slip is thick and chalky. The only decoration is a thin B line paralleling the lip, inside and out. H 73 mm, D 192 mm, H/D 38%.

## Outside-Painted Bowls of Shapes *Ba–c* and *Ea*

Here follow descriptions of about a dozen outside-painted bowls from Aja B, arranged in order from the lowest to the highest in percentaged H/D. I would class most of the lot as of shape *B*, gambreled, with H/D 35–41%, but the two last as *E* shape (flat nonflaring bowl), H/D 44–45%. The true *E*-shape bowls also have a nearly flat bottom and nearly straight (noncurved) sides in profile. The *B*-shape bowls tend to a more-rounded or even somewhat pointed bottom, which lifts the gambrel turn where the side begins to rise more conspicuously into a view. The extreme of this is shown in Figures 140 and 145, in which the rise of the bottom nearly equals the rise of the width of the side. The result is that the design band on the side is narrow. In both these specimens the side also slopes inward toward the mouth. These specimens, and occasional others (such as Kroeber 1956, pl. 32c, 32d, and 37a) justify the original (Gayton and Kroeber 1926) name of "point-bottom bowl." Shape *Bb* is an exception, appearing almost flat bottomed. However, practically no Nazca bowls are actually truly flat bottomed, not even the *E* and *D* shapes. The majority of bowls here illustrated have a moderately rounded bottom, not appreciably more rounded in *B* than in *E* (Fig. 90).

## *Low Bowls, B Type*

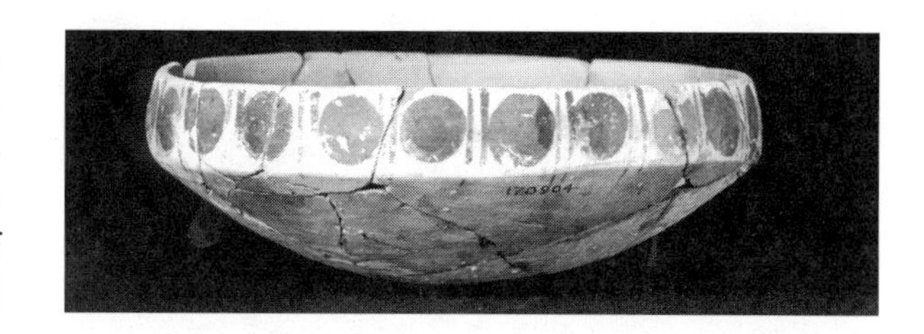

**FIGURE 140, 170904 (N2).** Grave 6; shape *Ba*. H 50 mm, D 143 mm, H/D 35%. The rising sides slope inward, the rim (137 mm) having only 95% the diameter of the gambrel shoulder. Width of the design band is under half the total H. Base and interior are unslipped. Background of design band W; no outlining. Design, twenty-two solid ovals or circles alternately DR and B, separated by pairs of vertical B lines. Colors three: W, DR, and B.

**FIGURE 141, 170914 (N2).** Grave 9; shape *Bb*. H 65 mm, D 180 mm, H/D 36%. Sides concave. Width of the design band with B background is under half the total height of vessel; the nearly vertical side below is (medium) DR wash as is the interior. Lip and lower edge of design band are W lines. Design consists of seven or eight right-facing fish, all alike in color; G back and tail; belly LR, separated by B line, also eye pupil, mouth, three gills, B; eye W; no outlining. Five colors: W, LR, DR, G, and B.

**FIGURE 142, 170916 (N2/3).** Grave 9; shape *Bc*. H 52 mm, D 141 mm, H/D 37%. Sides slightly concave. Design band width about three fourths of total H. Design background W, outlines B, lip stripe B, base and inside DR. Design, twelve 3-steps with downslope to right alternately DR and B, with complementary W background filling as many squares. Colors three: W, DR, and B.

**FIGURE 143, 170903 (N2/3).** Grave 6, shape *Bc*, H 71 mm, D 185 mm, H/D 38%. Sides slightly concave. Design band width about 3/4 of total H. Background of design band DR, base B, lip stripe B with W line below, interior DR. Design, eleven lozenge diamonds formed by a broad W line and filled by six B lines (three in opposite directions). The execution is hasty and imprecise. Colors three: W, DR, and B.

**FIGURE 144, 170908 (N2/3).** Grave 6; shape *Bc.* H 51 mm, D 133 mm, H/D 38%. Sides nearly vertical, slightly concave, bottom evenly rounded, gambrel turn abrupt, modeling precise. Design-band width ca. 57% of total H. Design background W, seemingly no outlining except of beak; lip stripe B; base DR; interior LR. Design, four right-facing long-necked, heavy-beaked, crested birds, mainly B, with beak and belly area DR, W eye, two barred wing stripes, and one tail stripe. The execution is stiff but controlled. Colors four: W, DR, and B in design, LR in interior of bowl.

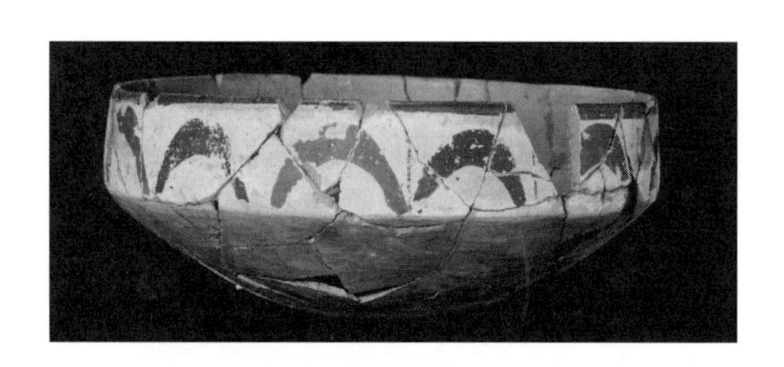

**FIGURE 145, 170902 (N2).** Grave 6; shape *Ba.* H 72 mm, D 178 mm, H/D 40%. Sides slightly constricted toward mouth, base a rounding cone (point bottom), H of side (design band) slightly greater than H of base (ca. 48–52%). Background W, no outlining, lip stripe B, interior surface and exterior base unslipped. Design, twelve crescents, ends downward, alternately B and DR, mostly separated into panels by thin B lines. Colors three: W, DR, and B.

**FIGURE 146, SHOWING BOTH HALVES OF BOWL 170915 (N2/3).** Grave 9; shape *Bc.* H 53 mm, D 130 mm, H/D 41%. Sides sloping apart, without curve, bottom slightly rounded, almost flat, gambrel angle definite. Design width 80% of total H. Background W, outlines B, lip stripe B, base and interior LR. Design, three right-facing, sharp-beaked birds, spotted on head and shoulder. Beak, throat, belly LR; tail G, head and wing shoulder, G with B stippling; eye, wing stripe, tail stripe, W; pupil, wing pinions, B. Colors four: W, LR, G, and B.

**FIGURE 147, 170918 (EARLY N3).** Grave 9; shape *Bc.* H 73 mm, D 179 mm, H/D 41%. Sides spread to top, nearly straight, bottom flattish, angle rounded, modeling good. Design band (excluding rim stripe) ca. 56% of total H, considerable base shows. Background W, outlining B, rim stripe DR, lip a B line, base DR, interior DR. Design, thirteen black-tipped fruits separated by vertical thin B lines. Nine of these fruits each contain five curved lines, but four contain a mass that forms a sort of solid stripe. Colors five: W, LR, DR, DBr, and B.

**FIGURE 148, 170897 (N3).** Grave 3; shape *Bc.* H 55 mm, D 135 mm, H/D 41%. Sides slope apart, are nearly straight in profile, the (broken) bottom is flattish, approaching the *E* shape. Design band about 57% of total H. Background LR bordered by W lines, no outlining, base B, lip B, interior LR. Design, eleven s-shaped, wormlike, interlocked, two-headed snakes in W, carrying a B center stripe and three B dots at each end. Painting slovenly, as usual when there is no previous outlining. Colors three: W, LR, and B, the LR showing pretty dark in the photograph.

## *Medium-Height Bowls, E Type*

**FIGURE 149, 170893 (N3).** Grave 3; shape *Ea.* H 67 mm, D 152 mm, H/D 44%. Sides not spreading much, nearly straight in profile, bottom rounded and flattish. Design-band width (excluding lip stripe) ca. 75% of total H. Background B with W border lines, outlining W; rim stripe, base, and interior DR; lip line B. Design, ten three-step figures descending to right, complemented by B background to form as many squares. The execution is precise. The design color sequence is LR, G, DR, LBr, LR, G, DR, LBr, DR, and LBr. Colors six: W, LR, DR, LBr, G, and B.

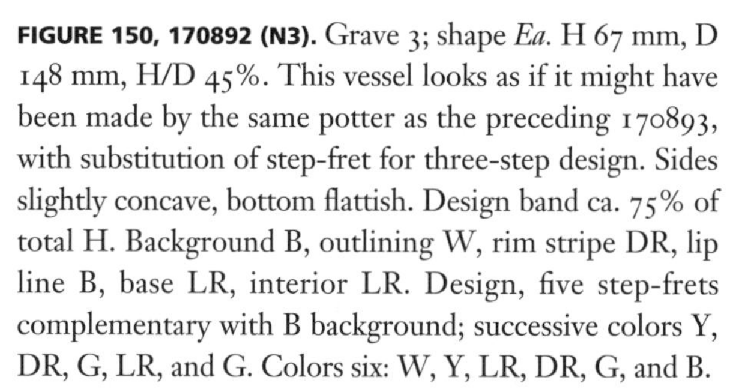

**FIGURE 150, 170892 (N3).** Grave 3; shape *Ea.* H 67 mm, D 148 mm, H/D 45%. This vessel looks as if it might have been made by the same potter as the preceding 170893, with substitution of step-fret for three-step design. Sides slightly concave, bottom flattish. Design band ca. 75% of total H. Background B, outlining W, rim stripe DR, lip line B, base LR, interior LR. Design, five step-frets complementary with B background; successive colors Y, DR, G, LR, and G. Colors six: W, Y, LR, DR, G, and B.

170894 (not illustrated) is the mate of 170892, also from Grave 3. Apart from the order of the frets being Y, G, DR, G, and LR, 170894 is identical except that the fret comes out from the step to the right, but in 170892 to the left. There is no set rule for direction of figures in Nazca, although left-facing definitely prevails. This case of difference in paired vessels is characteristic. But was the potter intending a reverse or merely unobservant?

### *High Bowl, F Type*

**FIGURE 151, 170925 (N3).** Grave 7. H 139 mm, D 79 mm, H/D 57%. Colors six: W, Y, LR, DR, G, and B. Design, deity with conspicuous W mouth mask. There is some similarity to fragmentary large bowl 171105 picked up on the surface of Cahuachi Ag, also six colors.

### Double-Spout Jars, Shape *U*

**FIGURE 152, 170891 (N3).** Grave 3; shape *U1*. H of body 156 mm, D 170 mm, H/D 92%; H of spout 194 mm, H/D 114%. Background W, outlining in fine B lines, spouts DR, stripe at base DR. Two identical cat gods on opposite sides. The central part of the face is DR, with B-centered W eyes and mouth, long LR tongue; the peripheral, or whisker mask (not closed above mouth) is W; eyebrows LR, above these a DBr band, then a LR headdress. The profile body contains a B lenticular stripe with alternate W and LR bars across it. Top and bottom of body are V, containing B (DR) rectangles in the back, lines in the belly. The four legs are paddle shaped and are colored in transverse bands as follows: V (with adjacent body), W line, B, W line, V, W (the claws). The front feet are divided by four B lines into five digits, and the rear feet by three B lines denoting four digits. The long up-looped tail is V with B stripes. Colors six: W, LR, DR, DBr, V, and B. The W is creamy and was first so designated by us; the V may be G pigment applied thinly; DBr occurs only in unimportant areas.

The design painted on this piece is very close to Seler (1923), figures 1, 2, and 3, the first of which was painted in similar position on a double-spout. Characteristic features are the strictly feline body and tail; the mottling of the body; the rectangular or paddle-shaped four feet; the continuity and identity in color of lips, cheeks, and eye area, so that the mouth mask is broken above the lips; the extension of the whiskers or mouth mask upward and to a point instead of horizontally and spreading, as was the case in most later representation; and the absence of both human and cultural features such as staff, beads, clothing, and so forth. In the three Seler figures, the eyes are not far from round; in our present piece, they are fully round.

Seler's figures 8–16 show this same feline with fruits "tied" to it by lines. We have regarded these attached fruits as characteristic of phase *B*. If this is so, the Nazca *A1* feline was perpetuated with little change into Nazca *B*. If not, attached fruits are not distinctive of Nazca *B* (although most frequent then) but were already being drawn in early *A1*. 170900 is a fragment of spout and bridge found with a few other sherds in Grave 5.

**FIGURE 153, 170901 (N2/3).** Grave 6, an unusual *U* shape (*U3*) from which the double-spout portion has been wrenched out. The body of the vessel is basically a very wide-mouthed, broad-collared jar, with two perforated lug handles, all now polished solid B. But before firing, the mouth had been covered with a modeled domed top from which the two spouts rose, this whole being baked on to the base jar. Later the spouts and bridge were broken out. It is the W domed top that bears the design painting.

H 150 mm, D of body 142 mm, H/D 106%; D across handles 158 mm, H/D 95%; neck D to handle D, 66% (neck D 105 mm); lip (or dome) D to handle D, 78%; H of neck collar to total H, 21% (collar H 32 mm).

Design background of dome W, outlining B. Design, four fish, two large, two smaller; in all these the head, back, and tail are B, the rest of the body LR and W, although divided by B lines into W belly and LR lateral stripe and the latter subdivided again; eye and mouth W, containing B. The colors seem to be only three: W, LR, and B; DR was perhaps once present on the spouts.

We consider this pot an early Nazca experiment that was not permanently followed up, although the prevalent associated ox-heart-shaped double-spout went on all through Nazca *A* and beyond it. Wide-mouth jars (shape *R*) begin in Nazca *A*, narrow-mouthed *(S)* are typical of *B*, two-handled narrow-mouthed *T* are also Nazca *B*. The early-*A* of the present site and Cahuachi A still used unpolished, unpainted, sometimes rim-incised cookpots in place of the polished and design-painted *R* jars of later *A*. Also, the opening of the these cook-pots is relatively greater than of the *R*-shape jars. Here we have such a handled cookpot polished and painted black to serve as the main body of a double-spout; but all painted design is still reserved for its added dome. The result is a hybrid from the point of view of the Nazca style as it subsequently developed, and a hybrid that evidently did not thrive.

### Head Jar, Shape *Y4*

**FIGURE 154, 170924 (N3).** Grave 7. H 205 mm (bottom broken out), maximum D 176, H/D 116%. The nose is modeled and so is the turbaned or merely gathered mass of hair; all other features are painted on. The colors are only three: W, LR, and B; all detail is either B on W or W on B, except for the LR mouth and a LR band at the rear.

Grave 7 held a headless skeleton, some braided hair ties, a broken bowl 170925 (Fig. 151), a broken plate 170926 (Fig. 137), and the present jar, which evidently represented the corpse's missing head.

Kroeber (1956, 357) set up this type of vessel as a Nazca A subclass, *Y4*, of the generic shape class "*Y*, head jar" postulated by Gayton and Kroeber in 1927. The present piece is really very close to Gayton and Kroeber, plate 7a. The modeling, the sling tied around the massed hair, the drooping lids (of a trophy head), the triangular check point, and the shapeless lips all correspond. The H/D ratio of the Aja piece is 116%, of plate 7a 105%, and Seler's (1923) figures 141 and 142 are both in the vicinity of 108%. They both show the hair mass, the sling, and a similar mouth, but the eyes in Seler are respectively lozenge shaped and circular, and 141 has the falcon design painted around the eyes, 142 has a horizontal stripe; 141 also has low bosses for ears. It is evident that this is a highly specific, valid shape class, definitely associated through our present piece with early Nazca *A*, quite likely limited to it, and possibly serving at burial the function of replacing a head lost in the interminable trophy-taking.

### Three-Handled Large Jar, Class *TTT*

**FIGURE 155, 170911 (N3).** Grave 8. Fragment of a vessel similar in size to Figure 128, 171302, from Cahuachi A, also unslipped, but less rough and porous and hence the painting is more effective. The size is indicated by the distance between the handle bases in Figure 155, which is 270 mm. Colors three: W, LR, and B, stripes of W serving as background and being bordered by LR when the wavy contained band is B, and vice versa. The paste of this ware is quite thick.

These two pieces and Kroeber and Strong (1924), plate 28i from Ica Ocucaje Site C are all early Nazca *A*, and there is no evidence that the type persisted after *A*.

### Unslipped Utility Vessels

**FIGURE 156, 170919 (EARLY N3).** Grave 9. H 116 mm, D 140 mm, H/D 83%. Cambered collar, two strap handles. Ratio of neck D to body D 58%, of collar (estimated) 64%. There was probably a punctated face on the collar like that of Figure 130 from Cahuachi A: the right eye punctation of such a face is visible near the edge of where the collar is broken off.

There is a thin LR painted decoration on the brownware of this vessel, which the photograph wholly fails to show. This painting consists of vertical lines or narrow stripes alternating with vertical rows of four or five dots. These run from collar to near the base, and there are four or five of each kind on each panel between the handles. It will be remembered that Cahuachi A, Figure 130 shows similar faint painting, also in LR.

Graves 6 and 3 contained portions of three similar pots, too fragmentary to restore and photograph, but that deserve description.

170899, from Grave 3, is similar to the last but smaller. Collar cambered, two vertical handles probably at shoulder, unslipped, LR stripes from lip to shoulder.

170910, from Grave 6 is also like Cahuachi A, 171319, but larger (H of collar 3.5 mm, as against 2.5 mm). Two vertical strap handles on shoulder, cambered collar bears punctate and modeled face on opposite sides, LR vertical stripes from lip to shoulder.

170898, from Grave 3, is a crude bowl with pairs of nipple-like projections, crumbled to bits from decay caused by intermittent groundwater. The disintegration has gone too far to permit mending the vessel, but a detailed reexamination shows that it was probably a small, almost miniature, handled cookpot, of unslipped and unpainted buff to reddish ware, 4–5 mm thick, and never fired very highly. Along the rim, just below it outside, are a series of blunt, rude, nipple-like projections, averaging about 6 mm in diameter, 2 mm in projecting height, and each with a 1.5-mm-wide hole impressed in its center. They come in pairs, 13–16 mm apart between centers; ten of them occur on one large sherd. Two small handles are preserved, coming off below the nipples; they measure 12–13 mm along their outside periphery, 6 mm wide, the aperture 3 mm by 4 mm clear. It would be hard to estimate the size of the pot, but the handles show that it must have been very small. It was somewhat similar to Cahuachi A 171319, Figure 130, but smaller, unpainted, and the handles set higher.

These pieces—the two from Cahuachi A, one from Ocucaje F10 (Kroeber and Strong 1924, pl. 28f), two others from Ocucaje F13 (Kroeber 1956, pl. 34e–f), and one from Ocucaje A (Kroeber and Strong 1924, pl. 29d), numbering ten in all—are of significance as criteria for distinguishing earlier from later phases of Nazca style *A*.

These handled, unslipped, rarely or slightly painted but sometimes incised or punctated cookpots or utility vessels have been discovered only in early-*A* associations. From these same early associations, collared jars of shapes *R*, *S*, and *T* with slip and painted design are, to date, absent. It is therefore probable that it was from our rough utility vessels that shape *R* developed in later phase *A* with uncambering of the collar, loss of handles, addition of polishing, slip, and formally painted design. Such later Nazca-*A R* jars are represented by Kroeber (1956, pl. 38h), by Kroeber and Strong (1924, pl. 28p from Ocucaje F near Grave 6 but not in it), and by Seler (1923, figures 63 and 180).

From these later Nazca *A* jars there then developed the *R*, *S*, *T*, and *W* jars by pointing of Nazca *B* type (in *R*), narrowing of mouth (in *S*), redevelopment of handles (in *T*), and widening of lip and painting a face on body (in *W*).

## Aja Graves Excavated by Tello

When Tello began to excavate the cemetery at Aja B and opened Graves 1, 2, and 4 with Mejía Xesspe and his crew, he permitted Kroeber to make sketches of most vessels. The central Grave 1, a large stone-lined tomb, had been previously opened and partly refilled, but Graves 2 and 4 were intact, and Kroeber drew designs of about five vessels from each. Some of these are reproduced in Figures 157–162. His draftsman of course saw only Kroeber's pencil drawings and had no way of distinguishing unintended defects from the original execution, nor would Kroeber be able to supply in 1959 omissions made in 1926. Pieces are identified by the National Museum of Peru numbers assigned them on the spot in 1926.

### *Aja B, Grave 2*

**FIGURE 157, MAP 30/54 (N3).** Probably *B*-shape bowl. Colors: W, Y, LR, DR, G, and B. Feline, flanked by capsicum pods, but these are not attached to the animal's body, but in fact occur in panels separated by dividers. The face and whisker mask are similar to 170891 of Grave 3, as shown in Figure 152 above, especially as regards the head, although this is in line with the body, which is scalloped and backboned much as Seler (1923), figures 58–67.

**FIGURE 158, MAP 30/55 (N3/4?).** *Ac* plate, center panel painted R, W, and B. The bottom is shown somewhat too flat and the lip rises too steeply as reproduced.

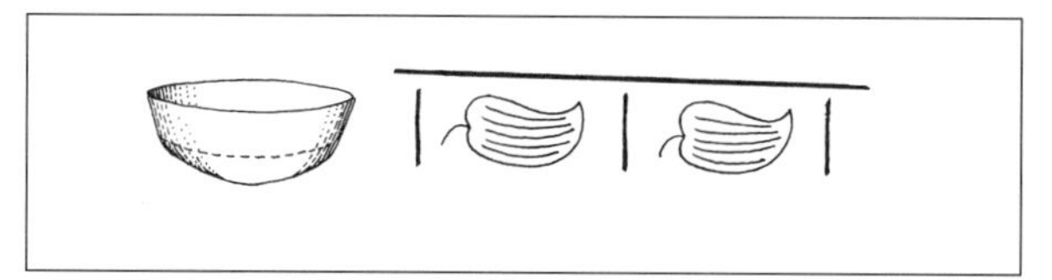

**FIGURE 159, MAP 30/56 (N3/4?).** *B*-shape bowl. The broken line indicating the turn from bottom into side is of course too high. Design, capsicum pods outlined in B, separated by B paneling lines and containing five horizontal lines, Y, B, Y, B, Y and G, B, G, B, G in alternate fruits. The bottom of the bowl was buff Y, the interior R.

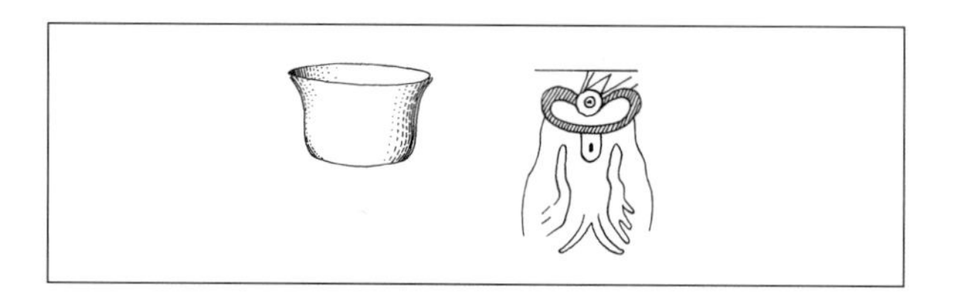

**FIGURE 160, MAP 30/57 (N3).** *F*-shape bowl if the proportions are right. The design is of swifts or nighthawks (Seler's *"Nachtschwallen,"* 1923, his figures 289–293), not outlined. The colors were obscure and the design was not clear in detail.

**MAP 30/58** *(not pictured).* Bowl, feline design similar to MAP 30/54 but without the fruits below. The crescents in the backbone were as in Figure 152 but without the compartmenting by cross-lines. The long whiskers of the cat's face were straighter than in Figure 152.

**MAP 30/53** *(not pictured).* Bowl, shape *B.* Colors: W, LR, DR, and G, no B. Hook-fringed design unit repeated in panels, apparently no outlining except for panels.

**MAP 30/52** *(not pictured).* Double-spout. Colors: W, Y, LR, DR, G, and B. Four flowers and ten vertical hummingbirds with high-humped head and single-toed feet. The colors varied for certain parts in the repetitions of the birds.

## *Aja B, Grave 4*

**MAP 30/70** *(not pictured).* *B*-shaped bowl. Colors: W, LR, and B. Background B. Design, long-tailed cat in panels; three repetitions plus a fourth compressed one. Alternate figures had (the body) W inside LR, then LR in W. The feline is very close to 107891 (Fig. 152) from Grave 3.

**MAP 30/72** *(not pictured).* Inside-painted plate shape *Ac.* Colors: W, Y, LR, DR, and G. No B outlining. Four salamanders with stumpy legs and short straight tails.

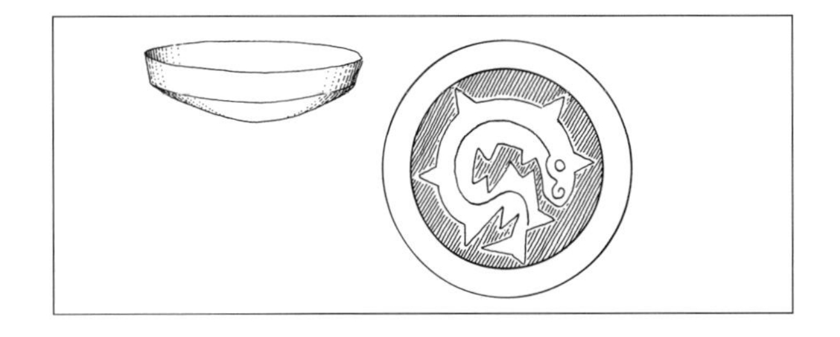

**FIGURE 161, MAP 30/75 (EARLY N3).** Inside-painted plate *Ac.* Colors: W, Y, LR, and G, no B. Background LR, outlining W. Looped-up fish, 170907 from Grave 6, Figure 135.

**MAP 30/76** *(not pictured).* *B*-shape bowl. Colors: W, Y, LR, and G, no B. Background LR. Broad W-outlined slings, no panels.

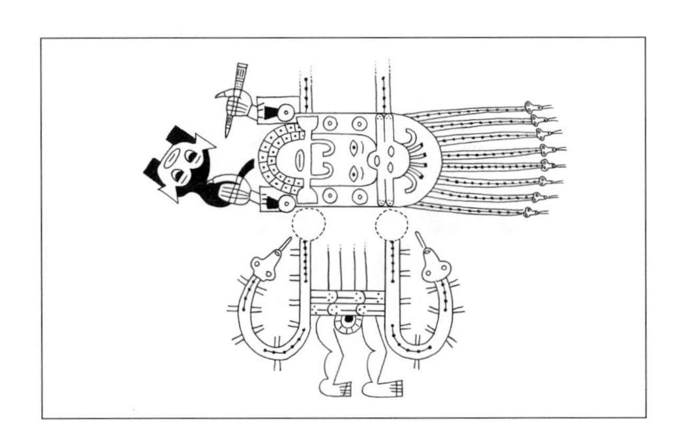

**FIGURE 162, MAP 30/74 (N3).** Cat deity design painted on double-spout, as seen from above and unrolled; dotted lines show place of spouts. Colors: W, Y, LR, R *(sic)*, DR, G, and B (one of the three Rs is probably a Br). This is perhaps the most elaborate design yet identified for this early phase *A.* The complexity suggests generic *B* phase, yet there is no single stylistic feature of *B* present, even though themes more frequent in phase *B* are represented. The closest parallels are in Seler (1923), figures 26, 27a–c; and his figures 28–30 are similar, plus reproducing the position of the design with reference to the two spouts.

## MAJORO CHICO A: PHASE *A1*

Majoro Chico was the second hacienda in which the 1926 expedition excavated in Nazca Valley. We prospected and dug at five subsites, which were designated A, B, C, D, E. Of these, locus A was the most productive, and we dug 20 graves there. Some of these were duds, some contained only bones, some were late *B* or *Y*, and five were Nazca *A*. The Nazca *A* graves run nearly consecutively from Graves 14 through 20 (16 was Nazca *B* and 19 was empty or a false clue), and they probably were fairly well grouped together, so that one led us to the other (Fig. 22).

However, they differ in one respect from the phase *A* graves at Cahuachi and Aja: they are not all of one and the same chronological moment, not a pure-style lot. In line with this, no interconnections were noted as occurring through parts of one vessel having been deposited in two graves. Of the five graves opened, two (18 and 20) are early Nazca *A* or *A1*, the same as Cahuachi and Aja; two (15 and 17) are A2 or later Nazca *A;* the fifth grave (14) was certainly an *A* and probably an *A1* interment, but the contents were few, so it is best not to press the subphase assignment.

### Majoro A, Grave 18

Besides its much-deteriorated skeleton, this grave contained four inside-painted plates, six outside-painted bowls, one bowl painted both in- and outside, one double-spout, a pair of figure jars, and a "water jar." Some of these were wholly intact, none were badly shattered, and only two were seriously deteriorated. It is apparent that the proportion of shapes is much as at Cahuachi A and Aja B.

### *Inside-Painted Plates, Shape Ac*

**FIGURE 163, 170530 (N3).** D 192 mm, H 65 mm, H/D 34%. Background, center, and rim, DR; exterior rim DR; outlines B; lip line B. Colors about five: W, Y?, LR?, DR, and B; the near mate 171528 has also G, which was not noted here. Design, a loop-necked, long-beaked bird with webbed feet and solid-color ovoid tail; the neck is curved under to bring the head below the feet. Seler's (1923) figures 298, 305, and 306 show birds with oval tails, 307 and 308 with long-looped necks. The rim has fourteen pairs of radial stripes, alternate pairs B and W.

170528 is a near mate of the last, not figured here. D 194 mm, H 63 mm, H/D 32%. In spite of the surface being more deteriorated, six colors are discernible, the same as in the previous plate plus G. The pairs of rim stripes determinable in sequence are G, Y, and W.

**FIGURE 164, 170523 (N3).** D 158 mm, H 46 mm, H/D 29%. Single fish or cetacean; whichever it may be, Seler's (1923) nearest designs are his figures 343 and 344. Background W stippled with DR, outlines B, rim DR, exterior rim DR, lip edge line B. Colors only three: W, DR, and B.

**FIGURE 165, 170526 (N3).** D 142 mm, H 42 mm, H/D 30%. Ten-pointed B star, W center; LR ring on DR background, outlining W and B; rim DR, underside of rim DR, lip edge line B. Rim bears eleven pairs of W radial lines, set on without reference to the ten-star points.

## *Bowl Painted Inside and Outside*

**FIGURE 166, 170522 (N3).** Inside of 170522, bowl of *E* shape, slightly gambrelled toward bottom. D 110 mm, H 54 mm, H/D 49%. The design is the same inside (photographed) and out and consists of four s-shaped slings, the central one differing from the three peripheral in that it has two symmetrical cords at each end—four in all. The cords are W (central), W, LR, and DBr. The sling beds are half LR and half DR, in the two W-corded representations, in the two darker-corded pieces the bed is a pattern of right angles successively B, W, B, LR, and B. The background is B, no outlining, one short stretch only of the lip edge seems to be W. Five colors: W, LR, DR, DBr, and B.

## *Outside-Painted Bowls of Shapes Ba–c and Ea*

**FIGURE 167, 170525 (N3); PLATE 2.** Shape *E*, 170524 is a broken duplicate. D 161 mm, H 71 mm, H/D 44%. Vertical fish, similar to Seler's (1923) figure 336, repeated sixteen times on B background, no outlining except a W border line top and bottom of background panel. Bottom and interior DR, lip B. The schematized fish all have W belly and eye, the back and tail are alternately G and LR. Colors five: W, LR, DR, G, and B.

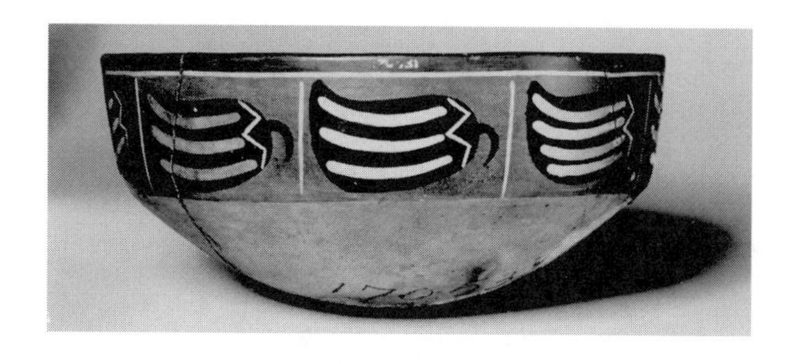

**FIGURE 168, 170531 (N3).** Shape *Bd*, with design panel narrower than height of rounded base. D 218 mm, H 93 mm, H/D 43%. Background LR with vertical W lines paneling it, rim band DR, lip edge B. Design, nine B capsicum peppers (similar to Seler 1923, figures 387–394), mostly with three light stripes each, uniform in each fruit, but W or LBr stripes in alternate fruits. One fruit (right in Figure 168) has four stripes of varying colors, in order downward: bright O, W, O, and W. Colors six: W, LR, DR, LBr, B, and O.

**FIGURE 169, 170527 (N3).** Flattish shape *B*. D 122 mm, H 59 mm, H/D 48%. Background of design band W, rest of bowl outside and inside DR, lip B. Heavy outlines B, panel dividers DR. Design, thirteen up-pointing fruits similar to Seler's (1923) figures 396–397, palm(?). Alternate fruits DR, in-between ones alternately Y, LR. Colors five: W, Y, LR, DR, and B.

**FIGURE 170, 170529 (N3).** Shape *B*. D 155 mm, H 78 mm, H/D 50%. Design background W, outlines B, base LR, rim band DR, lip line B. Design, two B-outlined continuous zigzag bands, LR and DR intercrossing (the LR prevailing where they meet), and thus forming a series of sixteen W diamonds, each of which is centered by a large B dot. Colors four: W, LR, DR, and B.

**FIGURE 171, 170532 (N3).** Shape *E* or flattish *B*. D 152 mm, H 66 mm, H/D 43%. Background W, design of nested B-line rectangles (eight sets). Rim band DR, lip line B, interior LR. Colors three: W, DR, and B plus LR only on inner side of bowl. This nested-box design appears also below in Grave 20, and in Kroeber and Strong (1924), plate 27u, from Ocucaje Grave F4 with Nazca *A1* associations.

## *Double-Spout, Shape U1*

**FIGURE 172, 170533 (N3).** Elongated high ox-heart shape, smallish. D 117 mm, H body 121 mm, H/D 103%; H spouts 159 mm, H/D 136%. Background W, outlining B, base DR, spouts B. Cat-deity face DR, eyes, mouth, W, mouth mask, not closed above lip, Y; three disks on each side face; headdress G; LR body carried over tip of jar between spouts to opposite rear where there is a double girdle(?) of shingled snake heads, W, then G, and below it DR human legs and feet and B-zigzag-bordered tail to left and up, ending in a trophy head on lower right of front side. The figure's right hand seems to hold a staff or club; its left hand, below the face, holds a trophy head by its hair. Colors six: W, Y, LR, DR, G, and B.

## *Human-Figure Jars, Shape X*

**FIGURE 173, 171534–5 (N3).** Pair of mates, the latter photographed. D 103 mm, H 185 mm, H/D 180%. The figure is seated, wearing a fox skin headdress whose front legs it holds. Face, arms, legs DR; outlined in B. Eyes, mouth, nails, fox's eyes, teeth, W. Necklace G, tunic LR; a base stripe and rim stripe are B. Fox's skin is flesh color (verging toward orange) stippled with B; hind legs and tail hang down wearer's head, where most of a DR projection is broken off. Total colors six: W, F, LR, DR, G, and B. This pair of jars is very similar to Figures 126 and 127 (171292, 171295) from Cahuachi A, Grave 1.

## *Small-Mouthed Jar*

**FIGURE 174, 170540 (EIP 3; PISCO).** Jar shape unusual in *A1*, apparently did not continue. It differs from *R*, *S*, and *T* jars in several respects, although generically related. The greatest D is near the bottom; the mouth tapers instead of flaring; there is a single small handle or pierced nubbin (near the neck) instead of none or two; and the greater part of the surface is unpainted. The D (246 mm) is somewhat greater than the H (241 mm) including mouth. The neck or spout constitutes 15–16% of the total H. The painted pattern of fishes is Nazca *A1* in manner.

[The body and neck form of vessel 170540, Figure 174, are not congruent with Nazca shapes of this early period. In the editor's opinion, this vessel conforms better with the contemporary Carmen ceramics from the Pisco Valley and is likely a trade piece.]

The fifteen vessels here described from Majoro Chico A, Grave 18 contain no features previously undescribed in the *A1* style phase except the in- and outside painting of Figure 166, the bowl 170522. Kroeber (1956), plate 41, shows six bottom-painted *F-H* bowls, most of which he assigns to post-*A1*, viz. late phase *A* or early *B* (former *X*). However, there is this difference: the 1956 bowls are *F-H* shape, H/D range 59–77%; but 170522 is shape *E* (or *B*), H/D 49%.

## Majoro A, Grave 20

Grave 20 contained three bowls and a shell spoon.

**FIGURE 175, 170539 (N3).** Shape *E* (or *B*) bowl. D 158 mm, H 77 mm, H/D 49%. Design of nested rectangles is very similar to 170532 from Grave 18, Figure 171, even to the use of the same three colors: W, DR, and B, in the same places. The pieces are not duplicates however; the proportions are different, and the first one is better executed.

**FIGURE 176, 170536 (N3).** Shape-*Bd* bowl. D 202 mm, H 89 mm, H/D 44%. Recalls 170527 of Grave 18 (Fig. 169) in its design band of fruits, except that these are here laid on their sides and their points are solid B. Even the same five colors are used in the two pieces. There are eleven fruits in the circuit, their interiors alternately DR and Y.

**FIGURE 177, 170538 (N3).** Shape *E* or *B*. D 129 mm, H 57 mm, H/D 44%. Colors four: W, LR, DR, and B. Step blocks, complementary. The background (viz. alternate steps, overhanging to left) is LR; the in-between ones are DR. There are nine blocks of each color, plus an insufficient space for a tenth pair. This contains merely a LR rectangle on end and a vertical DR stripe. Above and below, this band of complementary steps is framed by DR lines. Two blocks are partly outlined in W; there seems to be no other W on the bowl. The remaining pairs of blocks are not outlined. The rim band of this bowl is DR, the base B.

### Majoro A, Grave 14C

The data on Grave 14, 400 cm deep, are incomplete and unsatisfactory. There were three bodies; the first two were 5 m apart (!) and the position of the deepest in relation to the two others is not clear; it was with this last body [14C] that the *A1* pottery was associated.

An undeformed (post-Nazca) skull was found at 120 cm, no doubt from a later interment. At 300 cm there was a child's skeleton. At 400 cm there was a miniature plate and part of a regular shape-*Ac* plate; presumably also there was, or had once been, the principal body of the grave, but the records now available do not say. Kroeber was not present at the excavation and Schenck is no longer alive. This grave has the greatest depth recorded for Majoro Chico A, the next being 370–380 cm for the gold sheet and several of the pottery vessels in the phase *A2* Grave 17. The depth of 400 cm is also equaled by only one grave at other Majoro Chico sites, namely, E, Grave 1, Nazca *Y*.

The two vessels indubitably associated with the bottom of the grave are both interior-painted plates of shape *Ac* and radially striped on the rim and therefore would be *A1* in phase. They were numbered 170494/5.

**FIGURE 178, 170494 (N2/3).** Intact plate, miniature. D 80 mm, H 21 mm, H/D 26%. (Compare the five miniature double-spouts from nearby A2, Grave 17.) The entire background is W stippled or mottled LR, the lip edge is B, the outer rim DR. In the center is a black guanaco or llama head. The eye, from the pupil outward, is B, W, and LR; the tongue is LR; the neck or collar, DR. On the rim are ten pairs of radial B lines.

Except for size, this miniature seems a typical *A1* plate. The LR stippling or mottling recurs in the background for fish painted on plate 170905 (Fig. 133) from Aja B, Grave 6. B on W stipple occurs in 171301B, Cahuachi Ag, Grave 2, and on head and body of bird (Fig. 109); B on G mottling on fish painted on a plate from the same grave (Fig. 100); and B on flesh on a fox skin in the figure jar just described from Grave 18.

We incline to regard this painting as the representation of perhaps a trophy head of a guanaco. This species still occurs wild occasionally in the vicinity of the Río Grande drainage. Kroeber saw a tame captive in Nazca Valley during his 1925 reconnaissance.

**FIGURE 179, 170495 (N3).** Restored from seven sherds, also at the very bottom of Grave 14C, part of an inside-painted *Ac* plate. The background is W bordered by a B line, the rim is LR, the outer rim DR, the lip line B. The design is LR and B, depicting several kidney-shaped roots or fruits, each with two sprouts from it (or a heart with aorta?). This piece is somewhat similar to Kroeber (1956) plates 31b, 36b, and figures 4a–b. These last (Ocucaje pieces) are all Nazca *A*, early *A*, corresponding to what we here call Nazca *A1*.

The size of this *Ac* platter can be estimated approximately at D 200 ± mm, H 75 mm, H/D 38%. The colors are W, LR, DR, and B.

Numbers 170496–98 are sherd lots that contain Nazca *A* and Nazca *B* fragments from a goodly number of vessels; but as they have no sure associations they are disregarded here.

## FREQUENCIES OF *A1* VESSEL SHAPES AT THREE LARGER SITES

The frequency of shapes occurring in our three largest series of *A1* graves; those excavated at Cahuachi A, at Aja B (including two of Tello's graves), and at Majoro Chico A, are summarized below. Shape distributions at the three sites run strikingly uniformly, considering the variability expected in such a large sample. Nine shapes are represented in at least two of the three sites, and three shapes occur at all three. The number of plainware pre-*R-S-T* jars might have been somewhat increased with some effort to save badly broken ones. The shape categories listed in Table 2 are illustrated in Figure 90.

## OTHER *A1* SITES AND GRAVES

We return now to description of phase *A1* graves found scattered or isolated, not in pure-style sites. We begin with two at Ocongalla West A, which were less rich than the three at Majoro A.

### Ocongalla West A, Graves 4 and 5

**FIGURE 180, 170657 (N4).** The only vessel in Grave 4, an *E* bowl. H 71 mm, D 154 mm, H/D 46%. Colors five: W, F, DR, G, and B. The flesh may be a perception variant of LR or Y rather than a distinct pigment. The slip is DR within the design band, B above and below it, with W outlining. The design consists of five parallel horizontal

TABLE 2

**FREQUENCIES OF *A1* VESSEL SHAPES**

| | Aja B Cahuachi A Graves | Majoro A Graves, including Tello's | Graves 18, 20, 14 | Total |
|---|---|---|---|---|
| Plate *A* | - | 1 | - | 1 |
| *Ac* | 13 | 10 | 6 | 29 |
| Bowl *B* | 13 | 5 | 2 | 20 |
| *Ba* | - | 1 | - | 1 |
| *Bb* | - | 2 | - | 2 |
| *Bc* | - | 6 | - | 6 |
| *Bd* | - | - | 2 | 2 |
| Bowl *B* or *E* | 2 | - | 3 | 5 |
| Bowl *E* | 3 | - | 2 | 5 |
| *Ea* | - | 2 | - | 2 |
| Bowl *F* | 1 | 1 | - | 2 |
| Bowl *GG* | - | 1 | - | 1 |
| Double-spout *U1* | 3 | 3 | 1 | 7 |
| *U3* | - | 1 | - | 1 |
| Z | 1 | - | - | 1 |
| Figure Jar *X* | 2 | | 2 | 4 |
| Head Jar *Y4* | - | 1 | - | 1 |
| Water Jar *TTT* | 2 | 1 | - | 3 |
| Small-mouthed Jar | - | - | 1 | 1 |
| Plain Jar (pre-*R-S-T*) | 2 | 4 | - | 6 |
| **TOTAL** | 42 | 39 | 19 | 100 |

zigzag lines, each of about two dozen double angles. In order downward, these lines are F, W, DR, G, and F. The pattern effect is similar to Kroeber and Strong (1924), plate 29g, from Uhle's Ocucaje Site A (which may be *A0* rather than *A1*) and which is also an *E* bowl of H/D 46%; Kroeber (1956), plate 33d, an *F*-shape bowl (H/D 62%) from Uhle's Ocucaje Site F, Grave 14; and same, plate 45b, from Nazca, with five rows of festoons.

Grave 5 contained five vessels, two plates, and three shape-*E* bowls with shape-*B* leanings.

**FIGURE 181, 170659 (N3).** *Ac* plate, with three pairs of W and three of B radiating stripes across rim. H 62 mm, D 178 mm, H/D 35%. Colors four: W, LR, DR, and B. The design is of four pallar beans with sprout or rootlet, two being DR, and two B, all four sprouts LR on W ground. For the design, compare Kroeber (1956), figure 4 and plate 31b, all on plates from Ocucaje.

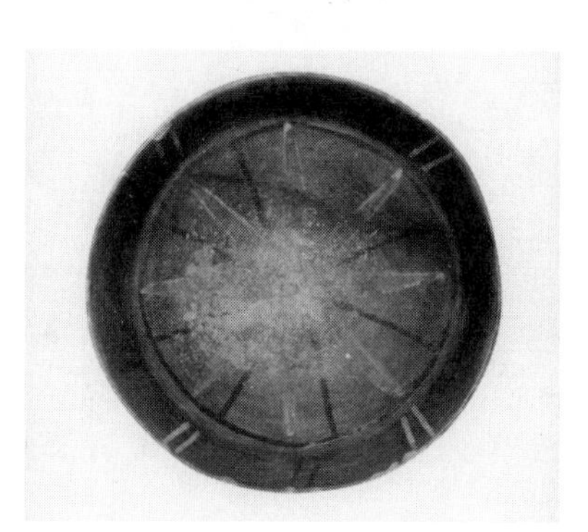

**FIGURE 182, 170663 (N3).** Another *Ac* plate. H 60 mm, D 195 mm, H/D 31%. Colors three: W, LR, and B. The background is LR; on this is a W-outlined (hollow) eight-pointed star with seven B radii between its rays (one radius omitted). On the interior rim are four pairs of alternatingly B and W paired vertical lines.

The three bowls from Grave 5 are *E* shape in H/D proportion, but with a definite *B*-shape turn in profile below the design field.

**FIGURE 183, 170660 (N3).** H 87 mm, D 184 mm, H/D 47%. Colors five: W, Y, DR, LBr, and DBr, the last replaces B or perhaps is a thin-painted B. The design is a hummingbird four times repeated, with colors rearranged as follows:

| | Wing Shoulder | Wing Stripe | End | Throat | Thighs | Tail |
|---|---|---|---|---|---|---|
| 1 | DBr | LBr | W | LBr | Y | DBr |
| 2 | DR | Y | W | Y | LBr | DR |
| 3 | LBr | DR | W | DR | DBr | DBr |
| 4 | Y | DR | W | DR | LBr | Y |

Apart from the recurrently W wing end, the colors tend strongly to vary in repeats of the figure, but DR, DR, LBr, and DBr are used twice on wing stripe, throat, thighs, and tail respectively. The background (like eyes and wing ends) is W; all outlines, DBr. This involves a darker brown (B?) enclosing DBr areas, as in the tail in Figure 183. The interior bowl is polished DR.

**FIGURE 184, 170661 (N3).** Similar bowl. H 88 mm, D 177 mm, H/D 50%. Design of four left-facing flamingos instead of hummingbirds as in the last. The colors are four: W, LR, DR, and B. The feet are LR, the bills DR, the rest of the birds B, and the background W. A rim stripe is DR, the lip edge B, and the base LR.

**FIGURE 185, 170662 (N3).** *E* (?) bowl with rather rounded turn and bottom. H 87 mm, D 171 mm, H/D 51%. Colors five: LR slip on base and interior; B lip and design background; and DR, W, and G, each repeated once in that order, in a double-spiral pattern, except that the last spiral is single for lack of room. Each spiral consists of three and a half to four turns. Kroeber (1925), plate 46b; also Kroeber and Strong (1924), plate 26h, from Ocucaje.

## Soisongo B, Grave 11

Grave 11, presumably of Nazca *A1* phase, was the only early grave that the expedition located at Soisongo B. At 30 cm down there was a plain, sooty-black bowl, 170817, broken, suggestive of Nazca *Y1;* and portions of two wooden implements, 170818–9. These objects probably got into the ground much later than the grave below them, which was 180 cm deep. In this was a skeleton with slightly deformed skull (170820). There were four textiles described on the spot as 170822 and 170823, fragments of "pinkish" cloth, one with green embroidery in the corners; 170824, a "yellow" wool belt; and 170825, fragments of a *turbante,* a yellow cloth wound three times around the head.

**FIGURE 186, 170821 (IMPORT?).** At the same depth of 180 cm was a single pottery vessel, the crude, unpainted, three-handled jar 170821. The dimensions of this, H 192 mm, D body 145 mm, H/D 132%, minimum D neck 53 mm, minimum W of three strap handles 15 mm, maximum D of apertures in three handles 16 mm. The ware, of red paste, was slipped grayish white and was smoothed only rudely. The collar is strongly cambered and carries a low lip, which is smaller outside than the neck constriction. Three small pinches or fillets of clay had been applied in the upper part of the collar. Two of these, opposite each other, are short and in a vertical plane with a horizontal perforation, and seem to represent ears. Between them is a less protruding and narrower horizontal fillet with four (or five) slight indentations immediately above that may represent a mouth.

The three strap handles are best described by reference to Figure 186. They almost certainly indicate that the vessel served as a water jar. As the whole height is under 20.5 cm, of which nearly a quarter was in the collar, the total inside height was not over 6 inches and the diameter less. The quantity of water held was therefore inadequate for household use, and the vessel may be considered a canteen for travel.

The Nazca *A* culture knew three-handled water jars, which we have named type *TTT*, but most of them are much larger, and although they are rough and largely unslipped, they do carry B and R paint ornamentation on W.

Equal or greater resemblance of this piece 170821 is to what seem to be two-handled cookpots and handleless cambered water jars, which are wholly without paint and usually bear small applied fillets or punch marks or both.

Neither of these two types of kitchenware appear in the Nazca collections ordinarily assembled, but the associations of the few other exemplars of both types are with Nazca *A1* material, and they may ultimately prove to extend before this phase. They seem to be cookpotlike and wide-mouth-jar-like types made as utility ware in *A1*, but then succeeded from *A2* on by smoothed, polychrome, and polished jars of shapes *R* and *T*, the handles, if retained, being reduced from three to two.

That our attribution of this grave to A1 may be confirmed or corrected, we add the following description, by Donald Collier, of the textiles found in it. They seem for some reason not to have been made accessible to O'Neale for analysis in 1937.

### Textiles from Soisongo B, Grave 11

Object 170822 is a fragmentary plain-weave cotton mantle dyed rose color. Medium twist yarn, texture finer and more open than coarse muslin. Made of two pieces seamed together. One piece has a loom width of 64 cm and an incomplete length of 295 cm. Assuming that the second piece (mostly missing) was of equal size, the total dimensions were 128 cm wide and 295+ cm long.

Object 170823 consists of fragments of five pieces, which have been lettered a through e.

a. Three fragments, each about 15 cm x 25 cm, of plain-weave cotton cloth dyed rose brown. Texture similar to 170822.

b. Fragment, 50 cm x 35 cm, of plain-weave, undyed (white) cotton cloth. Heavier and more closely woven texture than 170822. Portion of selvage present. Remains of embroidery in blue and blue-green wool on one edge; this appears to be to finish the raw edge at right angles to the selvage.

c. Small cotton warp-striped bag, 12 cm wide and 12+ cm long (the bottom is missing; judging by the remains of the needle-knitted side stitchery, which seems to be nearly intact, the length was close to 12.5 cm). The stripes (warp runs vertically on bag) are 1–2 mm wide and alternate as follows: blue, white, blue, white; blue, brown, blue; white, blue, white; blue, brown, blue; and so forth. The top edges and the side seams are stitched with a thick needle-knitted band of red wool.

d. Fragments of a two-piece plain-weave mantle or tunic of cotton; probably white but badly stained and darkened. Embroidered in bands of green (or blue) wool. The edges are finished in the same wool. The two different designs discernible are sketched in Figure 51. The two pieces of the garment are seamed edge to edge with a loosely stitched cotton thread. The original dimensions are indeterminable.

e. Small fragment of fine white cotton voile, plain weave.

Object 170824 is a woven, warp-faced belt of wool, 3 cm wide and 613 cm long. The length is notable: it would pass many times around a waist. White yarn (yellowish tinge) with dark brown and light brown warp stripes on borders. Center eighteen warps are two-ply white yarn; the outer four warps on each border are double, being a twist of a two-ply light brown yarn and a yarn composed of a light-brown and a dark-brown ply. As a consequence of these double warps, the borders are noticeably thicker than the center section of the belt. The weft is a two-ply yarn with twisted light-brown and dark-brown elements, like one of the yarns of the double warp. The weft is double, that is, two weft threads are manipulated together through the same shed, but they are parallel rather than twisted together like the double warps. There are 1.6 wefts per cm (4 per inch). The wefts are inserted in a simple over-under technique. The double wefts show plainly as a welt where they pass around the outermost warp, but otherwise they are invisible. At the ends of the belt the outer brown warps are finished off and the inner white warps are gathered into three strands and braided into a flat braid 1.5 cm wide; these end braids are 24 cm and 29 cm long respectively. They are tied together in a granny knot 10 cm from the ends.

Objects 170825 is a group of fragments of plain-weave white cotton voile, badly rotted and in sections "burned" dark brown (from body juices?). It is folded in many layers. It has the sheer texture of cheesecloth, but the yarn is a little thicker. Mixed with the disintegrated cloth are the remains of a considerable number of yellowish red feathers. The whole is too badly destroyed to determine if and how the feathers were attached to the cloth. As the name given it by the native excavators suggests, it was evidently a feathered cloth or veil wound around and around the head.

There seems little doubt that all these textiles as well as the jar are Nazca *A1*.

## Soisongo C, Grave 10

Soisongo C, Grave 10, at 50 cm down, held parts of two large jars, a painted one covering a wide-mouth jar or pot that contained an infant's skeleton.

**FIGURE 187, 170845 (N3).** Cover, which was the upper half of a three-handled coarse water jar *TTT*, similar to those previously described. D 308 mm, remaining H 165 mm. In the museum, this half vessel mended to so even an edge as to suggest either that it had originally been joined there or that it had been ground off there after breaking; or possibly both. The base of the constricting neck is 97 mm in D, or 31% of maximum remaining D. The colors, limited to panels as usual in this *A1* type, are W, DR, and B. The thickness of the ware is 6–8 mm.

**FIGURE 188, 170846 (N3).** Two-handled jar or pot covered by the last. It was described as "reddish" when found, and as unpainted in the museum. It is utility ware, from 7 to 9 mm thick. H 335 mm, D 337 mm, lip D 237 mm, H/D 99– 100%, the lip D 70% of maximum D. On the photograph, neck D is 83% of lip D.

### Cantayo D, Grave 6

Grave 6 at Cantayo D was 2.5 m south of Grave 5. Some 40 cm down was the bottom of a large jar, inverted above the head of the elderly male mummy; at about 90 cm were two vessels, one on each side of the body, whose feet were at 140 cm.

The large jar was not saved. It was about 400 mm in D, around 350 mm high in what remained of it, this portion consisting of the conical-rounded bottom plus some 150 mm of constriction upward; if there were handles, they were in the discarded portion. The ware was red, rather coarse, and 6–7 mm thick. This was almost certainly a water or food container, not a cooking vessel, its bottom later used as a grave cover. It is dated by the accompanying painted vessels.

**FIGURE 189, 171012 (N4); PLATE 5.** *F* bowl. H 104 mm, D 140 mm, H/D 74%. The colors are W, LR, DR, and B. There are eight DR panels divided by W lines; each contains a fruit or seed, which Seler (1923, figs. 396–397) suggests may be palm nuts, alternately LR and B, bordered and tipped in W. See also Kroeber (1956), plates 32a and 33b, both Nazca *A1* from Ocucaje.

### Cahuachi O

At the west foot of Cahuachi A, in what Kroeber named Cahuachi O (Figs. 61 and 66) was Grave 16, 200 cm deep, in which were an *Ac* plate, a shape-*Bd* bowl, and a cookpot, all thoroughly in the style of the vessels in the top of Terrace A.

**FIGURE 190, 171344 (N3);** H 45 mm, D 164 mm, H/D 27%. There are four colors: "flesh, with strong pink tone," DR, G, and B, the flesh may be a variant of either W or LR, perhaps a mixture of the two. It serves as background of the circular central panel. On it is overpainted a nine-pointed G star; this G is unusually light in the photograph. There is a free B line between each ray of the star, and it has a flesh center, B bordered and B centered. The inside rim of the vessel is DR bordered by B.

**FIGURE 191, 171345 (EARLY N3).** *Bd*-shape bowl. H 82 mm, D 203 mm, H/D 40%. Colors four; the conventional W, LR, DR, and B. The nine fruits are alternately LR and DR, separated into panels by B dividers. Rim is B, inside LR, base outside unpainted.

The cookpot, 171343, not shown here, is very similar to vessel 171320 from Cahuachi A, Grave 5 (Fig. 131). The Grave-16 piece is H 122 mm, D 183 mm, H/D 67%. The rim is 23 mm high and 8–9 mm thick; the exterior neck diameter is 111 mm.

## NAZCA *A1* OBJECTS WITHOUT SURE ASSOCIATIONS

The foregoing had burial association at least with a grave. What follows consists of objects without even that; objects identifiable by their style as Nazca *A*, but lying unassociated in the ground, on the surface, or found in test pits or trial excavations.

### Cantayo D or E, Surface

Three vessels were brought in by one of the expedition's local workmen, who was presumably also a private pot-hunter at times, as having been dug at a spot where there was no visible grave, so that the catalogue entry was "Surface"; although Tello's assistant Mejía affirmed to Kroeber that the vessels were from a grave that the digger was misrepresenting in order to loot it for himself later. The museum numbers are 171018–20.

**FIGURE 192, 171018 (N4) (MISLABELED 170984).** Phase *A1* bulbous jar, shape *P*. H 150 mm, D 140 mm, H/D 107% (typical H/D for shape *P* runs about 90 to 105%). Simple pattern of six R, B, and W disks of concentric circles, each in W field, separated by B dividing lines. For the disks, Kroeber (1956), plates 33a, 34d, 35b, and 35f; for the shape, the same, plates 31f, 34a, which also show the considerable unpainted area below.

**FIGURE 193, 171019 (N4).** From the same grave, is an *Ac* plate. H 82 mm, D 201 mm, H/D 41%. Colors four; W, LR, DR, and B. The design is of a conical seed or heart-shaped tuber with two sprouts from it. For this, Kroeber (1956), plate 36b.

**FIGURE 194, 171020 (N4/5?).** Small, unpainted but smooth, matte-finished, reddish two-handled jar with nearly cylindrical but somewhat constricting mouth. H and D are the same, 133 mm; lip D 55 mm, or 41% of maximum D; measurements on the photograph give the neck and lip Ds as 46% and 42% of maximum D. So few plain Nazca vessels have been described that this one is perhaps more important than its two painted associates. This is one of the smallest plain Nazca vessels recorded: about 13.4 cm. It is therefore not surprising that the ware is thin, from 2.5 mm to 3 mm in the body, from 3.5 mm to 4 mm in the neck.

## Cantayo M, Surface and Trial Pits

This group of pieces has only a floating location and no real associations. They all seem to be good Nazca *A1*. They occurred broken and were pieced together at the Museum.

**FIGURE 195, 170967 (EARLY N3).** Preserves enough of *Ac* plate to show the design. The colors appear to be W, DBr, DR, and B. The central panel is filled with one sprouting tuber similar to Kroeber (1956), plate 36b and to Figure 193 from Cantayo D or E. The rim was crossed by some 35 radiating W lines, the spaces between which are painted in alternating colors. The painting is sloppy. Approximate dimensions are H 66 mm, D 183 mm, H/D 36%.

**FIGURE 196, 170974 (N4).** Shape-*Bd* bowl. H 70 mm, D 145 mm, H/D 48%. Colors five: W, Y, LR, DR, and B. Background of design band is DR, with vertical W-line dividers. In each panel is a W-line inverted v, and beneath it a triangle, these being filled in succession with B, LR, and Y.

## Unknown Grave, Paredones (?)

**FIGURE 197, 170192 (N3).** On Kroeber's 1925 reconnaissance tour to Nazca, he acquired from huaqueros operating just upstream from Paredones a classic Nazca *A1* bowl of shape *Bd*. This bowl measures H 87 mm, D 193 mm, H/D 45%. There is a B rim stripe, then, on a W background, without paneling, six maize ears in order G, LR, and Y in color, cleanly executed. Kroeber did not see the piece *in situ*, and he doubts whether it is really from Paredones but it is good *A1*.

### Purchased at Yapana

**FIGURE 198, 170864 (N5)** is a narrow-mouth handled jar, shape class *T*, which was purchased at Yapana (located a few km above Cahuachi, Fig. 2). We would class it as Nazca *A*, probably *A1*. It measures H 149 mm, D 189 mm, lip D 88 mm, neck D 81 mm, H/D 79%, lip D to maximum D 47%. (On the photograph the lip D is 49.6% of maximum D, the neck D 45%, the collar H 14% of H.) It is evident that the orifice is only barely on the narrow-mouthed side of the arbitrary 50% separating fundamental shapes *R* and *S*. The vessel looks wide mouthed; this is owing to its rather low total H compared to D. It has not yet departed far from the presumable utilitarian cookpot origin of the type. The two small handles are as usual near the neck.

The colors observed are six: W, F, LR, DR, LBr, and B, which may correspond to the standard pigment slots W, Y, LR, DR, G, and B, since the F was noted as varying to Y, the LBr to G. The W-edged main panel is slipped DR, the collar and base band LR. On the DR panel are painted twenty-eight figures of a bird, six in the upper row, nine in the middle, thirteen in the lowest. Contrary to the usual Nazca *A* practice, these birds lack outlining, possibly because of the DR background. Although somewhat crudely slapped on, the color application is consistent in the twenty-eight figures. The bird's body is Y (F). On this are twelve to fourteen DR spots. The eye, the four *(sic)* legs, the hind wing feather are W; the middle feather is G (LBr); the front feather and the beak are LR; and the tail is B.

The four legs on birds are surprising, and so are the vertical wing feathers, the direction of which is horizontal in both Nazca *A* and Nazca *B* typical design painting. However the elongated and spotted body recurs in Seler (1923), figures 297, 298, which are evidently Nazca *A*. [Also see vessel 170981, Figure 221, from Cantayo M, Grave 1, described in Chapter 7.]

CHAPTER 7

# *Pottery of Phase A2*

WE NOW COME TO EXAMPLES OF A LATER SUBPHASE of Nazca *A* than heretofore considered. We designate it as *A2*. The occurrence of *A2* shapes differs consistently from that which we have considered previously for *A1* Graves 14, 18, and 20, from the same cemetery of Majoro Chico A. There are no more *Ac* plates in *A2;* bowls are *F* and *F–H,* or over-all-painted instead of *B* and *E* side-painted; there is a set of miniature double-spouts; there are a wide-mouthed *(R)* and a narrow-mouthed *(S)* jar, unpainted but polished or smoothed, instead of rough as in Nazca *A1;* and a cookpot-shaped vessel with a bail handle and design-painted sides. The designs in *A2* seem to show less change from *A1* than the shapes.

## MAJORO CHICO A, GRAVE 17

Grave 17 of Majoro Chico Site A was one of the deep Nazca *A* graves at Majoro, twelve vessels being encountered at around 350 cm, three more at 370, and a thin sheet of stamped gold (turned over to the Peruvian government) at 380 cm.

**FIGURE 199, 170511 (N4) (with MATE 170512).** *F-H* bowls. D 143 mm, H 97 mm, H/D 68%. Background B, W-bordered top and bottom, W vertical dividers for panels, base LR, rim stripe DR, lip line B, inside rim DR scallops against W. Design, ten upright lozenges (rhomboid diamonds), B and W bordered and each containing twelve rectangular dots, giving a lattice effect. Alternate lozenges are LR; those in between, successively Y, Y, DR, Y, and DR. Total colors five: W, Y, LR, DR, and B. Somewhat similar in design are Kroeber and Strong (1924), plate 26e from Ocucaje F7, shape D, and plate 27c from Ocucaje F22; also, above, Figure 143, 170903, shape *Bc* from Aja B, Grave 6.

**FIGURE 200, 170513 (N4).** *F-H*-shape bowl. D 171 mm, H 112 mm, H/D 65%. Background B; base, rim stripe, DR; lip line, B; vertical dividers W. There are fifteen panels, each containing three vertical stripes, the top rounded and broad bottom tapering with a small irregular transverse mass above the three. These fifteen figures may represent capsicum peppers; Seler (1923), figures 394, 395. The middle one of each set of three stripes is lighter colored and carries twelve or thirteen B dots. The basic color pattern seems to be YWY, GYG, LR, ?, LR, five times repeated, with the question mark in between the two LRs standing for W once, Y once, and areas of deteriorated pigment. Colors six: W, Y, LR, DR, G, and B. For the design, compare Kroeber (1956), plate 45c, d, which are also *F-H* shape.

**FIGURE 201, 170516 (N4).** Hemispherical *GG*-shape bowl. Overall-painted outside. D 122 mm, H 56 mm, H/D 46%. Background DR, rim stripe B. Colors seven: W, Y, F, LR, DR, G, and B. Design, cat deity with LR mouth mask continuous above mouth and three W disks on each side beyond. The upper face is DR, the ear tabs and chin tabs flesh. The LR right hand holds a Y dart, the space between it and the head is gray.

Overall, outside-painted bowls appear in Kroeber (1956), plate 31e, lizards, *E* or *F* shape, D 116 mm, H/D 57%, Ocucaje Grave B5; plate 33a, disks, *E* shape, D 116 mm, H/D 39%, Ocucaje Grave F4; plate 37h, birds, *E* shape, Uhle Nazca collection; plates 41a–d, 41f, designs respectively snake, bird deity, cat deity, maize ears, all shape *F*, D 116–120 mm, H/D 64–77%, Uhle Nazca collection; plate 41e, dancers, shape *H*, D 152 mm, H/D 59%, also from Nazca; and Gayton and Kroeber (1927), plate 9h, from Uhle Nazca collection.

**FIGURE 202, 170519 (N4).** Shape-*P* jar. D 161 mm, H 168 mm, H/D 104%. Design background W, bordered by B stripes, lip B, base LR. Black "suspending staves" of the four parabolic design elements, which are alternately LR and DR, unoutlined. This is a Nazca *A* vase, shape *P*, H/D around 100%, as compared with Nazca *B* shape *P* vases with H/D 124–156%, according to the distinction in Kroeber (1956), page 347.

**FIGURE 203, 170514 (N4); PLATE 9.** Double-spout jar. D 164 mm, H of body 165 mm, H/D 101%; H spout 213 mm, H/D 130%. Colors eight: W, Y, F, LR, DR, DBr, G, and B. Background W, spouts B, outlining B. Design, bird deity identically repeated. Some color areas are Y, head, one wing feather; flesh tongue root, breech clout, legs and feet, trophy head at shoulder, one wing and one tail feather; LR end of tongue, throat, middle wing feather, lowest tail feather; DR stripe bordering W background below, beak, lowest wing feather, next-to-lowest tail feather; DBr middle tongue, trophy head on tail; and G back of neck, top wing and tail feathers. Every color appears two or more times. The painting is clear and precise.

This is the first occurrence (it seems lacking from phase *A1*) of the profile bird-deity figure characterized by curved neck, transverse head, single eye, beak curving apart, with trophy-head tongue and human legs, first identified by Seler (1923) in his Section 4 and shown in his figures 101–107, 111–115. The vessel shapes of these are not shown. Other illustrations are all on *F-H* bowls but none with period associations, Kroeber (1956), plates 41b, 44a, 44b.

The present specimen is also the first in the present time-sequenced description to show three other features: 1) wing and tail feathers rendered by multicolored round-ended stripes (instead of long black triangles); 2) spines or scallops along upper edge of wing; and 3) full-face trophy heads with eyes, mouth, and lip-skewers indicated by mere black lines.

All three of these features, like the bird deity himself, continue into the *B* phases of the Nazca style; the present instance is the earliest one datable by association.

**FIGURE 204, 170515 (N4).** Four of five miniature, toy-size, double-spout jars all given the same number. The sizes are, from left to right: D 51, 47, 50, and 50 mm, body H 52, 49, 48, and 44 mm, spout H 69, 65, 65, and 65 mm, yielding for body H/D 102, 104, 96, and 88% and for spout H/D 135, 138, 130, and 130%. It is clear that the little pieces are essentially uniform in size and proportion, and that the proportions are those of full-size spouts. The absolute dimensions are less than one-third of the full-size vessel just described, the volume about one-fortieth. Colors are at least six: W, F, LR, DR, DBr, and B, perhaps also Y (they are considerably eroded). The spouts are unpainted. Each little vessel is painted with one cat-deity representation. In the vessel on the left, the mouth mask is incomplete above the upper lip and a tongue hangs down; there were also W disks beyond the mask. In the next to the left, the mouth mask is continuous above the lip.

**FIGURE 205, 170510 (N4); PLATE 10.** Unique in shape. First of all, it has a bail handle—an ornamental imitation in pottery of a withe that might have been tied onto the two small side handles. The shape *(R2)* might be construed as a modified wide-mouth jar *R1*, but more significant are the nearly spherical body, the size of the mouth, and the lowness of the collar. D 222 mm, H body 177 mm, H/D 80%; mouth D/body D about 67%; neck D/body D about 64%; H collar/H body about 8%; H design band between W stripes/H body around 55%. Colors five: W, Y, LR, DR, and B. Background B, with W line dividers and borders, rim DR, lip line B, small handles LR. The bail handle is unslipped but carries LR and DR frets on its upper surface. The twelve vertical fish all have W bellies, but their backs and tails run Y, DR, LR, Y, LR, DR, Y,

LR, DR, Y, LR, DR—that is, a basic sequence Y, LR, DR with the last two interchanged once; the sort of repetitive rhythm with some irregularity that is characteristic of Nazca coloring.

The small handles at the lip recur in phase *A1* cookpots, Figures 130, 131, and 156, and Kroeber (1956), plate 34e, Ocucaje; but these pots are not only unpainted, they are not even polished, only roughly smoothed and incised.

**FIGURE 206, 170517 (N4).** Smallish wide-mouth jar, somewhat aberrant shape *R*, the neck and lip being very short and the body shouldered. The surface is a fairly well polished reddish buff, unslipped and wholly unpainted. D 135 mm, H 123 mm, H/D 91%; mouth D/body D 70%; neck D/body D 67%; flat base D/body D about 61%. The vertical H is distributed as follows: rim to neck 7%, neck to shoulder 36%, shoulder to bottom 57% (= 100%). With these proportions compare the unassociated but obviously early jar of Kroeber (1956), plate 38h: H/D 92%, D mouth/D 68%, D neck/D 64%, and H collar/H 11%; the collar also is straight and nearly vertical, but the piece is painted.

**FIGURE 207, 170518 (N4).** Smallish narrow-mouth jar, somewhat aberrant shape *S*, unpainted and unslipped, smoothed but not polished, brownish with dark firing clouds. D 159 mm, H 131 mm, H/D 82%; mouth D/body D, 36%, about half that of the preceding piece; H of vertical collar (lip)/total H, 11%.

These two jars are slightly offside yet generally intermediate between the cookpot-derived, camber-collared, unslipped, mostly unpainted but often punctated or incised jars of phase *A1* and the elegantly turned, polished, slipped, and painted shape-*R* and -*S* jars of Seler and of Gayton and Kroeber in phase *B*. They have lost the pair of small handles of their predecessors (preserved however on the painted bail pot in the preceding figure); later on (sometime in phase *B*), some of the *R* and *S* jars were to reacquire such handles to become shape *T*.

## MAJORO CHICO A, GRAVE 15

**FIGURE 208, 170500 (N4).** Bowl shape *Bd.* D 160 mm, H 75 mm, H/D 47%. The width of the band of painted decoration is 60% of the height of the bowl. Background DR, dividers and outlines W, rim stripe B, bottom unslipped. Colors five: W, LR, DR, G, and B. Design, nine fruits, each with two solid circles, alternately LR and G. This double-spotted fruit seems not to be illustrated by Seler.

**FIGURE 209, 170501 (N4); PLATE 11.** Shape-*H* bowl. D 168 mm, H 97 mm, H/D 58%. Background DR, outlining B, lip line B. Colors eight: W, Y, F, DR, LBr, V, G, and B, LBr in place of more-usual LR. Design: cat deity with compressed body, twice: the feet and curved tails to right of heads. Mouth-mask projections above lip touch but are not fused; four whisker bunches on each side, beyond them four W disks. Fox skin on forehead much conventionalized. A trophy head, LBr in profile, at shoulder; tail ends in Y; flesh cat face with pointed whisker bunch, not visible in photograph. Some color distributions are LBr face, pleated body, hands; G necklace, dart in hand; V legs (G and V contrast in this piece); Y "sleeves" above hands, tail, cat face on tail; and F only on part of this tail face. The figure on the opposite side has some color transpositions, such as the necklace in Y instead of G. The painted design extends over part of the bottom but not to its center, which is slipped a muddy LR.

The eight colors on this piece are a greater number than we counted on any *A1* vessel described in preceding pages but are equaled on the *A2* double-spout from Grave 17 (170514; Fig. 203 [Pl. 9]). The fruit-design bowl in this grave might still be phase *A1;* the present deity bowl seems definitely later than *A1*.

These two vessels were found at 310 cm, 10 cm lower than the deformed skull and the skeleton. They were the only contents of the grave except for some sherds and a spindle whorl found near the surface and in the upper portion of the grave shaft.

### UNCERTAIN *A2* MATERIAL

[The following material from Cantayo and Agua Santa is of uncertain context and association, and several pieces exhibit *A* and *B* features. Kroeber chose to discuss them under this heading.]

#### Cantayo M, Grave 4

From Cantayo M, Grave 4, there are two vessels. Vessel 170988, not illustrated, is a section of a *B*-shape bowl with a band of rhomboidal diamonds, which by precedent would be Nazca *A1*.

**FIGURE 210, 170989 (N4).** A bulbous-concave vase of shape *P*. H 155 mm, D 142 mm, just barely within the H/D limit of 109% of P, characteristic of Nazca *A* but with more bulge or belly than is typical of *P* vases from phase *A*. The D of the rim is 74% and that of the high waist only 67% of the maximum D lower down where the painted pattern ends. The design consists of six much-abbreviated or distorted trophy heads in supine position, separated by B double-line dividers. From each head two unusually long locks or masses of hair are suspended. Of the six heads, alternate ones are DR, the intervening ones Y, DBr, and LR, with W background and B hair; total of five colors.

This shallow grave cannot be assigned to a phase with assurance, but *A2* is probably not far off. There is an added uncertainty in that the burial was shallow and the bowl was found at 30 cm, the vase at 50 cm.

#### Cantayo Cax Deity Bowl

**FIGURES 211a–b, 171036 (EARLY N5).** A finely made and painted shape *F-H* bowl, which was found in Cax at Cantayo by wall A (Fig. 59). Cax was an early structure, and some of its contents have been tentatively assigned to period *A1*, others to *A0*. This bowl is incomplete, and as the elaborate design extends over the outside bottom—the feet of the represented deity being on the side opposite to its head—and nearly half of the representation is lost, our photograph does not give an adequate idea of it. We append, therefore, a drawing (Fig. 211b), which shows that the shoulders or upper body occupied the outer bottom of the vessel and that it was viewed by setting the vessel bottom up. The head then hung down the front, the legs down the opposite back, while wings

PLATE 1 (FIGURE 97)

PLATE 2 (FIGURE 167)

PLATE 3 (FIGURE 105)

PLATE 4 (FIGURE 112)

PLATE 5 (FIGURE 189)

PLATE 6 (FIGURE 122)

PLATE 7 (FIGURE 125)

PLATE 8 (FIGURE 126)

PLATE 9 (FIGURE 203)

PLATE 10 (FIGURE 205)

PLATE 11 (FIGURE 209)

PLATE 12 (FIGURE 212)

**PLATE 13 (FIGURE 223)**

**PLATE 14 (FIGURE 222)**

**PLATE 15 (FIGURE 226)**

**PLATE 16 (FIGURE 236)**

**PLATE 17 (FIGURE 275)**

**PLATE 18 (FIGURE 252)**

**PLATE 19 (FIGURE 269)**

**PLATE 20 (FIGURE 272)**

**PLATE 21 (FIGURE 271)**

**PLATE 22 (FIGURE 321)**

**PLATE 23 (FIGURE 314)**

**PLATE 24 (FIGURE 316)**

PLATE 25 (FIGURE 354)

PLATE 26 (FIGURE 340)

PLATE 27 (FIGURE 345)

PLATE 28 (FIGURE 351)

**PLATE 29 (FIGURE 367)**

**PLATE 30 (FIGURE 372)**

**PLATE 31 (FIGURE 374)**

**PLATE 32 (FIGURE 379)**

extended down the right and left sides. The arrangement is similar to that of Seler (1923), figures 73 and 74, where the same winged cat deity is draped over the top of a double-spout jar, head, right wing, legs and tail, left wing respectively each over a quarter of the vessel's side.

The colors are given as seven: W, Y, LR, DR, G, B, and LBr with a reddish tinge. Height is 79 mm, D at rim 119 mm, D at base about the same as H; the H/D 66% is well within the range of both *F* and *H* bowls. The painting is definite and well polished, and the shaping of the bowl is elegant.

We are uncertain where to place this bowl in time. It seems more *A2* than *A1* and has a few stigmata of *B:* the dotted feather ends, for instance. Elaborate deity figures are often particularly difficult to assign to a style phase.

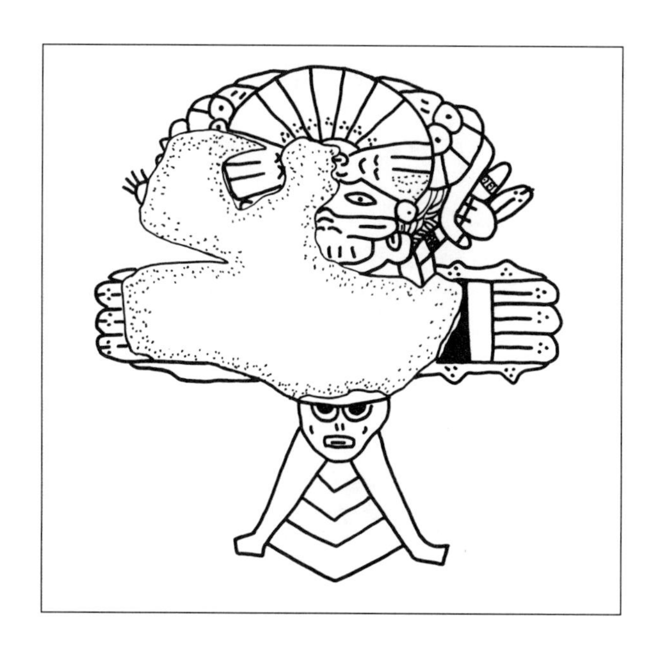

### Agua Santa, Grave 16

A lot of four vessels was purchased from a peon who alleged he had excavated it at Agua Santa (Grave 16 in a *B2* area), but his allegation is evidently untrue because some of the pieces are *A1*.

**FIGURE 212, 170648 (EARLY N3); PLATE 12.** This is a rather puzzling piece, which is a nearly cylindrical cuplike vessel, a little too lacking in flare for an *F* bowl, a little too lacking in bulge and flare for a bulbous-concave *P* vase of phase *A*. It is 112 mm H, 123 mm maximum D, H/D 91%, which is around the limit of tallness for period-*A F* bowls and of squatness for *P* vases. It is about as near to being truly cylindrical as Nazca low vessels come. The D at rim is 123 mm, at waist 119 mm, at bottom bulge 120 mm. The colors are five: W, F, LBr, DR, and B. The design shows three darts in a cluster repeated seven times. The darts in each cluster are alternately DR, LBr, and F, outlined, feathered, and tipped B; the exterior and interior vessel rim have a DR band, lip B, exterior base unpainted.

As will be seen below, we have set darts (arrows) as one of the criteria of phase *B*, and the occurrences known to us as corroborated by associations seem to validate this attribution. The present vessel in most respects of shape and color seems to be Nazca *A*, perhaps *A1* or even *Ao;* but it is not anchored to firm associations. Perhaps our criterion of darts as characteristic of phase *B* may have to be given up; or again, the shape and color of this vessel make it style *A* prolonged into *B*.

[The other vessels from Grave 16, purchased with 170648, are described from Collier's notes below.]

**FIGURE 213, 170647 (N2/3).** Shape *Ac*. H 46 mm, D 147 mm, H/D 31%. Colors five: B, F, DR, LR, and W (yellowish W).

**FIGURE 214, 170649 (N3/4).** Shape *T* without handles. H 107 mm, maximum base D 141 mm, H/D 76%. Colors five: B, W, DR, Y, and DBr.

**FIGURE 215, 170650 (LATE N4).** Shape *U1* miniature. Body H 66 mm, D 71 mm, H/D 93%, H to top of spouts 90 mm. Colors six: DR, W, B, V, G, and Y.

## OF PHASE *A2* OR *B1* (?)

[Three gravelots are now presented that contain a mixture of *A2* and *B1* elements. Kroeber placed Ocongalla West A, Grave 6 under this heading; Carmichael added Cantayo D, Grave 5 and Cantayo M, Grave 1, as these had not been covered elsewhere and appear to exhibit traits of *A2* and *B1* as defined by Kroeber.]

### Ocongalla West A, Grave 6

Grave 6 of Ocongalla West A, only 20 cm deep, contained a child. It also contained 170664–5, netlike cloth and a child's striped wool garment, the latter illustrated in O'Neale (1937), plate 37i. It also contained two pottery vessels, 170667 and 170668.

**FIGURE 216, 170667 (N4).** Originally a jar with large flaring mouth and two small handles. The lip was broken and the neck was then ground off to form a new, lipless edge. The handles were also broken off, although their stubs remain. With its original collar, the jar may have been nearly as high as broad. It now somewhat resembles the lipless jar shape *Q*, although its remaining upper part curves more. The present H is 138 mm, D 174 mm, H/D 79%; on the photograph, the mouth D, measured outside, is about 57% of maximum D. The colors are five: W, LR, DR, LBr, and B. The background of the wide design panel is B. The design is of fish or dolphins plunging, mostly from left to right, but some smaller ones in opposite direction or diagonally upward, as recognizable in Figure 216 from their W tails. The eyes and most of the bellies are W, but at bottom and top are some DR bellies. The backs are LR, DR, or LBr. There are also heavy spirals (of one-and-a-half turns), some W and some LR or LBr; it is unclear what these represent. It looks as if the B background had been applied as a slip, and then the W and reds overpainted on it.

In its general shape and dark background, the present jar in its original condition was probably more-or-less like Kroeber and Strong (1924), plate 28p, (which is *A1* from Ocucaje) and like Gayton and Kroeber (1927), plate 4c, in its handles. There are also some points of resemblance (fish, B background, jar with small handle), as well as sharp differences from Figure 174 above from Majoro A, Grave 18. There is also a resemblance of design—plunging fish or dolphins on a B background—to that occurring in three zones on a *Pb* bulbous-concave vase (H/D

120%) in Kroeber (1955), plate 35c from Uhle's Ocucaje Grave F3, which Kroeber construed as later than most of Uhle's Ocucaje material, in the "A-plus phase"; which would mean, in our present terminology, *A2* or close to it; with which the Nazca *B*-period shape of the vase concurs.

With this finding vessel 170668 is in accord. We leave it unillustrated because it is not only broken but incomplete. It is, however, a (trophy) head jar of type *Y* (specifically *Y1*, now) as Gayton and Kroeber constituted it in 1927 (p. 5, illustrated in pl. 7f). It is a well-known form (Seler 1923, figures 138, 143, 145, 146, 151, and 153), whose occurrence is Nazca *B*.

It is of course possible that the *Y1* head jar began to be made in Nazca *A2;* or that the plunging-fish jar, though still retaining *A* features, is from phase *B1*. But the two pieces together take Grave 6 out of *A1*, just as the fish jar prevents them from being allocated to *B2*. We must leave the grave as in the range of *A2* to *B1*. If it had contained two or three more vessels, they would probably have sufficed to tip its attribution one way of another.

### Cantayo D, Grave 5

**FIGURE 217, 171005 (N5).** Shape-*P* vase. H 114 mm, maximum D 115 mm, H/D 99%. Colors six: W, B, DR, LR, Y, and DBr.

**FIGURE 218, 171006 (N4/5?).** Shape-*H* bowl. H 73 mm, D 127 mm, H/D 57%. Colors two: W, B.

**FIGURE 219, 171007 (N4).** Rounded shape-*GG* bowl. H 43 mm, D 90 mm, H/D 48%. Colors three: B, DR, and LR.

[The vessels from this burial were not discussed in the original manuscript. The grave was 90 cm deep and was without a roof. It contained the remains of an individual 14–20 years of age. According to the field catalogue, all of the vessels and the skeleton were found 90 cm below the surface. Period affiliation is given as *X?*, which corresponds to *B1?* in the current work. Vessel 171005 is a good *B1* candidate, and the shape of 171006 is congruent with this phase designation. However, the small bowl, 171007, appears to be much earlier (*A1* in the current classification), and its presence in this gravelot has evidently caused some confusion. This grave is not well documented, and there may have been an error when it was excavated. It is also possible that 171007 was originally from an adjacent burial encountered when Grave 5 was being prepared, or it may be an heirloom.]

### Cantayo M, Grave 1

**FIGURE 220, 170980 (EARLY N5).** Shape *T*. H 137 mm, D 133 mm, H/D 103%.

**FIGURE 221, 170981 (EARLY N5).** Shape *P* to *Pb*. estimated H 150 mm, D 137 mm, H/D 109%. Colors five: B, W, Y, DR, and LR.

[These vessels were found with a baby interred in a large coarseware jar. The plainware vessel, 170980, was inside the jar with the infant, while 170981 lay just outside the burial jar. The contemporaneity of these two vessels is therefore inferred but not conclusive. They were not described in the original manuscript, and we cannot be sure how Kroeber would have classified them. Vessel 170981 provides the best clues. The type of bird design in the upper panel was earlier attributed to Nasca *A*, possibly *A1* (Chapter 6, Purchased at Yapana, 170864, Fig. 198), although the birds on the current piece are not spotted. The vessel shape falls in the *P* to *Pb* range (more of an *A2-B1* shape), and the double bands below the birds and lower plain area are most typical of *B*. This vessel would fall within the *A2-B1* range of Kroeber's classification. The smoothed surface of the plainware vessel, 170980, also fits comfortably in this range.]

## DISCUSSION OF PHASE *A2*

A summary is hardly called for on so few graves, some of which are of unsure phase and provenience. We do not know why the expedition should have found so few *A2* graves compared with the many of *A1*. The discrepancy suggests that there is something skewed in our division of *A* into *A1* and *A2*. Correspondingly, in phase *B*, though in reverse, *B2* is much more abundantly represented by graves than is *B1*. As expected, among the four, the contrast would be greatest between *A1* and *B2*. Quite possibly our typing is fundamentally based on the distinctive *A1* and *B2* qualities. Then, whatever seemed still allied to *A1* but divergent became *A2* as a residue; and similarly, what was allied to *B2* but less distinctive became an anticipating *B1*.

As there is no evidence of invasion, conquest, or other overturn in the Río Grande drainage during the Nazca period, one would assume that stylistic change was continuous. Our *A1*, *A2*, *B1*, and *B2* sequence conforms to this assumption. One might also make the assumption that the four style phases were about equal in duration and represented by equal quantities of graves and remains, or that we ought to have chosen the criteria distinguishing them in such a way as to make the remains come out essentially equal in numbers. Whether the low frequency of *A2* and *B1* is the result of our skewing the classificatory criteria, or whether these two middle phases left actually fewer graves because they were briefer, may ultimately be determined; we cannot at present answer the question.

When Gayton and Kroeber in 1927 first systematically classified the Nazca style on the basis of Uhle's 600 ceramic pieces brought to California, secured mainly without grave data, they started with the *A1*-*B2* contrast, *A1* being given as a historic unit by several pure-style lots or sites at Ocucaje in Ica Valley. *A1* represented the formative peak, *B2* the elaborative peak, Nazca *Y* the period of decline or gradual dissolution of the style. These authors then bridged the *A1*-*B2* contrast by inventing an intermediate *AB*, or *X*, phase. In a sense, this *X* phase was a hedge, a relatively undistinctive transition between two stylistically more salient style phases; and, as a hedge, Kroeber in 1956 dissolved it away again. Phase *X* obviously was about what we here denominate *A2* plus *B2*. The fact that the Nazca style was continuously changing is probably assumed by everyone. Whether now calling the middle span of the style *A2*+*B2* is better than formerly calling it *X* is of no moment if our whole emphasis is on the continuity of change within the style. If, however, a style contains more than mere continuity, if it has a peak or peaks, if it contains points of organization of the style itself that are the nuclei of stretches in which the direction of the style is different, then *A2*+*B2* would carry more meaning regarding the history of the style than a mere bridging *AB* or *X*, which presumably remained on the same level and maintained the same direction as *A2* and *B2*. *A2* implies prevalent continuation of the direction of *A1*, and when *B2* is reached the implication is that such continuation is now being outweighed by changes in direction or manner that reached their culmination later in *B2*.

Perhaps such an approach to the history of a style carries an inherent probability that the crucial nodal points will be self-weighting, so that they must tend to be recognized more clearly and to seem represented by more numerous examples. In other words, the greater frequency of *A1* and *B2*, as against *A2* and *B2*, may be founded on perceptual formulation—on the way one sets up or defines the situation. Or again, it may be a historical fact that the middle phases *A2* and *B2* lasted fewer years. We see the problem; we cannot now answer it. There is something involved that bears on what a style is and how, theoretically, it tends normally to develop.

CHAPTER 8

# *Pottery of Phase B1*

## NAZCA *B* AND ITS PHASES

Nazca B graves were encountered by the 1926 expedition at several sites in Nazca Valley. The most prolific was Ocongalla West B, about half a kilometer west of the hacienda house, where Graves 3, 4, 7, 8, 9, 10, and 12 yielded some sixty whole or restorable vessels. Graves 1 and 11 at this site were of early *Y* phase *(Y1)*, and their contents will be described in a later section. At nearby Ocongalla Zero, Graves 1, 2, 3, 4, and 6 were less rich than those at West B but of the same period.

Agua Santa was considerably mixed. Graves 10, 11, 12, 14, and 15 were Nazca *B*. The former were opened intact; contents of the latter were purchased. Graves 1–9 proved to be Nazca *Y* or Late. The four Soisongo sites, A, B, C, and D, were again mixed, with Nazca *Y* predominant, but Grave C5 was Nazca *B*. At Majoro Chico A, only Grave 16 was of phase *B*.

Scattered *B*-type material was encountered elsewhere, was purchased, or was presented to the expedition. However, most important are the four richer of the six Ocongalla West B graves, because of the range of associations afforded by the ten to fifteen vessels in each. By means of these and previously recorded associations, we have tried to subdivide phase *B* of the Nazca style into an earlier and a later phase, as with phase *A* and, below, the *Y* phase. But we are less confident of the result here, because the overwhelming proportion of *B* material obtained by the expedition, following the criteria decided upon, is later *B*. We did look for other criteria that might be substituted and yield a more-even distribution of earlier and later *B*, but we were unable to find workable ones.

The designs that can be listed as characteristic of early phase *B (B1)* are fewer than *B2*, since we have fewer *B1* than *B2* graves and none that contain large assemblages of vessels. Also, it would seem that many *B1* designs continued on into *B2*. Perhaps *B1* designs are most significant in designating vessels as being post-*A*, viz., as made sometime in period *B*, the separation of *B1* from *B2* being in our present stage of knowledge dependent largely on *B2* criteria.

### Criteria for Phases *B1* and *B2*

The following list of traits first appear in Nazca phase *B1*. The parameters used to assign *B1* or *B2* status to them are explained immediately after.

1. Scalloped upper edges of deities' backs or wings.
2. Such scallops developed into spaced large spines, either empty or filled with trophy heads, swift (bird) heads, and so forth.
3. Feathers indicated by contiguous parallel bars of different colors, the distal end rounded and containing three dots to indicate a trophy face (?), with a thin-tip line projecting like a tongue.
4. Atlatl darts (arrows) in series as ornaments.
5. Square, unrayed (human?) trophy heads, full face but cut off above, across the eyes or brows; single or in series.
6. Full-face human figure wearing conical cap seamed in front, the base of which cuts across the eyes as in the trophy head just described. The figure usually carries fruits or vegetation.
7. Feet on birds indicated by a longish cursive horizontal line, the leg portion being slanting and short.
8. Interlocking fish or snakes.

Sometimes doubtful between *A* and *B* are whiskered cat deities. These were surely painted in both phases. But *A* designs may have gone on into *B*, and *B1* into *B2*, or again new special features were sometimes devised that were collocated with older ones in synthetic figures. It will take a great mass of material documented for provenience and associations before these complex relations in cat-deity designs can be worked out with assurance. A few features can be suggested at least as being post-*A*, such as a body striped into a sort of pleatings, and an "eye" somewhere near navel position.

Pastel-like colors begin to appear in phase *B1* but are carried further in *B2* and are characteristic of it, together with an increase in fine-drawn, small-area, delicate, and elaborate designs.

Our criteria for separating the later *B2* from earlier *B1* were the following:

1. The bent-over ray.

2. The rayed trophy head (which would presumably be a deity's head). While the bent-over rays most often come on such a head, they also occur separately. It should also be noted that a special form of the rayed trophy head will be used below as a marker for separating phase *Y* from phase *B*. This is the deliquescent trophy head, with the rays as if dissolving and the face features lost except for a single central eye. In phase *B*, however, the eyes are two, a mouth or tongue is present, and the rays are definitely shaped, in no sense degenerate or slovened, although they may be hastily executed.

Otherwise occurring as parts of the rayed trophy or deity head in its later *B2* form are:

3. Rays cut off square at the end.

4. Rays expanded into one or two (rhomboidal) diamonds before they end in a sharp point. These occur characteristically also in staves or sceptres carried by deities, such as the "jagged-staff divinity," or *Zackenstabdämon*, of Seler, for which a more accurate translation would be "angled (or zigzag) staff spirit (or deity)." The German *dämon* has the sense of the Greek *daimon*, not the evil connotation of the English word *demon*.

5. Sets of three rays on top of the head, resembling a crown, and consisting of two bent-over rays flanking a central angled (rhomboid) or square-cut or simply pointed one, the whole having a sort of fleur-de-lis effect.

From these rays and the deities who wear them, we can go on to other designs that occur associated with them either on the same vessel or in the same grave and can therefore also be reckoned as signaling the *B2* subphase. Such are:

6. Women's yellow faces, front view, with long almond eyes, trimmed hair, and often with cheek paint. These come singly or more often in horizontal series, filling a band around a vessel. They run on into phase *Y* but are much simplified and schematized there. They never occur in phase *A* and probably not in *B1*.

7. Profile figures of men (or ghosts? at any rate, unrayed) dancing, hunting, fighting, carrying parrots on sticks, seem not to occur before *B2*.

8. Darts flying among hunted guanacos or darts attached to deities seem to be *B2*, whereas loose darts in rows or darts replacing a deity's tongue appear in *B1*.

9. Schematic triangular faces, outlined only, single, grouped, or in series, seem to be *B2*. These, with appendages, may be derived from women's body tattooing (see Figure 254 and Seler [1923], fig. 206).

10. Short black-line tips or projections—Junius Bird's "cactus spines," although some of them fork—are restricted to *B2*. Their meaning is unclear, probably not cactus. [Junius Bird was a noted Andeanist at the American Museum of Natural History, New York.]

11. Interlocking step-frets in complementary colors of course go back to Nazca *A1*, but a special variant in which at least one of the pair is broken or double in color (color 1 for the step, color 2 for the fret) seems to characterize the later *B* and go on into *Y*.

12. Vertical short bars in rows, suspended, or sometimes alternately stood up and suspended, are *B2*.

13. Quartering of bowl bottoms by lines or coloring or both is also a *B2* feature.

14. Wingless or pin-feathered birds, often in series, are characteristic of *B2* associations, but it is not yet certain that they are limited to *B2*.

## GRAVES OF PHASE *B1*

When we review the Nazca *B* graves opened by the 1926 expedition, there are only three that we would designate as *B1*, namely, Ocongalla West B, Graves 3 and 4 and Majoro Chico A, Grave 16. These three graves contained thirteen vessels. As against these, there were at least seventeen documented *B2* graves at four sites, with a total of ninety or more vessels.

### Ocongalla West B, Grave 3

This grave, 300 cm deep, contained six more-or-less cylindrical vessels (vases and goblets) and one wide-mouthed spherical jar. The change is conspicuous from the phase *A* preponderance of open bowls and plates with a sprinkling of double-spouts.

**FIGURE 222, 170684 (N5); PLATE 14.** We will begin with the spherical jar, shape *S.* H 133 mm, D 148 mm, H/D 90%. The mouth or rim D is 54% that of the body, the neck 48%. Height of the B collar is 15% of body H. The width of the B band limiting the design below is also about 15% of body H. The colors are seven: W, Y, LR, DR, LBr, G, and B. The limited background within the design band is W, design-element borders are B. The face and legs are DR, the trophy-head band over the forehead LR, the border above this G, the body pleats Y, the whisker mask LBr, the scallops at top edge LR, the square trophy head at far left of figure DR, the penis dart and rectangular "ears" (?) Y.

Design features probably significant of period (as against Nazca *A*) are the pleated body, the navel eye within, the penis or dart, the rectangular ears, the upper-edge scallops, and the square trophy head with cut-off eyes and rectangular mouth.

**FIGURE 223, 170688 (N5); PLATE 13.** Bulbous-convex vase of shape *O.* D 104 mm, H 131 mm, H/D 126%; mouth D 85 mm, mouth D/body D 65%. There are eight colors: W, C, Y, LR, DR, Violet, G, and B. The W serves as background. Cream occurs on the necklace; Y on the adjacent disks and other small parts; LR on the mouth mask, to the right of the head, in the ridge and spines; DR on the face; violet on the legs (not shown in Fig. 223); G below the necklace and on the torso; and B in the border lines and in the swifts' heads between the back spines.

A cat deity encircles the vase. Characteristic are a forehead eye and a navel eye (not visible), a pleated or "planked" torso, two large down-pointing appendages from lower jar (transposed bunches of whiskers?), and above the back large erect spines with swifts' heads filling interstices.

**FIGURE 224, 170687 (N5).** Can be construed as either shape *O*, bulbous-convex, or shape *M*, tapering vase. It is bulbous-convex below and tapers straight above. D 102 mm, H 120 mm, H/D 118%; mouth D/body D is 77%, which expresses the greater taper of this vase compared with the preceding. The colors are seven: W, Y, LR, DR, LBr, DBr, and B. There is no G; the background is W. Some examples: LBr back spines, DBr upper of two middle bands, Y lower band, LR base band, DR swifts' heads (v-shaped, haired) between the spines, B alternating with W squares. The drawing is rapid yet clean, but the colors were applied thinly and are watery.

This is a three-zoned pattern: swifts and spines above, as if taken from Figure 223; a double band in the middle; and a checker design below.

**FIGURE 225, 170685 (N5).** Shape-*M* tapering vase. D 125 mm, H 140 mm, H/D 112%, mouth D 9.9 mm, mouth D/D 88%. Colors five: W, Y, LR, DBr, and B, applied somewhat thinly as in the preceding piece. The s-figures at the top and dividers below are LR, the two horizontal stripes Y and DBr, the top and bottom stripes B, the empty background W. The patterning could be construed as triple-zoned, but as the s-panels and girth bands together are narrower than the lowest zone, double-zoning is the actually more appropriate term. Designwise, this is a pretty meager vessel, although both painting and modeling show practical skill.

**FIGURE 226, 170682 (N5); PLATE 15.** The modeled nose puts this vessel into shape *Y1*, face jar. However, apart from the pinch of clay pressed on as nose, the "faceness" of the vessel is wholly in the painting. Disregarding this, we have a bulbous-concave vase of shape *P*.

Diameter is 100 mm (both below and at rim), H 125 mm, the ratio, of course, 125%. The minimum external diameter is 82 mm, its ratio 82% of the maximum; the long concavity of the silhouette has considerable elegance.

Colors are five: W, LR, DR, G, and B. The face is creamy W; because of the hair bangs, it presumably is a woman's face. Around the eyes is falcon's head(?) face painting in LR, with a tear-line bar in G down and outward across it. The hair, ears, mouth painting or tattoo, and the latticework above are B; the band separating lattice from face is DR. All essentials of the depiction are carried out in W, LR, and B.

**FIGURE 227, 170686 (N5).** Waisted goblet, shape *J*, specifically *J1*, unusually flat-bottomed for a Nazca vessel. D (at top) 111 mm, H 116 mm, H/D 105%; the minimum at waist and maximum at base are 92 mm and 100 mm, 83% and 90% of the rim D.

Colors are thin but clear and number eight: W, Y, LR, DR, LBr, DBr, G, and B. The background above is W, then comes a LR band, the lower part is DR. The bird's body is LBr, the trophy heads along its back mainly DBr, the beak Y. At the far left of the photography are G round-ended tail feathers with tip spines; in order downward, these are LR, G, DR, DBr, LR, and Y. The second feather is the only G area on the goblet.

The subject is a bird with an open beak directed

downward, a rhomboidal eye, a crop, and crest. The body is striped or pleated; below are three- or four-toed feet, and a Y breechcloth/trophy head. The trophy-heads arrayed supine along the back are heavily distorted; they are not separated by spines as in many other instances.

### Ocongalla West B, Grave 4

This was shallower than Grave 3, 180 cm deep as against 300, and held fewer vessels.

**FIGURE 228, 170689 (EARLY N5).** Figure vase, shape class *X*. As it is neither a seated man of phase *A* nor a seated woman of late *B*, it could be put into a subclass *X3;* but it may be unique. In distinction from all other shape-*X* specimens, it has neither modeling nor painting in its lower half and might be described as a human bust growing out of a round-bottomed bowl. The nose is modeled, the mouth swells into a low cone with a punched-hole perforation in the middle, the arms stick out stiffly and are hollow and seem to have been open at the end.

The effigy is 114 mm high. The maximum diameter is toward the bottom; H/D is about 169%. Left-to-right side diameters, in terms of the left to right maximum near the bottom, are below arms, 91%; neck, 62%; at ears, about 65%; and rim, 53%.

Colors are four: overall slip LR; rhomboidal eyes W; eye pupils, outlines, brows, B; collar at vessel lip a creamy Y.

All in all, there is very little of Nazca style apparent in this vessel. It may represent a sport or experiment, or it may be an import from the Andes or copy of such an import.

**FIGURE 229, 170690-1 (N5).** Face (really trophy-head) jar, shape *Y3*, or equally well *Qn*, lipless jar with modeled-on nose (Kroeber 1956, 357, 381). D 185 mm, H 164 mm, H/D 89%; lip D/maximum D, about 52%. Colors four: W, Y, LR, and B, plus color of the unslipped paste outside the black-line framing. The face is Y; hair and bordering of eyes, mouth, and cheek painting B; trapezoidal cheek paint LR, also lower border of head hair; W occurs only in minute dots on mouth, to indicate teeth. The lips are skewered together in B; the eyes are closed, their top and bottom fringes probably indicating brows and lashes. There is no doubt that the representation is of a prepared and dried head.

**FIGURE 230, 170690-2 (EARLY N5).** Shape *Y1* or *P*, like Figure 226 (Pl 15) in the preceding grave. D 112 mm, H 121 mm, H/D 108%, which is low for phase *B*. The rim D is 87% of body D, the neck 82%. Colors five: W, Y, LR, DR, and B. The upper bands are W, LR, and W. The face is Y, the triangular cheek paintings DR, the mouth LR; all outlining is in B, also the solid hair painted at the back. The eyes are closed: this is another indubitably trophy head vase.

**FIGURE 231, 170691 (EARLY N5).** This interesting piece is a waisted goblet of subtype *J1*, characteristic of phase *B1*. This is indicated by its proportions: D (below) 136 mm, H 128 mm, H/D 94%; the rim D is 95% and the waist D 81% of the maximum body D. With its waist constriction, this vessel bears some resemblance to *F-H* bowls, but these flare out from bottom to top, whereas this piece flares less in its upper third than it constricts in its lower two-thirds. Also its H/D ratio is 94%, while the maximum found in bowls classed as *F* is 81%, in *H* bowls only 72% (Kroeber 1956, 368).

The colors are three: W, B, and DR, the last confined to the lip edge and a stripe near the bottom. The pattern is therefore B and W, with the W applied first, although there is more B area. The fish or snake heads do not strictly interlock, as they sometimes do in textiles and as step frets normally interlock complementarily; but the painted panels in which they are set do interlock in the sense of meshing or interdigitating.

A near parallel to the design of the present piece is the inside-painted plate 20f in Gayton and Kroeber (1927). It also is an overall design, and the fish do essentially complement one another; but what in the present piece are lines framing the cell or panel for each fish are also backbones (as it were) in the fish themselves in 20f.

Another parallel is in Kroeber (1956), plate 37c, on a shape-*D* bowl of presumably period *B*. The fishes (if that is what they are) are in a tandem series here, but the backbones and painted panel ends recur.

Seler (1923) shows the interlocking pattern in his figures 352–356. (Care must be exercised not to read his Chancay parallels, figures 351, 357–360, and 362–363 as Nazca.) To judge by the vessel shapes and supplementary designs, all five of his Nazca illustrations are of Nazca *B*. His figures 353 and 356 are paneled and more-or-less interlocking; 352, 354, and 355 are complementary interlocking.

The interlocking fish or snake is not a common Nazca pattern. It has not been found in phase *A* association. It may have been taken over from a textile development. If it really represents a snake rather than a fish, as seems likely, it may be a development out of Nazca *A* s-shaped, double-headed snakes interlaced as in Seler's (1923) figures 313–315, to which our Figure 148 corresponds. The present phase *B1* piece is the earliest period-dated occurrence and is of the simpler or paneled type which strictly does not interlock. It remains to be seen how long it continued in use at Nazca. As far as we know, it does not occur in Nazca *Y*. Its use in the Interlocking Style of the central coast of Peru has generally been assumed to be derivative from Nazca. If so, its zenith of frequency in ceramics may have come there after the design had been abandoned in Nazca. Or, could the central coast have developed the design and imparted it ready-made to Nazca? If the relative chronologies allow this interpretation, it makes the simplest explanation, especially since it is clear that the greatest frequency of occurrence was on the central coast.

## Majoro Chico A, Grave 16

Grave 16 at Majoro Chico A was dug within the sequence of Graves 14 and 20, which were Nazca *A*, and, having some miscellaneous sherds in its upper portion, was for a time regarded as also of period *A*. It is, however, a shallower grave—200 cm—than the associated phase *A* graves, which ran from 250 to 400 cm deep. Moreover, exclusion of everything not at the bottom of interment 16 leaves only three vessels, though those are indubitably Nazca *B*. Above the bottom, at 150 cm down, was found a bowl that stylistically is very probably *A*, so that it presumably came originally from a neighboring phase *A* grave that was disturbed when Grave 16 was dug in phase *B* and was then reinterred, though above the *B* burial.

**FIGURE 232, 170506 (N5).** Triple-banded *Pb*-shape (bulbous-concave) vase. D 127 mm, H 151 mm, H/D 119%. Mouth D is 93% and minimum D 87% of maximum D. The nearest in H/D proportion to this vessel is the jar in Kroeber (1956), plate 35c from Ocucaje Grave E3, whose H/D ratio is 120%, and which comes from one of two or three post-early-*A* graves in a cemetery otherwise early *A*. Inasmuch as the Nazca *A1* vases of shape *P* previously illustrated (Kroeber and Strong 1924, pl. 25h, 28 mm; Kroeber 1955, pl. 31f, 34a) average H/D only 96% (92–102), and the one newly shown as of *A2* in the present monograph (Fig. 202, 170519, from Majoro

Chico A, Grave 17) is 104%, but eleven *B2* phase *P*-shape jars (from Ocongalla West B, Kroeber 1956, 347 and below) average 135% (124–156%), it is clear that the present piece at a ratio of 119% and the Ocucaje E3 vessel at 120% are probably post-*A1* and presumably post-*A*, but also somewhat pre-climax *B* or *B2;* which would make them *B1*. In terms of Kroeber's subclassification (1956, 347, 379) into *P1* or *Pa* of phase *A* and *P2* and *Pb* of phase *B*, the present piece would be nearer Pb.

It must be noted that while we have five *Pa* vases recorded from as many separate graves of phase *A1* at Ocucaje on the Ica River, the 1926 expedition did not recover a single such vase from all its *A1* graves at Cahuachi A, Aja B, and Majoro Chico A. This may be an accident of numbers, but it more likely expresses a substylistic difference between the Nazca *A1* of Ica and Nazca Valleys, such as exists also in the relative scarcity and frequency of radial stripes on the rims of shape-*Ac* plates.

With the determination of 170506 as *Pb*, there is in accord its triple-zoning, which has not been found in any clear phase *A* specimen and which tends to identify the post-early-*A* Ocucaje F3 grave (vessels shown in Kroeber 1956, pl. 35a–e) as late *A* or early *B* transitional in time.

The colors of 170506 are six: W, Y, LR, DR, G, and B. The topmost zone has a W background with black dividers, each panel containing one dart; the color sequence for these is G, LR, Y, and DR, repeated as a unit.

The middle zone is traversed by a LR zigzag band bordered in DR. Of the triangles left by the zigzag, pairs adjacent to an upper-left-to-lower-right slope are (with some irregularity) alternately W and G. Of thirteen such pairs of triangles five are G, two pairs are W, plus three double pairs of W. Above, the band of zigzags and triangles is bordered by a LR stripe, below, by a DR one.

The lowest zone consists of a W line, a 9-mm-wide LR(?) stripe [others might call this a brown color], and a B band 25 mm wide.

**FIGURE 233, 170507 (N5).** Bulbous-convex *O*-shape jar. D 110 mm, H 150 mm, H/D 136%. Colors four: W, LR, DR, and B.

Kroeber (1956, 348) has stated, "Shape *O* has no known antecedents in pre-*B* period." If this is correct, the *B* age of Grave 16 is further confirmed, in agreement with the painted design of this piece.

However, the same design as here occurs on two roughly cylindrical jars in Gayton and Kroeber (1927), plate 9g and 9i. These are wider at top than bottom and definitely concave in outline, and they were therefore classified as shape *J*, goblets. Kroeber in 1956 suggested renaming the class "waisted goblet," and subdividing it into *J1* (H/D 90–110%, early or middle B), and *J2* (H/D 130–140%, full or late B). While this subclassification of *J* cannot be directly contravened by our present *O*-shape specimen with a H/D ratio of 136%, it leaves us doubtful. It is possible that an *O* shape of early *B* transformed to the *J* shape of full *B;* nothing more is involved than slight remodeling of overall profile. The design of the conical-hatted figure, holding vegetation, lends itself equally well to both shapes. What we need is more *J*-shape and *O*-shape jars of identifiable period.

Seler (1923, 238–241) construes the painted figure as a spirit of vegetative growth—he always carries fruits—and calls attention both to the skewered seam in the front of his cap and to the fact that this head-piece comes partially down over the eyes so as to make the face look like that of a trophy head. However, his illustrations 122, 123, and 126 give no indication of the shape of the vessel that bore them; his 124 is a narrow-collared *S*-shape jar, and his 125 a tall cylindrical vase (H/D 195%, shape N1).

The conical-cap figure recurs in climax-*B* phase *(B2)* association below, in Figure 270, 170780, from Ocongalla

West B, Grave 12, and Figure 309, 170983, from Cantayo M, Grave 2. It must accordingly be construed as a design that went on through the whole or most of phase *B*.

**FIGURE 234, 170505 (N5).** *F-H* shape bowl. D 150 mm, H 98 mm, H/D 65%. Base Y, background of the design W, with narrow B borders and figure outlines. Colors eight: W, Y, LR, DR, DBr, V, G, and B. The violet occurs on the middle one of three long feathers (partly visible in the illustration), the G on the legs (partly visible), Y on the breechclout, DR on arms, LR on the tongue, DBr replaces LR in repetition of the figure on the far side of the bowl.

The following features of design are B in period: 1) scalloped or serrated edge of wing; 2) wing feathers parallel, rounded with three-dot face at end; 3) darts held, and tongue a dart; and, probably, 4) mouth mask reduced to (or replaced by) a lenticular mass.

Following are the three vessels with *B* features from the bottom of Grave 16. The remaining piece was encountered 50 cm higher.

**FIGURE 235, 170504 (N3).** Found part way up in Grave 16, 150 cm deep, an *E*-shape bowl. D 167 mm, H 76 mm, H/D 46%. There are five colors: W (outlining and dividers), Y, LR, DR (rim, base, interior), and B (background). The pattern consists of five step-frets, successively LR, DR, Y, LR, and DR. These are not complementary with the background. That is, the end of the colored fret extends down to the base, dividing the background for each fret into three separate pieces: a hanging step, a square enclosed by the fret, and a narrow strip between the fret and the next vertical divider. The effect is that of an incomplete or disjointed step-fret, owing to the last element in the figure being lengthened somewhat and cutting up the background. In short, the idea of the complementary step-fret, a naturally pleasing running pattern, seems botched and perverted.

This piece seems *A* phase, and probably *A1*, for the following reasons: 1) the shape *E*, 2) the black background, 3) the white outlining, and 4) the white dividers into panels for each of the repeated design units. Since its placement in the grave was separate from the *B*-style objects in the grave, position confirms stylistic judgment and the simplest interpretation is that the bowl was buried in an *A* grave, disinterred in the digging of the subsequent *B1* grave, and there reinterred, but separately.

## GIFTS FROM CANTAYO

**FIGURE 236, 170603 (N5/6); PLATE 16.** Shows a type-*Pb* bulbous-concave vase presented by Sr. José de la Borda of Hacienda Cantayo, said to have been found in its confines. The H is 160 mm, D of the base 116 mm, D of the waist 101 mm, D of the rim 111 mm, with H/D respectively 138%, 158%, and 144%. The four colors are W, F, DR, and B (if there is only one red, it is usually LR). The flesh color occurs in the narrow bands separating the zones; for the rest, the distribution can be recognized in Figure 236. All three zones show only animals, in the upper and lower, small and right-facing; in the middle zone, larger and left-facing. This change of direction is unusual within the same vessel. The small animals (8, 9, 10, and 11 in number in successive rows) are tailed, so they cannot be guinea pigs; they are probably mice or rats, in spite of their humped backs. The three large animals in the middle zone may be dogs or foxes; they have only three legs and a seven- or eight-pointed star for a heart(?). The curved object with four knots or nodes that they seem to be holding in their mouths and eating may represent vegetation. Something like it appears in a representation of hunted camelids (Fig. 259). The current piece is phase *B*, probably *B1*.

**FIGURE 237, 170599 (N4/5).** Also from Cantayo and received as a gift, this vessel is a shape-*Pb* bulbous-concave jar with modeled nose and painted face, also belonging to shape class *Y1*, face vase. The H is 180 mm, D of base 135 mm, D of middle 116 mm, D of rim 140 mm, with H/D respectively 133%, 155%, and 129%, the base D being exceptionally smaller than the rim. The colors are W, DR, and B.

**FIGURE 238, 170596 (N5).** [Another vessel received as a gift and said to be from Cantayo is 170596, shape *S-T*, H 189 mm, D 202 mm, H/D 94%. The design parallels that of vessel 170505, Figure 234.]

## SUMMARY OF *B1* GRAVES

It is evident that small as the foregoing sample of *B1* ceramics is, it is markedly different in its vessel shapes from Nazca *A1* and *A2*, with their predominance of bowls and plates and sprinkling of double-spouts. Of thirteen vessels from burials, only one is a bowl. That there is no double-spout is no doubt an accident of small sample, since spouts recur in *B2;* but their diminution probably began in *B1*. There is one narrow-mouthed spherical jar, and one anomalous figure or effigy jar. A full ten of the thirteen vessels are goblets and vases, all but two taller than wide: shapes *J1* (twice), *M*, *M-O*, *O* (twice), *Pb*, *Pn* (twice), and *Qn*. The ten pieces of these seven shapes, lumped together, seriate in H/D ratio thus: 89, 94, 105, 108, 112, 118, 119, 125, 126, and 136%. If proportionally greater height is a sign of later place in time, the sequence of the three graves would be Ocongalla 4, Ocongalla 3, and Majoro 16. The present series is too short to warrant serious faith in this particular construal, but with abundance of material, the method might yield subdistinctions of chronology.

Three of the aforementioned vessels are also head jars, *Y1* or *Y3*, seen as variants of *P* and *Q* shapes with additions of a modeled nose. Neither of these forms has been found in phase *A*.

Phase *B1* also at times runs to a larger gamut of colors than found in *A1* or *A2*—witness the eight colors in 170688. This is associated with the tendency to increased height: tall vessels with design in several zones not only invite more variety but have more surface for it. The average number of different colors per vessel is six on the jars and vases from Ocongalla Grave 3 but only four on the lower vessels from Grave 4. This difference also serves as a reminder that caution in inference is necessary when the numbers are small.

CHAPTER 9

# *Pottery of Phase B2*

## GRAVES OF PHASE B2

GRAVES OF PHASE *B2* are 7, 8, 9, 10, and 12 of Ocongalla West B; 1, 2, 3, 4, and 6 of Ocongalla Zero; 10, 11, 12, 14, and 15 of Agua Santa, 5 of Soisongo C, and 2 of Cantayo M— seventeen in all. There are also some purchased vessels from Taruga and Tunga on southern tributaries of the Nazca River.

### Ocongalla West B, Grave 7

**FIGURE 239, 170700 (N5).** One of a pair of shape-*Y1* trophy-head jars, which can also be considered bulbous-concave vases with modeled nose, or *Pn* (Kroeber 1956, 348). D 115 mm, H 150 mm, H/D 130%; D mouth 90 mm, mouth D/maximum D 78%. The colors are six to eight: W, F, Y, LBr, LR, DR, G, and B. Of these, flesh and Y may be different applications of one pigment, and possibly LBr and LR also. There are three zones of design. Zone 1, the head or face is Y, toothed eyebrows are B, eyes are W rhomboids outlined in B, mouth DR also outlined in B, cheek painting LR circles not outlined, but each bearing four B triangles in from rim: the hair behind, not showing in the photograph, is B. Zone 2 is a plain LR band above which are two rows of B three-step blocks making squares with complementary W blocks. Zone 3 has a W background into which rise a series of rounded LR spikes from a continuous base. Between the spikes are swifts with heads and abbreviated bodies separated by a transverse horizontal bands or collars. Above and below these transverse bands the body and head of each bird is a uniform color, but the bands are of contrasting hues. In the four repetitions visible in the illustration, the colors are, from left to right: above and below, G, LBr, LBr, and F; transverse band, Y, G, F, and LBr.

Most of the business of design on this vessel is carried out with W, Y, LR, and B; the four other colors, F, LBr, DR, and G occur in restricted areas, touching up the design effect. Vessel 170701 is the mate of 170700.

**FIGURE 240, 170702 (N5).** Bulbous-concave *P* jar. H 158 mm, D 117 mm, H/D 135%; mouth D varies from 90 to 97 mm, so ratio of mouth D/maximum D runs 77–83%. Concavity of the profile of the upper half is very slight, but perceptible; there is no actual diminution of D from lip down. The design, B-outlined on W, is of a cat divinity, whose body extends around the jar to the right; he holds a trophy head under his own face. The colors are

W, F, Y, LR, DR, G, and B. The mouth mask appears to be Y, the staff on each side flesh color. The body tail, not shown in the photograph, contains Y, LR, DR, and G. There is a wide B bottom band. The spikes on the back or top of the body (only the beginning of one shows in the illustration) are LR. The interspike pattern, similar to that of the last piece described, shows the following coloring of its elements:

| | | | | |
|---|---|---|---|---|
| 1 | LR | DR | Y | B |
| 2 | LR | | F | B |
| 3 | LR | | G | B |
| 4 | Y | F | LR | B |
| 5 | LR | | G | B |

**FIGURE 241, 170704 (N5).** One of a pair (with 170703) of flat-bottomed flaring bowls of shape *D* (which is a Nazca *B* shape). D 142 mm, H 60 mm, H/D 42%. The colors are seven: W, Y, F, LR, DR, G, and B. The background is W, outlines B. The flesh color appears only twice in one of the six bird repetitions as a variant of Y. All bodies of the birds are LR with DR spots; all wing tips are LR; other parts vary alternately or irregularly, thus:

| | 1 | 2 | 3 | 4 | 5 | 6 |
|---|---|---|---|---|---|---|
| Beak | Y | DR? | Y | DR | Y | DR |
| Wing | G | DR | G | DR | G | DR |
| Tail | Y | DR | F | DR | Y | DR |
| Wing Feathers | ? | Y | F | DR | Y | G |
| | G | LR | G | LR | Y | |
| | DR | DR | DR | DR | | |

Corroborating the bowl shape, the rudimentary faces and tongues at the ends of the wing feathers are characteristic Nazca *B*. The bottom or outside of the bowl is quartered in B and W.

**FIGURE 242, 170705 (N5).** Shape-*S* narrow-mouthed spherical jar. D 163 mm, H 150 mm, H/D 92%; mouth D 72 mm, neck D 56 mm, mouth/maximum D 44%, neck/maximum D 34%; vertical H of collar 25 mm, collar H/H 7%. As the arbitrary turning point between shapes *R* and *S* is mouth D/maximum D 50%, this vessel is narrow-mouthed and shape *S*.

The colors are eight, the most usual six plus LBr and DBr, but no flesh. The main design, which is repeated on the opposite side, is obviously Nazca *B*. Background W; outlining, bottom band, collar, B. The design is of a flying deity. We find nothing closely similar to it in Seler, although he has many of the elements. The two main figures are separated by narrower panels containing five horizontal rows of four quadrilaterals, each divided by a stepped diagonal into white and black halves; the whole panel is framed in LR lines. Specific criteria of *B2* are the bent-over rays and the forked projections forward from the face.

**FIGURE 243, 170706 (N5).** A case of outline-only design, which seems not to appear before *B2* and continues into Nazca *Y*. The shape is between an *F-H* bowl and an *I* goblet; it is low for a goblet (D 111 mm, H 84 mm, H/D 76%) but too flat bottomed for a bowl. We have classed it as an angled goblet, characteristic of *B2* and *Y*. The angle at the waist is 160 degrees, that is, there is a bend of 20 degrees. The colors are only three: W for background, B and LR for alternate renderings of the deity. One of the LR is, and not for lack of space, reduced to a head: body, arms, and legs are replaced by fruits, the chin round instead of pointed, ten round dots attached to the outline of the face. The deity represented is that of fruits or vegetation, according to Seler (1923, 238–241). In his figure 124, Seler shows him in outline, as here, but as painted on an *S*-shape jar.

This Grave 7 clearly is fully developed if not late *B2*.

### Ocongalla West B, Grave 8

**FIGURE 244, 170708 (N5).** This was the only vessel, an excellent one, in Grave 8. This is a bulbous-concave vase *P*, of subvariety *Pb* characteristic of Nazca *B*, definitely higher than wide. D 103 mm, H 136 mm, H/D ratio 132%. There is a barely measurable narrowing of D below the lip at about one-sixth of the way down. The colors are five: W, LR, DR, G, and B. The W is for background, mouth and eyes; the LR for the face and appendages; DR only on the tongue; G in the eye panel; B is used for eye pupils, outlines, and top and bottom bands. The face is repeated three times. A similar figure occurs in Kroeber (1956), plate 39d, on a *K* or double-curve goblet, and in Seler (1923), figure 238, on a wide-mouthed *R*-shape jar, as also in his figures 237, 239, and 240. We suggest that this is the trophy head (note half-closed, cut-off eyes and tongue like a carrying cord) of a deity, as shown by the rayed appendages, pointed, bent-over, jagged rhomboidal, and twisted up. In some representations the end of the tongue is replaced by a diffuse (not outlined) red area for blood.

The execution in the present piece is elegant, forcible, and effective, especially as contrasted with its amoeba-like successors in Nazca *Y*, or even with exceptional Figure 256 in Grave 10 below.

### Ocongalla West B, Grave 9

Graves 9 and 10 are interconnected by sherds from vessels of one appearing in the other: they must therefore be essentially synchronous. In Grave 9, field catalogue number 355 (museum number 170714) consisted of fragments of a bowl painted with a cat-deity design. In Grave 10, field number 369 was assigned to another bowl with "monster" (cat-deity) design; but sherds from this also fit into 355/170714. In addition, at least one sherd of 369, after it had been marked 170728 at the museum, was found to fit into vase 170730; this is still visible in the photograph of 170730 (Fig. 256).

Grave 9 was deep, 380 cm for the most part, and the skeleton was too decayed to preserve. South of the body was an oval bowl, 170719, of a type that otherwise we construe as of Nazca *Y* phase. On the southwest of the body was the miniature vase 170710, a mate to which, 170716, stood north of the body, or nearly opposite. West of the body were 170711–713; of these three, 170713 strongly suggests Nazca *A* style. To the northwest were 170714–715. Then to the north came the second miniature vase already mentioned, but at 20 cm greater depth, or total of 400 cm. To the northeast, also at 400 cm, was spherical jar 170717. At 400 cm depth, but without record of precise position in the grave, there were also a bowl, listed originally as "359, two (?) vessels in fragments," but reconstructing at the museum into one whole bowl, 170718. Also at 400 cm were field numbers 360–363, beads, pendants, and pebbles, all of stone (170719–723).

The arrangement looks as if the body had been seated at the southeast or south of the grave well, looking more or less west, with vessels ranged around facing it. (Depth of the body seems not to have been recorded. At 400 cm there is often not much left of the bones, and in such case they were usually not saved.) The variation from 380 cm to 400 cm does not throw light on the style discrepancy, because one pair of mates was divided between the two levels.

We must accordingly leave the problem open and proceed to a description of the eleven vessels, beginning with the two stylistically aberrant pieces.

**FIGURE 245, 170709 (N8).** Oval bowl, almost rectanguloid, similar to vessels 170473, 170482, 170746, and 170748 from Majoro Chico A, Graves 7 and 8, and Ocongalla West B, Grave 11, all of which we have designated Nazca *Y1* on account of their paste, shape, design, and associations. However, the association in the present is with indubitably fully developed Nazca *B*, or *B2*. This bowl type evidently overlapped *B2* and *Y1*, and perhaps *Y2* also.

The H is 112 mm, D lengthwise 145 mm, D crosswise 117 mm, yielding D/H ratios of 77% and 96%. The paste, where unpainted (outside the four design panels) is light buff; the applied pigments are W, LR, DR, and B. There are four panels, separated by three vertical stripes containing dashes. The larger figure on the left of the illustration, a very deliquesced rayed deity, has all four colors. The smaller figure, more-or-less an abbreviation of the larger, in the end panels is W with LR (and B outlines) in one of its two renditions, W with DR in the other.

**FIGURE 246, 170713 (N3/4).** Bowl that in both shape and design suggests Nazca *A*. H 67 mm, D 154 mm, H/D ratio 44%. It is nearest to shape *Bd*, gambreled bowl, a Nazca *A1* form, or to shape *E*, flat non-flaring bowl, also Nazca *A*. Both these have a straight or slightly convex rim in the upper part of their profile, as this piece has. It can be construed as gambreled from the line with which the design begins. The colors are W, Y (cream), LR, DR, G, and B. We construe the design units as heads or faces with either tear lines or cheek paints. Everything interior is W; the hair, in successive units beginning at the left of the photograph, is B, G, Y, G, LR, B, Y, G, and LR. The background is DR, a Nazca *A* trait. The design recurs, better executed and on a *P1* vase, in Kroeber and Strong (1924), plate 28m from Ocucaje, Uhle's Grave F1, a Nazca *A* vessel. Seler apparently does not show an example of it. Nor did Kroeber unearth a recurrence of the design in his 1926 excavations in Nazca that yielded the collections described in this monograph, except for the following remote resemblances. Of phase *A* is a cat-deity head on 170891 (Fig. 152) from Grave 3 at Aja B. This is a well-painted multicolor, full-face head, the top framed by two W arcs above two round eyes. On the sides, two W whisker bundles come up to meet the arcs, giving a W frame for the face that is somewhat reminiscent of our present design. There is also a pair of globular jars showing highland (?) influence and representing skulls, from Cantayo Ca, Grave 21, 171016-1-2 (Fig. 401). They are crudely overpainted with round W eyes and W brows or forehead. Their period is uncertain; they are described in Late context but may be earlier.

It is difficult to see the present piece from Grave 9 as anything but Nazca *A* or *A*-influenced in spite of this grave and the associated Grave 10 being otherwise *B2*. The *B2* vessels in the grave will now be described.

**FIGURE 247, 170711-1 and 170711-2 (N4).** Field number 352 proved to include two inside-painted plates. 170711-1 is illustrated. These are of shape class *Aw*, as defined by Kroeber (1956, 361): small, shallow, of uniform curvature, painted inside center and rim, often in quartering, and late *B* or *Y* in design. The piece shown is larger (H 74 mm, D 206 mm) than those tabulated in 1956 (D 122–138 mm) as well as relatively higher : H/D ratio 36% as against 29–35%. The colors are W, F (variant of Y?), LR, DR, G, B. The center quarters are alternately G and F, separated by LR stripes. Each segment has a full-face trophy head sketched in with black lines, dashes, and dots, the lips (and eyelids?) being pinned with thorns. The rim is DR, each quarter with three (or four) W transverse bars. The only paint on the exterior or bottom side is a DR rim band. There are no areas of W paint larger than the rim transverses, and the B consists wholly of outlines or cursive touches.

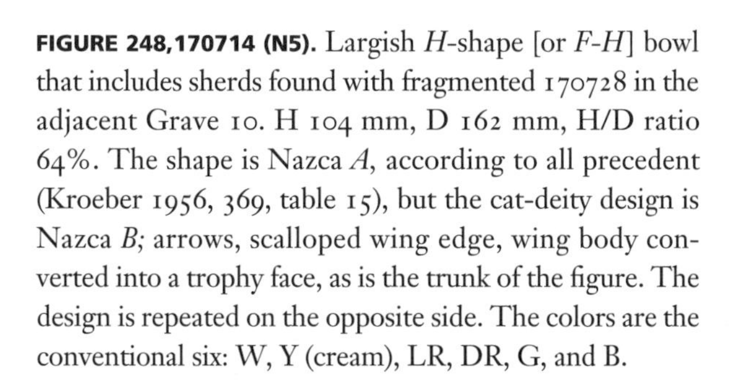

**FIGURE 248,170714 (N5).** Largish *H*-shape [or *F-H*] bowl that includes sherds found with fragmented 170728 in the adjacent Grave 10. H 104 mm, D 162 mm, H/D ratio 64%. The shape is Nazca *A*, according to all precedent (Kroeber 1956, 369, table 15), but the cat-deity design is Nazca *B;* arrows, scalloped wing edge, wing body converted into a trophy face, as is the trunk of the figure. The design is repeated on the opposite side. The colors are the conventional six: W, Y (cream), LR, DR, G, and B.

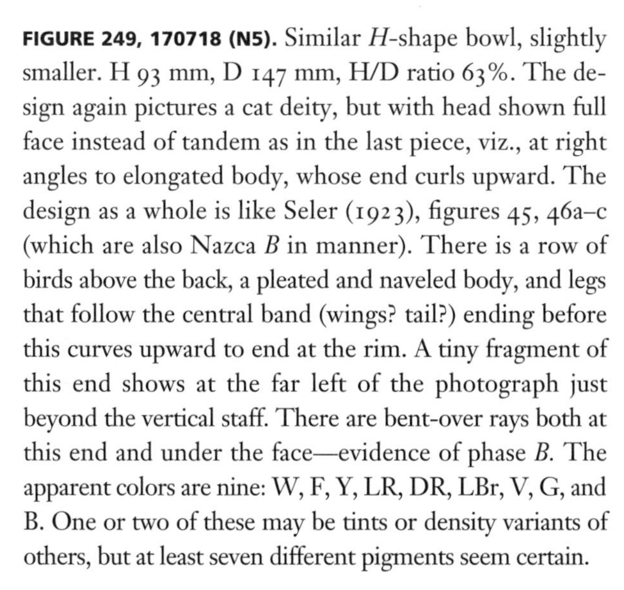

**FIGURE 249, 170718 (N5).** Similar *H*-shape bowl, slightly smaller. H 93 mm, D 147 mm, H/D ratio 63%. The design again pictures a cat deity, but with head shown full face instead of tandem as in the last piece, viz., at right angles to elongated body, whose end curls upward. The design as a whole is like Seler (1923), figures 45, 46a–c (which are also Nazca *B* in manner). There is a row of birds above the back, a pleated and naveled body, and legs that follow the central band (wings? tail?) ending before this curves upward to end at the rim. A tiny fragment of this end shows at the far left of the photograph just beyond the vertical staff. There are bent-over rays both at this end and under the face—evidence of phase *B*. The apparent colors are nine: W, F, Y, LR, DR, LBr, V, G, and B. One or two of these may be tints or density variants of others, but at least seven different pigments seem certain.

**FIGURE 250, 170715 (N5).** Another flaring bowl of approximate *H*-shape, largest of the three. H 133 mm, D 220 mm, H/D ratio 60%. The design is in three continuous bands, the repeated units apparently derivative from elements or parts generally associated with the cat deity. The colors are the usual six: W, Y, LR, DR, G, and B. The upper zone is similar to the top of the back of some cat deity representations, characterized by a series of erect spikes. The customary filling between the spikes varies among trophy heads, birds, fruits (?), flowers (?), and so forth. In the present piece we consider the filling units to be malformed or degenerate trophy heads. As the background in all three zones is B, the hair of the heads is represented by G blobs. The lower zone has the spikes reversed to point downward, and the misshapen heads are much as in the upper zone, but the hair seems to be in an elongated mass instead of two rectangles as in the upper zone. The filling figures as a whole may be derived from full-face trophy heads like Seler (1923), figures 174 and 175 or from profile ones like his 181, 191, 192, and 194–199. The face portion of both upper- and lower-zone heads is executed in a regular repeat of colors W, Y, and G.

The middle zone consists of keyed or interlocking rectangularized figures in a Y-LR-G repeat. We consider these also derivative from trophy heads, this time surely full face, much as in Seler (1923), figures 175 and 177. In fact, one of these two designs may have been the prototype from which the pattern of 170715 was developed.

**FIGURE 251, 170712 (N5).** Shape *P* bulbous-concave vase. H 157 mm, D 123 mm, H/D ratio 128%. There are eight colors: the usual six plus LBr and DBr. The Y can also be construed as cream. The LBr appears in a stripe separating the upper tier of trophy heads and tail feathers from the lower tier; the DBr appears in the bird's beak, in the farthest right head in the upper tier, and in the lowest tail feather.

The painted representation that surrounds the vase is that of a bird, in two units or a repeat, shown by Seler (1923), his figures 284 and 285 with a longish beak, crest or comb, loop neck, and distinctive coloring on jaw and throat: he calls it a "maize bird." In the painting on our vessel there are no feet, and the body and tail extend around the vessel in two tiers, at first of squarish, full-face trophy heads (three each, one beyond the other, tandem) and then of four horizontal feathers in each tier that end in spines just below the bird's head.

**FIGURE 252, 170716 (N5); PLATE 18.** Vessels 170710 and 170716 are a pair of miniature shape *N* vases. H only 104 mm, D 72 mm, H/D 144%. Technically, they are *Nn* because a nose is modeled on the lower third of the vase, which portion represents a human head, the upper part of the vase perhaps standing for a turban or cylindrical headdress. Vessel 170716 more than 170710 shows a sudden stricture where the headdress meets the head, as if the two parts had been modeled separately and then joined before firing. With literal logic these two vessels could be considered head jars, shape *Y* (or shape *Y1* as elaborated in Kroeber 1956, pl. 356); but the original *Y1* pieces, as shown in Gayton and Kroeber (1927), plate 7c-f, are more globular below and then usually concave above, and their painting is in two zones; whereas our present miniatures are pretty evenly cylindrical and the painting forms three definite zones, in both of which respects they resemble *N*-shape vases. In fact, our pieces show the three slight bulges and two concavities characteristic of the *N2*, or wavy silhouetted variety of *N* (Kroeber 1956, 346). Strictly, then, they might be designated as *N2n*. Of course, a designation like this is formal; its significance is in indicating the interplay of patterns of shape—the basic tall cylindrical form, its wavy swellings, and the assimilation to a face by means of a modeled nose and painted eyes and mouth.

The painting on Figure 252 (Pl. 18) has seven colors: W, Y (cream), LR, DR, LBr, DBr, and B. As so often when there are two browns, there is no G. The design comes in three tiers. The face is Y with W eyes, LR mouth, B border to eyes and mouth, B pupils and eyebrows, and B-grid cheek paint of the falcon-head type, with LR dots between the bars. The middle tier perhaps represents the band of a turban or other headdress, and is bordered by two LB stripes. Between these is a continuous band of complementary (interlocking) step-frets, whose sequence in part runs DBr, Y, DBr, Y, LR, DR, Y, with customary half rhythm. The third tier, the top of the turban, is W with a row of hummingbirds (cf. Seler 1923, figs. 280–283) stuck head downward around it. The wings are more in the manner of phase *A* birds, but in a miniature vessel only a handbreadth high there would scarcely have been space to paint the typical period-*B* wing feathers. There are ten birds in the circuit; the wing stripes are all LR while the body colors are LR, Y, LBr, LR, Y, LBr, LR, DBr, LR, and Y.

**FIGURE 253, 170717 (N5).** The final pot from Grave 9, narrow-mouthed jar of shape *S*. H 155 mm, D 175 mm, H/D 89%. neck D is 36% of body D, lip D 47% of body D. H of the collar is 20% of the total H, measured on the photograph. There are seven colors: the usual six plus LBr, which appears on the mouth mask. The colors are brilliant. There are two units of design, each representing a cat deity with human legs and bird wing and tail. Seler (1923), figure 85, comes closest of his figures to our representation except that this has the head supine or tandem with the trunk, but Seler's has the head upright.

### Ocongalla West B, Grave 10

This grave, which is tied to the preceding Grave 9 by interfitting sherds, was a meter deeper—500 cm—and is even richer. There are no disturbing inclusions of apparent earlier or later period. Every vessel is well-stylized Nazca *B2*. There are nine tall, near-cylindrical vessels of shapes *P*, *M*, or *K*; four bowls of *H* and *D* shapes; and one magnificent head-and-spout of a naked tattooed woman. We will begin the descriptions with her.

## *Figure-and-Spout*

**FIGURE 254, 170727 (N5).** Handled figure head-and-spout, shape *V*. 183 mm high, with its opening at the top of the head. It is similar to Seler (1923), figure 208, from the Gretzer collection in Berlin. The major difference is that Seler's piece has neither handle nor opening, being a clay figurine (Thonbild). Beyond that, Seler's seated lady has her legs outstretched forward and holds her hands level in front of her, whereas ours has tucked her legs under tailor fashion and has set her palms on her knees. The tattooing is similar on buttocks and abdomen; the Chicago specimen in addition has tattooed designs on her arms and legs.

Our piece represents a woman giving birth to a W-eyed and W-toothed baby, evidently a deity or demon. Strictly, it is the mouth interior that is W; six minute B lines in this are interstices, delimiting the separate teeth. The baby's emerging head (18 mm long, 16 mm wide) does not show in the photograph because it is being born head first but face downward.

Both Seler's piece and ours have a deity head painted or tattooed on the abdomen, the head on ours being completely radiating, Seler's having bent-over rays, square mouth, and tongue. Possibly these figures not only represent tattooing but symbolize the god about to be born or his father.

Our specimen uses the motif of fruits attached to the heads tattooed on the arms, legs, and hips, as Figure 208 shows; the Berlin specimen uses rather the jagged-staff deity with bent-over rays and other typical accoutrements. In both cases, all designs on the body are found elsewhere on Nazca *B* pots. In addition, our piece has a figure-representing tattoo on the small of its back. This represents a broad full face with rectangular mouth and short protruding tongue, the face being surrounded by thirteen rounded outline triangles each containing three short dashes—in other words, reduced trophy heads. From each of these trophy heads there come off one or two solid B rectangles (clubs of hair, twenty-three in all) that give the main deity head an effect of a fringe of blunt, short rays.

The colors are W, C, LR, DR, LBr, and B. The body is cream throughout. Other colors occur in areas as follows: W eyes in face on abdomen and eyes of infant being born; LR seven dots between B lines around wrists, also wavy subvaginal lines; DR spout (5-mm orifice) and the bridge, also the woman's own mouth; LBr large triangular face tattooed at navel; B woman's own and baby's hair and the lumbar face's blunt-ended rays, and also all the remaining linear representations of tattooing wherever.

Seler (1923) illustrates two other women's figures (figures 205, 206) that have a head opening but no spout, lack arms and legs, but are considered by Seler to be naked and tattooed.

These birth scenes and tattooed women are of interest both because of the light they throw on Nazca customs and because all the design elements that appear on them are good touchstones for the fully developed Nazca *B2* style.

## *Shape-P Bulbous-Concave Vases*

We come now to the tall vaselike vessels. Five of these of shape *P*, the bulbous-concave vase in its later and more-slender Nazca *B* form *Pb*, can be considered together as regards shape (Figs. 255–259).

| | **H/D** | **MILLIMETERS** | | |
|---|---|---|---|---|
| | % | H | D | Concavity |
| 170732-1 | 156 | 170 | 109 | 2 |
| 170730 | 149 | 162 | 109 | 3 |
| 170740 | 141 | 178 | 126 | 6.5 |
| 170723 | 133 | 150 | 113 | 4 |
| 170736 | 131 | 197 | 150 | 1.5 |

The five *Pb* vases are here seriated according to their H/D percentage ratios. The mm figures for H and D are measured on the vessels. Concavity is measured on photographs by subtracting the minimum D of silhouette from the exterior D of the lip and reconverting the difference into the mm size of the original. As the figures are for diameters, a concavity of 4 mm means that the vessel at its narrowest girth is 2 mm concave on each side as compared with the lip. It is obvious that amount of actual concavity is quite slight—just enough to impart elegance to the profile.

It will also be convenient to present the color scheme comparatively:

| | | | | | | | | |
|---|---|---|---|---|---|---|---|---|
| 170732–1 | W | Y | LR | DR | | G | B | (6) |
| 170730 | W | Y | LR | DR | V | G | B | (7) |
| 170740 | W | Y | LR | DR | DBr | VG | B | (8) |
| 170723 | W | Y | LR | DR | LBr | G | B | (7) |
| 170736 | W | LR | DR | G | | | B | (5) |

It is not clear how many pigments are represented by seven or eight colors as compared with six. The LBr and DBr may be owing to different densities of paint on the brush, and V might be a variant of G or of G with LR, for all we know. The same holds for cream and flesh as regards Y in other pieces.

The designs painted on these five bulbous-concave *Pb* vases will be treated individually.

**FIGURE 255, 170732-1 (N5).** Design is painted in two zones on W background above a solid DR base. The upper zone about balances the base in width and consists of LR step blocks, leaving pendant W complementaries between. Below are a G and Y encircling band. The middle zone takes up half the total height and contains vertical bars that alternately spring and depend for about five-sixths of the width of the zone. They are neatly right angled in B outline, and their filling colors are, in order of no regular repeat, DR, LR, V, LR, W, LR, DR, LR, W, LR, B, LR, G, and LR—fourteen of them. The pigments seem to have been applied somewhat thinly and not polished much but the pattern is simple, open, and elegant.

**FIGURE 256, 170730 (N5).** Also has three zones, the lowest being a plain DR, the middle much the widest. The top zone shows B amphibian larvae (Seler 1923, fig. 319) with W eyes and mouth (?) and LR gills (feathery, not outlined). The middle zone has three repetitions of a deity face on W background. The face comprises a crest of three blunt rectangular rays (Y); upper face (DR) containing eyes (W) cut off at top; mouth or mouth mask with inward-facing points (G); a jagged staff at each side (LR); two rectanguloid panels (trophy heads?) at each side (V); the mouth cavity is filled with LR blobs or smears, no doubt representing flowing blood. Compare Kroeber (1956), plate 39d.

**FIGURE 257, 170740 (N5).** Double-zoned, the lower one narrow and solid DR, the upper filling the remainder of the surface on W background, of which little shows because of the crowding of the parts of a cat deity. He carries a V staff in his G right hand, a trophy head in his left. His crest is G and LR, upper face DR with W eyes, LR mouth mask, DBr chin or collar. The body extends around the vessel, curling upward at the tail. Above and below, fourteen diagonal darts project from body and tail, whose irregular color sequence is: LR, DR, LR, DR, G, LR, V, Y, DR, DR, G, LR, DB, and V.

**FIGURE 258, 170723 (N5).** So narrow a LR base band as to be essentially single-zoned. On W background are painted eight lizards with vigorously swished tails, the bodies slightly diagonal, scales indicated by a cross-hatched area. Their colors are lizard body, LR, Y, LR, DR, Y, G, LB, and LR; lizard body, LBr, LR, G, LR, LR, LR, LR, and LR. Between the lizard tails are lenticular elements in heavy DR outlining. Seler (1923) cites no paintings of lizards. Two that might be so interpreted (1923, his figs. 323, 326) he interprets, we think correctly,

as salamanders. They have heads narrower than the lengthwise-striped bodies; our lizards have heads wider than their scaled bodies. Salamanders are shown below on our Figure 334 from *Y1* Grave 8 at Majoro Chico A.

**FIGURE 259, 170736 (N5).** Single-zoned on W, vigorously if sloppily painted, appearing fuzzy because the main figures are not outlined. It shows camelids being hunted with arrows (? or darts) and probably sling stones indicated by LR, DR, G, and B small solid circles. The darts are outlined in B. The animals are LR with white eyes; thin branching lines, B or G, issue from their mouths. These may indicate breath or blood or perhaps only their pasture. Compare Gayton and Kroeber (1927), plates 6e, 10b.

## *Shape-M Tapering Vases*

We come next to two cylindrical vessels that can be classed as shape *P* like the foregoing or as shape *M*, tapering vase. The later seems the more appropriate because, while like *P* they bulge most near the bottom and show a concave profile toward the top, there is no actual constriction below the top. They are both rather short for vases, around the six-inch range, almost identical in proportion, but the first, 170725 (Fig. 260), is single-zoned; the second, 170739 (Fig. 261), three-zoned in design. The dimensions are, respectively, H 144 mm, D 113 mm, H/D 127%; and H 160 mm, D 127 mm, H/D 126%. Measurements on photographs raise the H/D ratio slightly, to 131% and 133%, and yield (more reliably) rim D/maximum D, 81% and 78%. The colors are the same on both pieces, the standard *B*-period minimum six: W, Y, LR, DR, G, and B.

**FIGURE 260, 170725 (N5).** Single-zoned, the pigments are powdery and partly effaced. Visible are a dancing figure in G, Y, and LR, with flying breechclout or tail; behind it, remnants of Y and LR barbed rays; and below this, an unidentified representation of three crossing rectangles connected with two solid circles in Y, LR, and B. The dancing figure evidently represents a ghost, perhaps of a trophy head—compare the large eye and socket and grinning mouth; also Kroeber (1956), plate 40b; Gayton and Kroeber (1927), plates 5b, 10a; and in Seler (1923), figure 186, which he calls "dance of the trophy heads" and which is also accompanied by some unidentified paraphernalia and lenticular objects (disks?). This trophy head or ghost dance is one of the few themes in Nazca art that successfully captures motion.

**FIGURE 261, 170739 (N5).** First and third zone alike on a B background with curvilinear design; the middle zone is on W background with angular design; plus there is a base band of solid DR. The U-curved design element with a third straight arm in the middle is obscure. It is perhaps to be thought of as sitting on its convex base, with three prongs up, and each of these carrying at its end a small W perforated disk with B center. For this design there is parallel in Kroeber (1956), plate 46a, except that from four to six tiny W dots are lined along both edges of the three arms instead of one larger one at the ends only. The figure is here actually set pointing up, and its repeats are in panels set off by dividers; the background is B, as in 170739. Seler (1923) shows something similar in his figures 410 and 412, also on B background and with the arms pointing upward. His 412 has U-shape outline, and there are three W spikes, rays, or petals radiating from the end of each arm. The arms themselves are also lined by minute W dots. His figure 410 is evidently more representative: the convexity has become a flat base, the three arms have become irregularly zigzag, and there are fine thorns raying out from them all the way up; at the tips, there are again the large triple spikes or petals. Seler suggests that 410 represents a cactus and that 412 is conventionally derived. He may or may not be right; we have no suggestion of our own to offer. At any rate, the figures are evidently related. Since all but 170739 sit individually with the arms upward, ours must have been turned 90 degrees to face left and run tandem in a continuous band. The B background to this design in all cases is remarkable. While B backgrounds are not uncommon in Nazca *A*, they are rare in full *B2*.

In the present piece, the u-shape ornaments are alternately G and LR.

The middle zone of 170739 holds a continuous band of six complementary step-frets, with the steps somewhat slanted. A peculiarity is that the small quadrangle forming the hooked-in end of the fret is sometimes differently colored from the rest when it rises. There is considerable irregularity of shape execution, but most of the continuous pattern around the vase can be described thus as regards color: Ww, DR, Wlr, G, Ww, DR, Wlr, G, Ww, DR, and W. The underlined letters indicate frets set on the bottom, lower-case letters the color of the terminal hook-in, and capitals not underlined are frets hanging from above with their hook-in always the same as themselves. The color scheme is wholly regular, a unit Ww-DR alternating with Wlr-G.

## *Shape K, Double-Convex Goblets*

We come now to two double-convex goblets, shape *K*, both multiple-zoned and executed with elegance of form and precision of design.

**FIGURE 262, 170732-2 (N5).** H 139 mm, maximum D (at top and bottom) 123 mm, H/D ratio 113%. Measurements on the photograph show that the minimum D in the middle is about 11% less than above and below. They also show that the tapering in at the lip is scarcely more than 1 mm on each side, although it seems marked to the eye.

This is the vessel with nine seeming colors. The upper and wider zone of design contains four tandem cat deity heads with crest of bent-over rays, mouth mask ends turned into fleur-de-lis, and mouth with points turned inward and no lower jaw or bottom like 170730 (Fig. 256) from this same grave. Instead of blood in the mouth, a forked rectangular tongue protrudes from it. Five colors are given to five successive parts of the head: crest, eye region, mouth mask, mouth, and tongue. In the four repetitions of the head, these colors are:

| | | | | | |
|---|---|---|---|---|---|
| 1 | G | Y | LR | DR | DBr |
| 2 | Y | DR | LR | G | V |
| 3 | G | Y | LR | DR | DBr |
| 4 | Y | DR | LR | G | F |

The lower zone contains seven pendant and seven standing bars, colored in order DR, LR, V, LR, W, LR, DR, LR, W, LR, DBr, LR, G, and LR. Every even bar is LR, but the odd ones seem to come randomly, sometimes darker and sometimes lighter than LR. The painting is cleanly and firmly executed.

**FIGURE 263, 170735 (N5).** Taller and more-slender *K* shape, with two narrow zones of design at the rim, one geometric, the other representative; a third zone as wide as the other two together; and a broad base band of solid dark red. H 115 mm, D 104 mm, H/D ratio 111%. The incipient convex constriction toward the lip is obviously a matter of a very few mm only, though without it the goblet would present an aesthetically quite different shape.

The background of the two lower zones is W, tinged however enough to suggest description of it as creamy. There are six colors, the usual six with LBr replacing Y: W, LR, DR, LBr, G, and B.

The uppermost design band shows pairs of interlocking step-frets, with three peculiarities: 1) alternate LR step-frets arise out of continuous base band of the same LR; 2) between these and the complementary ones there is a slanting series of mere steps of color contrasting with both; and 3) the fret hook of the non-G element differs in color from its triangular step-block and agrees with the slanting mere steps. This third feature we have already encountered in a vessel from this same grave, the *M* vase 170739 (Fig. 261), though without feature 2; whereas this feature (2) recurs in *Y1* association below, in Majoro Chico A, Grave 7, 170471 (Fig. 324, between step-frets) and 170472 (Fig. 325, alone, in series of itself).

The color scheme of this abnormal step-fret band is intricate but nearly regular. Every rising step-fret is LR like the base out of which it emerges. To its left are the slanting, free-floating steps; these are either G or LBr, in this order, left to right: G, G, LBr, G, LBr, and G. To the right of the LR rising fret is a depending one that engages it. This depending fret has separate colors for its two parts, namely the hook and the step-block. Designating the hook by lower-case letters, the coloring of the depending frets is gW, lbrW, lbrW, gW, lbrW, and gW. In short, the hanging frets are all mainly W, their hooks are either G or Lbr, the choice between these two being the same as the color of the slant, free steps next following (except that in the second of six units the hook is Lbr but the free steps G).

The second zone of 170735 shows tailless rodents, probably guinea pigs, in procession. They are B with LBr pupils of their eyes and LR feet.

The third zone contains, similar to that on the preceding *K* goblet, pendant bars on W. Again every even bar is LR; the odd ones run (left to right) G, LBr, G, DR, and LBr.

## *Shape-D Bowl*

**FIGURE 264, 170726 (N5).** Flat-bottomed flaring bowl of shape class *D*. H 70 mm, D 184 mm, H/D ratio 38%. The colors are four only: W, LR, DR, and B. The theme of the painting is the dance of thirteen trophy-head ghosts, as in 170725 (Fig. 260) of this same grave, and, as there, the execution is somewhat hasty but vigorous. Head hair and clubs, if they are such, are B; odd dancers are DR, as are the right or hind ends of their breechclouts, the left or front ends of those on the even dancers, the base of the bowl, and its lip stripe; the remaining dancers and breechclouts are LR; and the eyes and the background are W.

## *Shape-F-H Bowls*

Four *F-H* high flaring bowls were in this grave; three of them are illustrated. They are, in series as to height:

| | H | D | H/D | Comment |
|---|---|---|---|---|
| 170731 | 122 mm | 215 mm | 57% | 2 birds |
| 170724 | 89 mm | 150 mm | 59% | 3 zones of design |
| 170729 | 88 mm | 139 mm | 63% | near mate of last |
| 170734 | 142 mm | 210 mm | 68% | 1 cat divinity |

**FIGURE 265, 170731 (N5).** Bears two representations of the bird shown in Seler (1923), figures 101–106, with a jagged crest as in Grave 9 (Fig. 251). The colors are the usual six, except that LBr replaces the more-common G. Y, LR, DR, and LBr occur both on the body and in the tail feathers, although in diverse order; DR also for the crest and neck. Black is limited to outlining, bars, and dots. White occurs in all eyes, including those of the trophy heads forming the creature's back or wing, and as background.

**FIGURE 266, 170729 (N5).** Triple-zoned. Upper tier has twelve LR crest spikes with the spaces between them filled with figures that are probably conventionalized swifts (Seler's "night swallows," 1923, figs. 289–293). They are less common in this place than are trophy heads, but both occur in phase *B2*. The wings and certain other peripheral parts are B throughout, the body and collar alternate between DR, Y and LR, DR. The background is W. Second tier, eight right-facing fish, B and LR, with trophy-head eyes, also on W background.

Bottom quartered Y and B, separated by LR stripes. Total colors five: W, Y, LR, DR, and B.

Vessel 170724, not illustrated, is a near mate of 170729, though somewhat higher, and differs in details of design and colors, of which there is a sixth, G, used both in the swifts and the fish. The swifts are proportioned somewhat differently. The fish are left-facing, and their bellies alternate between LR, G, and DR instead of being consistently LR. The basal quartering contrasts DR and Y instead of B and Y. Pieces such as these two, probably made by the same potter, illustrate the free variation allowed, or preferred, while adhering to a generic pattern of shape, color, and design.

**FIGURE 267, 170734 (N5).** Cat deity with long body curving upward at the tail and ending in a trophy head much like 170775 (Fig. 275 [Pl. 17]) of Grave 12 and carrying on its back a series of spikes and trophy heads. It is in these that the sixth color, Y, occurs. The main head has a G top, LR forehead, DR eye area with W eyes, LR mouth mask, and G chin or collar, all with B outlining. The composition is crowded as compared with the *P* vase 170740 (Fig. 257).

### Ocongalla West B, Grave 12

This grave was deep, a full 5 meters. It was also a rich grave in pottery, containing no less than twenty-six vessels, most of them in pairs. All perishable objects had decayed, however, and only part of the bones of the skeleton could be saved, although these included the deformed skull [female, age 35+].

#### *Double-Spouts*

**FIGURE 268, 170777 (N5).** Double-spout of shape *U2*, typical of full *B* style in shape, color, and design. There are altogether nineteen painted trophy heads shown on the vessel; two, eight, and nine respectively in three tiers. These are reminiscent, in their general form, of the trophy heads on vases in Figure 244 from Grave 8 and Figure 262 from Grave 10 of the same Ocongalla West B cemetery. The bent-over rays, the diamond-headed staff or ray, the triple crest of quadrangles, the eyes cut off above, and the type of tongue are all late *B*. All the triple crests as well as the base of the pot are Y in color. The spouts and bridge, the outlines of designs, the eye pupils, the area in which the eyes are set, and the tongue are B; the remainder of each head is LR; eyes, mouth, opening, and overall background are W. The vessel is unusual in containing no DR; usually the eye area and tongue would be of that color. Gray occurs only for the mouth.

The sharp turn in the profile of the vessel, with approach to lenticular overall form, is characteristic of phase *B2*. The dimensions are H to top of spout 141 mm, H of body 99 mm, D 142 mm, with H/D ratios of 99% and 70% for spout and body respectively.

The trophy head of a deity, as we incline to construe the design on this vessel, is characterized by a simplification of the endlessly proliferating complexity of entire cat-face deities. Hence the firmness and boldness both here and in the specimens from Grave 8 and 10. Seler (1923) deals with this particular type of head briefly in his figures 237–241 under the general caption of the jagged-staff deity, which he first treats, in figures 221–236, as it becomes increasingly complex, and later, in figures 245–255, as it is further complicated and slovened or degenerated. Our point is that the present head figure represents a reversal of the general trend of Nazca design toward complexity, confusion, and ultimate deliquescence. This head is always isolated, without a body; and its traits, although characteristic of divinity, are decisive and few instead of endlessly multiplied. Some of its rays appear on the whole-figure jagged-staff deity and were possibly first developed there; but stylistically they are put to quite different use in these present detached heads. We suggest that they represent heads cut off from a divinity; but there is nothing to show that this divinity was *the* jagged-staff god, or in fact that there was a specific, particular jagged-staff god in Nazca mythology. These heads are certainly stylistically distinct, and perhaps thematically as well. We therefore suggest a distinctive name for the design: "rayed trophy head" or "god trophy head."

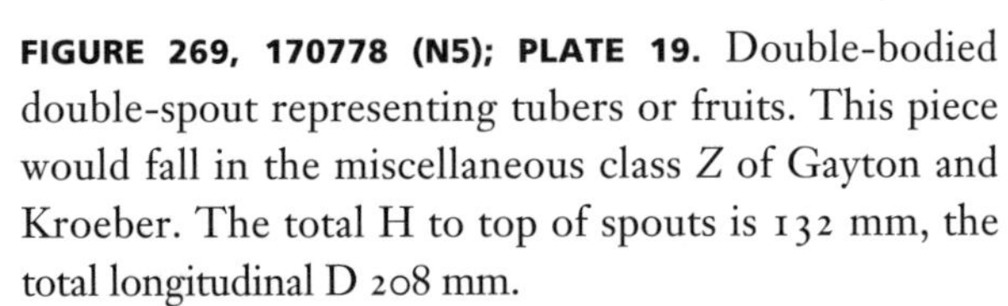

**FIGURE 269, 170778 (N5); PLATE 19.** Double-bodied double-spout representing tubers or fruits. This piece would fall in the miscellaneous class Z of Gayton and Kroeber. The total H to top of spouts is 132 mm, the total longitudinal D 208 mm.

The colors are W, LR, and B, the LR limited to a rectangular stretch at the center of the bridge. The rest of the bridge, both spouts, and the painted bases are B, as are all the painted figures. These are wholly in outline, the largest masses of B being the hair clubs of the full trophy heads below, and next to them, the middle fingers! Compare this motif and mode of rendering with our Figures 243 and 291.

## *Wide-Mouthed Spherical Jar, Shape R*

**FIGURE 270, 170780 (N5).** The one wide-mouthed jar in this grave (and in fact from the *B2* part of Ocongalla West B cemetery, though there are several narrow-mouthed *S* shapes). As the lip D is 54% of the maximum D, the vessel is shape *R*, wide-mouthed jar, by definition, 50% being the limit between *R* and *S*. The H is 92 mm, the maximum D 91, the H/D ratio 101%. With mouth and neck measuring 47 and 41 mm, their ratios to body D are 52% and 45%. Perhaps more significant is the height of the collar, which is 21% of the total H. Collars are generally low in Nazca *A* but tend to become bigger in both directions in *B*.

The design shows the conical-capped vegetation deity of Seler (1923), figures 122–124. The cap is always seamed in front and covers the top of the eyes; the figure has vegetation, fruits or roots, attached to it. Other examples pictured in this volume are Figures 233 and 309.

There are seven colors: W, Y, LR, DR, DBr, (G), and B. They occur as follows: lip, collar, B; background of design zone creamy W; vertical stripes separating front and back figures LR; base band DR; deity's cap LR; eyes W; face Y; body LR; belt DBr, breechclout Y; legs DR; attached fruits Y, LR, DR, and DBr. The figure on the jar side not shown has the same color disposition except that one (!) eye and the mouth are G instead of W. This is the only use of G and seems an oversight or mistake.

## *Shape P, Bulbous-Convex Vase*

There were three of these vases in this grave, or four, counting the mate (170774) of 170773. We summarize the principal comparative data.

| | 170771 | 170772 | 170773 | 170774 |
|---|---|---|---|---|
| H (mm) | 147 | 130 | 201 | 199 |
| D (mm) | 106 | 105 | 155 | 154 |
| H/D % | 137 | 124 | 130 | 129 |
| Colors | W Y LR DR DBr V G B | W Y LR DR V G B | W Y LR DR B | W Y LR DR B |
| Design | rayed heads | camelids | darts | |

We now discuss the designs and color distribution of individual vases.

**FIGURE 271, 170771 (N5); PLATE 21.** Has four rayed trophy heads on W background in an upper zone and nine pendant vertical bars on LR background in a lower. The two bands are separated by a V band; there are only three occurrences of the color, which makes it difficult to judge whether or not it is phonemic, that is, produced by a separate pigment. The heads have W rhomboidal eyes, W lips, and a narrow wormlike tongue. They are surmounted by a triple ornament of a spike flanked by bent-over rays, plus four separate such rays on each side. Below the face there also extend two hand- or paddlelike objects. The four heads vary in coloring in their repetitions, thus: face, LR , DR , LR , and G; proximal "hand," Y, DBr, Y, and LR; distal "hand," G, V, DR, and V. This yields no clear sequence pattern.

The bars in the lower zone run, from left to right (beginning with the bar at far left in Fig. 271), Y, W, DR, W, DBr, W, G, W, and DR. This analyzes into W alternating with varying dark colors, plus a single leftover Y.

It will be noted that the color V (besides its zone-dividing band) occurs twice in small areas in the upper zone, and DBr once there and twice on bars below.

The heads are of the god-trophy-head type discussed in connection with the double-spout Figure 268 (Pl. 21) from the present grave, Figure 244 from Grave 8, and Figure 262 from Grave 10.

**FIGURE 272, 170772 (N5); PLATE 20.** Also double-zoned, camelids above and barbed darts below. The upper background is G, which is unusual, from which the camelids stand out in LR, with W eye and mouth. Curious symmetrically branching W figures issue from their mouths, which three times enlarge to circles and have a LR dot in the center. Two of these circles look like bird heads, which, however, have no meaning in this context; and both total shape and the W color argue against construing the figures as blood from a lung wound. It will be remembered that in Figure 259 (of Ocongalla West B, Grave 10) the hunted camelids also had branching protrusions before their mouths.

In the lower zone, on W ground, are two rows of eight darts each. They are staggered, but identical color ties each upper dart with the lower to its left. These pairs, left to right, run LR, V, LR, DR, LR, Y, DR, and G. This starts out as a LR-and-other alternation, but the sequence breaks down—a not infrequent Nazca happening.

The horizontal bands on this vase are, downward, Y at the rim (below a black lip line), LR in middle, and B below.

**FIGURE 273, 170773–74 (N5).** The first of the pair of mates illustrated by Figure 273 is above average size for a *P* vase but is single-zoned for representation and has only five colors, G being absent. The zone extends over more than half the height, below which is a solid DR band for about a sixth of the height, the remainder being unpainted. The design is of a continuous band confined above and below by a border band of LR rising above (and falling below) into about twelve triangles, reminiscent of the scallops or spike series that often delimit the upper edge of the back or wing of cat and bird deities in phase *B* painting. The total enclosed area is then divided into five nearly square panels by LR vertical bars. Each panel contains three horizontal darts or arrows, varicolored with B barbed points. Adjoining the butts, each panel background is B; at the tips, W. The dart colors, from above down, are: DR, Y, DR, Y, and Y; LR, LR, LR, LR, and LR; Y, DR, Y, DR, and DR.

This pattern changes into a three-color sequence in panels 1 and 3, with the reverse in 2, 4, and 5. The design zone general background is W; it is separated from the wide DR band below by a narrower Y band. The bottom of the DR band falls at the maximum diameter of the vase. Both design and execution lack grace; there is no elegance in either darts or frame, and the B and W halving of the panels is unnecessarily crass. A clumsy effect is produced by there being no taper of diameter down from the mouth to a minimum just below it; even a shrinkage of a mm or two here would have helped the shape, as in the two preceding vases.

## *Waisted Goblet*

**FIGURE 274, 170764 (N5).** One of a pair of shape-*J3* waisted goblets (or near-bowl goblets) with three zones of design. H 83 mm, maximum D (at mouth) 95 mm, minimum D (at waist) 66 mm, bottom D 71 mm, yielding ratios of H/D 87%, minimum D/maximum D 70%, bottom D/maximum D 75%. The colors are the usual six plus LBr. Not showing in Figure 274 is the exterior bottom, which is quartered DR and W. The background of the lowest zone on the side is DR; for the two upper zones, it can probably be construed as W. The design of the lowest zone consists of W pendant bars. The two upper zones have the same design, a complementary step-fret variant, the lower one slightly smaller.

This design can be construed in two ways. In the first case, the alternate W step-blocks are considered as background. Intervening is a series of step-frets plus a differently colored fill-in of the fret end. The units (fret color first, fill-in second) are DR-LR, Y-LR, LR-DR, G-LR, DR-LR, LBr-DR, LR-DR, and Y-LR. This gives two Y, two LR, two DR, one LBr, and one G frets. The only pattern visible is DR, Y, LR, and G, with Y and G interchanged on the repeat and LBr substituted for G. The fill-ins are five LR, three DR.

In the second case, the design is without background and consists of continuous complementary step-frets of which alternate ones are W, but with their tails (fret ends) cut off and colored (the fill-ins). This imposes a pattern of triple-color contrast on a pattern of complementary or double form in the design unit. This construal probably reflects the history of the development of the design, but the eye sees more readily the first construal.

We have found this variant of the complementary step-fret band, or closely related ones, also in *D*-bowl Figure 280 below, and in Grave 10, Figures 261 and 263.

## *High Flaring Bowls, Shape H*

There were, in this Grave 12, five high flaring *H*-shape bowls, two pairs and a single. We illustrate opposite sides of one pair in order to give the full design, although the two vessels of this pair differ appreciably in size. The group is ranked by proportional height.

| | H (MM) | D (MM) | H/D | COLORS |
|---|---|---|---|---|
| 170776 | 154 | 204 | 75 | W Y LR DR DBr G B |
| 170775 | 137 | 200 | 69 | W Y LR DR DBr G B |
| 170779 | 82 | 138 | 59 | W Y LR DR G B |
| 170770/69 | 63 | 109 | 58 | W LR DR LBr B |

**FIGURES 275, PLATE 17; and 276, 170775–6 (N5).** Almost the full design of this large and high pair is visible; the staff and right hand are repeated, and a middle section of the body is omitted. While the head is in erect position, the striped body, as shown by the feet, is prone. Above it is a "backbone" of darts that curves down and then up in a tail, which in turn ends in a cat-deity head upside down. Above this is a row of erect spikes with profile trophy heads between. Beyond the figure's feet, the spikes and trophy heads transfer to the underside of the tail—probably in answer to a problem of space and not for any symbolic reason. It will be observed that the mates vary most in height. Vessel 170776, which we use to show the tail end of the design, is perceptibly higher to the eye as well as by measure.

The color placing is background W; main head (downward), headdress DR, forehead LR, eye area DR, mouth mask LR, necklace DR; right and left arm and hand, DR; staff Y with LR transverse areas; trophy heads above body between LR spikes successively are DBr, Y, DR, LR, G, Y, DR, LR, and G; cat-deity head on the tail has headdress DR, face Y, hands (paws) DR with W nails.

This is about as large as *H* bowls ordinarily come. (Kroeber 1956, 368, cites one with D 227 mm, as against 204 here, but the next largest there is only 173 mm.)

We do not discern a single design element on these two bowls that is exclusively *B2* in phase, though it is true that darts, spikes, and so forth, do occur in *B1*. The generic cat-deity design goes back to Nazca *A*, as does the *F-H* shape group of high flaring bowls. This pair of pieces is well executed and polished, no doubt had value and may have been heirlooms. In any event, if followed traditional models.

**FIGURE 277, 170779 (N5).** *F-H* bowl proportionally lower than the last pair, and the simple double-zoned design is wholly *B2* in style. The exterior bottom is quartered DR and W with LR dividing stripes. The upper zone has twelve DR spikes arising from a base stripe, and the elements between them are stalked, suggesting flowers to our eye, although they are also fairly similar to the swifts sometimes placed there. Seler (1923), figure 386, shows a similar form of interspike elements, also with trophy heads. The color sequence of the elements on the present bowl is upper object, Y, LR, Y, G, Y, Y, LR, LR, Y, Y, LR, and LR; stalk and cup, LR, G, DR, Y, LR, LR, Y, G, LR, DR, G, and Y. There is certainly no repeat order here. Y and LR occur nine times each, G four times, DR twice.

The lower zone shows a much-geometrized object consisting of a three-dotted triangle of varying colors, from the base of which a narrower B triangle streams back to end in a wavy edge. The objects may be fish, snakes, pollywogs, or overconventionalized trophy heads (compare Seler 1923, fig. 176). These latter sometimes shrink to a triangle with dots for eyes and mouth, and in other cases the B hair of trophies is a simple or indefinite mass. The face triangles are successively G, LR, Y, DR, LR, DR, Y, G, LR, Y, DR, and G, which is a random playing with the order of the four colors, although there are three occurrences of each.

**FIGURE 278, 170770 (N5).** Still smaller *H* bowl. H 63 mm, D 109 mm, H/D 58%. The LBr color occurs only in a stripe between a LR stripe and the DR base band. Its lightness in the photograph shows it as distinct from both the adjacent reds, but it might be muddied or deep Y. The bean pod design elements are alternately LR and B. Published analogues to them are in Seler (1923), figures 375–378 (mostly three-lobed as here), in Kroeber (1956), plate 45e (five-lobed), and in Kroeber and Strong (1924), plate 25h (four-lobed). This last figure shows a Nazca *A* low variant of bulging-concave vase *P* and comes from Ocucaje Site B, which is Nazca *A1*. It should be added that vertical dividers between repeating figures on bowls are also an *A* phase characteristic. However, the shape of the present vessel, with its degree of flare, is phase *B* rather than *A*. We must assume that the bean-pod design carried through.

## *Shape-D Bowls*

**FIGURE 279, 170768 (N5).** One of a pair of bowls. H 49 mm, D 118 mm, H/D 42%. This is too shallow for an *F-H* bowl (Kroeber 1956, 368), but it fits in shape class *D*, flat-bottomed flaring bowl (Kroeber 1956, 366–367, see pl. 38a–c), whose H/D ratio runs 35–47% (mean 41%). All the bowls of this type whose designs are identifiable are *B* phase. But the present design is seen in other cases of phase *A* (see Kroeber and Strong 1924, pl. 26e, pl. 27c). We seem accordingly to have a phase *A* design (or at least one that originated then) on a phase *B* shape, which is about the situation for the preceding piece.

The sixteen diamonds are outlined in B. Beginning with a LBr one, they group thus:

| | | | |
|---|---|---|---|
| LBr | G | LR | |
| LBr | G | LR | |
| LBr | DBr | LR | |
| LBr | DBr | LR | |
| LBr | DBr | LR | G |

This suggests that DBr and G were based on the same pigment, or were like enough in appearance to replace each other. The extra unit is attributed to the Nazca habit of letting a circuit come out as it happens instead of calculating or estimating ahead. The listed color scheme is W, LR, LBr, DBr, G, and B, which is unusual in having two browns but no Y.

**FIGURE 280, 170762 (N5).** One of another pair of flat-bottomed flaring bowls of shape *D*, more flat and larger bottomed than the last and therefore less flaring, is illustrated in Figure 280. This is only 58 mm high, but 173 in diameter, with a H/D ratio of 34%. This is low for shape *D*, whose previously measured lower limit is 35% (Kroeber 1956, 367), but also low for shape *E*, which goes down to 37% (1956, 365). Shape *E* is normally phase *A*, whereas *D* is phase *B*. The design, however, is definitely phase *B* in this bowl. It is a continuous band of complementary step-frets with the W ones having the interlocking tail of their fret changed to B; the LR ones are LR all through; so there is an asymmetrical effect, as in the waisted goblet 170764 described above from this grave.

The colors are five: W, LR, G in the design, B only in the outlining, and DR only in stripes at base and lip.

The diagonal steps in the center of Figure 280 are the result of crowding, not of a desire for variety: the painter had not left space enough for the last step to be square.

## *Plates Ar, Inside-Painted on Rim Only*

**FIGURE 281, 170765 (N5).** One of a pair that includes 170766 is a rim-painted plate of aberrant shape class *Ar* [not shown in Fig. 90; see Kroeber 1956, 351]. The *Ar* shape is of *B* phase, contrasting with the center-painted plates *Ac* of phase *A*. H 63 mm, D 189 mm, H/D 33%. The colors are W, Y, LR, DR, and B. Of these, DR is used only at the rim of the plate. The center is unpainted reddish buff. This is bordered by a W line. Then the rim zone was painted solid B, on which W, Y, and LR were overpainted. The LR fared the worst in this, or partly came off; hence the bodies of the tadpoles or salamander larvae (as in Seler 1923, fig. 319) are scarcely visible. Their feathery gills were done in W, which shows much better; as does the Y of the single triple cross and of the very irregular quadrilateral, pairs of which intervene between successive larvae, and whose denotation remains problematical. There are ten larvae in the circuit.

Overpainting on black is uncommon in Nazca ceramics, but it goes back to phase *A*. Compare Kroeber and Strong (1924), plates 26b, 28m, 29c, and 29g; probably also Kroeber (1956), plates 43d, 45b, and 46g. These are all early Nazca; but the rim-painted plate is definitely late *B*. Compare also Figure 246, 170713, in Grave 9 of the present site.

Thus we have in most of the bowls and plates of this grave some features of shape or design that look retained from phase *A* alongside others that are definitely *B2* in style. It is not clear why this should be true particularly of bowls, unless it is because they no longer received primary interest from the makers.

### *Undecorated Spheroid Jars*

Grave 12 also contained three pairs of undecorated, unhandled spherical jars, 170755–56, 170757–58, and 170759–69. All six vessels are unslipped buff in color, with a very thin wash of white. [None of these vessels have use-wear markings; if utilized outside of the mortuary context it must have been for liquid or dry storage.]

**FIGURE 282 and 283, 170758 (N5) and 170760 (N5).** The two pairs from which these illustrations were made are respectively somewhat larger (225 mm high) and smaller (194 mm high) than the preceding numbered. The D of these two are 237 mm and 180 mm so that in 170758 H is exceeded by D (95%), in 170760 the reverse (108%). Measurement on the photographs shows other minor difference in proportion.

| | LIP D/MAX. D (%) | NECK D/MAX. D (%) | COLLAR H/MAX. H (%) |
|---|---|---|---|
| 170758 | 43 | 39 | 8 |
| 170760 | 53 | 49 | 6 |

The first of the two (170758, Fig. 282) is more definitely shaped, and if slipped, polished, and painted would be an acceptable *S*-shape jar; whereas, on the basis of mouth, the second vessel (170760, Fig. 283) would be *R* shape, except that it is too high and the collar is too indecisive to fit the class very well. Both jars seem somewhat heavier than most painted Nazca vessels. The thickness of the ware is around 10 mm in 170758, 7 mm in 170760.

We know very little about Nazca-style utility pottery. Perhaps these jars replace in period *B* the three-handled *TTT* shape of phase *A*, which evidently served to hold or carry water and therefore were only partly and simply painted. It is also noteworthy that these six jars come from the richest grave discovered in the cemetery at Ocongalla West B and that no similar jar appeared in poorer or shallower phase *B2* graves.

### Ocongalla Zero

This site must be distinguished from Ocongalla West A and West B (Fig. 11). It was the first site excavated by the expedition in Nazca Valley. Six graves were opened (Fig. 12), all presumably of phase *B2*, although one (Grave 5, 80 cm deep) contained no artifacts. Grave 3 contained two bodies: at 60–80 cm an infant in a pot with two vessels; and at 180–200 cm was an adult with some fragments of plain white cloth and three vessels. All five of the ceramic pieces, however, were *B2*. Graves 1, 2, 4, and 6 were respectively 225, 225, 270, and 290 cm deep and contained one vessel each, or a pair of mates in Grave 4.

Near the graves, in the upper 50 cm of the soil, was what seemed to be part of a house wall or enclosure, from which some canes and cord were recovered (170426) as well as a pair of corner posts (170425); also a skewerlike piece of wood, a fragment of cotton cloth, a broken crystal (170427–29), and some sherds (170424). These remains seem to have been from a Late Period [Late Intermediate Period] occupation not connected with and probably ignorant of the *B2* burials near by.

#### *Grave 1*

**FIGURE 284, 170409 (EARLY N5).** A near-bowl goblet, shape *J3* as in Kroeber (1956), page 345, found at the left foot of the skeleton. The proportions are H 119 mm; maximum D (at base) 136; minimum D (waist) 110; mouth D 128. These yield percentage proportions of H/maximum D 88%; minimum D/maximum D 81%; and mouth D/maximum D 94%. Measurements on the photograph make minimum D/maximum D 84% and put the position of the minimum D at 25% of the total H down from the rim. The proportions are intermediate between *F-H* bowls (which are lower, flare more, and have rounder bottoms) and waisted goblets of shape *J* (which are taller, flatter at the bottom, and show a definite minimum diameter or waist). Shape class *J3* was set up in 1956 to accommodate three phase *B* vessels from the cemetery at Ocongalla West B (Graves 3, 4, and 12) and Uhle's Ocucaje F2 piece (Kroeber and Strong 1924, pl. 28j). The present 170409 will now have to be added to the group, which occurs in phases *A*, *B1*, and *B2*.

The pattern zone, including its borders, has a height of 66% of the total height of vessel. There are five colors in the painted design: W, B, Y, LR, and DR. It shows, although hardly recognizably, the bird with large down-pointing profile head, one eye between upper and lower beak. From the trophy-head tongue a long protrusion is swung around upward to become a trident, each prong ending in a bent-over ray. This last feature makes the vessel B2 in phase by our criterion. The bird figure is repeated four times in the design panel. In one repetition, the tongue ends bluntly instead of in a trident. The DR and W (slip) areas mostly are the same in repeats of the figure, the Y and LR areas mostly alternate; B is used only in outlining and on the vessels' lips. The shape of the bowl is much more elegant than the badly controlled painted design.

### *Grave 2*

**FIGURE 285, 170410 (N5).** Smallish narrow-mouthed jar of shape *S*. H 146 mm, D 155 mm. Found at left foot of body with frontally deformed head. The shape proportions are H/D 94%, lip H/total H 19%, neck D/maximum D 35%, mouth D/maximum D 48%. There are five colors: W, Y, LR, DR, and B. On the upper part of the body are two rows of wingless (fledging) birds with pinfeathers. These birds are in unbordered DR stippled with W. Their beaks are Y, outlined in B, the two-toed feet solid B. The background is W with short LR horizontal lines or dashes on the W. For flightless birds see Seler (1923), figures 300–301. Our jar was found in fragments, which, however, sufficed to restore the pot.

### *Grave 3*

**FIGURE 286, 170411 (N6).** Shape-*J2* waisted goblet. H 157 mm, D 140 mm, H/D 112%; minimum D 118 mm, minimum D/maximum D 84%. The maximum D is virtually at the lip, the minimum about one-third the way up. Height of the design band (including disk-bearing lower border) is about two-fifths of the vessel height. There are six colors, G being added to the usual five. The design is double with one repeat. Half is taken up by three tentacled deity heads in tandem connected by their tongues; they are LR, G, and LR; their five double tentacles fold over and carry forking black cactus spines. The LR camelid has a Y dart flying over its back, whereas from its mouth issues a Y bent-over jagged staff, also with forked cactus spines. There is thus an abundance of features characterizing *B2*. Again the painting is hasty and poorly controlled but the vessel shaping excellent.

**FIGURE 287, 170412 (N5/6).** *F-H* bowl 112 mm high, 167 in diameter, H/D 67%. The concavity of the sides is 4.5–5 mm (measured as per Kroeber 1956, 368, n. 21); the slope or spread of the sides from vertical is 20 degrees. This is a well-shaped vessel, W with B lip and about thirty-four units, just below the rim, of wide-stroked figures resembling the mirror image of a capital N; below each, a somewhat narrower-stroked diagonal x. The Ns are alternately LR and DR, the corresponding Xs LR and B.

This is a puzzling piece. The nearest analogue we can find is Kroeber (1956), plate 35d, described on page 390, which is from Uhle's Ocucaje Grave F3, in turn classed as of Nazca *A*-plus phase, that is, *A2*.

It is these two vessels that were with the pot-buried baby in the upper part of Grave 3. While the second is difficult to place stylistically, the first is surely *B2*. The next three vessels were more than twice as deep in the same grave with an adult skeleton.

**FIGURE 288, 170414 (N5).** Large bowl, original H about 125 mm, D about 300 mm, H/D 42%, vertical H of design band 92 mm. There is a definite turn in vessel profile at the lower edge of the design band, which would make the vessel of shape *Bd*, gambreled bowl. These *B* bowls, however, run from 127 mm to 188 mm in diameter as against 300 mm in the present piece; similarly, the vertical height of the design band in twelve *B*-shape bowls analyzed in Kroeber (1956, 363) runs from only 48 mm down to 26 mm, as against 92 mm here. The piece is just too gigantic to fit into the category of gambreled bowls. Moreover, the design painted on these is almost always of repeated small units, whereas here we have the whole cat god. Also, the gambreled bowls are typically of style *A*, while the darts with this cat god are typical of full *B*.

If we turn, alternatively, to shape *D*, the flat-bottomed flaring bowl, there is still size discrepancy, although less of it, the measured shape-*D* specimens being from 178 mm to 201 mm across. They also show a concave profile (see Kroeber 1956, pl. 38a–c). The *D* bowls mostly bear phase *B* designs, corresponding to the darts here. On the whole, the fit of the piece is better with shape *D* than with shape *Bd*, even though the oversize is certainly abnormal.

The painting is somewhat crude and hasty, executed in the six colors W, Y, LR, DR, G, and B, unless one differentiates a seventh flesh color (of the breechclout) from the Y of the whiskered mouth mask and shaft of the grasped dart.

**FIGURE 289, 170415 (EARLY N5).** Head vase of shape *Y1*, equaling bulbous-concave vase shape *Pb* converted by addition of a modeled nose, which is a phase *B* type. H is 149 mm, the maximum diameter 118 mm, H/D 126% (range of other measured specimens 125–150%), D at top about 89 mm. Above there are three bands, B, LR, and B, on white background. The face is Y, the eye and lip areas W, the painting below the eyes LR, the hair at the ears B, the back hair DR striped with B, a total of five colors.

**FIGURE 290, 170416 (N6).** Waisted goblet of shape *J1-2*, but somewhat squat. H 159 mm, mouth D 149 mm, H/D 107%, waist D/mouth D 79%. The bottom diameter equals the waist diameter, which is an aberrant feature for waisted goblets. Of the three subtypes described in Kroeber (1956, 345, 378), the present piece is nearer *J1* in its total height proportion but nearer *J2* in its low-lying waist. Subtype-*J2* occurrences seem to be late *B* in their painting, as indeed the present piece is. (For subtype *J3*, see Ocongalla West B Graves 3, 4, and 12 above.) The five colors are the usual W, Y, LR, DR, and B. The profile trophy heads above and below are very degenerately ragged and jagged; the trapezoid portion of each head is LR, the nose portion alternates between DR and Y. The wide central band of the goblet is closely filled with DR broad-stroke irregular stippling, except for two rows of reserved W circles, each containing eight or nine DR dots surrounding one larger LR one. This painting suggests very late *B* approaching *Y*. The degenerated trophy heads recall Seler (1923), figures 182–185 and 244 and are surely at least late *B*.

In this double grave, two pottery vessels, 170411 and 170416, are quite clearly late *B* stylistically, in their painting; the face jar 170415 is at least full *B*; the *B*- or *D*-shape bowl 170414 is also clearly *B* in its painting, although aberrant in shape and size; and the white *F-H* bowl 170412 has its nearest analogue in a late-Nazca-*A* specimen from Ocucaje. Also we have not observed other *F-H* bowls with specifically late-*B* painting or association, though they do continue into early *B*. One difficulty is that the pattern on the white *F-H* bowl 170412 is really too simple for sure stylistic attribution; the brush strokes by which the capital-N figures were painted might well have been decadent *B*-style. The general attribution for both burials is *B2*.

## *Grave 4*

**FIGURE 291, 170418 (N5).** The first of a pair of *N1*-shape cylindrical vases (170418–19). Actually the form approaches that of a waisted goblet, shape *J2*. The H/D of the present piece is 160% (H 147 mm, maximum D, at top, 92 mm); the *N1* proportion is around 200%, the *J2* type 130–140%. The upper diameter of 170418 exceeds the lower by 6 mm and the middle by 9 mm, so the waist constriction is slight, but elegant.

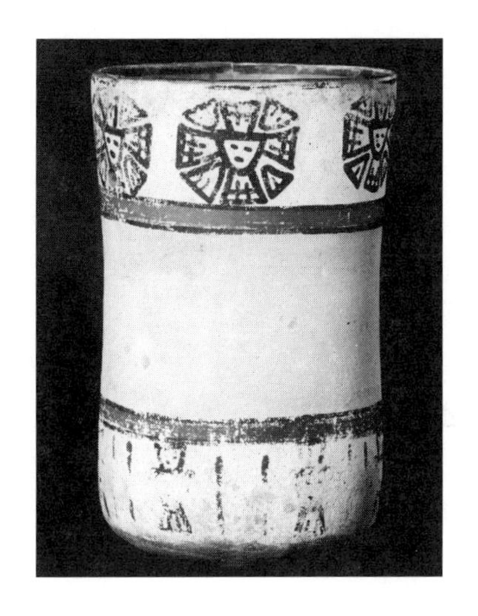

The painted design is triple-zoned, which is a feature particularly of *N2*, or triple-bulge cylindrical vases, although it also occurs in the near-cylindrical *N1* type (Gayton and Kroeber 1927, pl. 11a; compare 11b–d). The middle zone is a plain Y in color and is set off by LR bands from the upper and lower, which contain a repetition of radiating trophy heads outlined in B. Those in the bottom zone are reduced as compared with the top, and divided into panels by vertical LR lines. The colors thus are four. The outlined trophy heads (cf. Seler 1923, fig. 178 and our own Fig. 269), the zoning, the *N1* shape, and for that matter the *J2* waisted-goblet shape, are all in developed *B2* style.

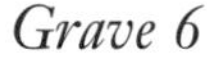

## *Grave 6*

**FIGURE 292, 170423 (N6).** Shape-*W* flaring-rim head jar. H 142 mm, D 153 mm, H/D 93%. The flaring rim accounts for nearly half the total height. The mouth D is 75% and the neck D 60% of maximum D.

There are six colors: W, Y, LR, DR, G, and B, and three zones of design. Below the rim are six complementary step-frets, alternately W-G, W-Y, and W-DR, once repeated, with additional free-floating steps within each pair. Next down but still on the flaring rim there is a true (complementary) interlocking fish (snakes) pattern, W and LR. On the pot's body is a Y almond-eyed face (trophy head?) with W eyes, LR mouth in DR lips, and on the cheeks stepped quadrilaterals of LR face paint (one mostly peeled off). Outside the face the lower zone is B. The bottom of the vessel is merely slipped. The brush strokes are firm, the colors saturated, the texture hard.

The step-frets with inserted free line of steps, the interlocking fish, the yellow full face, and shape *W* are all definitely phase *B*, mostly if not always *B2*.

## *Summary*

The five graves and the ten pottery vessels are all unqualified Nazca *B* and largely *B2* in style, except for two bowls, one associated with the upper and one with the lower body in Grave 3, that show a few features possibly reminiscent of late Nazca *A*. This stylistic discrepancy is unexplained. It may possibly be resolved when more period-dated Nazca bowls become available.

## **Agua Santa, Nazca *B* Section**

Graves 1–9 at Agua Santa were Nazca *Y* or post-Nazca in period and are described below. Graves 10–12 and 14–15 were Nazca *B2* (there was no Grave 13).

### *Grave 10*

This grave, in which at 100 cm there was seated a body with frontally flattened skull, contained three ceramic pieces, 170634–6, and a slip of incised wood, 170637 (Fig. 40). All three of the vessels are *B2* in general effect, although none of the most characteristically late-*B* design features occur.

**FIGURE 293, 170635 (N5).** Waisted goblet, whose H/D of 139% puts it into shape class *J2*, which class is taller (130–140%) and later than *J1* (90–110%). The goblet's H is 118 mm, D near base 85 mm, D in middle 77 mm, and D just below rim 83 mm.

The allover painting comes in three zones. At the top is a row of prone profile trophy heads on W background between LR spikelike dividers. The heads are successively DR, LR, and Y, this sequence being repeated. These trophy heads are similar to Seler (1923), figures 195–196. The middle zone has four horizontal stripes, DR, Y, LR, and G in order from top to bottom. From this depend six widely spaced LR bars with folded-over ends, extending across the lowest zone, which is DR. The color array is the usual one for six: W, Y, LR, DR, G, and B.

**FIGURE 294, 170634 (N5).** Tapering vase, shape *M*, H/D 185%. Height is 172 mm, bottom D 93 mm, top D 84 mm. There is no measurable actual constriction below the top; the effect is of a very gentle concavity where the slight cone-taper of the profile changes to a cylinder as it nears the rim. The painting is on a W background and uses seven colors, V in addition to the six of the last specimen. The main design is of a winged cat deity, painted twice in the dominant middle zone, with subsidiary slightly ornamented bands above and below. The face is Y, so is the scalloped back and the breechclout, while the arms and legs are G. The proximal part of the wing and the eyes are W. The pleated belly(?) is V; and B is used for all outlines, for two stripes on the W wing, and for the triple-domed top of the headdress. The remainder of the headdress is LR, W, and DR in order down; the serpent-headed feathers of the tail are respectively LR, V, W, LR, G, and DR. The head lacks mouth mask and has an archaic air about it, but many of the details are characteristic of the developed *B* period. A similar creature is shown in Seler (1923), figure 90.

**FIGURE 295, 170636 (N5).** Vase which is neither quite shape *M* (tapering) nor *N1* (cylindrical). H 146 mm, D 90 mm, H/D 162%. The greatest diameter is near the bottom. The diameter at top is 90% of this, and at the constriction (a little way down) 87%. The constriction thus is real, in which respect the shape is like that of a waisted-goblet *J*, even though higher up and accompanied by greater slenderness of the profile than *J* vessels have. The shape would be straight *N1* except for showing a taper-plus-flare profile instead of a cylindrical one; and the flare at the top is too slight for it to be counted in *N2*, which has three rounded curves and two concavities in its silhouette. This is not a badly turned-out piece, but it falls between several shape classes.

The design is zoned but very simple. The two upper zones are W with light design; the lowest is solid DR. The upper-zone design and the lip are B; the middle-zone designs, spaced pairs of diagonally crossed lines, are LR. The upper zone contains two bands of encircling pattern: parallel festooned lines, concave upward, with three dots above each concavity, possibly derived from outlined trophy heads. Color scheme: W, LR, DR, and B.

## *Grave 11*

**FIGURE 296, 170639 (N5).** Waisted goblet *J2*. H 168 mm, maximum D (at rim) 127 mm, H/D 132%; waist D 100 mm, base D 106 mm, waist/rim D 79%, base/rim D 83%.

Six colors: W, Y (pale or flesh), LR, DR, G, and B. There are three zones of decoration. Upper zone, band of five complementary step-blocks separated by W slanting zigzag band of free-floating, intervening steps. The steps of the blocks are set at an acute angle; their borders are prolonged into the block. The right-hand (hanging) blocks are Y; the left-hand ones are successively G, LR, LR, DR, and LR. This design occurs also in phase *Y1*. Middle zone, solid DR, bordered by B-lined Y stripe above and below. Lowest zone, a W simple rectangular meander, with DR field above, LR below, lower edge of meander (toward LR) outlined in B. For the total vessel, shape and painting agree: phase *B2*.

## *Grave 12*

The two vessels in Grave 12 also show decisive *B2* stigmata.

**FIGURE 297, 170640 (N6).** Waisted goblet *J*, intermediate in its proportions between *J1* (H/D 90–110%) and *J2* (H/D 130–140%). H 173 mm, D 152 mm, H/D 114%. The vessel is not complete, but measurements on the photograph suggest that there was no actual constriction, only a slow increase of diameter from the minimum at the bottom, to nearly halfway up, then an ever more rapid increase to the top. The profile is definitely and elegantly concave, but only *seems* constricted.

The design is in six colors (W, Y, LR, DR, G, and B) and in three zones.

The upper zone has facing pairs of step-blocks separated by W background—very similar to the free or intervening steps on goblet 170639 in Grave 11. The block pairs are mostly DR-LR, varied occasionally to G-LR.

The middle zone twice depicts a tentacled deity, probably flying. Eyes, mouth, and tongue appear twice at the head, facing both forward and back. The face with tentacles or rays (ends folded over) has a long angled tongue of jagged-staff type. There are cactus spines all over, thick, longish, and even three-pronged!

The bottom zone contains eleven supine profile trophy heads, with long hanging B locks, quite crude, somewhat resembling Seler (1923), figure 191. The color sequence is two LR, two DR, two LR, two G, one LR, and two Y.

**FIGURE 298, 170641 (N6).** Another waisted goblet, at the border of *J2* proportion. 170 mm, D about 130 mm, H/D 131%. While the vessel is incomplete, there is an absolute decrease of diameter at the waist, which is about 7% less than at the bottom, and 19% less than at the rim (estimated).

There are only three colors, W, LR, and B, and the painting is very crude. Most of the design zone is B; on this is an elaborate, barely recognizable deity (head?) with tentacles, overpainted in W. Below is a W band containing B-outlined LR figures, butterfly-shaped. A pair of cactus spines on each may be antennae. The bottom of the vessel is unslipped buff. All the design painting is hasty and slovenly, and both vessels are close to *B1* in style and quality.

## *Grave 14*

**FIGURE 299, 170642 (N5).** Tapering vase *M*. H 197 mm, D 135 mm, H/D 146%. The rim D is around 84% of the maximum D about one-third up the vessel's height. In spite of the concave profile, there is no actual constriction, only a diminishing taper.

The colors are the usual six: W, Y (flesh), LR, DR, G, B. They are applied with a degree of neatness. The design is in four zones, on W slip. Zone 1, at rim, a dozen or more Y trapezoidal figures with rounded top alternately LR and DR, with B dividers. Zone 2, widest, contains four rectangular deity or trophy heads, half-eyed, oblong-mouthed, with the tongue and four parallel tentacles represented as darts. Successive faces are G, Y, Y, and DR. The tongue and outside darts are all LR; the medial darts (second and fourth) are Y, except for one DR on the third face, one G on the fourth. Mouth and eyes are W; forehead band, LR. Zone 3 repeats zone 1 inverted. Zone 4, at bottom, solid DR. Below this the bottom is unpainted.

This vessel seems stylistically somewhat stiff and precise. The grave was not excavated by the expedition, but the vase was bought from a workman living nearby who pointed out its provenience.

## *Grave 15*

Graves 14, 15, and 16 at Agua Santa were not excavated by the 1926 expedition, but by a local peon who alleged he had previously dug them up there; he sold about ten pottery vessels to the expedition as having been found in three tombs near the phase *B2* tombs excavated by the expedition (Fig. 37). Consistency of style among and especially within the three lots is the obvious precondition for credence due his allegation. His Grave 14 held one *B2* vessel. Grave 15 held four, all excellent and clearly *B2* stylistically; so this lot can be treated with probability as if it were a genuine grave. The lot called Grave 16, however, contained *A* as well as *B* vessels and is evidently a synthetic mixture of pots from graves of different period. We now describe the four *B2* vessels called Grave 15.

**FIGURE 300, 170643 (N5).** Shape *Pb* bulbous-concave vase. H 174 mm, D (lower half) 119 mm, minimum D (toward top) 105 mm, lip D 109 mm; H/D 146%, min. D/max. D 88%, lip D/max. D 92%; the concavity toward the top is a real constriction, not a mere seeming one owing to the outward bulge below. Colors W, LR, DR, and B. The slip is W; the design consists of three horizontal bands painted on, giving five zones: DR, W, LR, W, and DR. These are separated by B lines, and the lip edge is B.

**FIGURE 301, 170644 (N6).** Vase very similar to the *Pb* one just described but without bulge below and only minimal constriction above, so it best fits shape type *M*, tapering vase (discussed in Kroeber 1956, 345–346). When a difference of two or three millimeters more-or-less of D in profile can throw a vessel from one shape type into another, it may seem that the basis classification must be overly artificial. We think, however, that the shape types or classes have genuine aesthetic validity, but when two or more classes are fairly close together in silhouette, a very slight increase of concavity here or convexity there will alter vessels enough in effect to warrant their description by another name or letter symbol. In other words, the ancient Nazcans probably did not consciously distinguish or name all our classes, but they unconsciously aimed at certain modal points of shape and then let execution flow back and forth between these by transitions.

In the present case, H is 158 mm, max. D just above the turn of the base is 103 mm, waist D (high up) is 92 mm, lip D 93 mm; yielding H/D 153%, rim D/base D 90%, min. D/base D 89%. Remeasurement on the photograph of the two upper diameters confirms that the difference is not over a millimeter and may be less. For all nonaesthetic purposes, the sides of the vessel run straight upward with a perceptible overall taper of 10%; but if the potter had made the silhouette lineally straight, the aesthetic effect would have been quite different and rigid. Or if he or she had left the upper half as it is, but had bulged the lower half out only one mm more on each side, the upper half would by contrast have looked much more concave and the silhouette more flowing.

The colors are seven: W, F, LR, V (instead of usual DR?), LBr, G, and B. The V is "dark, muddy, almost purple." The F is clearly distinct from W, but may correspond to Y in descriptions of other vessels. The design disposition is in seven zones. Zones 1, 3, 5, and 7 are W slipped, overpainted with supine profile trophy heads in 1 and 5, with two rows of B-outlined squares bisected by B diagonal steps in zone 3, and without design in zone 7, the base. Zones 2, 4, and 6 are plain F (Y?). The seven trophy heads in both zones are much distorted by long previous hasty rendition. We think the projecting point above represents the forehead-nose line; and the two short vertical lines below the end of the forehead are the closed eyelid of the trophy; beyond this is a W crescent that we cannot identify; and then, radiating out from this, are B lines (three of them double width and forking at the end), which evidently represent strands or locks of hair. An irregularly quadrilateral or triangular (unoutlined) blob below, at the nape or occiput, may originally have represented a mass of hair; but if so, the painter of this vase had forgotten its significance, since she or he regularly varied its color to contrast with the skin of the face, whereas human hair is invariably B in Nazca ceramic representation so far as we know. The color contrasts are (face before diagonal, blob after), beginning with left head in Figure 301, top row: LBr-V, V-LBr, G-V, LR-V, V-LR, LR-defaced, and G-V; and in bottom row: V-LR, LR-V, G-V, V-LR, LR-V, V-LR, and G-V. The total frequencies are LBr two, LR eight, V thirteen, and G four. The appearance of LBr in only one pair of adjacent heads raises the question whether it was there capriciously but deliberately substituted for LR by the painter or happened to come out somewhat denser or dirtier in this pair and was then read by us as a separate LBr pigment. The most common combination is of LR and V, usually inverted in the following head and reinverted in the third. Gray occurs four times, always for the face only and always with V as counterpart; its occurrences are spaced about as evenly and far apart as a total of seven figures allows. The rest of the pattern is free minor variation of combination and place in series, in typical Nazca manner.

**FIGURE 302, 170646 (N5).** Trophy-head vase *Y1* or *Pb* (bulbous-concave vase *P* with modeled-on nose); the two shapes come to the same thing. This piece is standard in every way except for being at the upper limit of its type in tallness and consequent slenderness: H 226 mm, D 152 mm, H/D 149%, lip D/body D (at lower edge of eyes) 85%, and this ratio persists for about the upper fifth of the total height, which thus is fully cylindrical. The tallness of this piece suggests that it was made in full or late *B2* phase.

**FIGURE 303, 170645 (N6).** The fourth piece in this lot, an angled goblet of shape *I* whose upper edge rises into four scallops and thus appears quadrilateral, although the base is cylindrical. H 98 mm, D at base also 98 mm, max. D 151 mm; H/max. D 65%, H/base D 100%, rim D/base D 154%. It is evident that this piece, and angled goblets as a class, are not far from flaring bowls of *F-H* type (Fig. 90). Roughly, they also tend to replace them in phase, bowl shapes *F-H* flourishing in Nazca *A*, and *I* goblets in *B2* and going on into *Y1* under the type designation *AGY* (Fig. 91), in which the angle is usually exaggerated, in comparison with the *B2* form of *I*.

The colors are seven: a yellowish buff slip, W (for eyes), LR, DR, V (muddy, toward tan, first construed as LBr), G, and B.

The upper design is of a cat deity with extended paws, a trophy head hanging down his back, legs, wing of rectangular feathers, and a staff. This is a design that basically goes back to Nazca *A1*, and in fact pre-Nazca Paracas, but the execution here is modified to conform to the manner of advanced phase *B2:* eyes cut off by forehead band to resemble deity trophy head (plus repeated or false eyes above headband); headdress of bent-over rays; the worn or suspended second trophy head as large and elaborate as the first; cactus spines (mostly forking) around the peripheries; and staff enlarged jaggedly into two pairs of quadrilaterals. All these are characteristic *B2* stigmata. The color distribution is hands or paws B; mouth mask of cat whiskers V; forehead band and rayed headdress LR; face and rays of second had V; rump or breechcloth B but containing two LR areas; legs DR; blunt wing feathers successively LR, V, and W; zigzag staff LR. On the rear, the color distribution is the same except that the three feathers are LR, V, and G—which last thus appears on one side and in one spot only. The two deities do not quite cover the round of the vessel, so there is a small abbreviation of the main figure (in B outlines and LR triangles) inserted as filler.

In the lower zone of the vessel is a line of nine supine profile trophy heads somewhat like those of Figure 301, but facing in opposite direction and wearing what looks like a tall headdress (compare the headdress in Kroeber 1956, pl. 40a, which also shows hair in strands or locks). This headdress is rendered in LR, the face in V, and the hair, of course, B.

This goblet in Figure 303 shows certain phase *Y1* features: the yellow-brown slip or background color (Gayton-Kroeber 1927, pl. 9d, 15d); the quadrangularity (ibid., pl. 9d, 13e, 15c, 15d, and 16a); the false eyes anticipatory of the single eye in *Y1* deliquescent amoeboid heads (below). But as *B2* and *Y1* were contiguous, and one merged into the other, some *Y1* features undoubtedly began to occur in *B2*. There still is in this piece a complexity of design and a control of its execution which entitle it to be attributed to *B2* like the rest of its lot, which aim at a simpler product and therefore seem to come out somewhat less advanced in stage.

## Soisongo C, Grave 5

This is clearly a *B2* tomb, containing five vessels at 300 cm.

**FIGURE 304, 170837 (N5).** A handled or *T*-shape jar. H 179 mm, D 183 mm, D mouth 77 mm, D neck 67 mm, H of collar 27 mm. These yield proportions of H/D 98%, mouth D/max. D 42%, neck D/max. D 37%, H collar/total H 15%. Colors six: W, Y, LR, DR, G, and B. A cat deity is painted on W background on each side, facing right—left is usual. There is a DR trophy head projecting from the mouth-masked deity's head; its eyes are cut off. From the trophy head issue five darts: LR, Y, G, LR, and Y. The four-striped or pleated body is Y and dotted; loincloth (not showing in photograph) is Y.

**FIGURE 305, 170838 (N5).** Waisted goblet of shape *J* (between *J1* and *J2*) which got laterally flattened, especially above, while its clay was still wet. The result is that it is oval instead of circular in cross-section: about 115 mm x 93 mm at the mouth (average 104 mm), 97–102 mm (average 100 mm) at bottom. With H 118 mm, H/average D is about 113% at the mouth and about 118% at the bottom. The waist is definitely concave, but not heavily so. Colors six: W, Y, LR, DR, V, and B. The V appears in top headdress and chin band of the deity, both of which are G. Along the top of the body are LR spines, and between these inverted Y trophy heads.

Cat-deity representations change slowly through the sequence of Nazca culture phases, and it might be difficult to define in either Figure 304 or 305 criteria distinctive of *B2* as against *B1*. But the remaining three vessels from the grave are unqualifiedly *B2*.

**FIGURE 306, 170839 (N5).** *Pb* bulbous-concave vase. H 157 mm, body D 118 mm, mouth and waist D each 100 mm (i.e., concave profile but no actual constriction); H/D 133%, mouth D/body D 85%. Colors six: W, F, LR, DR, G, and B. There are two horizontal zones of pattern each containing about eighteen repeats of what to modern eyes inevitably suggests a human fetus, but whose meaning to ancient Nazcans we cannot divine; they might be peculiar distortions of human trophy heads, that most persistent of Nazca symbols. The upper and lower row vary only in colors: upper, B with F eyes and LR pupils; lower, DR with F eyes and B pupils. The four bands are, from top down, DR, LR, G, and B; lip also B; background W.

**FIGURE 307, 170840 (N5).** Another bulbous-concave *(Pb)* vase, slightly smaller than the last, slightly less bulbous below, slightly less concave-seeming above. There is in fact no actual concavity, since by measure the vessel continues to taper very slightly all the way to its mouth. H 150 mm, body D 110 mm, H/D 136%; the mouth D is 88% of body D. The vessel is thus a bit slenderer than the preceding and a bit nearer a cylinder. The design zone occupies much the same proportion of the surface as in the last, but is in a single broad zone. In this is the horizontal figure of a personage or deity without mouth mask but carrying two zigzag or jagged staves. His headdress and penis show rhombus rays. The design colors are nine: W, Y, LR, DR, LBr, DBr, V, G, and B. The repeat on the opposite side of the design shown in Figure 307 aims at reproducing the lines but deliberately varies the color in the corresponding area. As this is one of the technical aesthetic devices of the Nazca ceramic painter (and textile embroiderer), we give the color correspondence in full.

| | | | |
|---|---|---|---|
| head and headdress | Y | LR | |
| outline of body and arms | LBr | V | |
| two panels in body | B | B | (same) |
| left staff above | LBr | DR | |
| left staff below | DR | LBr | |
| right staff above | LBr | G | |
| right staff below | LR | Y | (same) |
| belt | V | Y | |
| breechcloth | LR | LR | (same) |
| penis | Y | DBr | |
| legs | G | DR | |

**FIGURE 308, 170841 (N5).** Example of the rather infrequent although recognized shape *Q*, lipless jars. The greatest diameter is low down; then the vessel rounds in profile into an almost straight inward slope to the rimless mouth, a slight concavity being just perceptible. H 104 mm, D 132 mm, mouth D 75 mm, H/D 79%, mouth D/max. D 57%. These proportions are close to those of other measured phase *B* examples (Kroeber 1956, 351–353). The colors are four: W, LR, DR, and B, but mainly W background with B outline designs (lacework). The LR is limited to center stripes and tongues of serpents; DR, to a radiating disk or head very low on the side. The main design is of heart-shaped faces with about fourteen appendaged rectangles (probably fruits or food) radiating out from the faces. Below and between the faces are worm-shaped, jagged-edge serpents.

The last three vessels make this grave unmistakably Nazca *B2*.

## Cantayo M, Grave 2

[There were two pots found in this grave, both of phase *B2* as previously defined. The original discussion of these vessels has not been located. Descriptions are below.]

**FIGURE 309, 170983 (N5).** Shape *P*. H 167 mm, D 135 mm, H/D 124%. Colors seven: W, Y, F, LR, DR, G, and B. Design: conical-capped vegetation deity; compare with Figures 233 and 270, and Seler (1923), figures 122–124.

**FIGURE 310, 170984 (N5).** Shape *S*. H 155 mm, base D 169 mm, base of neck D 54 mm, rim D 74 mm, H/D 92%, neck D/base D 32%, rim D/base D 44%. Colors six: LBr, DBr, G, W, Y, and B. Design: cat deity, similar to Figures 304 and 305.

## Nasca *B2* from Tunga

Figures 311–316 (Pl. 24) picture a series of Nazca *B2* vessels purchased at Tunga, the southernmost of the tributaries of the Río Grande. They are probably all from one cemetery—certainly from one period—but unaccompanied by data.

**FIGURE 311, 171349 (N7).** Narrow-mouthed, lenticular *S*-shape jar. H 107 mm, D 153 mm, H/D 70%, lip and neck respectively 25–26% and 22% of D. Colors five: W, Y, LR, DR, and B. Design: three Y-faced deities, bent-over rays, spines, attached fruits, with heads curiously cleft above. Collar B, lower wide band DR below B stripe.

**FIGURE 312, 171350 (N7).** Shape *C*, flaring-sided bowl. H 77 mm, D 142 mm, H/D 54%. Five colors: W, Y, LR, DR, and B. Bottom quartered DR and Y divided by LR stripes. Design: trophy heads with mouth mask, bent-over long rays, spines; one of the two adds Y to LR, DR, and B. The *C* bowls (Kroeber 1956, 366–377) are a *B2* type but average lower than this piece, and their design is normally geometric; but this one is at least highly angular.

**FIGURE 313, 171352 (N7).** *L*-shape conical goblet. H 136 mm, D at mouth 123 mm, H/D 111%. Six colors: W, Y, LR, DR, G, and B. Bottom quartered W and Y. At rim, band of supine trophy heads alternately LR and Y. Main middle zone contains two deity trophy heads, one in five colors, the other lacking Y, general design similar to Figure 312, but squarer; mouth mask, trident tongue, bent-over rays, and spines.

**FIGURE 314, 171353 (N6); PLATE 23.** Shape *N1*, double-zoned cylindrical vase. H 203 mm, D 103 mm at mouth and again two-thirds of the way to bottom, H/D 197%; D at neck about 9% less. Colors six: W, Y, LR, DR, G, and B. There are two zones of design. The lower contains seven pendent units, foliage-like; half of each is LR, the other half Y, DR, G, Y, DR, Y, and G in succession; subject of representation is uncertain. The larger upper zone contains three repetitions of a dancing hunter(?) carrying what is probably an atlatl on which stands a parrot(?); his other hand holds three darts, below which is another parrot walking on the ground; compare Seler (1923), figures 133–134. The turbans are LR, DR, and Y; men's heads and trunks DR; sash and breechclout Y; legs G; and birds LR. Seler's figures are also mainly naked, except for a high hat and breechclout with sash.

**FIGURES 315, 171354 (N7) and 316, 171355 (N7) or PLATE 24.** The first of two four-zoned cylindrical vases, bulging three times, and hence shape *N2*. Figure 315 dimensions are H 209 mm, D at mouth 113 mm, H/D 185%; D at middle is a little less than at mouth, and near bottom again slightly less. The colors are five: W, Y, LR, G, and B; it is DR that is lacking. Upper-zone design: two rayed trophy heads abbreviated, with folded-over and pointed rays, spines and blood(?) in mouth. Second and bottom zone: women's heads, full face, Y, with W eyes and mouth, LR cheek paint. Third zone: series of squares of interlaced wavy lines alternately LR and B, perhaps representing blood(?) as in zone 1.

Figure 316 is similar *N2* but more slender and elegant. H 186 mm, mouth D 94 mm, H/D 198%; D at base a shade greater than at mouth. Colors same as in Figure 315 but with the usual DR present, that is, six hues in all, clear, painting sharp. The second and fourth zones contain women's Y faces, as in preceding vase, with similar cheek paint (or tears?). The third zone contains repetitions of an element with W trident folded-over rays at each end, perhaps allied to the plant represented in Seler (1923), figures 220, 410–412. The upper zone, widest, depicts a battle scene with darts and slingshots(?) flying and a victor seizing the vanquished by the hair; on the side not showing, one man has been beheaded. The general subject is something like Seler (1923), figure 137.

These six pieces are obviously all *B2* in phase. The following are less certain.

## Tunga: Period Not Certain

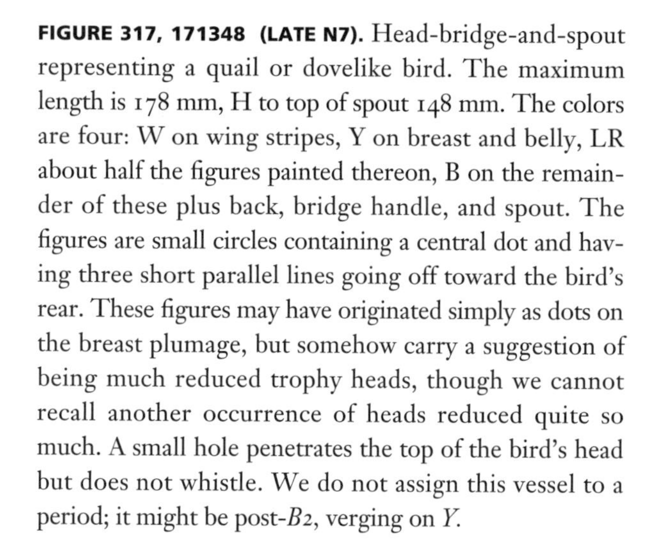

**FIGURE 317, 171348 (LATE N7).** Head-bridge-and-spout representing a quail or dovelike bird. The maximum length is 178 mm, H to top of spout 148 mm. The colors are four: W on wing stripes, Y on breast and belly, LR about half the figures painted thereon, B on the remainder of these plus back, bridge handle, and spout. The figures are small circles containing a central dot and having three short parallel lines going off toward the bird's rear. These figures may have originated simply as dots on the breast plumage, but somehow carry a suggestion of being much reduced trophy heads, though we cannot recall another occurrence of heads reduced quite so much. A small hole penetrates the top of the bird's head but does not whistle. We do not assign this vessel to a period; it might be post-*B2*, verging on *Y*.

**FIGURE 318, 171351 (N5).** Seeming *F*-shape bowl, which is a phase *A* form. H 103 mm, D 144 mm, H/D 72%. Colors six: W, Y, LR, DR, V, and B. Four birds, probably parrots; wing edge LR; wing feathers, in order down, V, LR, Y, and DR; tail and beak B; spotted body LR and Y in alternate birds. The scalloped wing edge and the feathers with face suggestions or a spur on their tips, are definitely Nazca *B*, although more likely *B1* than *B2*. The procession of free-standing birds certainly recalls Nazca *A*. We leave the bowl's phase unassigned. It certainly does not seem to be *B2*.

### Nasca *B2* from Taruga

At Taruga, which is the stream next south of the Nazca River, an assembled collection was purchased, the larger part of which went to the National Museum in Lima, but twenty vessels were reserved for Chicago. These are numbers 171076–95, of which the last five were roughly classified on the spot as Nazca *Y*, the remainder as Nazca *B*. A few of the latter, *B2* in type, are briefly discussed here.

**FIGURE 319, 171077 (N7).** Not quite either a waisted goblet of shape *J2* or an unbulged cylindrical vase *N1*. This piece is definitely waisted, rather too much so for a cylindrical vase; but it is the same diameter top and bottom, whereas a goblet should be larger at the rim. Nor does this vessel quite fit shape *P*, bulbous-concave vase, because there is no bulbousness below. This intermediacy is owing to a quality of the Nazca style that does not press forms into slots but aims at modes of style between which there is interflow. At any rate, this is a vase of elegant form, with well-chosen disposition of its design zones. H 150 mm, D at rim and base 90 mm, D at the narrowest around 78 mm, H/D 167%. The colors are five: W, LR, DR, G, and B. The zones of painting are four, the first and third similar interlocking step-frets, except that the first has and the third lacks "floating drifts" of W steps. The largest and second zone contains an intricate deity design, black, without color, apparently on unslipped background. Such merely outlined designs are not too common in Nazca but are *B2* when they occur. The lowest zone is of irregular DR blobs on the unslipped paste, apparently; but there may have been some scaling off of paint. The total design is intricate in plan but less precise in execution.

**FIGURE 320, 171079 (N5).** Shape *C* flaring bowl (close to *J3*). H 116 mm, D 165 mm, H/D 70%. Colors six: W, Y, LR, DR, G, and B. The bottom is quartered W and B; the zone above contains two considerably modified feline deities.

**FIGURE 321, 171082 (N7); PLATE 22.** Much lower proportioned and more flaring *C* bowl than the last, much the same in diameter (168 mm), but only 69 mm in height, H/D thus being merely 41%. The base is B and W quartered again. The main design is an elaborate, much-compressed deity, with numerous folded-over rays and forked spines, squeezed into a curved oval panel, repeated. Colors five: W, Y, LR, G, and B (DR lacking).

**FIGURE 322, 171087 (N7).** A smaller bottom-quartered *C*-shape bowl. H 62 mm, D 134 mm, H/D 46%. The main zone contains innumerable B tadpoles on W interspersed with short, fine DR lines. A LR line separates this zone from the B and W quartering. This makes four colors, to which might be added a reddish flesh-color slip over the designless inside.

CHAPTER 10

# *Nazca Y Phase*

NAZCA *Y*, IN THE GENERIC SENSE, represents the breaking down of the Nazca style as represented in its *A* and *B* developmental phases.

While we present the principal phase *Y* results of the 1926 excavations with a subdivision into *Y1* and *Y2* (or *BY* and *Y*), this subdivision deals with a minor distinction intended to carry out the developmental reconstruction as far as possible; and for the moment, in presenting an outline of the concept of the phase *Y* style as formulated to date, it seems most effective to make this presentation refer to generic *Y* as a whole—everything past phase *B* and yet in some measure still within the orbit of total Nazca style.

## THE NAZCA *Y* STYLE: GENERALITIES

This larger phase *Y* style is deteriorated from *A* and *B* in almost every way. The ware is heavier, coarser, little polished, and tends to be unevenly turned and crudely modeled. There are fewer colors used per vessel, on the whole, and these tend to be applied rather thinly, giving a wan or weathered effect. The lines and the outlines of designs are also mostly rendered carelessly, without precision and sometimes with actual slovenliness. Fine repetitive detail like dots, small crosses, close parallel lines are perhaps the most neatly executed. Elaborate designs are simplified and blobby, with an effect of something soluble having been allowed to get wet.

The principal vessel shapes listed below are recapitulated from and referenced to the compilations in Kroeber (1956), pages 374 and 381; the corresponding plates shown in Gayton and Kroeber (1927); and see our Figure 91.

## PHASE *Y* VESSEL SHAPES AND DESIGNS

*AGY*, angled goblets of *Y* type, lower portion cylindrical, upper flaring: another type carried over from Nazca *B2*. Plate 16f, perhaps also 15d.

*ArY*, flattish plates painted inside on rim wholly or chiefly, still another type carried over from Nazca *B2*.

*CJY*, cylindrical-collared jars. Plate 13c–d, 13f; also 14a–b, 16e, Tiahuanacoid influence. They may be plain, three-handled, with one lug.

*DBY*, deep bowls, segments of spheres, height two-thirds or more of diameter, sometimes lip slightly incurved. They are somewhat like the early Nazca shape *GG*, but higher and thicker. Plates 15e, 16b–c. A subvariety is oval instead of round.

*FPY*, strap-handled face pitchers, more-or-less spherical body, cambered mouth roughly modeled into a head or face, with almond eyes painted on. Plates 12a–f; also 13e, without modeled face (and see below, Fig. 326).

*OBY*, oblong rectangular bowls. Plates 15c, 16a. These begin to occur in late Nazca *B2*, but are proportionally more frequent in *Y*.

*QY*, incurved or lipless jar; plate 16d, carried over from Nazca *B2*, compare 5e. Pseudo-*QY* jars, convexly incurved bowls, also occur.

*WJY*, wide-mouthed jars. Plates 13b, 15f.

These eight shapes account for most of the *Y* inventory excavated by the expedition in 1926, although bowls lower than *DBY* have to be added as well as some occasional shapes.

The most prominent Nazca *Y* designs are these:

1. Detached deity heads, deliquescent, even amoeboid; and allied to them, armed or rayed suns, flowers, stars, usually with a single eye. We suggest that most of these are slovened, abbreviated, or degenerated forms of a rayed full-face trophy head of the type shown in Gayton and Kroeber (1927), plates 5e and 9e and in Kroeber (1956), plate 39d. The rays seem to be attributes of divinity (as in the jagged staff figure). Possibly an idea of deity and of deity's magical trophy head became blended in this concept. The radiating extensions are various: bent over, enlarged to a diamond and then pointed, simple pointed, cut off blunt or squared, or various combinations of these. In their more derivative of degenerated forms they may be

bent, elbowed, or otherwise modified. This is the most characteristic and perhaps the most frequent Nazca *Y* design.

2. Circular panels left unpainted, or slipped white, or filled with a rayed figure derived from or approximated to the rayed trophy head.
3. Rectangular design panels, sometimes alternating with circular ones.
4. Narrow stripes, in framed panels or loose, with black dashes, white dots, or plain.
5. Contrasting compound geometric patterns, such as rectangular areas of checkers adjacent to zigzag, or of stripes to crosses.
6. White-eyed diamonds in rows; white dots in rows.
7. Step-frets, complementary interlocking, often one or two pairs in a frame; one set of the step-frets may be two-colored; or an intervening series of diagonal steps is developed.

It is evident that Nazca *Y* rests in Nazca *B* but has also developed some new features, although these are usually simple; and that its qualities, whether of continued or of novel traits, are stylistically deteriorated.

## NASCA *Y* MATERIALS EXCAVATED IN 1926

The fuller graves opened by the museum's expedition are here separated into two series, *Y1* and *Y2*, according as on stylistic grounds they seem either earlier and less altered from preceding Nazca *B*, or later and changed farther away from it.

The initial criterion used by us in distinguishing *Y1* from *Y2* is the absence *(Y1)* or presence *(Y2)* in graves of the face-pitcher jars, *FPY*. There is of course a certain risk in basing on a single feature, since there is always the possibility that the furniture of some *Y2* graves happened to lack an *FPY* jar. Ultimate judgment therefore will rest on whether the two lots of material here designated as *Y1* and *Y2* are each internally consistent in the majority of their total features, in addition to the one critical face pitcher shape.

This question will be reviewed after the two lots of ceramics have been described.

## GRAVES OF PHASE *Y1*

The most important *Y1* tombs were Majoro Chico A, Graves 7[A and B] and 8, and Ocongalla West B, Graves 1 and 11. These contained twenty-nine pottery vessels. To these, Soisongo A, Grave 2, and Soisongo C, Graves 1, 2, 3, and 13 add on thirteen more pots. Perhaps the most conspicuous traits of these vessels are the deep sphere-segment bowl shape *DBY* and a black-painted slip or background.

### Majoro Chico A, Grave 7A

**FIGURE 323, 170467.** Large two-handled *T*-shape jar with its rim broken out. It was uncovered 3 m away from Grave 7B, at a depth of only 1 m, and therefore represents a separate interment. H 268 mm to tip of broken-out rim, D 340 mm, H/D 80% or more. Diameter of the neck is about 51% of that of the body. The vessel is unpainted and soot blackened and contained 170468, a lot of feathers, threads, spindles, comb, bits of weaving, and so forth. Its rim resembles the rim of the presumably early Nazca *A* black jar 171031 (Fig. 382) found at Cantayo Cax Grave 11.

## Majoro Chico A, Grave 7B

**FIGURES 324, 170471 (N8); 325, 170472 (N8); and 326, 170473 (N8).** Three vessels in Grave 7B were deep rounded bowls. Only one of them is black and has its design in two panels on opposite sides: 170471, Figure 324, H 100 mm, D 176 mm, H/D 57%. The two others have a yellowish background (at least one of them of unslipped paste) and a continuous band of design: 170472, Figure 325, H 93 mm, D 191 mm, H/D 49%; and 170473, Figure 326, H 114 mm, D 160 mm, H/D 71%. The last is deep enough to be classed as shape DBY. The lowest of the three has a superficial resemblance to the *B*-shape gambreled bowls of earlier phases, but its silhouette is more continuously rounded and the design band is narrower. Of colors, all three bowls have W, LR, DR, and B and show the unslipped Y-buff paste (in 170471 in the panel corners and dividing band). To these colors 170472 adds G.

The panel of 170471 contains as design two pairs of complementary interlocking step-frets separated by a diagonal zigzag band of steps. This design recurs in Figures 342 and 343 from Ocongalla West B, Grave 11, and it goes back to Nazca *B2* (Kroeber 1956, plate 37b); it has not been found in *A*. In 170472 there is only the dividing zigzag band, without the steps, repeated over and over in four colors, but without quite regular sequence, thus G, LR, DR, W, G, DR, W, LR, G, W, DR, G, and so forth. In 170473 we have the typical deliquescent rayed trophy head, with inner eye, a sort of W-centered stem, and a fringe of bent-over rays plus a few loose rays strewn in.

**FIGURE 327, 170474 (N8).** From this same Grave 7B. H to broken spout 170 mm, D 180 mm. There are four colors: W (in two densities), LBr, R, (probably DR), and B. The lower half of the body and the handle are unslipped and unpainted. The upper half of the body carries a thin white slip, which is finished below by a B and R band. What is left of the neck or head above its greatest diameter is R. The pattern consists of a broad zigzag encircling most of the body. This zigzag consists of three parallel stripes, R, W, and R. The R stripes are B bordered; the W stripe is more opaque than the W slip, and each section of it is diagonally crossed by three short B lines besides containing a longitudinal one. Near the front middle of the pattern, five or six slightly larger B lines hang down outside the zigzag.

A careful examination of the broken orifice shows that this vessel did not carry a face. The neck of the vessel carries up on one side to where the cheek should begin in a face pitcher without sign of either modeling or painting. Also, there is pronounced camber, which would interfere with a face. Further, the R paint on the upper slope of the camber does not carry to the back (where the strap handle begins), whereas in true face pitchers R or B paint does appear here to represent hair. Figure 326 was evidently much like Gayton and Kroeber (1927), plate 13e, which has always been construed as phase *Y* and has a plain cambered neck and orifice.

### Majoro Chico A, Grave 8

This grave is puzzling in some of its features, and its record should have been noted and kept in more detail. It contained two bodies, one with undeformed skull (170484) at 230 cm deep, the other with heavily flattened skull (170486) at 240 cm. This disparity is somewhat disconcerting, since Nazca *A* and *B* regularly deformed heads, Nazca *Y* usually so. With these skeletons was a matching pair of bowls (170483, 170485) at 230 cm. A meter above, at 120 cm and 130 cm, five fragmented vessels were found, of as many different shapes, only one a bowl and that both deeper than the pair at 230 cm and black slipped. A note recorded at the time said that the upper-level objects were more in Nazca *Y* manner than the pair below, which seemed Nazca *B*. This might suggest a *Y* interment that happened to be made in an old *B* grave; but the differentiation noted in excavating proves to be only partly true, now that smashed vessels have been reconstituted in the museum. And finally, the depth of a fourth bowl, 170482, with quite indubitably Nazca *Y* design of deliquesced and one-eyed god's trophy head, failed to be entered in the record.

On review of the pottery as a lot, it seems stylistically poised on the very boundary of late Nazca *B* and early Nazca *Y*, with some pieces inclining more to one, some to the other period, but those more akin to *B* regularly bearing some stigmata of slovening or deterioration from good Nazca *B*. They might therefore have all been made in one lifetime, but by different potters; or there might have been two separate interments not too long a time apart.

There was another complication: one vessel, 140475, the first one encountered in the grave, is aberrant from any other we know at Nazca, but with several stylistic traits suggestive of Nazca *A!* These *A* traits are not decisive because of the abnormality of the piece in both shape and design, but they are prevalent.

A number of loose sherds found at 150–230 cm were also saved (170478). They are mostly phase *A*, some *B*, a few possibly *Y*; but since there are no further notes as to their relative position, we shall not illustrate them and merely enumerate the subjects of some of their designs.

We shall now describe the ceramic contents, specifying the respective leanings of each piece to phase *B* or *Y*, and leaving the seeming *A* vessel and the loose sherds to the last.

## *Bowls*

**FIGURES 328, 170481 (N8); 329, 170482 (N8); and 330, 170485 (N8).** First we will deal with the four bowls in the grave. Two of these are mates, so the number illustrated reduces to three, Figures 328, 329, and 330. The first, 170481, Figure 328, from 120 cm, is a typical *DBY* shape: H 101 mm, D 168 mm, D/H 60%. The second bowl, 170482, Figure 329, (depth unrecorded) is broken: H about 103 mm, D 175 mm. The upper silhouette is straight, looks somewhat like a shape-*B* gambrel and is certainly not a sphere-segment. Figure 330 shows 170485, one of the pair found at 230 cm: H 78 mm, D 162 mm, H/D 48%. It is difficult to assign to a shape class.

As for color, 170481 is slipped B, the panels LR in background, the disks W; the others have the design area showing the unslipped Y-buff of the paste as background, with LR bands bordering it. Only the base of 170482 has a thin black slip; the base of 170485 is the same as the design area, but the interior, which also carries design, is slipped LR. The total colors are, respectively, W, LR, B; W, LR, DR, and B with Y-buff paste; and W, LR, G, and B with buff paste.

The designs are wholly typical *Y1*. Figure 328 has pale (overpainted?) disks, rectangular panels, W-studded short parallel bars or stripes. Figure 329 has the formless, amoeboid, deliquesced rayed trophy head, with interior eye, stem or mouth, and both cut-off and bent-over rays; its long outlined rectangular extensions may be a square form of bent-over rays. Seler (1923) does not seem to illustrate the design. (Seler's Berlin collections seem to have included almost no Nazca *Y* pieces.) Figure 330 has paneled pairs or capital-L-shaped bars (fret hooks without blocks?) outside, and eight step-blocks (without frets) paired into four pyramids inside, pendant from the rim. This painting both inside and outside is unusual in any Nazca phase; the position of the inner designs pendant from the rim suggests and perhaps foreshadows the design arrangement of Late Period bowls, in the manner of I. T. Kelly's (1930) "cumbrous bowls," especially those from Ica and Nazca.

## *Human-Figure Jar*

**FIGURE 331, 170477 (N7).** Female figure jar, shape *X*. Seler (1923) has no representation of this type, but a startlingly close example is Gayton and Kroeber (1927), plate 8b. It is there given as Nazca *B*, which is undoubtedly correct, as shown by the almond eyes and yellow face. Both vessels represent a seated woman carrying a large receptacle, probably a basket, on her back; its opening is the mouth of the vessel. The 1927 specimen shows the basket texture, the present one its carrying bands. Position of the hands, coiffure, tattooing on chin and upper lip, face paint across nose and cheeks, are all substantially identical. Only the large DR disks on the shoulders are unique to the present specimen.

Both pieces show an interesting relation to the cylindrical vases of shape *N*, the tallest of Nazca vessels, especially to the subtype *N2* (Gayton and Kroeber 1927, pl. 11), which has three bulges and two concavities in its silhouette and carries design in four zones. Plate 8b (ibid.) has three bulges, at feet, shoulders, and basket rim; the present 170477 has four, at feet, elbows, face, and basket rim. Both of these modeled pieces are also de facto zoned into feet, body, and head plus basket; in Figure 331 this is formalized by the two dark horizontal straps or dress borders. The *N* vases normally carry two zones of women's yellow, almond-eyed, and bang-haired faces seriated in a tier or row—the same face as is modeled and painted on the figure jars. The *N* vases tend to have their height more than twice the diameter. Our two effigies run: plate 8b, H/D 156%; 170477, 166% for H/D of mouth, 150% for H/D of base; 8b, like the vases, is widest at the mouth, while the present Majoro piece is widest near the base.

Between the two effigies, plate 8b is presumably the earlier: the painting in Figure 331 is hastier, more sloppy, like a many-times-made copy; compare the fingers, the bracelets, the blobs rendering the basket texture. It could thus well be an early *Y* rendering of a conception originating in late *B*.

170477 has six colors: W, Y, LR, DR, G (the belt, below), and B. H 187 mm, D at base about 125 mm.

## *Rim-Painted Plate*

**FIGURE 332, 170480 (N7/8).** Rim-painted plate. D 162 mm, H 54 mm, H/D 33%, about average for *A* plates. The colors are three: creamish W, LR, and B. The design is serpentine and continuous, although broken into eight parts by transverse bars.

The nearest parallels to 170480 are, first of all, Gayton and Kroeber (1927), plate 4a, there misclassed as a *C*-shape conical bowl; it is a rim-painted plate with two striped and cross-barred snakes, each in four curves and having round heads that have seized salamanders. Next similar is Kroeber (1956), plate 38e, H/D 40%, somewhat high for *A* shape but within limits. Its design has eight panels, four short ones empty, two long ones containing a black-dotted headless snake of five curves; the two others containing a W-dotted B right-angled meander of three convolutions.

It is evident that these three pieces are related in design theme as well as design disposition: 4a (1927) is the most realistic, the current Figure 332 next, 38e (1956) the most geometric. Two other inside rim-painted vessels are more different, though still related to 170480: Gayton and Kroeber (1927), plate 4b; and Kroeber (1956), plate 38f. Measurements show that as relative height increases in these five vessels, the width of rim relative to center also increases. All of the pieces show qualities of late *B2*, but all contain also some elements foreshadowing of *Y1*.

## *Angled Goblet*

**FIGURE 333, 170479 (N8).** An angled goblet of shape *I2*. H 111 mm, D at mouth 157 mm, D at neck 70 mm, D at base 85 mm, H base to neck 41 mm; this gives the smaller basal portion or stem 37% of the total height. The relation of the present specimen to six other previously accredited examples of shape class *I* is best shown by a comparison based on Kroeber (1956), table 3, page 341.

| | **FIGURE 333** 170479 | 1956 MIN.–MAX. OF 6 | 1956 MEAN OF 6 |
|---|---|---|---|
| Rim D | 157 mm | 105–161 mm | 131 mm |
| H/D rim | 71% | 66–92% | 80% |
| D base/D rim | 54% | 55–69% | 62% |
| D neck/D base | 82% | 86–106% | 98% |
| Neck angle | 145° | 155–162° | 158° |

Figure 333 is thus just within the range of the previously measured angled goblets in two features, just beyond their range in three features. This may be because it seems of *Y1* phase (as shown by its painting), but the six compared goblets are more prevalently of *B2:* the exact phrasing in 1956 was "definitely (i.e. markedly) late *B*—really *B-Y* transition."

The colors of this angled goblet, Figure 333, are only two: four good-sized W disks on overall B-slipped surface. These disks are a phase *Y* characteristic, or at least of *Y1*. They have not been recorded in any clear and exclusive *B* association.

It is evident that the *B*-type pieces from Majoro Chico A, Grave 8, are all late *B: B2+*, we might say. The woman vase seems later than the other piece of its type, and this other already is fully developed *B2*. The plate's affiliations seem all to be terminal *B;* and the goblet, finally, has outright *Y*-style painting. If these three were originally deposited in an earlier burial that was disturbed by a straight *Y1* interment, it was presumably not many generations earlier. Yet a simpler explanation is to attribute all six vessels so far considered as from the very border of *B* and *Y*, transitional between *B2+* and *Y1*.

## *Collared Bowl with Nazca A Resemblances*

**FIGURE 334, 170475 (N4).** We come now to the one seemingly Nazca *A* vessel which was found in fragments with the upper-level pieces at 130 cm depth. There is of course only stylistic likeness of this piece to phase *A*. Yet several of its features do point that way: the black background; the LR vertical dividers; the lizards or, as indicated by their mottling, more likely newts or salamanders; and the radial stripes on the inside rim of the collar.

Salamanders or amphibians occur in Kroeber (1956), plate 31e from Ocucaje Grave B-5 of *A1* period; Kroeber and Strong (1924), plate 26b, also from Ocucaje, Grave B-5, frogs; and Kroeber (1956), plate 41d, salamander(?) at end of cat deity's serpent tail, also on B background, phase post-early *A*. Seler (1923, figs. 319–322, 324–325) shows larval forms of frogs and newts and, in his figures 323 and 326, tailed (though gilled?) newts or salamanders. Of these, figure 323 is on an *R*-shape wide-mouth jar that might be either Nazca *A* or *B*, and figure 326 is on an *Ac* plate that is surely phase *A*. In his figure 312, Seler (1923) distinguishes a lizard from the foregoing salamanders; it is accompanied by arrows, which show it to be phase *B*.

Tailed amphibians are rare in South America except for an introduced species. Seler (1923, 313) says that tailed salamanders *(geschwaenzte Lurche)* occur only as far south as Ecuador, but (ibid., 315, figs. 323, 326) he shows tailed forms as well as patent larval ones. Does he mean that newts occur farther south but do not develop beyond the gill stage? It is of course also possible that fully mature salamanders with lungs did formerly occur as far south as Nazca and have since died out.

The colors of 170475 are four: W, LR, G, and B. The animals' spots alternate between LR and G. The rim stripes are LR, G, and B, separated by W lines.

The shape of style-*A* vessel 170475 is, so far as we know, unparalleled in the Nazca area: a cambered bowl body with a straight collar or lip one-fifth the height of the vessel. This collar flares very slightly: the neck is 91% of the body D, the lip 95%; D 170 mm, H 111 mm, H/D 65%, or without the collar 52%. Other Nazca bowls never have collars, jars and even cookpots do not have them so wide as this, nor are their bodies so low. Figure 334 is therefore unique, and unique shapes occur chiefly in Nazca *A*. All stylistic considerations thus point to this piece really dating from Nazca *A*, yet they are only stylistic.

There remain the miscellaneous sherds (170478) from a number of vessels strewn through the depth of 150–230 cm in the grave. Clearly *A* style among these are hummingbirds, paneled fruits, paneled profile trophy heads, and plunging dolphins. Clearly late *B* are a pinfeathered bird and a rayed deity trophy head. Dubiously *Y* are two fragments with parallel bars containing longitudinal lines or wiggles.

## Ocongalla West B, Grave 1

This tomb, only 120 cm deep, held six vessels, two of them mates of others.

**FIGURE 335, 170671 (N7).** One of a pair of angled goblets shape *I*, but with conical-rounded instead of cylindrical and flat base. It is very similar in shape to Kroeber (1956), plate 38g, except that H/D of that is 102%, of the present piece only 69%. (This last is near the medium range of shape *F-H*, flaring bowls, but these always have a gently rounded flat bottom, which fact precludes 170671 from being classed with them.) Diameter is 116 mm, H 80 mm; colors four: W, LR, DR, and B. The upper design panel has a W background, the lower merely the light orange-red paste. In the upper zone are two panels each of six pairs of bent-over rays (with spines—rarer in *Y* than in *B*) set between two DR rectangles. The lower zone contains triangular-outline trophy heads (indicated by four, five, or six dots!) and between them pendant trophy tresses.

The vessel in Kroeber (1956), plate 38g also has trophy heads, or women's yellow faces, in its lower zone, indicated by four horizontal dashes in a square. The upper zone shows pinfeathered birds, a late *B* theme, here executed with typical *Y* slovening. There can be no doubt that this goblet 38g (ibid.) and 170671 are closely akin in style.

**FIGURE 336, 170673 (N7).** Flattish bottom and flare, H/D 55% (H 51 mm, D 93 mm), and is therefore of bowl shape *F-H*. The bottom is quartered in alternate W and flesh quadrants. The upper zone contains seven or eight deliquesced one-eyed rayed heads, alternately B and LR. Colors four: W, F, (only on two quadrants), LR, and B; painting hasty.

**FIGURE 337, 170675 (N7).** One of a pair of matched quasi-*B*-shape bowls. H 64 mm, D 134 mm, H/D 48%, narrow above the gambrel (one-third of total height, W design band only a quarter). The bottom has W and flesh quadrants like the last piece. The upper zone contains two design panels separated by solid LR rectangles like 170671. Each of these panels contains three figures, of which the only sure interpretation is that each shows an eye. The figure as a whole may be meant to represent an animal, a rayed head, a tressed trophy head (cf. Kroeber 1956, pl. 39e; incipient *Y*, for the most likely derivation) but the reduction is carried too far for sure recognition. With each figure is a blobby LR cursive element, perhaps descending steps? Colors the same four as in last, with flesh only in quadrants.

**FIGURE 338, 170676 (N7).** Conical goblet, shape *L*, a phase *B* and *Y* form. H 172 mm, D 130 mm, H/D 132%, as compared with seven capital-L-shape Uhle pieces from Nazca, which run from 97% to 129%, mean 110% (Kroeber 1956, 342), but which include phase *B* as well as phase *Y* examples. Background black, colors four: W, LR, DR, and B. The lower design zone holds LR and DR blobby wiggles; the upper, triangles of four or five strokes each, latticed in opposite diagonal slope (also see Gayton and Kroeber 1927, fig. 3, no. 13, "overlapping lines"). Compare with the present piece Figure 372 (Pl. 30), below, from Majoro Chico E, Grave 1.

## Ocongalla West B, Grave 11

This grave contained five black-painted deep bowls of *DBY* shape, one shallower white bowl, one angled goblet *I*, and three inside-rim-painted plates. There is not one elegantly made or skillfully painted vessel in the lot.

The five *DBY* bowls are best presented together. Individual design features are:

**FIGURE 339, 170746 (N8).** Central eye, two loose eyes, mouth.

**FIGURE 340, 170753 (N8); PLATE 26.** Central eye, stem, three triple rays.

**FIGURE 341, 170748 (N8).** Two simplified heads at ends of twice-bent bar carrying pattern of folded-down rays, dashes down center.

**FIGURE 342, 170749 (N8).** Each complementary step-fret pair LR and G, separated from next by W step band.

**FIGURE 343, 170754 (N8).** Rectangular panels set on end; each contains one DR-W complementary step-fret plus unslipped band and two corners.

| FIGURE NUMBER | 339 | 340<br>PLATE 26 | 341<br>PLATE 27 | 342 | 343 |
|---|---|---|---|---|---|
| Catalogue number | 170746 | 170753 | 170748 | 170749 | 170754 |
| Diameter (mm) | 172 | 166 | 177 | 167 | 136 |
| Height (mm) | 120 | 116 | 129 | 125 | 96 |
| H/D ratio (%) | 70 | 70 | 73 | 75 | 71 |
| Color of vessel | B | B | B | B | B |
| Design background | W | W | W | W | |
| Design band | 11 | | | | |
| Rectangular panels | 2 | 2 | | | |
| Circular panels | 2 | | | | |
| White disks | 2 | 2 | 3 | 2 | |
| Deliquesced rayed head | ✓ | ✓ | ✓ | | |
| Step-fret pairs (number) | 5 | 2 | | | |
| With diagonal free steps | ✓ | ✓ | | | |
| Other colors: | | | | | |
| LR | ✓ | ✓ | ✓ | ✓ | ✓ |
| DR | ✓ | ✓ | | | |
| G | ✓ | ✓ | ✓ | | |
| cream | ✓ | | | | |
| unslipped | ✓ | | | | |

**FIGURE 344, 170751 (N8).** Shallower and oval bowl; if round it would be best designated as *GG*. H 77 mm, D at base 149 and at tip 174 mm, H/D 52% and 44%. It further differs from the five *DBY* bowls just described in that it has a W background, divided off by vertical LR bands. Adjacent panels both bear much degenerated rayed heads, but one has thirteen bent-over rays, the other six square-ended ones accompanied by fretlike branching appendages outlined in LR. This design comes at the short end, the thirteen-rayed one on the long side. The outlined parts of the design suggest Seler (1923), figures 178, and 208. Colors: W, LR, DR, G, and B.

**FIGURE 345, 170747 (N8); PLATE 27.** Unevenly modeled, smoothed, but unslipped angled goblet of shape *I2*, of exposed buff paste, except for the narrow base, which is painted LR. There are four crosses consisting of black bordered LR right angles with W between. In spite of the rectilinearity of the design, none of the right angles are true. H 103 mm, D 145 mm, H/D 71%. Diameter ratios, maximum below lip 100%, at lip 98%, at neck 45%, at base 47%. Height of base, 33–34% of total H.

**FIGURES 346, 170745 (N8), and 347, 170752 (N8).** Two LR plates, interior rim-painted with rectangular figure. The dimensions are 170745, H 79 mm, D 200 mm, H/D 40%; 170752, H 71 mm, D 197 mm, H/D 36%. If Figure 346 is slipped, it is with a wash of the clay that the paste consists of. The paste color of Figure 347 is LR buff; it may have been lightly slipped with W most of which has come off. The rim designs are 170745, four DR or G squat crosses outlined in B and containing crossed B lines (there is no W on this piece); 170752, five quite unequally spaced rectangles composed of short radial stripes of W, DR, Y, W, and LR, some containing a briefer B line.

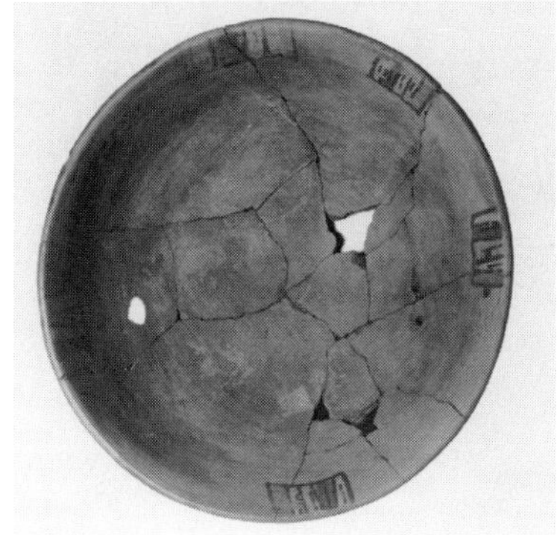

**FIGURE 348, 170750 (N8).** Another inside-painted plate with two opposite designs coming inward considerably from the rim. H 75 mm, D 218 mm, H/D 34%. The background is LR with a B line on lip. The plate is badly broken, incomplete, and somewhat decayed on the surface. The design is difficult to recognize: it suggests to one of us spread-wing thunderbirds, to the other it seems to resemble hawk moths; the heads would be toward the empty center. Both figures are DR outlined in B, and with three or four W bars or patches on each wing.

These three rim-painted plates differ from Figure 332 and other rim-painted plates in not marking the division of center and rim. In this they resemble the cumbrous bowls which seem to be post-*Y* phase.

In spite of its ten vessels, Grave 11 averages about as crude in the execution of its ceramics as any *Y1* grave.

## Soisongo A, Grave 2

At 150 cm, a square bowl and an angled goblet (shape *I2*) were found in Grave 2, certainly of phase *Y* and presumably of *Y1*.

**FIGURE 349, 170798 (N7).** The bowl nearly unique. H 60 mm, D 115 mm, H/D 52%. The D is from side to side, each of which is very slightly rounded, until it comes to a sudden corner. Similarly, the sides rise nearly vertically. The overall shape thus approaches closely to half a hollow cube. The ware is rather thick, its effect heavy. The base is slipped W; above this, for 37 mm up to the lip, the sides are painted B; over this apparently is painted a pattern in W and LR. On two opposite sides this overpainting consists of nineteen vertical lines, ten W and nine LR. On the other two sides is a pattern of dots or disks, slightly larger in D than the lines are wide. On each side there are three tiers of six dots each, each tier of one color: LR, W, and LR on one side; W, LR, and W on the opposite side. There are no colors on the bowl but these three. It is an unusual piece within the Nazca style, with a trait or two slightly reminiscent of Nazca *A* features, none of *B*, and most of *Y:* the squareness (cf. Gayton and Kroeber 1927, pl. 16a), parallel stripes, dots, and B background.

**FIGURE 350, 170799 (N7).** *I2*-goblet. H 104 mm, D at lip of 145 mm, H/D 72%; D at base 85 mm, base D/max. D 59%. The angle at the beginning of the flare is about 120 degrees. The colors are four: W, Y, LR, and DBr, this last probably a badly fired B. The base and inside are unpainted; all the outside flare is slipped W. At the waist is a LR band or girdle with B borders. The base is quartered by B lines into four sectors, two of which are painted Y, two plain. The flaring side above the waist is divided into twelve compartments by twelve B stripes, each touched up by three pairs of little W dashes. The stripes run from nearly vertical to 30 degrees off. Between each pair of B stripes run three LR lines eleven times; but the twelfth (center of Fig. 350), four lines. Between vessel shape, quartering, and cursive geometric design, this vessel might be late *B2*, more likely *Y1*.

### Soisongo C, Grave 1

This grave was 190 cm deep. It contained five vessels of rather good quality.

**FIGURE 351, 170826 (N7); PLATE 28.** Nominally a human-figure jar of class *X*, but actually has a modeled and carefully painted woman's head serving as orifice to a flash-shape or flattened jar of oval cross section. Height is 206 mm, D right to left 150 mm, D fore and aft 122 mm, H/D 137% and 169%; H of neck of vessel (the woman's head) 57 mm, which is 28% of total H; D of orifice 50 mm. There is resemblance to the basket-carrying woman of Figure 331, although Figure 331 is widest at the top; also to the face pitchers of *Y2*, though the handle of these is lacking. There are five colors: W, Y, LR, G, and B. The lowest quarter of the vessel is unpainted; the rest slipped W. The face is Y, the hair B, the almond eyes and part of the headdress W. Most of the body of the vessel is covered with a pattern of zigzag stripes seemingly representing the woman's cloak; the six longer of these stripes are, in order downward, G, LR, Y, G, LR, and Y, bordered or separated by B lines. The residue of area left by the wide zigzag areas is filled by B chevron lines on the W slip parallel to the colored stripes.

This type of vessel with the body made spherical, a strap handle added, and the cloak as usually replaced by other painting would make the *Y2* face pitcher.

**FIGURE 352, 170827 (N7).** *I2*-shape angled goblet whose main pattern is a simplification of the cloak in the preceding figure, the color filling of the stripes being omitted (only DR lines on W slip). The full design scheme is, top to bottom, B blobby zigzag units or wiggles; LR and then DR encircling band; the chevrons just described; again a LR and DR band; and short vertical B bars pendant from a B line on W slip. Colors: W, LR, DR, and B. H 107 mm, max. D at rim 139 mm, H/D 77%; base D 88 mm, waist D 80 mm, base D/max. D 63%, waist D/max. D 58%. It will be seen that there is a real waist constriction; the bend of the profile here is not far from 35 degrees, that is, an angle of 145 degrees is formed.

**FIGURE 353, 170829 (N7).** Very similar angled goblet: H 100 mm, max. D 125 mm, H/D 80%; base D 95 mm, waist D 85 mm, base D/max. D 76%, waist D/max. D 68%. The constriction is more pronounced than in the preceding piece; its bend and angle are respectively around 40 degrees and 140 degrees. The colors are three: W for slip, DR, and B. There are fifteen DR lines around the vessel. Black are: the lip; top and bottom line; sixteen or seventeen brush strokes, thirteen of them clear. These last correspond to the wobbly zigzags in the preceding goblet, as the parallel lines correspond to the parallel zigzags.

**FIGURE 354, 170828 (EARLY N8); PLATE 25.** Hemispheric *GG* bowl, more specifically *DBY*, deep bowl of *Y* phase, with banded design. H 96 mm, D 150 mm, H/D 64%, rim D is about 5–6 mm less than maximum. Colors: W, Y, LR, DR, and B. The upper zone, on seeming Y slip, has been overpainted with repeated DR diagonal floating steps of three rises, left to right, B-outlined. The Y spaces intervening are somewhat wider but, of course, remain similar free, three-rise steps; they contain a B diagonal line and six B dots. The lower zone was slipped LR, over which were painted two rows of tandem B bars, each with four (or five) W dots.

There is a curious suggestion of Ica (Late) style about the dots and steps in the upper zone, but we consider the resemblance fortuitous. Significant features of phase *Y* are the floating diagonal steps above and the dotted end-on dark bars below.

**FIGURE 355, 170830 (EARLY N8).** *Y*-style cylindrical-collared jar, shape *CJY* (Kroeber 1956, 374) similar to Gayton and Kroeber (1927), plates 13c, 13f, and (with handles) 13d; this last bears a disk or medallion similar to Figure 355. H 161 mm, D 130 mm, H/D 124%. Without the collar or neck, the vessel would be close to spherical. Colors: W, DR, and B. The neck collar is crude DR; the shoulder B, below which is a DR stripe; everything below unpainted. The finer painting is poorly preserved: three or four DR disks with D nearly equal to width of B shoulder band containing a smaller central B disk with W dots or short dashes. Larger and smaller disks and upper and lower edge of B shoulder band are bordered by thin W lines, which have largely disappeared, perhaps because overpainted (or painted under by B or DR).

There is overpainting of W on dark color also on Gayton and Kroeber (1927), plates 13f and probably 13c; a shoulder zone of design in the same two; black or dark slip again in these two; disks of design, and handles, in 13d (ibid.); and rather shapeless collar neck in all three.

This grave seems to be good *Y1* in style, although it does not show any tentacled or deliquescent trophy heads.

### Soisongo C, Grave 2

This is a puzzling grave. The skeleton was that of a young person, age 12–20 years. A red, white, and yellow tapestry band was wound twice around the head; this textile will ultimately help fix the period of the interment. The bottom of the body was at 125 cm; at 80 cm was encountered the top of a large reddish jar, broken, which had been set above the body. This jar is sketchily outlined in Kroeber's 1926 field notebook as approximately spherical below a wide, somewhat flaring mouth. What the museum possesses (170831, original field number 470) is the upper half only of the body of the vessel, without mouth or flaring collar, as shown in Figure 356. There is no possibility of mistaken identity, because Kroeber sketched in his notebook the peculiar painted design visible in Figure 356: the mouth and lower half of the vessel body must have got separated from the rest and were either lost or mislaid, possibly newly numbered.

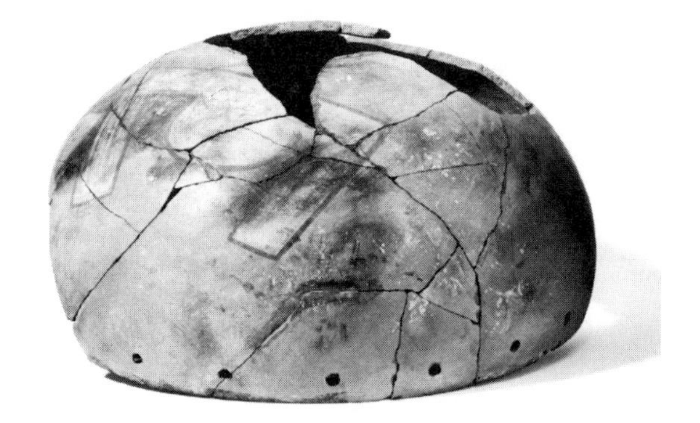

**FIGURE 356, 170831 (N7/8).** Part shown has H of 225 mm (suggesting ca. 450 mm for the whole body), D 433 mm, body H/D around 100%. The D of the orifice from which the neck collar rose is 155 mm; since the collar flared, its lip would have been 200 mm or so in D. The thickness of the ware is around 10 mm. The present lower edge runs precisely around the former equator and is straight but not ground smooth. Mend holes, 70–80 mm apart, run halfway around the circumference and are smeared with gum, as is the edge below them. We assume that the vessel was made in two pieces, or in fact three, counting the neck. Quite likely the upper and lower body halves were made successively in the same mold and then joined before firing, as was done on the north coast of Peru in Tiahuanacoid times. Joints of this sort tend to break or crack along the seam. When this pot cracked partway, it was drilled and lashed and made watertight with the gum. So far as we know, this two-piece mold manufacture has not been reported for the Nazca area; but, then, large pots there have not been examined for the technique.

There is some W and B paint on the shoulder preserved: two giant capital-E figures in thin W, outlined in black. We have no idea what they represent. In place of a middle horizontal projection, this E figure, which is quite thick-stemmed, has a semicircle. The two other horizontals are turned somewhat off the parallel to converge slightly in both renditions.

Although we cannot interpret this strange and arresting design symbol, it furnishes the clue to the period of this grave. Grave 13 in the same Soisongo C locus was excavated by Tello, who recovered from it four vessels, which are probably still in the great museum at Magdalena under the numbers MAP 30/42–45 for 1926. One of these four vessels had a spherical body with a tall and wide cylindrical collar, as sketched by Kroeber in his field notebook and reproduced here in Figure 358. This had painted on its shoulder the almost identical capital-E figure, also pointing downward as in Figure 356. This figure was W or Y, outlined in B, on a blackish surface according to the notebook; the paste, texture, and shaping of the vessel were poor. The three other vessels in this grave are indubitably *Y*, in fact *Y1* by our subclassification: a rectangular bowl, a striped angled goblet, and a rim-painted plate (Figs. 359–361). We can then confidently construe the present grave as phase *Y1* on the basis of its capital-E-design painting.

## Soisongo C, Grave 3

**FIGURE 357, 170835 (N7).** The only vessel found in this grave. It is similar in shape to the lower half of 170671, Figure 335, from Ocongalla West B, Grave 1, which also has a line of simplified dot faces. Vessel 170835 is painted in three colors: W, LR, and B; a band of LR, 38 mm wide, encircles the interior rim. The remainder of the interior and the exterior base is unslipped, natural buff. H 97 mm, max. D 150 mm, H/D 65%; rim D 148 mm, base D 96 mm.

## Soisongo C, Grave 13

The expedition and the National Museum of Peru excavated the Soisongo sites jointly. Dr. Tello dug Grave 13 at Site C and permitted Kroeber to sketch the four Nazca *Y* vessels it contained (MAP 30/42–45). They are reproduced in Figures 358–361.

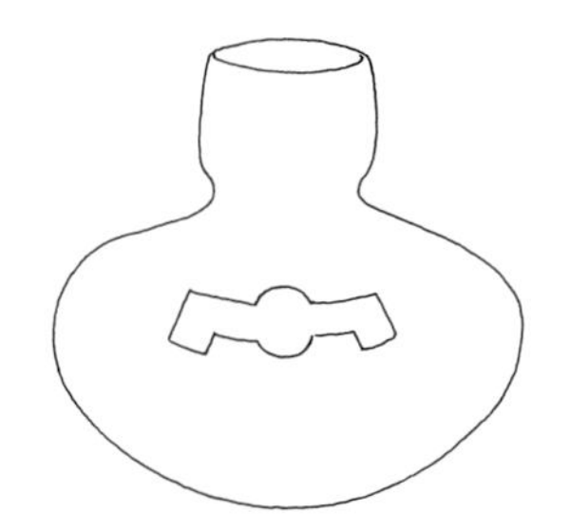

**FIGURE 358, MAP 30/42 (IMPORT?).** A jar with large cylindrical neck has already been discussed in connection with one (Fig. 356) from Grave 2 in the same Soisongo C cemetery.

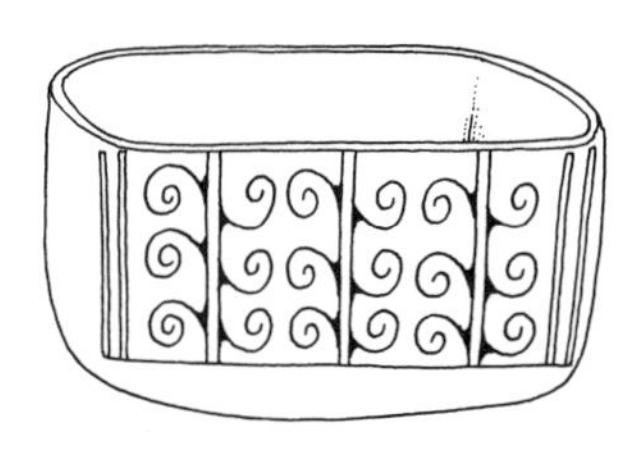

**FIGURE 359, MAP 30/43 (N7).** A rectangular bowl, very boxy in proportions, outside ends blank, the sides with oblong panels. These panels are each crossed by seven vertical bars, the two outside pairs red in color, the three middle ones W. These W bars cover the middle of three cursively painted s elements, all laid horizontally, the left half of each spiral being B, the right half red. (The notes do not specify the shade of red used.) The vessel is reminiscent of Figure 349 from Soisongo A, Grave 2 and Gayton and Kroeber (1927), plate 16a.

**FIGURE 360, MAP 30/44 (N7).** Angled goblet, shape *I* resembling the angled goblets in Figures 352 and 353 from Soisongo C, Grave 1 of phase *Y1* and especially Figure 350 from Soisongo A, Grave 2. Like the last, this goblet is diagonally striped with B darts, each with three W longitudinal (*not* diagonal, as drawn) dashes, LR head, and two LR parallel lines between it and the next dart. Below is a row of B "crow's feet," separated from the main design by a DR band. Colors four, as in preceding: W, LR, DR, and B.

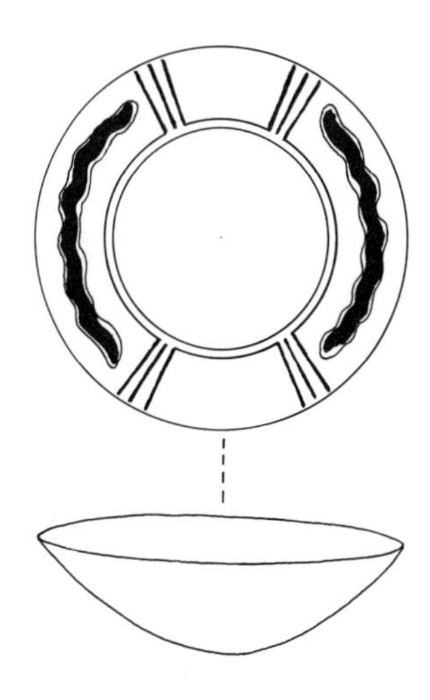

**FIGURE 361, MAP 30/45 (N7).** Interior rim-painted plate with two snakelike designs. Kroeber's notes read: "B on R; appar. lightly p'ted with W around the B (figures), and on this is a thin red border following the B. Outside (of vessel) has only a narrow border of DR." This plate recalls Figure 332 from Grave 8 of Majoro Chico A and Figure 348 from Grave 11 of Ocongalla West B, both phase *Y1*.

The present grave is clearly of phase *Y1*. There is a striking resemblance between Figures 349–350 from Soisongo A, Grave 2 and Figures 359–360 in this Soisongo C, Grave 13.

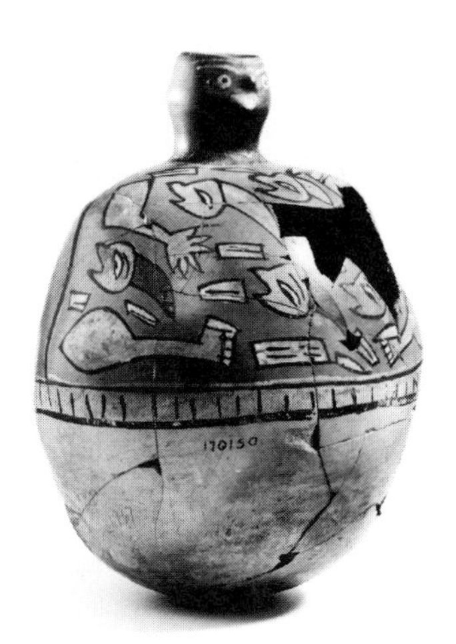

**Purchased at Paredones in 1925**

**FIGURE 362, 170150 (LATE N7).** When Kroeber visited the Nazca Valley on reconnaissance in the spring of 1925, a little over a year before the 1926 expedition, his guide, the intelligent huaquero Maldonado, who in 1942 excavated for Sr. Truel at Ocucaje, took him from Nazca city across the river to Paredones ruin and a large cemetery on the upstream side of it. Here some huaqueros were in the process of taking out of an open grave, by their piecemeal burrowing methods, sherds from a jar that interested him because of its design of detached human members. He returned at afternoon's end and they cheerfully sold him the accumulated sherds, which proved to restore to most of a jar with modeled and painted head, as shown in Figure 362 (170150). This has a degree of resemblance to the cambered-neck handled pitcher Figure 327 from Majoro Chico A, Grave 7B, to the camber-collared handled pitcher with bosses in Gayton and Kroeber (1927), plate 13e, and to the handled face pitcher Figure 381 from Agua Santa, Grave 1B, although these all have strap handles and the present specimen has none. It is also proportionally taller and slenderer than any of them: the measured H is 270 mm, D 205 mm, H/D 132%. The head is smaller, relative to the body, than in the foregoing or in the spherical-bodied *FPY* of Nazca *Y2* phase. In its round (or rhomboid) eyes and prolonged eyebrows it resembles the Agua Santa pitcher Figure 381.

The whole front of the upper half of our piece is framed in a slightly trapezoid panel. Here, on a LR background are painted yellow trophy heads, arms, and legs, together with smaller rectangles of unknown denotation. Eyes and toes are W, hair shocks DBr.

On the back, in another panel, are two large Y disks, outlined in B, 95 mm in D. These disks confirm the specimen as of phase *Y*.

The somewhat cambered head is B, with W eyes and brows painted on, a triangular LR mouth, and a modeled button of a nose. The whole piece is pretty well polished, and the painting, though sloppy like most Nazca *Y* representation, has a startling vigor from its very confusion.

CHAPTER 11

# *Later Phase Y2*

## GRAVES OF PHASE *Y2*

THE FIVE GRAVES CLASSED AS *Y2* contained a total of twenty-eight vessels. Majoro Chico E, Grave 1 is the most important as it alone accounts for fifteen of the vessels, including two face-pitchers. Two additional face pitchers were found with two *DBY* bowls in Soisongo B, Grave 9. A single face pitcher was present in each of the other three interments: Majoro Chico A, Grave 5; La Huayrona, Grave 1; and Agua Santa, Grave 1B; which contained three, four, and two vessels respectively.

### Soisongo B, Grave 9

This grave is the first of those containing face pitchers (shape *FPY*), which we have tentatively assumed to characterize the *Y2* phase; but it also contained two black-painted deep bowls *(DBY)* such as have characterized the preceding *B-Y* series of graves and which occur again in Majoro Chico E, Grave 1.

Grave 9 was 280 cm deep and contained two bodies and four vessels. The inference from the position of the objects in the grave is that the interments were not separated by any considerable interval.

**FIGURE 363, 170811 (N8).** *DBY* bowl. H 108 mm, D 180 mm, H/D 60%, below average in height for its type. Color, B all over except for two rectangular LR panels down from the rim. Each of these panels contains three rectangles, each of which in turn shows three horizontal B bean pods on Y. The small rectangles are finished at both ends by vertical stripes. Colors: W, Y, LR, and B.

**FIGURE 364, 170812 (N8).** Plain *B* bowl of *DBY* type, slightly higher than the last and without design. H 117 mm, D 175 mm, H/D 67%. It is painted B over all the outside and on the inner rim and was then polished, but much of the slip has worn away.

There are two face pitchers that differ in size, form, and painting; all they have in common is the general plan of big body, head with nose, almond eye, and strap handle. They were apparently associated with separate bodies in the tomb.

**FIGURE 365, 170814 (N8).** Smooth, somewhat polished body close to spherical; the only modeling is that of the nose. Eyes, eyebrows, neck lines, B; triangles of face paint under eyes DR; hair DR; arms DR, outlined in B; all this down nearly to the equator of the sphere on a LR slip background; below that, no slip. Black cross-stripes also on handle, which springs from halfway down the back of the head. The whole head tapers upward as a cone frustum in a characteristic Andean way. There is no W; the colors are LR, DR, and B. Dimensions are H 240 mm, D 212 mm, and H/D 113%.

**FIGURE 366, 170815 (N8).** Much smaller, the head flares instead of tapering upward, the handle sweeps down from the rim, and the body is roughly biconical (made by joining two halves?) instead of spherical and has four prominent bosses. The eye and mouth seem slightly modeled as well as painted. The dimensions are H 132 mm, D 142 mm, and H/D 93%.

There are indications of a whitish slip over the whole vessel, with a B or DR horizontal band just above where the body is biggest. The face is indicated by B outlining, with W for the eye and a LR stripe (for face paint) below it. A defaced, rayed painted head (in B) radiates out from a front boss, here against a LR background. There is no sign of arms painted on. The bosses on this piece carry a suggestion of plates 13e and 15f in Gayton and Kroeber (1927).

## Majoro Chico A, Grave 5

We have already discussed Graves 7 and 8 from this site as of phase *Y1* as well as Graves 14–18 and 20 of phase *A*. See Figure 22 for the relative position of the graves at this site.

Grave 5 was 200 cm deep. Only the long bones of the adult skeleton were saved, the skull being broken. Artifacts were fragments of cloth from near the bones and three pottery vessels.

**FIGURE 367, 170461 (N8); PLATE 29.** Well-made and intact face pitcher, the best preserved found by the expedition. It is unusual in that it has a low shoulder or step at about shoulder height of the figure. Probably the top and bottom of the jar were joined here, and this may account for the superior evenness and smoothness of the vessel. The larger lower part was lenticular, like a low shape-*Q* jar. The shoulder-step also no doubt suggested dividing the body design into two zones. The head is shaped into a definite neck, with maximum width at cheek height tapering up to the vessel's lip. The nose is the only feature modeled; eyes and hair are merely painted on. The H is slightly greater than D: 208 mm and 205 mm, H/D 101%. Relative to maximum D, the D at shoulder is 66%, at neck 28%, at head maximum 36%, at lip 28%, width of handle somewhat less but widening toward the shoulder. This seems to be near the ideal for face pitchers. We consider the face probably meant for that of a woman because its long eyes on yellow are a characteristic late *B* representation of women.

The background of the face and shoulders is the unslipped yellowish buff of the paste. On this the hair, eyebrows, eye outline, and pupil are B; the eye iris is W; and there is a LR stripe under each eye and down the bridge of the nose. On the shoulders are painted four much deliquesced rayed heads, alternately LR and R; outlined in B, with W eye, mouth, and crown. Below the shoulder, extending down not quite to the maximum diameter, is a W band bordered by LR stripes; on this are painted four pairs of design elements like a capital E, back to back in each pair; the pairs are alternately LR and DR.

**FIGURE 368, 170459 (N8).** Inside-rim-painted plate, perhaps verging on shape *GG*. H 72 mm, D 215 mm, H/D 33%, of reddish paste, unslipped. On this are painted four designs: adhering to the rim, each is LR, lenticular, with three W lines; away from the rim, each has a B scallop-edged band bordered by a W line. The position and generic shape of these designs (plus lack of slip) foreshadow Kelly's (1930) cumbrous bowl type.

Vessel 170460, not illustrated, is a plain bowl of similar shape and proportions but larger. H 85 mm, D 262 mm, H/D 32%. It was slipped B but this is now mostly eroded away.

## Majoro Chico E, Grave 1

This was a rich grave as Nazca *Y* graves go. It was also deep—four meters. Every vessel in it was broken, and the bones in such bad shape that none were saved.

**FIGURES 369a, 170543 (N8) AND 370a, 170553-1 (N8),** the *FPY* face pitchers, are near mates; meant to be duplicates in size and shape, they differ in their ancillary painting. We show photographs of both because one is more complete in the head and the other in its body painting; and again (in Figs. 369b and 370b) we show drawings of the quite different designs painted on the shoulders behind each elbow.

The respective dimensions and proportions are not quite identical:

| | **170543** | **170553-1** |
|---|---|---|
| H (mm) | 184 | 187 |
| D (mm) | 165 | 165 |
| H/D body (%) | 112 | 113 |
| D lip opening/D body (%) | 30 | 23 |
| H collar (face)/H total (%) | 24 | 22 |
| Width strap handle/D body (%) | 22 | 21 |

The colors are W, Y, LR, and B on both, plus DR in 170553-1 on the back only. The faces are Y, hair LR, eyes B and W. The shoulders are W (a thin slip), bounded by a B band above the equator; the arms and throat pendants are LR outlined in B with W showing across the hands.

The differing pairs of figures painted on the back, of which only a distorted edge shows in the photographs, have been drawn in Figures 369b and 370b. They are, in 170543, a central-eyed five-rayed, jagged but squarish deity trophy head in B; in 170553-1, a LR band ascending and descending in four steps above a DR smaller three-step one.

The faces have only the nose modeled plus a bit of depression for mouth. The collars formed by the heads are somewhat cambered, but the necks are greater in diameter than the pitcher opening. This constriction toward the top looks Andean, as does the painting of the arms and pendant. The painting of the eyes on the Y face and the back designs are definitely in the Nazca tradition still, for all their crudity.

**FIGURE 371a, 170553-2 (N8).** Shape-*V* head-bridge-and-spout jar on an oval (instead of spherical) body, has a small DR nubbin on the breast and another at the rear. The length is 156 mm, the breadth about 120 mm, height to top of spout 178 mm, to top of body about 99 mm; H/length 114%, H/breadth 148%.

Colors four: W, LR, DR, and B. Background W except for B base and B spout and bridge. The modeled head is LR with B hair and W cheek stripe. The W body of the vessel is latticed in B and divided into four sections by DR bands.

**FIGURE 371b.** A swimming human body is painted on the top in LR, with W finger- and toenails and with the modeled head arising out of the painting. The arms and legs cross the painted latticing, which seems to represent a fish net.

The nearest analogues are Seler's (1923) figures 347–349, which are better modeled and better painted and show the man swimming and holding an indubitable (and less-pervasive) net or two with fish in it. These Seler vessels looked like Nazca *A* ware to Kroeber (1956, 355). The degeneracy in the present Nazca *Y* piece is obvious, not only in the inept handling of clay and paint brush, but in the senseless way in which the fisherman is entangled in his net: one suspects that the painter of the present vessel no longer cared or knew precisely what he or she was representing.

If this *Y2* piece is really decadent from a Nazca *A* type, Nazca transitions ought also to turn up sooner or later.

**FIGURE 372, 170547 (EARLY N8); PLATE 30.** One of the rare shape-*L* conical goblets, which seem to be late *B* and *Y*. Uhle's *L* goblets from Nazca are late *B* and *Y* and have H/D ratios running from 97% to 130% (Kroeber 1956, 378). The present vessel is slightly taller than any of these, perhaps because it is later: H/D is 132% (H 178 mm, D 135 mm). The silhouette is slightly convex below, slightly concave above.

The colors are the familiar four: W, LR, DR, and B. The design was appropriately cataloged by Schenck as "stars and stripes." It is wholly geometric, in four lower and four upper square panels, alternating. One set contains a B and W checkerboard, twenty-seven of each, the W squares with a diagonal LR cross ("star"). The four alternate panels contain eight narrow W horizontal stripes bordered by B and seven wider LR ones. A rather narrow rim panel has a W-bordered B background on

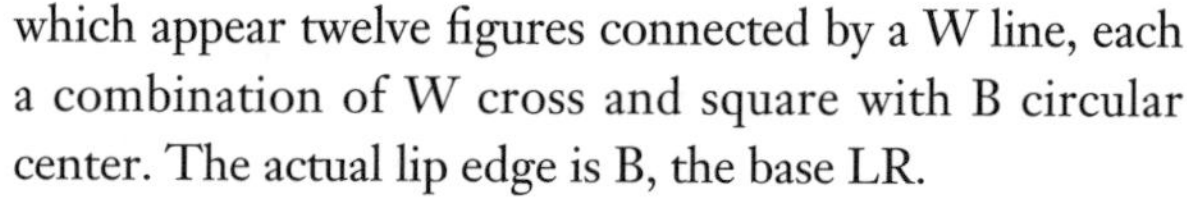

which appear twelve figures connected by a W line, each a combination of W cross and square with B circular center. The actual lip edge is B, the base LR.

Design and shape are too angular to be elegant, but the execution is with a neat firmness not common in Nazca *Y* vessels.

**FIGURE 373, 170549 (N8).** A mass of sherds numbered 170549 proved to consist of fragments of no less than four *DBY* black-painted bowls. The one shown here measured H 115 mm, D 152 mm, H/D 76%. Dimensions of the three other pieces were within 1 mm of these. Diameter of mouth was 80% of body D, indicative of the degree of incurve. In face we were at first inclined to class these vessels as lipless bowls of shape *Q*, but that form trends rather toward the biconical, with a nearly straight slope toward the lip, whereas the *DBY* shape is nearer a lopped-off sphere.

As standard in this type, the background is B. Besides this, W, Y, and LR occur. There are two large, square-ended LR crescents bordered in W. Each contains four half-length curved B bands in which there are five to eight W round dots. There are also two Y (nearly cream-colored) disks about 60 mm in D. The B background was put on after the disks and crescents, carelessly, so that the paste shows between them at times.

Vessel 170548, not figured, is a fifth *DBY* bowl, similar to the preceding in design but slightly different in dimensions and proportions. H 118 mm, D 145 mm, H/D 81%; ratio of mouth to body diameter 76%. It is peculiar that this one piece should differ somewhat when the others were made as identicals. The expedition found no other instance of five mates in a grave.

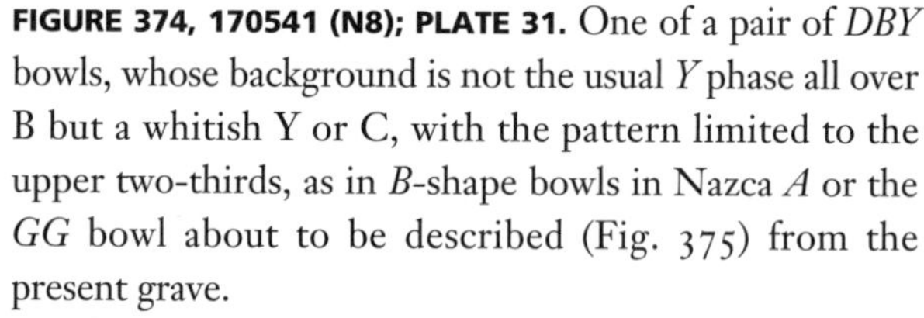

**FIGURE 374, 170541 (N8); PLATE 31.** One of a pair of *DBY* bowls, whose background is not the usual *Y* phase all over B but a whitish Y or C, with the pattern limited to the upper two-thirds, as in *B*-shape bowls in Nazca *A* or the *GG* bowl about to be described (Fig. 375) from the present grave.

There are about thirty-eight vertical B-bordered stripes in the upper pattern band, alternate ones cream-Y, and the rest in a recurring sequence DR, LR, G, and LR.

The base is unpainted, the horizontal band B, the lip and upper part of the inside also B. The five colors are cream-Y, LR, DR, G, and B. The cream or Y is probably a W that came out thick, since vessels wholly without W are rare in all Nazca periods. The G is the only occurrence in this grave. It is not a very common color in Nazca *Y*.

Height of 170542 (Fig. 374) is 123 mm, D 157 mm, H/D 78%, D lip/D body 73%; 170541 is 2 mm less in D, 1 mm less in H, H/D 79%.

In spite of their entirely distinct painted design, this pair of vessels conforms closely in shape to the five preceding black ones:

| | H/D (%) | LIP D/D (%) |
|---|---|---|
| 170549 (4) | 76% | 80% |
| 170548 (1) | 81% | 76% |
| 170542 (1) | 78% | 73% |
| 170541 (1) | 79% | |

**FIGURE 375, 170552 (N8).** The bowl just mentioned as of shape *GG* measures H 81 mm, D 140 mm, H/D 58%, and the D at mouth is only 1.5% less than the maximum of body D; in other words, the incurve at the opening is negligible as compared with that of the *DBY* bowls. The H ("width") of the design area is about 70% of the total H; of the design proper, around 45%. The design is a repeat of bent-ray fleur-de-lis alternately two-part and three-part, separated by pairs of diagonal bars; this all in B-bordered LR on a cream background, which, as in the previous vessel, very likely stands for W; the probable colors thus are three only.

Now follow three rim-painted plates, with designs that are precursors of the Kelly (1930) cumbrous bowls.

**FIGURE 376, 170544 and 170545 (EARLY N8).** Mates. The former measures H 63 mm, D 212 mm, H/D 30%; 170545 is 1 mm broader and 4 mm higher, H/D 31%. There is a thin whitish slip. On this are painted ten repeats of three concentric B-line arcs extending inward from the vessel rim. In alternate repeats, the spaces between concentric arcs are LR, in the other five W. There are three colors only: W, LR, and B.

**FIGURE 377, 170551 (N8).** Also a rim-painted plate. H 76 mm, D 178 mm, H/D 43%. Colors three, as in last: W, LR, and B. There are again arc-designs in from the rim; but there are only seven, are larger than in the last, and contain B two-sided steps. There is also a black band to delimit the rim design area.

## La Huayrona, Grave 1

Most the graves excavated at La Huayrona, at the southeast corner of Hacienda Pangaravi, were Ica or post-*Y* in period, but Grave 1, 200 cm deep, was Nazca *Y*. The pottery consisted of a face pitcher, two inside-rim-painted plates, and a bowl.

**FIGURE 378, 170581 (N8).** Face pitcher is intact and unusually neatly made. H 221 mm, D 217 mm, H/D 102%; mouth D/body D 23%. The colors are three only: W, DR, and B. The W is a thin slip. All face and head painting and the strap handle are B except for DR spots on cheeks. At the level of where the handle merges into the body is a B horizontal band. From the neck three sets of bands (three wide, four narrow in each set) radiate down to the horizontal band. The set in front is B, the two on sides DR. These take the place of arms in other pitchers.

**FIGURE 379, 170582 (N8); PLATE 32.** Inside-painted plate. H 83 mm, D 202 mm, H/D 41%. Colors again three: W, LR, and B. The slip is pinkish, probably LR. The three designs, at the rim, are rectangular, each consisting of four conjoined longitudinal B-bordered panels, the two middle ones W, the two outside LR, with a B straight line in the LR panels and a B wavy line in the W.

**FIGURE 380, 170583 (N8).** Inside-painted plate. H 87 mm, D 235 mm, H/D 37%. Colors four or five: a pinkish interior slip, Y or cream not far from W, LR, G, and B. There are five rim designs of arcs flattened nearly to rectangles, each consisting of three zones: at rim G, next Y or cream with B dashes and dots; farthest from rim LR. The three zones are B edged. The painting is poor and thin, the placing of the design units ragged.

Number 170584, not illustrated, is a plain brownish *DBY* bowl. 197 mm in D, 102 mm high, H/D 52%.

## Agua Santa, Grave 1B

This grave was encountered 50 cm below an Ica Period interment (Grave 1A). It contained two vessels but no body.

**FIGURE 381, 170610 (N8).** Face pitcher with the following dimensions: H 190 mm, D 193, H/D 98%. The upper half is painted red, the face and lower half are unslipped. The eyes, mouth, and three lines across the handle are black.

Vessel 170609, not illustrated, is a crude, heavy *ArY* plate, devoid of paint aside from a 25-mm-wide LR band around the interior rim. The sides are straight and expand outward from a flattened base. Dimensions are H 82 mm, D at rim 223 mm, D at base 60 mm; H/max. D 37%, H/min. D 137%. This vessel has higher sides and a more distinctly flattened base than are usually seen on *ArY* plates.

## COMPARISON OF PHASES *Y1* AND *Y2*

The ceramic content of ten phase *Y1* and five phase *Y2* graves has now been described, on the provisional assumption that *Y1* was marked by absence and *Y2* by presence of modeled face pitchers or flagons with strap handles. In each group there were several graves containing from three to eight vessels and one richer grave, containing respectively ten and fifteen. It seems fair to say that there seems to be a distinction, but that it is not very great and that the two phases overlap.

Phase *Y2* has proportionally more rim-painted plates, in designs of more parallel stripes containing dots, and more free-standing arcs or stepped triangles extending in from the interior rim of flattish plates. These last look like the initial stages of what Kelly (1930) has called cumbrous bowls, which have a wide distribution in Peru outside of the Río Grande drainage, where they are late phase *Y* and in which the design units are often placed along the rim.

Phase *Y1* has greater frequency of bowls of shapes *GG*, *B*, *F-H*, and oval, and also of angled goblets of shape *I*. Most of these have fairly close counterparts in Nazca *B* phase. As regards painted designs, the following, which occur also in phase *B* or have obvious prototypes there, are more frequent in the *Y1* than in the *Y2* graves:

1. Gray pigment.
2. Complementary step-frets separated by a stepped

diagonal band (cf. Fig. 292 with 342); or one of the frets two-color, the other remaining uniform.

3. The reduced or amorphous (deity?) trophy head, with central eye, sometimes a sort of stem, and rays bent over, cut off square, or combined into a sort of fleur-de-lis.

4. Right-angled lines, back to back.

5. Quartered bottoms.

6. Short black-line spines, cactus-like.

Phase *Y1* has more positive traits that become lost or rare in *Y2* than the reverse. There is less of the Nazca style left in *Y2* than in *Y1*, indeed less distinctive style of any sort. Beyond *Y2* one can no longer speak of a Nazca style; there is in fact already little Nazca left in *Y2*.

However, *Y1* grades into *Y2;* there is no sharp break. The black *DBY* bowls with disks and rectangular panel designs occur in both and with similar frequency. What is more significant is that, in our sample, *Y1* vessels are of thirteen shapes, none of marked frequency other than the deep black bowls, whereas in *Y2* there are seven different shapes: four-fifths of the vessels are made up of deep bowls, pitchers, or plates, the four other shapes having only one or two scattering representatives each.

The single *Y1* grave lacking *DBY* bowls is Grave 1 at Ocongalla West B, which in other respects shows more Nazca *B* features than did the other *B-Y* graves.

In short, *Y1* shades off into *Y2*. It can perhaps hardly be said that straight *Y2* is much further deteriorated qualitatively, but there just is less of the style left. However, *Y1* and *Y2* are only subphases and in most wider contexts can be subsumed as *Y*.

CHAPTER 12

# Pre-A1 Indications: Phase A0

## SUBSITE CANTAYO CAX

WE HERE BEGIN THE DESCRIPTION of pottery found at the intricate subsite Cantayo Cax, which somehow suggested in 1926 an antiquity greater than other sites dug in the Nazca Valley. It will be seen that some of these indications can be construed as correct.

### *Grave 11*

Contained a baby with a striped cloth over its head, buried in a wide-mouthed jar and set at a depth of 240 cm below the surface under a wall 170 cm high.

**FIGURE 382, 171031 (N 1/2).** The jar is a plain grayish brown vessel heavily encrusted with soot. The core of the paste is a dull reddish brown. Part of the bottom is gone; its present H is 345 mm, the estimated original H about 375 mm, the body D 330 mm; the original H/D would thus be around 114%. The most striking feature of the vessel is the enormous size of the mouth, both opening and neck, and the height of the flaring neck. This last is actually over one-fourth of the total height of the vessel in its present condition and must have been close to 24% or 25% while whole. The diameters, as measured on the photograph, are respectively 93 mm, 52 mm, 73 mm for body, neck, and rim, or 56% and 78% for the two last in terms of the body. These are much larger proportions than in Nazca *A* or *B* shapes. The two handles come off just below the neck but project beyond the body so as to make their diameter as great as the present reduced height. When Nazca *A* and *B* jars of basic shape *R* and *S* have handles, which converts them into our shape class *T*, they are usually less far spread opposite than the greatest diameter of body.

### *Grave 12*

About 0.5 m NE of Grave 11, under the wall D of the plot in Figure 59. In this was jar 171047, within which was another child (age 2–3 years), dried out, its skull deformed, the legs spread frogwise. Along with it was a guinea pig. This jar was of reddish ware, had the bottom broken out, and was set upside down. It measured about 450 mm in height (probably 470–500 mm when intact), about 500 mm in D, and around 130 mm in mouth D. The collar was very low and there were no handles.

### *Grave 13*

Contained the limb bones and skull of an adult, 171052; the latter was deformed long.

**FIGURE 383, 171053 (N 1/2).** Two fragments were kept from this large jar in which the body was buried. The rim fragment shown in Figure 383 is 45 mm thick at the lip, the folded rim is 80 mm to 125 mm, the shoulder 75 mm, and the lower margins of the sherd are 60 mm in thickness. The paste is coarse with a great deal of fine sand temper and mica flecks; paste texture is very similar to the small utilitarian pots from Cahuachi (Figs. 130, 131) and Aja B (Fig. 156).

The opening of this jar was about 300 mm across; its maximum D was around 900 mm; the bottom had been broken out by soil pressure; its original height was estimated at one meter; and the lip flared out.

### *Grave 14*

200 cm deep, contained a skeleton with natural skull, 171041, but no artifacts.

### *Grave 15*

Also along a wall, its skull showed some deformation, but again there were no artifacts.

### *Grave 16*

(See plot in Fig. 59.) 200 cm deep, contained a seemingly headless infant, in cloth wrapping, bedded on and in a mass of pacay leaves and covered by part of a jar, which unfortunately—perhaps because it was plain and coarse as well as incomplete—was neither described nor saved. The notes also mention a broken-handled olla (cookpot or water jar) just to the north of the body, but as if it were not part of the interment.

### *Grave 17*

Held only a child's deformed trophy head (171058, lacking the basal and occipital bones, age 8–9 years); contained both pottery and textiles. The head lay on pacay leaves and was covered by a red-bordered cloth (171059); on it lay a mass of wool strings, to which were attached three camelid metacarpal (or metatarsal) bones (171061). There were three pottery objects: a small, flat-bottomed bowl of blackware, 171065, containing food remnants and set by the head; most of a large angle-bottomed jar, whitish outside, blackish inside, 171066, covering the bowl; and a small double-barreled pottery whistle in the shape of a bird (171064).

Unfortunately, the blackware bowl 171065 cannot be located.

**FIGURE 384, 171066 (N2).** The covering vessel has H 173 mm, D just above base 191 mm, H/D 91%. The bottom is fairly flat for a Nazca-style piece, the turn into the side nearly right angled and rather abrupt, with neither an edge nor much rounding, the slope of the sides nearly straight converging, the lip without curve either in or out. The mouth D can only be estimated but was probably between 75% and 80% of the maximum D. We recall no Nazca *A* or *B* shape at all close to this one, except unpainted early Ocucaje F4-4701 and F7-4717, shown in Kroeber (1956), figures 1a and 1b, and there the rounding of base into side is greater. (The profile is a sort of hybrid of straight bowl *G* and lipless jar *Q* of the Gayton and Kroeber 1927 classification, but *G* has been given up as a standard shape and *Q* is round bottomed and round bellied.) Such affiliation as Figure 384 has is accordingly early Nazca *A1*. It is, however, painted with an all-W slip and B rim strip, with thin black slip inside. For parallels to this coloring, see Kroeber (1956), plate 37f.

**FIGURE 385, 171064 (N2).** This pottery whistle in Grave 17 is 60 mm long and double; that is, there are two blowholes and vents, parallel from tail to shoulders of the bird that is modeled. The painting is B on beak, head, back, and body with a W area around the eye and gizzard. The closest resemblance is to plates 34b and 34g, in Kroeber (1956), both from Uhle's Ocucaje, and to the Nazca two-barreled whistle 16-7852 (Kroeber 1956, 388).

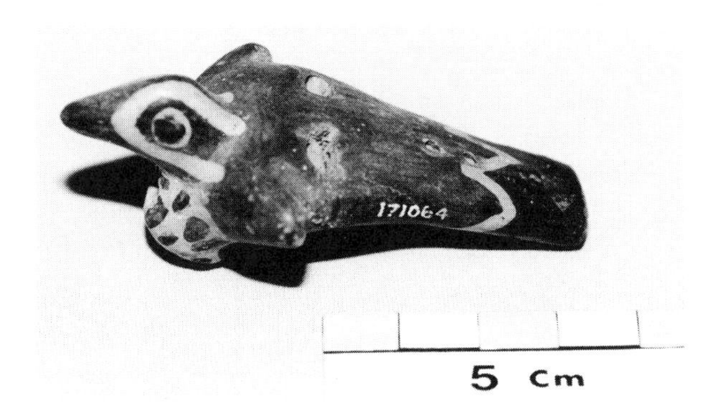


### *Grave 18*

Consisted of a child with deformed skull (age 6–8 years), 171067, at 260 cm below the surface.

**FIGURE 386, 171068 (N1/2).** A blackened, nearly globular jar with two handles, 80 cm above the skull. It was under Mejía Xesspe's direction that this recovery was made, and Kroeber's notes lack details, although he made one notation that suggested listing the jar and contents as Grave 18a and the child as Grave 18b.

[On the basis of the unique contents of this jar described below, vertical separation between child and jar, and the uncertain details of recovery, the editor agrees that these two finds should be treated separately. The jar and its contents fit better with the pattern of votive or ritual offering caches than with child burials. Also see Hair Analysis under Subsequent Research in the Preface, where hair artifacts found in the large jar are discussed.]

The globular jar has the following dimensions: current max. H 299 mm, max. D 348 mm, D at neck 187 mm, neck thickness 7–8 mm, shoulder thickness 10–11 mm.

The jar 171068 (Fig. 386) contained an astonishing collection of oddments, whose purport and use may become clearer on intensive analytic study. There were three lots. Numbers 17069a–b are a string or boa of pointed quills, and a small gourd. Numbers 171070a–m are a sack of felted (human) hair; three hanks of hair; a whistle of two canes; a hair wig; skeins of wool, of cotton, and of braided cord; four necklaces respectively of black seeds, of fruit husks(?), of joints of shrimp legs(?), and of blue beetle wings. Numbers 171071a–f are a brownish cotton cloth, a necklace of knitted fringe, an object of leather with a covering of yellow feathers, a cloth with border and fringe, a stone knife with a grip of netting, and its skin case.

Nothing nearly resembling this assemblage seems to have been reported with any other burial of Nazca culture. It strangeness strengthens the impression of the Cax finds representing a phase of Nazca culture separate in time from both Nazca *A* and *B*, and anterior—perhaps Nazca *Ao*.

As noted in the earlier chapter on excavations, the eight burials (Cax 11–18) were of three adults and five children, and of the latter one was represented by a prepared trophy head and one by a headless skeleton. Six of the eight were accompanied by textiles, and six were either contained in or covered by or associated with a large plainware jar or part of one. But the only pottery offerings were a blackened bowl, a white vessel, and a double whistle with the child's trophy head. This is certainly a different situation from the *A1* habit as exemplified at Cahuachi Site A or Aja B, where ceramic accompaniments, especially bowls, are standard, but the body was normally set on the floor of the tomb, not in or under a large pot.

**FIGURE 387, 171046 (TOP N3; BOTTOM N1).** We return now to five sherds, found not actually in Grave 12 but immediately above it. The two lower are most significant.

Figure 387, lower left, thin black sherd from interior of bowl, surface matte, with a pattern of stylus-polished lines. The outside is highly polished all over. This is what Strong calls "Cahuachi Stylus Decorated" (1957, 21, and figs. 7a–c, 9g–i) and lists as one of the criteria of his (resuscitatedly named) Proto-Nazca culture or period (preceding our Nazca *A1*), which terminates the Formative Epoch and is followed by his pure Nazca culture of the Florescent Epoch, subdivided into Early, Middle, and

Late Nazca. Strong's Early Nazca corresponds roughly to our *A1* (see Strong 1957, fig. 11); his Middle (ibid., figs. 13g–m) to our *A2;* his Late (ibid., figs. 13c–e, 14b–j) to our Nazca *B*. (Our Nazca *Y* he takes out of the Nazca style altogether, calling it Huaca del Loro—his fig. 15—and puts it into the Epoch of Fusion.) In short, stylus-burnished ware, according to Strong, is stratigraphically earlier than our Nazca *A1* and might therefore be designated as *A0* in our terminology.

Figure 387, lower right, is a rim sherd, 7 mm thick, from a large black bowl some 300 mm in D, polished inside and out. This is more *A0*.

Figure 387, upper row. Left: W, LR, and B; the fish-tail and dots are LR. Center: W, LR, DR, and B, the background being DR. Right: same four colors, background B, a LR and a DR oval both outlined in W and separated by a W line; the paste of this sherd is fine grained and verges on orange. These three sherds might be Nazca *A1* or *A0* like the two black sherds below them in Figure 387. These five sherds further tend to date Cax as prevailingly earlier than *A1*.

We list here the textiles from Cantayo Cax described by O'Neale (1937), most or perhaps all of which are likely to have been of Nazca *A0* phase as against the *A1* of Cahuachi.

### Cantayo Cax Textiles Described

| | | | PLATE |
|---|---|---|---|
| Grave 11 | 171033 | Striped wool material | 37g |
| Grave 11 | 171033 | Edge cord | 64c |
| — | 171045 | Kerchief edge | 65e–f |
| — | 171045 | Embroidered kerchief | 55b |
| — | 171049 | Embroidered band | 57b |
| — | 171050 | Cotton band, wool embroidered | 57d |
| Grave 18a | 171071a | Cross-striped wool material | 37a |
| Grave 18a | 171071b | Needle-knit fringed bands | 62c-d |
| Grave 18a | 171071c | Feather fringe | 66b |
| Grave 18a | 171071d | Check garment, fringed | 34d |
| Grave 18a | 171071d | Needle-knit band | 61e |
| Grave 18a | 171071d | Needle-knit technique | 63c |
| Grave 18a | 171071d | Weaving method | 68g |
| Grave 18a | 171071d | Looped fringe | 66c |

## VARIOUS *Ao* SHERDS AND FRAGMENTS

**FIGURES 388 (CENTER N2/3; BOTTOM N2), 389 (N2), 170890.** At site Aja B, which was a pure *A1* small cemetery, a test pit turned up sherds from 50 cm to 140 cm deep (?). Among these were several suggesting *Ao* or possibly earlier period.

One was a black rim sherd (Fig. 388, top left), about 21 mm x 25 mm and 3–4 mm thick, stylus-burnished inside; another, unburnished, was from the turn in a bowl wall (Fig. 388, top right); in both the paste was gray-black through, without any red. Most other pieces in the lot were or might be Nazca *A1*, as shown for instance by B and W panel dividers on DR of bowl exteriors (Fig. 388, center and bottom; exteriors shown). One rim fragment, Figure 389, is a bowl section with walls 3 cm high and 4 mm thick, max. D 180 mm. The exterior walls exhibit spattered R and B horizontally longitudinal stipples (6–10 mm long, 2–3 mm wide) transected by vertical black lines set 4–5 cm apart. Nearly all stipple marks tapered toward the left; the B occasionally lapped over the R. We do not recall any two-color stipples of this size on any Nazca *A1* vessel and suspect the design or technique may be characteristic of *Ao*.

In Aja B, Grave 8 there was a single glossy all-black rim sherd, 170913, bearing two vertical incisions made after firing. It appears to be from a bowl with nearly vertical sides and curved (not flat) bottom. Its significance lies in pointing to a pre-*A1*, or *Ao*, ceramic retaining Paracas traits, such as what Strong (1957) renames Proto-Nazca (logically enough, but likely to be confused with the older meaning of Proto-Nazca as originally named by Uhle to denote the total Nazca style). In fact, Strong illustrates a sherd from Cahuachi (1957, fig. 9a), which he calls "Cahuachi Polished Black Incised" ware, is very similar to our present Aja sherd. This *Ao* sherd, 170913, may have been in the ground when *A1* Grave 8 was dug.

**FIGURE 390, 171168 (TOP N1).** Cahuachi Site Ha, superficial excavations, yielded this "blackware sherd, graphitic lustre," that is, burnished (shown on top). The paste is fine, 3–4 mm thick, dark gray; both sides are well polished. The sherd has 21 mm of rim, maximum breadth 35 mm, maximum length from rim 43 mm.

Cahuachi Site Ea, trial pits in former diggings, yielded 171156, "incised sherd and 4 Nazca sherds." The incised piece is shown at bottom in Figure 390. Maximum length of the fragment is about 87 mm, thickness 3–5 mm, paste reddish buff with fairly large inclusions of white tempering material. The inside is smoothed a little, the outside smoothed fairly well and washed a pinkish buff. The incisions are about 1 mm wide; there are six longer and six short ones, the latter all tapering to a point as if the gouging tool had been swiftly dipped into and out of the still soft clay. Apart from the two upper left, the incisions are arranged to produce two point-to-point triangles, each containing three diagonal parallel lines; whether this was a repeated pattern or happens to be the preserved portion of a more complex design is not clear.

**FIGURE 391.** Two dark, unpainted, incised sherds were found on the surface of Soisongo Site C. A rim sherd reproduced from Kroeber's field notes, is shown in Figure 391. It was found by Mejía and is thought to have been deposited in the National Museum of Peruvian Archaeology, Magdelena (no other information available). The second piece, 170851, is a body sherd exhibiting one horizontal incised line and the ends of two vertical incisions; these three incised lines are along one edge of the sherd.

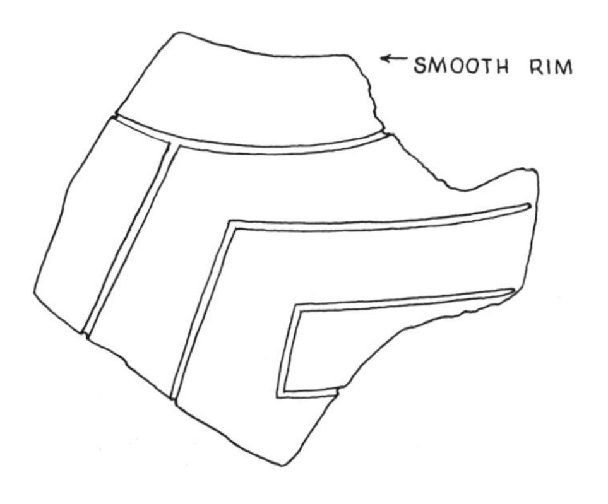


## PARACAS SHERD

In Ocongalla West B, Grave 12, sherd lot 170782, from one-third the way (170 cm) down this 500-cm-deep grave of period *B2*, there was one small sherd that was incised and post-firing-painted or encrusted with gum, in W, R, and B, with rectilinear pattern. This is the only Paracas post-firing-painted sherd found, or at any rate recognized, in the expedition's work. Another sherd from the same lot is a fine blackware piece and may have been Paracas or Nazca *Ao*.

## OCONGALLA WEST B, GRAVE 6: *A1* OR *Ao*

This was the only phase *A* grave found by the expedition at Ocongalla Site B. It was 100 cm deep; the adult skeleton was fragile, badly broken and the parts confused, and was not saved. Otherwise, the grave contained (besides a mussel shell) six bowls, or if interior painting is used as criterion of what constitutes a plate, there were four bowls and two plates. Three of the vessels were wholly plain; one had only two crossing stripes as painted design and had been stylus polished; two were painted with designs in generic *A1* manner but rather ineffectually executed. This grave is certainly not later than *A1* and may be *Ao*. We class it as doubtful between the two subphases.

**FIGURE 392, 170695 (N2/3)** is an inside-center-painted plate of shape *Ac*. H 65 mm, D 207 mm, H/D 31%. The inside rim and the outside bottom are DR. The lip edge is B. The center background is cream color or a dirty W. On this are painted two fish, parallel but head to tail. Their central body stripes and large round eyes are W. One is B on the back and DR on its belly, the other similarly G and LR.

**FIGURE 393, 170693 (N2/3)** is a *B*-shape bowl. H 74 mm, D 155 mm, H/D 48%. The base is DR, the design-panel background LR, a lip stripe B. The design consists of seven two-sided step blocks, poorly outlined in W, each one differing in the color of its left and right halves, and rather uneven in their steps and proportions. The three pairs shown in Figure 393 are, from left to right, G-B, unpainted-DR, B-DR; the four remaining ones, G-unpainted, B-DR, unpainted-G, and DR-unpainted. There is no regularity of repeat here. The four unpainted halves of blocks are in the orange-reddish paste. We cannot tell whether this absence of paint was intentional or whether this space was intended for a color that gave out or was not momentarily at hand and was forgotten when firing began. The total applied pigment scheme is W, LR, DR, G, and B. The manner is technically inferior Nazca *A1* style.

**FIGURE 394, 170698 (N2/3).** An inside-painted plate, with actual shape basically much like that of a *D* bowl, whose side viewed in profile shows a concavity of 1–1.5 mm. H 63 mm, D 167 mm, H/D 38%. The vessel might be described as semipainted. The exterior was slipped LR. The inside was unslipped but had a wide-striped cross painted on it from rim to rim in LR. It was then polished, but before the paint was properly dry so that the polishing strokes smeared some color on the unslipped quadrant areas, giving the simple design its fuzzy appearance, especially up and down across the arm extending horizontally over Figure 394. We do not recall other instances of this sloppily offhand manner of painting in the Nazca *A1* style.

**FIGURE 395, 170694 (N2/3), and FIGURE 396, 170696 (N2/3).** Also unusual for phase *A1* is to have three of the six bowls in a grave wholly unpainted except for an overall LR slip: 170694, shape *B* (Fig. 395); 170696, shape *Ba* (Fig. 396); and 170697, the last two being mates. The respective sizes are 170694, H 78 mm, D 200 mm, H/D 39%; 170696, H 63 mm, max. D 162 mm, rim D 157 mm, H/max. D 39%, H/rim D 40%; and 170697 about the same. Except for 170694 being somewhat larger, the three, plus the preceding one painted with a cross, are identical in size and in proportion (H/D close to 39%). Inasmuch as our basic definition of a plate as different from a bowl is that it is painted inside instead of outside, the distinction breaks down for three of these pieces and is trivial for the fourth because of the abnormality and slightness of the painting. Essentially what we have are four plainware reddish bowls, fairly flat bottomed, and differing from plates not only in averaging higher but in a steeper up-slope of their rims. For some reason, one of them was painted with an abnormally simple design, namely two red cross-stripes, which were then smudged by a hasty attempt at polishing.

CHAPTER 13

# *Post-Nazca Culture: Late Period*

[Descriptions of the recoveries from Cantayo Cb, Grave 5, Agua Santa, Graves 1A, 2, 4, 5, and 9; and the purchased vessels from Poroma have been added to complete the Late Period inventory.]

## SOISONGO B, GRAVES 4, 5, 6, 7, and 10

Apart from one early-*A* grave already described, Grave 11 near the center of the cemetery (see plot, Fig. 49), most of the graves opened by the expedition in Soisongo B were Late: Graves 5, 6, 7, and 10. Besides these, Grave 9 was Nazca *Y2*, which may have been antecedent to Late by only a brief period. These graves were clustered in the western end of the cemetery except for Grave 10, which lay close to the northeastern edge. The Late and near-Late graves opened were thus peripheral, the one early grave central in position. Grave 4, containing only an incised jar that we are unable to place as to period, was near Grave 5 but also not far from early Grave 11.

Both the Nazca-style graves, the terminal *Y2* as well as the early *A1* or *A0*, were fairly deep, 280 cm and 180 cm, and the skulls in them were deformed. The definitely Late Period graves were generally shallow, and the skulls, as recorded for Graves 5 and 6, were undeformed. The 40 cm depth of Grave 4 would tend to align this with the Late graves in general age.

Not only were the Late graves shallow, but they were poor, each containing only one vessel, a bowl or plate. In this feature, Grave 4 again resembles them, although the vessel was a spherical jar and incised.

We proceed now to a description of the pottery in these Late graves.

### *Grave 4*

**FIGURE 397, 170803.** This grave contained only a small-mouthed spherical jar. Dimensions are H 208 mm, D 245 mm, D lip edge 115 mm, D neck 90 mm, H/D 85%, lip D/maximum D 47% (small-mouthed by Nazca standard), neck D/max. D 37%. The outside is smooth and well polished, as is the inner side of lip. It is allover red, but with firing clouds; we are uncertain whether the red was applied or is the clay paste. There is no decoration except seven small incised curves on the shoulder, each like an inverted capital-U.

### *Grave 5*

20 cm deep, held only sherds (170804) and a belt or sling (170805). The skull (170806) was undeformed. This burial appears to be of Late Period.

## *Grave 6*

**FIGURE 398, 170808 (N8).** This grave, 190 cm deep, contained the inside-painted plate or cumbrous bowl. H 65 mm, D 188 mm, H/D 35%. The surface of the bowl is natural buff color, unpainted. The only design is eight double (parallel) arcs extending inward from the rim. Both lines of these arcs are B, as is the lip edge of the vessel. The circle segments contained by these arcs are painted alternately W and LR. The colors thus are three, plus background. The arcs are rather uneven in size and contour and their spacing is unequal.

## *Grave 7*

**FIGURE 399, 170809.** This grave also contained only one vessel, and that little superior in quality to the last. It is also inside-painted on the natural buff clay, but is deeper and more like Kelly's (1930) cumbrous bowls. H 83 mm, D 162 mm, H/D 51%. Although rounded, it approaches the conical, and it would certainly spill most of its contents unless bedded in sand. The colors are three: W, DR, and B, plus background. Basically the design consists of four arclike figures along the rim, extending toward the center. These begin with a low symmetrical pyramid of three steps, then a B-bordered band in a flat arc; this band is W and DR in alternate occurrences. A black double-step finishes off each arch at each end. Two B wavering lines connect the four arcs, crossing at the center. Each quadrant thus formed contains three parallel short B arcs and three B dots. The execution is sloppy, the design rather meaningless, as if the painter had had the impulse to produce something decorative but was without resources. There is some resemblance to Gayton and Kroeber (1927), plate 18f, Nazca Valley Late; also to Kroeber and Strong (1924), figure 11.

*Grave 10*

**FIGURE 400, 170816 (WARI, MH2).** An outside-painted, incurved open bowl. H 96 mm, D 159 mm, H/D 60%. As in the previous plates, most of the surface is wholly unpainted. Painting consists of B on lip; a 20-mm-wide W band below it containing about seven LR horizontal broad wavy lines; and below this a somewhat narrower solid B band. The B is not very deep, the W not clear, the LR might be DR pigment thinly applied.

## CANTAYO Ca, GRAVE 21

As detailed in the chapter on excavations, there is doubt whether this was a grave. Sr. Mejía Xesspe, who saw the digging, reported it was not a grave, and our workmen said there was no body but produced the bones of a leg (171017) with healed fracture. With or somewhere near this were a cumbrous bowl, 171015, and what was cataloged as 171016, a "smashed large bowl with W over-painted design," which however mended in the museum into two spherical bowls, evidently representing skulls, un-Nazca-like in style. They differ in size, the first H 232 mm (base lacking), D 270 mm, H/D 86%; the second H 207 mm (including base), D 233 mm, H/D 89%. They differ also in some minor features, such as only the first having perforated ears. They may represent husband and wife, or parent and child.

**FIGURE 401, 171016-1 (MH, VIÑAQUE INFLUENCE).** This is the only one of these vessels illustrated. The form of this pair of vessels is unlike anything Nazca; it would come nearest to shape *Q*, lipless jar. The opening is turned horizontal, without trace of collar. The bottom is quite flat, which is a north-Peruvian or Andean-highland trait. Only the W triangles on the cheeks, below the eye, suggest a Nazca-style face paint, although Nazca paints flat areas there, not outlines. The eyes are enormous W disks—quite different from Nazca-style eyes—B-bordered with large B pupils, evidently representing the cavernous eye sockets of skulls. The nose is cut off in the blunt shape of the nasal bones of a skull. The mouth is a white downcurve without Nazca parallel, so far as we know, B bordered and divided by four B borders into five schematic teeth. (Faint streaks below the mouth are acetate from mending, not original.) The forehead is painted unbordered W. The back of the head is

unpainted, except for a B looped stripe from which hang four B bands, two medial wavy, two lateral and smooth curved, representing hair. Besides W and B, the jar is painted red.

The triangles under the eyes may represent the sides of the mandible rather than paint. However, the effigies seem chinless. The downcurved mouth may represent the row of upper teeth with the lower absent.

With all its passion for trophy heads, the native Nazca population did not have the habit of modeling or painting representations of bare skulls. We incline to believe that these skull bowls represent an intrusion from the highland.

**FIGURE 402, 171015 (MH, VIÑAQUE INFLUENCE).** Also from Grave 21 at Cantayo Ca, along with the two skull jars reminiscent of Andean influence, an inside-painted flat-bottomed bowl of H 75 mm, D 258 mm, and H/D 29%, which would make it a plate. Colors four: W, Y, DR, and B, plus dun or buff unslipped paste. Painted design is limited to two pairs of units adjacent to the rim. One pair is bounded by a DR arc band and contains a B area with zigzag edge, with Y between the DR and B. The other pair of figures is five-sided, with two diagonal lines meeting concavely opposite the rim. The figure contains two triplets of adjacent DR bands, each ending in a W quadrilateral, bounding and dividing lines being B. While in detail of design this plate is somewhat aberrant, it conforms generally to the pattern of Late Coast plates, and it probably suffices to approximately date the "Andean" skull jars.

## CANTAYO Ca, GRAVE 3

**FIGURE 403, 171002 (LOCAL LIP).** The sole vessel found with body 2 (60 cm deep), below body 1 (40 cm deep), in Grave 3 of Cantayo Ca, and it establishes both burials as Late. It is a flat, low, inside-painted plate with bottom gently rounded from rim to rim. H 60 mm, D 228 mm, H/D 26%. The upper or design side was probably W slipped, as the illustration suggests. The design painting is in DR and B. In the central area are four sets of three B parallel lines, rather evenly wriggled, parallel also to the rim; and a fifth set of three in the middle. For about 15 mm in from the rim is a continuous DR band across which are painted a spaced pair of sets of three parallel wriggly B lines abreast each similar set in the interior central area. Between these transverse sets, most of the DR rim band is overpainted with a B band.

## CANTAYO Cb, GRAVE 5

Two elderly males were found with a mock or false mummy, and three vessels in this highland-derived grave of Coastal Tiahuanacoid period.

**FIGURE 404, 171026 (MH 1B/2A).** A cylindrical-collared jar, shape *CJY*. H 166 mm, D 145 mm, H/D 114%. It has an overall DR slip; the lip is B; and the chevrons on the rim alternate W, G, W, and G. The shoulder design is outlined in B; dots are W; and the vertical scrolls alternate W, G, W, and G.

**FIGURE 405, 171027 (LOCAL MH).** An incurved bowl. H 68 mm, max. D 146 mm, rim D 130 mm, H/max. D 47%. The exterior rim has a wide band of DR with a B line demarcating its lower margin; the lip is B. The pendant semicircles on the rim are B outlined in W dots. Between the semicircles are sets of five vertical bars; each set exhibits three bars in solid W outlined in B, between which are two B bars outlined in W dots. The white is closer to a cream or almost flesh color. The base is unslipped, natural buff.

**FIGURE 406, 171028 (MH 1B?).** A bowl. H 68 mm, D 167 mm, H/D 41%. The interior and exterior surfaces are painted DR. As with the previous bowl, 171027, the lip is B and the lower edge of the exterior design field is marked by a B line. The design consists of solid W panels outlined in B, between which are insectlike motifs (modified "stinger-creature"?) with four dots against a DR ground. The elements are outlined in B and painted W and G. Whether by design or accident, the exterior center base has a shallow indentation, which gives the profile a flat-bottom appearance.

## LA HUAYRONA, GRAVE 3

**FIGURE 407, 170586 (MH2, VIÑAQUE).** Very similar to Figure 400 of Soisongo B, Grave 10 is the incurved bowl, from Huayrona, Grave 3, at 150 cm deep. H 101 mm, D 180 mm, H/D 56%. The lower half is unpainted. From there to the rim is the design: a broad B encircling band, a red or DR band in which are nine broad-line W curving figures lying on their side, and then a B edge to the lip.

Graves 4, 6, and 7 at Huayrona contained no whole vessels, but were also classed as Late on the basis of some cloth and slings and their undeformed skulls.

## MAJORO CHICO B, GRAVE 1

Grave 1 at Majoro Chico B was Late. The skull was undeformed, and with it, at 120 cm, were some Late Period sherds (170435). There were three pottery vessels: 170432, not illustrated, small fire-blackened cookpot, at 75 cm; 170433 (Fig. 409), inside-painted plate or cumbrous bowl, at 85 cm; 170437 (Fig. 408), a flatter inside-painted plate, at 190 cm.

The differences in depth are unexplained. The first two vessels may be assumed to have been deposited together, but they are well above the body, whereas the third was 70 cm below the skull.

**FIGURE 408, 170437.** H 86 mm, D 253 mm, and H/D 34%. Colors three: W, LR, and B, all within rim band on upper (concave) side, the center and the underside being natural (unslipped) LBr or buff. The ground of the design band is W. The principal design consists of four repeats of side-by-side pairs of arcs, bowing from the rim inward, each arc containing three short transverse bars. Two opposite pairs of arcs are formed by wide B lines or bands; in two other pairs, the lines are LR. The bars are LR in the B arcs, B in the LR. There is also a pair of still wider B bars pointing inward from the rim between each pair of arcs. The painting is hasty and without precision.

**FIGURE 409, 170433.** A less-flat plate than the last. H 73 mm, D 173 mm, H/D 42%. Colors three: W, DR, and B. Again there seems to be no background slip; but there is design over the whole inside face. The design combines rim arcs with quartering and filling of quadrants. The four arcs are flat and are formed by a rather wide band, with a bar bisecting the enclosed space. The arc bands are B bordered; two of them are W, two DR. Deliberately wriggled B lines stretch across the plate between opposite arcs, crossing at center. In each quadrant thus formed are four or five B wriggly lines, parallel to the rim but without curvature. The design effect is disorderly and without attempt at precision.

## AGUA SANTA, GRAVES 1A, 2, 4, 5, and 9

The cemetery at Agua Santa contained Nazca *B* and post-Nazca graves in addition to several interments which lacked pottery. The Nazca *B* graves were clustered in the northeast part of the cemetery, while the Late Period graves lay close to the road on the western side (Fig. 37). Late Graves 2 and 9 were encountered just outside the Nazca *B* cluster. We now turn to a description of the pottery in the Late graves.

### *Grave 1A*

100 cm deep, contained an elderly woman wrapped in cloth with rope bindings, a small cloth bag tied at the back of her neck. Two vessels lay by her feet, a strap-handle jug (170607) and 170606, a bowl (or inside-painted plate) that contained a guinea pig.

**FIGURE 410, 170606,** the inside-painted plate. The vessel has no slip ground on either interior or exterior; designs are executed on natural buff. There is a narrow W band framed by B lines around the interior rim; all other designs are B. Dimensions are H 69 mm, D 179 mm, and H/D 39%.

**FIGURE 411, 170607,** is a strap-handle jug with geometric designs painted in B, W, and DR. H 126 mm, rim D 68 mm, neck D 50 mm, max. D 131 mm, H/max. D 96%.

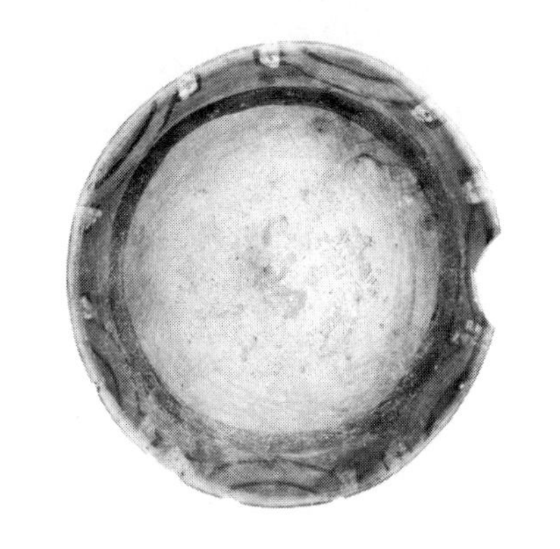

*Grave 2*

Contained two skulls, two vessels (170612–13), and thirteen sherds (170611) representing six to nine additional vessels, all at a depth of 150 cm. The sherds agree in period with the vessels described below. As postcranial elements were not present, this grave is better characterized as an offering cache or dedicatory skull burial.

**FIGURE 412, 170612,** is an inside-painted plate similar to Figure 410 in the absence of a ground color; all painting on natural buff. There are three colors; B, W, and DR. Dimensions are H 86 mm, D 235 mm, and H/D 37%.

**FIGURE 413, 170613,** a deep bowl *(DBY)*, with a DR band around the interior rim. The exterior design uses the same three colors as the previous piece: B, W, and DR. Measurements are H 85 mm, D 154 mm, and H/D 55%.

*Grave 4*

**FIGURE 414, 170618.** Grave 4 contained a single vessel with a woman and a child at a depth of 100 cm. The accompanying vessel, an inside-painted plate or bowl, is shown. As with Figures 410, 412, and 415, there is no ground color; designs are painted in B, W, and DR on natural buff. Dimensions are H 82 mm, D 173 mm, and H/D 47%. The vessel profile and dimensions are similar to 170620, Figure 415.

## *Grave 5*

**FIGURE 415, 170620.** Contained in a shallow burial approximately 110 cm deep (estimated), marked by a mass of cloth, hair, cordage, and sherds near the surface. Below a layer of small branches were the remains of an elderly woman with vessel 170620, which contained a guinea pig, set under her right arm. An inside-painted plate or bowl with natural buff surfaces; no ground color. The simple interior design, painted in B only, consists of two vertical, squiggly lines, on opposite sides of the interior walls, and two similarly opposed semicircles, pendant from the rim, each with a central dot. Vessel dimensions are H 80 mm, D 175 mm, and H/D 46%. (Compare with Figure 414.)

## *Grave 9*

In disturbed ground and contained the much-disarranged remains of an adult at 40 cm. There were two complete vessels near the body (170626, 170630) and sections of several others (170627–29). Of this latter group, 170628 cannot be located but was described as a partial bowl with "terrace design outside." Numbers 170627 and 170629 are sections of Nazca *B* vessels that were probably encountered when this Late Period grave was dug.

**FIGURE 416, 170626,** an inside-painted plate or bowl with a LR slip for ground on the interior. The bird or fish creature on the interior bottom is W, outlined in B, with LR eye and foot. The serpentine elements around the interior rim are W with B dots. The exterior rim exhibits spaced bands of slightly diagonal stripes, four stripes in each band, with bands alternating W, LR, W, and LR. Dimensions are H 58 mm, D 145 mm, and H/D 40%.

**FIGURE 417, 170630,** is a crude shape *Q* jar, which contained hard adobe. The surface of the vessel was roughly scraped but not smoothed during manufacture. Two large areas on the exterior were slipped W, but this is the only pigment applied. The dimensions are H 144 mm, D 184 mm, and H/D 78%.

## PURCHASED AT POROMA

A small selection of artifacts was purchased at Poroma in the southern Nazca drainage (Fig. 1). These materials all appear to be of Inca or Late Ica period. The four vessels described below are among the purchased items.

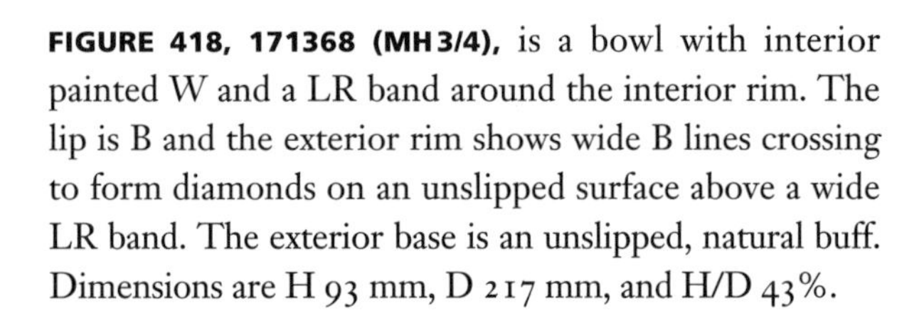

**FIGURE 418, 171368 (MH3/4),** is a bowl with interior painted W and a LR band around the interior rim. The lip is B and the exterior rim shows wide B lines crossing to form diamonds on an unslipped surface above a wide LR band. The exterior base is an unslipped, natural buff. Dimensions are H 93 mm, D 217 mm, and H/D 43%.

**FIGURE 419, 171369 (MH3/4),** a bowl very similar to the previous Figure 418. The interior rim has a DR band and the lip is B. The exterior rim exhibits a continuous DR serpentine design accompanied by short B horizontal lines against a W ground, above a B band. The lower exterior is unpainted. Dimensions are H 77 mm, D 180 mm, and H/D 43%.

**FIGURE 420, 171370 (MH3/4),** is a bowl with a LR band on the interior and exterior rim, lip also LR. The exterior rim carries Y squiggles and x shapes with circles on either side, all of these overpainted with B lines (B dots in circles). The bands below are B, W, and B respectively. The lower exterior is unslipped, natural buff. Measurements are: H 52 mm, D 162 mm, and H/D 32%.

**FIGURE 421, 171371 (MH3/4),** an inside-painted plate or bowl, similar in profile to Figures 418 and 419. On the unslipped exterior are traces of faint B lines, but design cannot be determined. The lip is B. The interior rim has a DR band with four nested v designs, two of these B and two Y. The central interior has a Y ground color on which lines, squiggles, dots, and the center x are B. Dimensions are H 45 mm, D 103 mm, and H/D 44%.

**APPENDIX**

# *Mineral, Plant, and Animal Identifications*

## MINERALS

Identified by Dr. Robert K. Wyant, formerly Curator of Economic Geology, and Harry E. Changnon, Curator of Exhibits in the Department of Geology.

170990
Cantayo M, Grave 4. Cataloged as lump of gypsum. About 12 x 7 x 5 cm. Very soft and friable. Would be useful for polishing.

171009
Cantayo Cb, Grave 2. Lump of friable, waterworn sandstone, about 12 x 9 x 6 cm. Contains coarse quartz grains, silica, and some iron. Could be used as an abrasive.

171299
Cahuachi Ag, Grave 1. About 198 grams of finely pulverized hematite pigment. Color is dark purplish red. Undoubtedly used as pigment.

171327
Cahuachi Ag, Grave 7. Quartz pebble, 7 cm in diameter and 4 cm thick. The surface is waterworn and shows no signs of polishing or abrasion to indicate human use. Traces of hematite on one face.

## PLANTS

Identified by Dr. Hugh C. Cutler, formerly of Economic Botany.

171044
Cantayo Cax, found with two sherds south of wall J. Large pallar bean, color ocher with brick red spots. A variety of *Canavalia ensiformis.*

171290
Cahuachi Aj, Grave 13. Lot of large, dried tubers, five nearly complete and several fragments. Identification: sweet potato *(Ipomoea)* or *yacón (Polymnia edulis).*

171326
Cahuachi Ag, Grave 7. Two pallar beans, one large and dark brown and the other smaller and red brown. Identification: *Canavalia ensiformis.* (Cutler thinks these two and the one in 171044 represent three varieties of *Canavalia ensiformis.*)

## ANIMALS

171239
Cahuachi Aj, Grave 11 (Fig. 73). Mummified parrot. Genus *Amazona*, probably *farinosa* species ("Plain colored parrot"). Range: tropical forest of South America; has not been reported from the Peruvian coast. Identified by Emmet R. Blake, Curator of Birds. [Genus *Amazona*, specie *farinosa* ("Mealy Parrot"), tropical lowland forest, reconfirmed by John Fitzpatrick and David Willard, Birds Division, Field Museum, 1986.]

171248
Cahuachi Aj, Grave 12 (Fig. 74). Llama bones: five metatarsals and two metacarpals. Three of the metatarsals have been drilled longitudinally, the holes vary from 3 mm to 6 mm in diameter. These bones are in a lot with a small wooden spoon, a wooden atlatl thumb rest, a small ball of black gum, an obsidian blade (retouched flake), a bone spatula (100 x 11 x 3 mm), a turquoise pendant, a heavy perforated stone disk (38 mm in diameter, 9 mm thick, hole 9 mm in diameter) that is probably a spindle whorl, and a piece of cotton cloth with blue stripes on selvage. Bones identified by Phillip Herskovits, Associate Curator of Mammals.

# Literature Cited


Gayton, A. H. and A. L. Kroeber. 1927. *The Uhle Pottery Collections from Nazca.* University of California Publications in American Archaeology and Ethnology, vol. 24, no. 1, pp. 1–46.

Kelly, I. T. 1930. *Peruvian Cumbrous Bowls.* University of California Publications in American Archaeology and Ethnology, vol. 24, no. 6, pp. 325–341.

Kroeber, A. L. 1926. *Archaeological Explorations in Peru. Part I. Ancient Pottery from Trujillo.* Field Museum of Natural History, Anthropology Memoirs, vol. 2, part 1.

——— 1930. *Archaeological Explorations in Peru. Part II: The Northern Coast.* Field Museum of Natural History, Anthropology Memoirs, vol. 2, no. 2, pp. 45–116.

——— 1937. *Archaeological Explorations in Peru. Part IV: Cañete Valley.* Field Museum of Natural History, Anthropology Memoirs, vol. 2, no. 4, pp. 221–273.

——— 1944. *Peruvian Archaeology in 1942.* Viking Fund Publications in Anthropology, vol. 4, New York: Viking Fund.

——— 1954. Proto-Lima: A Middle Period culture of Peru. *Fieldiana:* 44(1), pp. 1–157.

——— 1956. *Toward Definition of the Nazca Style.* University of California Publications in American Archaeology and Ethnology, vol. 43, no. 4, pp. 327–432.

Kroeber, A. L. and W. D. Strong. 1924. *The Uhle Pottery Collections from Ica.* University of California Publications in American Archaeology and Ethnology, vol. 21, no. 3, pp. 95–134.

O'Neale, L. M. 1936. Wide-Loom Fabrics of the Early Nazca Period. Essays in Anthropology. pp. 215–228. Berkeley: University of California Press.

——— 1937. *Archaeological Explorations in Peru. Part III: Textiles of the Early Nazca Period.* Field Museum of Natural History, Anthropology Memoirs, vol. 2, no. 3, pp. 117–218.

O'Neale, L. M., and A. L. Kroeber. 1930. *Textile Periods in Ancient Peru.* University of California Publications in American Archaeology and Ethnology, vol. 28, no. 2, pp. 23–56.

Rowe, J. H. 1956. Archaeological explorations in southern Peru, 1954–1955. *American Antiquity* 22(2): 135–151.

Seler, E. 1923. *Die buntbemalten Gefässe von Nasca in Südlichen Peru und die Hauptelemente ihrer Verzierung.* Gesammelte Abhandlungen zur Amerikanischen Sprach-und Altertumskunde, Band IV, pp. 169–388. Berlin: A. Asher & Co.

Strong, W. D. 1957. Paracas, Nazca, and Tiahuanacoid cultural relationships in south coastal Peru. Memoirs of the Society for American Archaeology, no. 13. *American Antiquity,* 22(4), 2: 1–48.

**AFTERWORD**

# NASCA RESEARCH SINCE 1926

*Katharina J. Schreiber*

When Kroeber began his work in Nasca[1] (Figure A-1), he had already developed a special interest in coastal Peruvian archaeology, having worked with collections made earlier in the century by Max Uhle. He had first worked with his student, William Duncan Strong, on collections from Chincha and Ica (Kroeber and Strong 1924a, 1924b), and then with student Anna Gayton on Uhle's Nasca collections (Gayton and Kroeber 1927). Having visited Nasca in 1925, his 1926 field work was designed to locate intact deposits of Nasca ceramics in order to answer questions that had arisen during the analysis of the Uhle collections. He therefore chose to focus upon and excavate only those sites pertaining to the Nasca culture, and this accounts for his lack of interest in sites dating to later periods. (See the obituary written by John H. Rowe for a more detailed discussion of the circumstances surrounding Kroeber's research [Rowe 1962].)

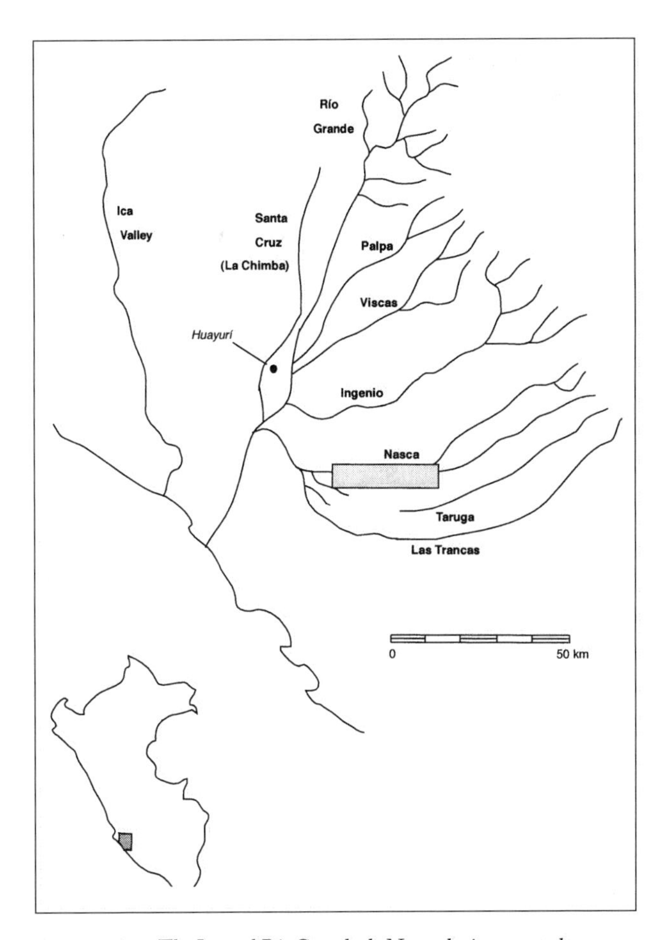


FIGURE A-1. *The Ica and Río Grande de Nasca drainages on the south coast of Peru. The site of Huayurí is noted. The shaded area is the portion of the Nasca Valley in which Kroeber conducted most of his research; see Figure A-2 for details.*

Our views of Nasca culture have changed substantially in the seventy-plus years since Kroeber's field efforts. In this afterword to Kroeber's detailed field observations, I provide a brief, general overview of Nasca prehistory as we now view it (and knowing these views in turn will change through the next century). Second, I summarize Nasca field and artifact research since Kroeber's time. And third, I provide data on the locations of Kroeber's sites and their state of preservation (or lack thereof) today.

My own experience in Nasca began in 1974 when I initiated what was to be a decade of research in the adjacent Andean highlands, in the Province of Lucanas, Ayacucho. During those ten years, Nasca was a haven to which we could retreat (after a harrowing two-day drive) to fill the gas tanks, get a good meal, and take a (sometimes) hot shower. My research interests in Nasca began in 1984, after political unrest in the highlands precluded doing any more field-work there. Most of this work has been devoted to intensive, systematic survey of the region, locating and recording all the archaeological sites still visible on the surface.[2]

Modern surveys are more intensive and systematic than they were in Kroeber's time; while Kroeber was only interested in a particular kind of site, our surveys recorded all visible remains, regardless of time period or type of site. In the 25-kilometer-long sector of the Nasca Valley in which Kroeber investigated 26 sites, we have recorded more than 150. In total we have covered some 75 kilometers of the valley, from Tambo de Perro to Ronquillo, plus 25 kilometers of the Aja tributary, recording over 300 sites just in the Nasca Valley. We have recorded an additional 300+ sites in the Taruga and Trancas valleys. I include this information so that the reader will understand my own research biases; my focus is on regional settlement patterns, rather than artifacts. Therefore, in my summaries of Nasca research I will focus primarily on the sites and the region, rather than on the ceramic artifacts.

TABLE A-1

| STANDARD CHRONOLOGY | | CULTURE NAMES | KROEBER PHASES | CULTURAL EVENTS |
| --- | --- | --- | --- | --- |
| Late Horizon | | | | Inca conquest |
| Late Intermediate Period | | | Late | regional cultures re-established |
| | 4 | | | societal |
| | 3 | | | collapse |
| Middle Horizon | 2 | Huaco del Loro | Nazca *Y* | Wari conquest |
| | 1 | | | |
| | 7 | Late Nasca | | reorganization |
| | 6 | | Nazca *B* | |
| Early Intermediate Period | 5 | Middle Nasca | | transition |
| | 4 | | Nazca *A2* | emergence of |
| | 3 | Early Nasca | Nazca *A1* | Nasca culture |
| | 2 | | Nazca *A0* | |
| Early Horizon (1–10) | | Paracas | | initial permanent occupation |
| Initial Period | | | | unoccupied (?) |
| Preceramic Period | | | | temporary hunter-gatherer occupations |

TABLE A-1. *Chronological chart of Nasca prehistory correlating the phase names used by Kroeber with terms currently in use*

**NASCA PREHISTORY: A Perspective from the End of the 20th Century**

A more detailed relative chronology has been developed for the region (Table A-1),[3] and the basic sequence of cultural events is generally known. In Kroeber's time, the distinctive Nasca style of ceramics and textiles had drawn the attention of anthropologists, but the social context within which those artifacts were created was not known. Indeed, it was generally assumed—based on the high quality of the artifacts—that the "civilization" was also highly developed. However, we now know that Nasca society was not a state or an empire; rather it was made up of loosely allied small polities, of a sort we might call "chiefdoms." Rather than a major political center, Nasca was a smaller and less-complex culture, but one that enjoyed an especially rich artistic tradition. Heir to the earlier Paracas and Topará cultures, Nasca also had elaborate burial traditions and massive cemeteries. (Unfortunately, these elaborate burials have produced an active modern tradition of grave robbing and looting on a massive scale.)

It is now known that the first occupants of Nasca were hunter-gatherers who lived in temporary settlements thousands of years before the modern era. The first permanent occupation began in the first millennium B.C., in what we call the Early Horizon, a few centuries before the emergence of Nasca culture. The valleys were colonized by people of the Paracas culture, who probably migrated from Ica or from other valleys of the north. Kroeber's tentative definition of Nazca *Ao* was the first evidence of an earlier tradition preceding the full-blown Nasca culture.

Nasca culture emerged around A.D. 1, and lasted about 750 years. Kroeber's Nazca *A* and *B* phases are generally correlated with what we now call Early and Late Nasca, respectively. Early Nasca people lived in small villages scattered throughout the Andean foothills. (Kroeber did not ascend the valley far above the modern town, so he never saw any of these sites.) The great ceremonial center of Cahuachi was in active use at this time. Mounds and pyramids were built and ritually remodeled, and religious offerings were left at the site. Cahuachi was also surrounded by dozens of cemeteries, suggesting that people made pilgrimages to the site to bury their dead in sacred space.

After four or five centuries of relative stability, Early Nasca society changed. Perhaps because of extended drought in the adjacent Andes, the already dry region became parched, and the people turned their efforts to constructing massive irrigation works in Middle and Late Nasca times. At the same time, they moved out of their small villages and into large towns, which indicates social reorganization, and perhaps conflict as well. While construction ceased at Cahuachi, it was still used in connection with the adjacent cemeteries where they continued to bury their dead. Kroeber's work not only has provided the best data on Nasca burial practices, but his division of the ceramics into earlier and later phases correlates very well with the changes that the Nasca society was undergoing. Indeed, this basic division of phases still forms the underpinnings of our analyses of social changes.

When Kroeber classified the later phases of Nasca ceramics as Nazca *Y*, he noted their association with what at that time was called Coastal Tiahuanacoid styles. The latter had been identified first by Uhle, in his excavations at Pachacamac on the central Peruvian coast, who noted their similarity to ceramics from the highland Bolivian site of Tiahuanaco.[4] In the 1930s, Julio C. Tello, the Peruvian archaeologist who had collaborated with Kroeber in Nasca, identified the source of the Coastal Tiahuanacoid ceramics as a site near modern Ayacucho, called Wari. Kroeber intuitively had felt that the Coastal Tiahuanacoid materials were from the sierra and that they represented an actual presence, or invasion, of highlanders. He could not have been more correct. It is now thought that Nasca—and most of what is today Peru—was conquered by the Wari Empire at about A.D. 750, beginning what we now call the Middle Horizon.

After the fall of Wari, Nasca (and most of Peru) underwent a period of collapse and reorganization. Only 500 years later another highland empire would rise; this time Nasca came under the control of the Inca Empire. Inca control lasted only from A.D. 1476 to A.D. 1533, when the Spanish Conquest caused the fall of the Incas. We still know relatively little about prehistoric events in Nasca after the fall of Wari and before the arrival of the Incas.

## ARCHAEOLOGICAL RESEARCH IN NASCA SINCE 1926

Most research that has taken place in Nasca since 1926 has focused on the Nasca culture of the Early Intermediate Period and the subsequent Middle Horizon, while very little attention has been paid to what Kroeber termed the Late Period. It is interesting that the research priorities set by Kroeber have changed so little, at least in terms of the periods to be studied. More recent research has focused on four overlapping areas of endeavor: 1) analyses of artifacts (especially ceramics and textiles), 2) investigation of particular cultural features (burial patterns, geoglyphs, puquios), 3) excavation of single sites, and 4) regional surveys. I shall deal with each of these foci in turn.

### Artifacts

Although nearly every museum with archaeological assemblages includes a collection of Nasca ceramics, almost none of those collections is the result of excavations made by professional archaeologists. Even Uhle's 1905 collections were probably purchased, not excavated. Kroeber's first interest was in ceramics and developing a chronological sequence that could be used to order the artifacts and sites in which they were found. Although after leaving Nasca he went on to other interests, he did return to Nasca research in the 1950s, certainly prompted by a new flurry of activity there. William Duncan Strong, his former student, was undertaking excavations there (Strong 1957); and a new University of California (Berkeley) project was underway in various valleys of the south coast, directed by John H. Rowe (1956). Never satisfied with the sequence he and Gayton had developed in the 1920s, Kroeber reanalyzed the collections and published a new revision (Kroeber 1956). And he returned to the writing of the present monograph, which he worked on until his death in 1960.

The study of ceramics has always been, and will continue to be, a major focus of Nasca research. Strong's work in 1952–1953 included excavations at the site of Huaca del Loro in the Trancas Valley, allowing greater refinement of what Kroeber had called Nazca *Y1* and *Y2;* Strong termed the substyles Loro Polychrome, Loro Polychrome Fine, and Tunga Polychrome Fine (Strong 1957, 36–43; Paulsen 1965). Lawrence E. Dawson, a member of Rowe's team, undertook to develop a seriation of Nasca ceramics and divided them into nine phases, which correspond generally to Kroeber's Nazca *A* through *Y*. Dawson's sequence is the one used today by archaeologists working in the region; unfortunately, it has never been published in its entirety. Various other archaeologists, many of them students of Rowe, have continued the work of refining the sequence and elaborating details of particular designs and phases (e.g., Proulx 1968, 1983, and 1989; Roark 1965; and Wolfe 1981).

Nasca textiles have also received a good bit of attention, some of it by Kroeber himself, in collaboration with Lila O'Neale (1937). Most textile experts are drawn to the earlier Paracas textiles, which overlap slightly in time with Early Nasca, but other studies deal directly with the textiles of the Early Intermediate and later periods (e.g., Rowe 1984).

## Features

**BURIAL PATTERNS.** Kroeber's collections are invaluable in that they include not only artifacts but also data on human remains, tomb construction, cemetery layout, site location, and so forth. His excavations provide some of the most reliable data on Nasca burial practices. Patrick Carmichael has been able to make direct use of Kroeber's materials in his seminal analyses of Nasca burial patterns (Carmichael 1988, 1995).

Related to rituals associated with death, the Nasca people also had a practice of taking severed human heads, preserving them, and suspending them from rope handles. These so-called trophy heads are depicted on Nasca ceramics and found in Nasca tombs and caches. While the cultural practices of taking, preparing, and displaying the heads are not yet clear, extensive anthropological studies have been made of the heads themselves, their depictions, and the archaeological contexts in which they are found (see Baraybar 1987; Carmichael 1994; Drusini 1991; Proulx 1989; and Browne, Silverman, and García 1993).

**GEOGLYPHS.** Kroeber was perhaps the first scientist to observe the Nasca geoglyphs, the now-famous Nasca Lines. He did not discover them in any real sense, given that they are mentioned in government documents reaching back at least to 1839, although he is sometimes awarded this honor. Ironically, it is the Lines that give Nasca its greatest fame today, and they are the biggest draw for tourists. In Kroeber's time they were virtually unknown. While interpretations of the Lines range from the ridiculous (landing strips for extraterrestrial space ships) to the sublime (power centers for New Age meditation), most scientific analyses would concur that they functioned as ritual roads or pathways of some sort. While neither their religious significance nor whether they pointed at sacred mountains or represented watercourses can ever be known with any degree of certainty, Kroeber was remarkably perceptive in seeing them as roads. (For summaries of current scientific research on the geoglyphs, the reader is referred to Reiche 1968, Aveni 1990, Hadingham 1987, and Morrison 1978.)

Kroeber noted geoglyphs at two locations, near their camp at La Calera and at Aja. In both cases he noted that lines radiated outward from small isolated hills; these are today called Line Centers, and there exist dozens of such places in the region (Aveni 1990). In the case of La Calera, he provides two discordant plans of the Lines; comparison with aerial photographs taken in 1944 indicates that Figure 9 is the more accurate of the two. Most of the Lines he noted there are badly damaged or gone today. The modern airport runway is now located just north of their former camp, adjacent and parallel to the road.

Likewise the lines he noted radiating outward from the hill at Aja B can no longer be seen, owing to the expansion of agriculture in the immediate area.

**PUQUIOS.** Kroeber was one of the first scientists to note the existence of underground aqueducts, or filtration galleries, in Nasca. *Puquios* are essentially horizontal wells that tap ground water and bring it to the surface where it can be used for agricultural and domestic purposes (Mejía Xesspe 1939; Schreiber and Lancho 1995). Kroeber, ever the astute observer, noted in several places that the "infiltration" of the Nasca rivers causes most of the length of their beds to be dry. The puquios were a way to overcome this difficulty and render the valley habitable. Puquios have underground galleries, with access shafts called "ojos." It is these shafts that Kroeber referred to as puquios; he thought they were individual wells connected by tunnels beneath the surface. He noted their existence in Taruga and Trancas and also included one on his plan of Cantayo.

The lack of water in most of the areas he worked, and the concomitant lack of early habitation sites in those same areas, resulted in an interesting bias in Kroeber's observations. He pointed out that there were very few substantial constructions in the Nasca Valley: only Paredones, Curvi, Cahuachi, and Estaquería. The former two sites are Late in date (established after the puquios were built), and the latter two are located far downstream, where perennial water is available. Had Kroeber ventured a few more kilometers upstream from the town of Nasca, to the point where water is available year-round, he would have noted dozens of archaeological sites of all time periods literally lined up along the sides of the valley (see Schreiber and Lancho 1995). Currently, an Early Nasca site is being excavated in this region by Kevin Vaughn of the University of California at Santa Barbara (UCSB), which will provide one of our first glimpses of Nasca domestic contexts.

### Site Excavations

**CAHUACHI.** Cahuachi is the largest site in the Nasca Valley, with the most impressive monumental architecture, and, not surprisingly, is the site that has received the most attention from archaeologists. Kroeber, although not the first to dig there, was perhaps the first to try to make sense of the entire enormous complex of ceremonial mounds and cemeteries as a single related entity. (See Silverman 1993, 14–29 for a summary of the history of research at Cahuachi.) In 1952–1953, Strong undertook excavations there in order to try to find stratigraphic associations between Nasca and the earlier Paracas culture. He concluded that Cahuachi was densely populated and served as the capital of the Nasca civilization.

In 1983, Helaine Silverman undertook a program of small excavations at Cahuachi, designed to test various ideas about Cahuachi's role in Nasca society. (See her 1993 monograph for the best extant plans of Cahuachi, as well as their correlation with Kroeber's plans.) She concluded that the site did not serve as the political capital of Early Nasca society, but rather was an empty ceremonial center, abandoned after Nasca 3. She also excavated a Loro phase room at the site (Silverman 1987).

Subsequent research by a long-term Italian expedition (1985 to present), directed by Giuseppe Orefici, has undertaken the excavation of several of the some forty-three mound complexes (see Orefici 1993), revealing the presence of massive construction efforts and major remodelings as well as numerous offerings ranging from single ceramic vessels to an offering pit filled with dozens of sacrificed llamas. Like Silverman, he sees the site as an empty ceremonial center, abandoned at the end of Nasca 3.

The jury is still out on Cahuachi, however. The excavations of Strong, Silverman, and Orefici have produced large amounts of habitation refuse, not to mention evidence of ceramic and textile production. It is clear that the site was not devoid of a permanent population, although the size of that population remains unknown. Further, although construction and remodeling of the mound complexes ceased by the end of Nasca 3, the site continued to be used as a religious center. Offerings there, as well as burials in the surrounding cemeteries, continued to be made through Late Nasca times and into the Middle Horizon.

**ESTAQUERÍA.** The temple complex recorded by Kroeber at Estaquería still stands, but most of the wooden posts have been removed. Kroeber did not write much about the site in the present monograph, but the reader is referred to his 1944 book in which he published several photographs of the site as it looked in 1926. Strong excavated there in 1952 but left as bewildered as Kroeber as to its nature, a state that persists to the present day. Estaquería is generally thought to be a religious site, pertaining to Late Nasca and/or the Middle Horizon. It may have replaced some of the functions of Cahuachi when constructions at that site ceased. The architecture of Estaquería is perhaps unique, but Strong (1957, 4) did observe a similar structure at Tres Palos II in the Grande Valley; later attempts to locate this site have not been successful. The Italian expedition plans to begin excavations at Estaquería in the near future, so our questions about the site may be answered soon.

**AGUA SANTA.** This small site was excavated in 1984 by the Italian expedition (Orefici 1993, 234–237; Isla, Ruales, and Mendiola 1984). While Kroeber's excavations focused on burials, the site apparently had a domestic component as well. (*Note:* The articles cited refer to the site as Pueblo Viejo; forthcoming publication by Isla Cuadrado will return to the original name, Agua Santa.)

**TARUGA VALLEY SITES.** Kroeber mentions only in passing two sites in the Taruga Valley. He described the "ruin" as an extensive town along the north side of the valley, but he probably only looked at ceramics from the west end. At the east end is an area that would appear to be a continuation of the Late town but is actually a very large Late Nasca town. In 1994, a UCSB project undertook test excavations at this site and found it to be a 16-hectare habitation site, occupied from Nasca 5 through 7, with most artifacts pertaining to Nasca 6; Middle Horizon Wari sherds were present but in extremely small number. Given extensive water damage to the site, no further excavations are planned. It is not unlikely that the vessels purchased by Kroeber at Taruga were from this site.

The Late Period Taruga "site" is actually a series of sites, habitation and cemeteries called Pajonal Alto. It is currently undergoing excavation by Christina Conlee of UCSB. The habitation portion of the site spans periods from the Middle Horizon (Loro phase) through the Inca occupation, and it is hoped that a ceramic sequence for Kroeber's Late Period will finally be developed, with stratigraphic control.

**LAS TRANCAS CEMETERIES.** Kroeber noted an extensive series of cemeteries along the south side of the Trancas Valley—still clearly visible today. These were the subject of excavations undertaken by Tello in the subsequent 1920s and 1930s; Tello did quite a bit of work in the Trancas Valley, although his field notes are yet unavailable, and he published very little about it. Materials from these cemetery excavations are currently being analyzed by Johny Isla, and those results will certainly further our knowledge of Late Nasca and the Middle Horizon.

**HUACA DEL LORO.**[5] Kroeber makes specific mention of this site, excavated by Strong in 1952–1953 (after Kroeber's field work, but before the present monograph was written); Huaca del Loro became the type site for defining the Loro styles of pottery, as discussed above. At the site, Strong excavated a round structure he designated as a temple. Also visible at the time were extensive remains of rectilinear architecture and burial areas (Strong 1957, 36–43). By 1970 the site had been largely bulldozed, but in such as way as to partially protect much of the site from looting; surface artifacts still cover an area of over 10 hectares. No subsequent work has taken place there, although excavations are being planned by Johny Isla and Mario Ruales.

**PACHECO.** Ironically, one of the greatest archaeological discoveries ever made in Nasca, Pacheco, was nearly made by Kroeber, but owing to a mix-up in plans he was never shown the site. Instead, his collaborator Julio C. Tello is credited with the discovery of this large Wari site, from which came a massive offering deposit of smashed fine ceramics. Tello excavated there in 1927, removing nearly three metric tons of sherds. Ronald Olson of the American Museum of Natural History also excavated there in 1930 (see Menzel 1964 for a discussion of the offering deposit.) By 1944 the site had been bulldozed to create new cotton fields, but traces of the site may still be seen along the edge of the first river terrace.

## Regional Surveys

Since 1926, three surveys have been conducted in the Nasca Valley, and individual surveys have been undertaken in most of the other Río Grande de Nasca tributaries.

**WILLIAM DUNCAN STRONG, 1952–1953.** Much like Kroeber, Strong was looking only for major sites, and specifically sites appropriate for excavation. He recorded sites in the Ica and Nasca drainages and along the coastline at San Nicolas Bay (Strong 1957). Unfortunately, he died before completing the writing up of his work, so we have only a map and a table of sites recorded, and no details. He did work in the same general region as Kroeber and recorded many of the same sites.

**DAVID ROBINSON, 1954.** Robinson's survey is the first that might be described as systematic and comprehensive. He noted the active destruction of sites in Nasca, especially cemeteries, and set about to make a record of them before they were gone (Robinson 1957). He was affiliated with Rowe's south coast project in 1954 and was given the responsibility for the Nasca survey and for developing a ceramic chronology especially for the late periods. He surveyed the Nasca, Taruga, and Las Trancas Valleys, the same valleys in which Kroeber had worked, and his recorded sites are almost exclusively cemeteries. His sketch plans and verbal directions for finding sites are unfortunately based on roads and structures no longer extant. He did provide map coordinates, but these can only be used with topographic maps produced in 1950, no longer available.

Robinson worked with professional *huaqueros* (looters) as informants, given that they knew best where all the major cemeteries were. And he bought a collection of ceramic vessels from them, indexed to the sites from which they were supposedly taken. This collection, the Wattis collection, is now housed at the Hearst Museum of Anthropology at the University of California at Berkeley (UCB).

**UCSB SURVEYS, 1986–1996.** As mentioned above, my own work has involved intensive, systematic survey of the Nasca, Taruga, and Trancas Valleys. We have covered all the areas in which Kroeber, Strong, and Robinson worked in these three valleys, recording all visible sites—to date over 600. The work has been done in collaboration with UCSB students, Peruvian students, and Peruvian archaeological colleagues (especially Johny Isla and Miguel Pazos.) Formal survey was undertaken in 1986, 1989, 1990, 1994, and 1996, and we believe it to be essentially complete. Publication of results is yet forthcoming, but some settlement data are reported in Schreiber and Lancho (1995).

**SURVEYS ELSEWHERE IN THE NASCA REGION.** Nearly every tributary of the Río Grande de Nasca drainage has been the subject of archaeological surveys, more or less comprehensive, in recent years. Carmichael completed a survey of the coastline and the lower reaches of the Ica and Nasca Valleys (Carmichael 1991). The Santa Cruz Valley (Kroeber's La Chimba) is currently being surveyed by Johny Isla and a Peruvian team. The Grande, Palpa, and Viscas Valleys have been surveyed by David Browne and Peruvian collaborators (Browne 1992; Browne and Baraybar 1988). And Silverman and Peruvian collabora-

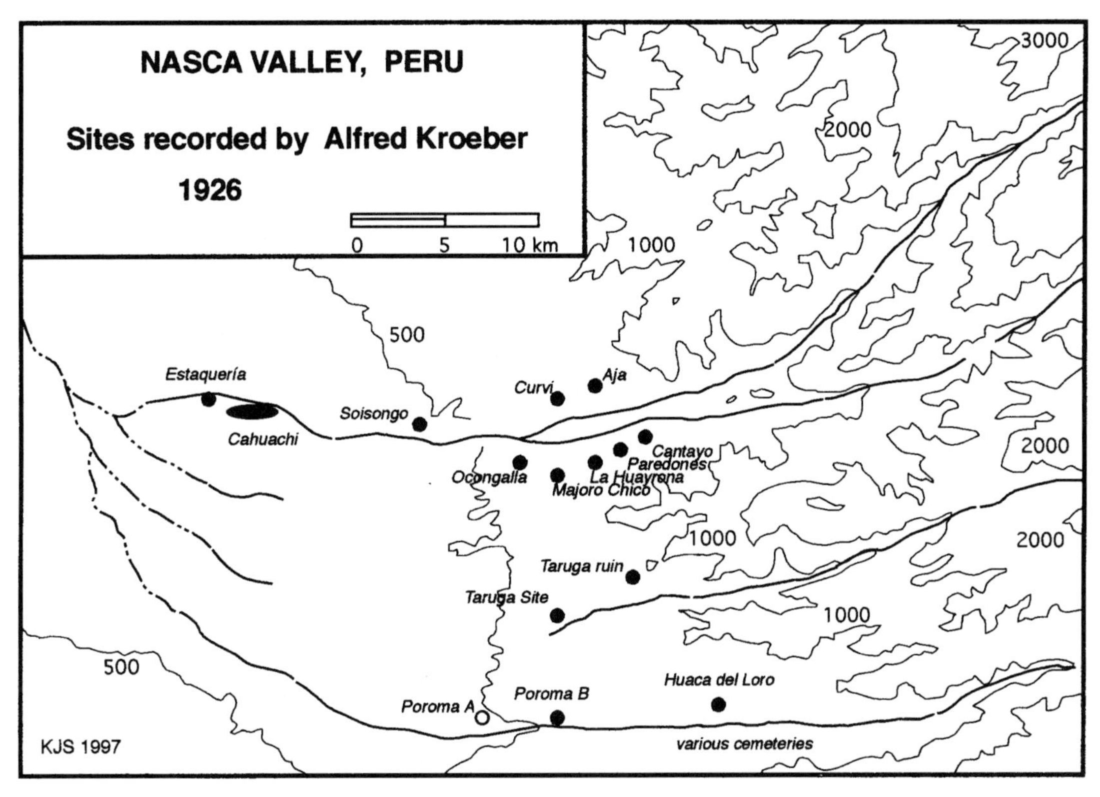


FIGURE A-2. *The Valleys of Nasca, Taruga and Las Trancas, showing the approximate locations of the sites recorded by Kroeber. As Poroma A could not be located exactly, its general location is indicated by an open circle.*

tors have completed a survey of the Ingenio Valley (Silverman 1993). Currently unsurveyed are the Jumana and Coyungo portions of the drainage, but Donald Proulx is planning to address these areas in the near future.

#### LOCATING KROEBER'S SITES

It is possible to locate many of Kroeber's sites with absolute precision, and even those that no longer exist can be situated with relative precision (Figure A-2). In order to locate Kroeber's sites, one must first begin with his sketch plans and verbal descriptions. Kroeber himself bemoaned the lack of existing maps when he did his field project and so was never able to use formal maps as his point of reference. (And in using his sketch maps one wishes that he had had an eye for topographic detail equal to his eye for ceramic detail.)

Second, one must consider what has happened between 1926 and the present and the current state of preservation of his sites. Of the twenty-six sites he discusses in the Nasca Valley, eleven have since been destroyed. By destroyed, I mean that there remain no surface traces of their existence; they may indeed (with one exception, Soisongo E) be preserved below the surface. Two factors account for the destruction: expansion of agriculture and construction of modern structures (including houses, commercial establishments, water control facilities, roads, and an airport). Expansion of agriculture is especially perilous to sites lying immediately adjacent to cultivated areas on ground that is only slightly higher than the cultivation. This accounts for the destruction of eight of the eleven destroyed sites.

The looting of sites also complicates their identification. While looting was already a serious problem in 1926, most looting has apparently taken place since then—and will probably continue for the foreseeable future. What were discrete sites in 1926 may now appear to be a single extensive looted area without obvious spatial subdivisions. Thus in some cases we can locate one or more of Kroeber's sites only as being within the boundaries of a much larger contemporary site.

Third, we may make use of maps and aerial photography not available to Kroeber. There exist good modern maps, all produced after 1970, at scales ranging from 1:10,000 to 1:250,000. Even more useful than maps are aerial photographs, available from the National Aerophotographic Service (SAN) of the Peruvian Air Force. A series of photographs taken in 1970 at 1:10,000 closely approximates the current landscape (as most alteration took place prior to the agrarian reforms of the late 1960s). But most useful is a series taken at 1:15,000 in 1944, only eighteen years after Kroeber's work. *Nearly every one of Kroeber's sites can be pinpointed on the 1944 photos.* Comparing the two sets of photos, along with the reports of the various archaeologists, one can determine specific dates by which particular sites were destroyed and had disappeared from view.

**Ocongalla**

On his Figure 11, Kroeber depicts a series of cemeteries and habitations at Ocongalla. This is a case in which subsequent looting has transformed what were once discrete sites into a single enormous looted site; both Robinson and Strong recorded the entire mess as a single site. The key to locating Kroeber's sites is the semicircular palisade and wall depicted on his sketch plan; these features are visible on the 1944 photos. To the east and west are also visible a series of discrete cemeteries that are arranged very much like those of his plan. In 1990, the UCSB project recorded several cemeteries in this area: Ocongalla Zero and Ocongalla West A, along with the Late cemetery between them, form our Site 90-C23. The adobe structure at Ocongalla Zero, whose location on Kroeber's two plans is not the same, is still visible, at least the higher portion of it; a very large looter's pit has exposed part of it. The Late cemetery between A and the wall-palisade is our Site 90-C24. We did not record the house walls inside the palisade as that entire portion of the site has been obliterated by modern houses and a new road leading north into the valley bottom. Just to the west is Ocongalla West B, which is our Site 90-C25. From this point to the west is a solid area of looted tombs, our 90-C26, which probably includes the two Late cemeteries. The site of Agua Santa is discussed below.

**Majoro Chico**

The knoll at Majoro Chico B is visible on the 1944 photos, but the site was already partially destroyed by then owing to plowing for agricultural production. Majoro Chico A is visible as a long narrow area of looting to the north of B, arranged along the valley edge and bisected by the old road leading out to the Majoro hacienda. Kroeber worked only on the east side of the road and noted (correctly) that the site may have extended to the west. The other three Majoro Chico sites cannot not be located precisely, except to place them between A and B and the three small hills to the east. Robinson's Site PV69-11 is located at the base of those hills, although he thought (erroneously) that he was at the same site recorded by Kroeber; Strong did not record Kroeber's site either. All traces of the five sites were completely obliterated on the surface sometime before 1970 and, aside from the occasional potsherd, are all but invisible on the surface. Carmichael and I visited the site in 1993 with the express purpose of locating precisely Kroeber's sites, but we were unable to do so. The 1944 photos provide our only data.

**La Huayrona**

Located just across the highway from the east end of what is now the airport runway, the site has been completely destroyed, first by agricultural expansion and then by construction of commercial buildings. It is visible, however, on the 1944 photos. It was recorded by Robinson as PV69-60 but was completely gone by 1970 and our subsequent surveys.

**Paredones**

Kroeber did not excavate at Paredones, but he did purchase ceramics from there. Paredones is an impressive Inca site located just south of Nasca, built adjacent to and over earlier cemeteries. Robinson recorded it likewise as a single site (PV69-14), but other surveys recorded the Inca center and the cemeteries as separate sites (Strong: #45 and #46, respectively; UCSB; 90-78 and 90-C12, respectively.) The Inca site is protected by the Peruvian National Institute of Culture, and the modern road was rerouted in the late 1980s to avoid passing through the site.

**Agua Santa**

This site is well known, given the Italian excavations there in 1984. It was recorded by Robinson as Site PV69-32; the UCSB survey did not assign it a site number in 1990, given recent work by other archaeologists. The site is now protected by a circumference wall and a guardian.

**Pueblo Viejo**

Pueblo Viejo is a large cemetery a few hundred meters to the west of Agua Santa. Robinson recorded it as PV69-32; the UCSB survey did not assign a site number, given its proximity to the Italian project.

**Soisongo**

Kroeber recorded five small cemeteries at Soisongo, all of which can be located exactly. The sites lie along the edge of an old alluvial fan adjacent to the mouth of the dry Socos quebrada. The sites are clearly visible on 1944 and 1970 photos. The easternmost (Soisongo E) has since been completely destroyed, both at and below the surface, by construction of a large, cement-lined reservoir. Kroeber's Soisongo A-D correspond to the UCSB Sites 90-C128 through C131. Robinson also recorded a cemetery at Soisongo, but it is located about a kilometer farther to the west. Kroeber's sites are not easily visible from the road, while Robinson's is.

### Aja

When Kroeber and Tello recorded the three small sites at Aja, they were located near the edge of a broad, gently sloping alluvial fan, very close to cultivation. Between 1944 and 1970 the limits of cultivation were expanded upward onto the fan, over and beyond the three sites. The only one of the three that can be located with absolute precision is Aja B, located at the base of a small hill. Despite being engulfed by agricultural fields, the hill still stands and the small cemetery is still visible; it was recorded as Site 96-208 by UCSB. We also recorded a sherd scatter to the east, Site 96-207, which was probably Aja C; no traces remain of Aja A. (Robinson's Aja sites are located farther to the east, along the road.)

### Curvi

Kroeber noted, but did not investigate closely, a cemetery and hillside habitation site just north of the Curvi hacienda buildings. The sites were recorded by Robinson as PV69-2, and UCSB as 86-2.1 through 2.7. The house terraces are clearly visible on the hillside just to the east of the Pan-American Highway as one drives northward out of the Nasca Valley.

### Cantayo

Tello divided the major cemetery complex into Cantayo (today usually spelled "Cantalloq") A through G. His divisions of the site, based on small arroyos running through the site, are easily made today on the same basis. His divisions between Sectors A and B and between Ca and Cb were arbitrary; while he did not say on what basis they were divided, it is clear on the 1944 photos that he was using the modern road as a division. The site was recorded by Robinson as PV69-12 and by UCSB as 90-C13. Cantayo has probably suffered some of the worst looting of any of the hundreds of cemeteries now known in this region. It is located near the town of Nasca, along a main highway connecting Nasca with adjacent highland regions, making it easily accessible to looters. The structure Cax, excavated by Tello, is only discernible with some difficulty owing to the extensive looting. What can be seen today are remains of architectural fill, including layers of corn stalks, a typical Early Nasca construction technique; this suggests that the structure was some sort of platform. Other remains of platform constructions can still be seen in Sectors D and E. Platforms in Sector G may also be Nasca in date or may be related to an adjacent Late Intermediate Period hillside village (UCSB Site 89-52) located just above and west of the cemetery. The site plan shows the upper end of the puquio Cajuca (today called Santo Cristo) just below Sector G.

The two small sites, Cantayo L and M (one wonders what happened to H through K) were included in Robinson's PV69-13, but were destroyed by 1970 by construction of a tract of houses; no trace of them was found by the UCSB surveys.

### Cahuachi

This well-known site has been discussed above; its location is not in dispute. It was recorded by all subsequent surveys, as was **Estaquería.**

### Sites in Taruga

Kroeber did not spend much time in Taruga and only mentioned two sites (discussed above) and one puquio. At the time of his visit. there were at least three puquios functioning in the valley, and he probably described the one closest to the Taruga hacienda, today called Santa María.

### Las Trancas

Kroeber's visit to the Trancas Valley was also brief; he mentioned only the cemeteries to the south of Huaca del Loro, all discussed above.

### Poroma

Poroma is a sector of the Trancas Valley downstream from Las Trancas. Site A cannot not be located with precision; the UCSB survey recorded at least eight cemeteries in that general vicinity, and we cannot know which of those Kroeber was describing. Site B is most likely UCSB Site 90-C65 and Robinson's PV71-1.

## FINAL OBSERVATIONS

I have attempted in this short piece to provide some context for Kroeber's 1926 Nasca field work, considering current views of Nasca culture history and the ways in which Kroeber's work contributed to our present understandings. I have provided an extremely brief summary of Nasca research that has taken place in the ensuing years, necessarily glossing over the details and controversies. Finally, based on my own experience in the region, having walked over nearly every inch of it, it has been possible to locate nearly all of Kroeber's sites. I hope the reader will find this information useful, as well as data on the current state of preservation of each.

That brings me to my final observation. Of the twenty-six sites recorded by Kroeber in the Nasca Valley, eleven have since been destroyed. What does this say about the current state of archaeological research in Nasca? Does this mean that 42 percent of all sites have been destroyed since 1926?

In truth, site destruction is a terrible problem for the archaeologist in Nasca. But the good news is that Kroeber's sample is probably not representative of site destruction throughout the region. He worked in the most densely occupied valley in the region, and most of his work took place not far from the modern town. La Huayrona and Cantayo L and M met their fate because of expansion of the town of Nasca; Aja A and C because of agricultural expansion very close to town. The five Majoro Chico sites were destroyed in one fell swoop by the owner of the adjacent hacienda,[6] hoping to expand his cotton fields. While the looting of cemeteries continues unabated, the wholesale destruction of archaeological sites is not as bad as we might fear from the fates of Kroeber's sites.

And here we are indebted one final time to Kroeber: the only data we will ever have regarding those eleven missing sites are the data that Kroeber collected.

### *Notes*

1. In Kroeber's time, and in fact until fairly recently, the convention was to spell Nazca with a "z"; modern usage prefers "Nasca." Except in referring to Kroeber's ceramic phases, the "Nasca" spelling will be used herein.

2. As all of this field work has been carried out since I joined the faculty of the University of California at Santa Barbara, I will refer to them as the UCSB surveys below.

3. The correlation of Kroeber's phases to the standard chronology is not as precise as this table would imply. As pointed out in the Preface, Kroeber's phases do not translate neatly into modern phases.

4. Today usually written "Tiwanaku."

5. This name was given to the site by Strong. Its original name was Tambo de Copara, but as there were two sites of that name, he renamed the one he was working at. The other, Tambo de Copara, has since been destroyed.

6. This owner, and members of his family, were particularly hard on archaeological resources back in the late 1940s and 1950s. He even destroyed an entire puquio.

# GENERAL BIBLIOGRAPHY: Nasca, Kroeber, and Later

I have endeavored to provide an overview bibliography of Nasca research, for the most part being work done since Kroeber's time in the field. In those cases where there exist multiple publications regarding a single topic, or by a single author, I have only included representative entries. No slight is meant to any colleague, either living or deceased, whose works are not included in their entirety.

I have included references to both Rowe's and Steward's obituaries of Kroeber; the latter includes a complete bibliography of Kroeber's publications, a subset of which is included with the former. I also include references to some treatments of Tello's life and works. Because he published incompletely, and because his field notes are yet unavailable to the professional community, some of our best information on his research comes from secondary sources.


Aveni, A. F. (ed.) 1990. *The Lines of Nazca.* Philadelphia: American Philosophical Society.

Baraybar, J. P. 1987. Cabezas trofeo Nasca: Nuevas evidencias. *Gaceta Arqueológica Andina* 15: 6–10.

Bird, J. B. and L. Bellinger. 1954. *Paracas Fabrics and Nazca Needlework: 3rd Century B.C.–3rd Century A.D.: The Textile Museum, Catalogue Raisonné.* Washington, D.C.: National Publishing.

Blasco Bosqued, C. and L. J. Ramos Gómez. 1980. *Cerámica Nazca.* Valladolid: Seminario Americanista de la Universidad de Valladolid.

Bolaños, C. 1988. *Las Antaras Nasca.* Lima: Programa de Arqueomusicología del Instituto Andino de Estudios Arqueológicos.

Browne, D. M. 1992. Further archaeological reconnaissance in the Province of Palpa, Department of Ica, Peru. In *Ancient America: Contributions to New World Archaeology*, ed. N. J. Saunders. Oxbow Monograph no. 24. Oxford: Oxbow Books.

Browne, D. M. and J. P. Baraybar. 1988. An archaeological reconnaissance in the Province of Palpa, Department of Ica, Peru. In *Recent Studies in Pre-Columbian Archaeology*, ed. N. J. Saunders and O. de Montmollin, 299–325. BAR International Series, vol. 421. Oxford: BAR.

Browne, D. M., H. Silverman and R. García. 1993. A cache of 48 Nasca trophy heads from Cerro Larapo, Peru. *Latin American Antiquity* 4(3): 274–294.

Carmichael, P. H. 1986. Nasca pottery construction. *Ñawpa Pacha* 24: 31–48.

———. 1988. Nasca mortuary customs: Death and ancient society on the South Coast of Peru. Ph.D. diss., University of Calgary.

———. 1991. Prehistoric settlement of the Ica-Grande littoral, Southern Peru. Research report. Submitted to Social Sciences and Humanities Research Council of Canada.

———. 1994. Cerámica Nasca: Producción y contexto social. In *Tecnología y Organización de la Producción Cerámica Prehispánica en los Andes*, ed. I. Shimada, 229–247. Pontificia Universidad Católica del Perú, Fondo Editorial, Lima.

———. 1994. The life from death continuum in Nasca imagery. *Andean Past* 4: 81–90.

———. 1995. Nasca burial patterns: Social structure and mortuary ideology. In *Tombs for the Living: Andean Mortuary Practices*, ed. T. Dillehay, 161–189. Washington, D.C.: Dumbarton Oaks.

Carrión Cachot, R. 1948. Julio C. Tello y la arqueología Peruana. *Revista del Museo Nacional* 2(1): 7–34.

Conklin, W. J. 1975. An introduction to South American archaeological textiles with emphasis on materials and techniques of Peruvian tapestry. In *Irene Emery Roundtable on Museum Textiles, 1974 Proceedings: Archaeological Textiles*, ed. P. L. Fiske, 77–92. Washington, D.C.: Textile Museum.

Drusini, A. 1991. Anthropological study of Nasca trophy heads. *Homo* 41(3): 251–265.

Dwyer, J. P. 1971. Chronology and iconography in Late Paracas and Early Nasca textile designs. Ph.D. diss., University of California, Berkeley.

Gayton, A. H. and A. L. Kroeber. 1927. The Uhle pottery collections from Nazca. *University of California Publications in American Archaeology and Ethnology* 24(1): 1–46.

González García, M. F. 1934. Los acueductos incaicos de Nazca. *Aguas e Irrigación* 2(2): 207–222.

Hadingham, E. 1987. *Lines to the Mountain Gods: Nazca and the Mysteries of Peru.* New York: Random House.

Isla Cuadrado, J. 1990. La Esmeralda: Una ocupación del período arcáico en Cahuachi, Nasca. *Gaceta Arqueológica Andina* 20: 67–80.

Isla Cuadrado, J., M. Ruales and A. Mendiola. 1984. Excavaciones en Nasca: Pueblo Viejo, Sector X3. *Gaceta Arqueológica Andina* 12: 8–11.

Kosok, P. 1965. *Life, Land and Water in Ancient Peru.* Brooklyn: Long Island University Press.

Kroeber, A. L. 1937. Preface to *Archaeological Explorations in Peru, Part III: Textiles of the Early Nazca Period. Anthropology Memoirs*, vol. 2, no. 3. Chicago: Field Museum of Natural History.

———. 1937. *Archaeological explorations in Peru, Part IV: Cañete Valley. Anthropology Memoirs*, vol. 2, no. 4, 223–273. Chicago: Field Museum of Natural History.

———. 1944. *Peruvian Archeology in 1942*. Viking Fund Publication in Anthropology vol. 4. New York: Viking Fund.

———. 1953. Paracas Cavernas and Chavin. *University of California Publications in American Archaeology and Ethnology* 40(8): 313–348.

———. 1954. Proto-Lima: A Middle Period culture of Peru. *Fieldiana: Anthropology* 44(1). Chicago: Chicago Natural History Museum.

———. 1956. Toward definition of the Nazca style. *University of California Publications in American Archaeology and Ethnology* 43(3): 327–432.

Kroeber, A. L. and W. D. Strong. 1924. The Uhle collections from Chincha. *University of California Publications in American Archaeology and Ethnology* 21(2): 1–54.

———. 1924. The Uhle pottery collections from Ica, with three appendices by Max Uhle. *University of California Publications in American Archaeology and Ethnology* 21(3): 95–134.

Mejía Xesspe, T. 1939. Acueductos y caminos antiguos de la hoya del Río Grande de Nazca. *Actas y Trabajos Científicos del 27 Congreso Internacional de Americanistas*, vol. 1, 559–569.

———. 1948. Apuntes bibliográficos sobre el Doctor Julio C. Tello. *Revista del Museo Nacional* 1(1–2): 1–34.

———. 1964. Julio C. Tello. In *Biblioteca Hombres del Perú*, ed. H. Alva Orlandini, vol. 28, 51–111. Lima: Editorial Universitaria.

Menzel, D. 1964. Style and time in the Middle Horizon. *Ñawpa Pacha* 2: 1–106.

———. 1971. Estudios arqueológicos en los valles de Ica, Pisco, Chincha y Cañete. *Arqueología y Sociedad* 6.

———. 1976. *Pottery Style and Society in Ancient Peru: Art as a Mirror of History in the Ica Valley, 1350–1570*. Berkeley: University of California Press.

Menzel, D., J. H. Rowe and L. E. Dawson. 1964. The Paracas Pottery of Ica: A Study in Style and Time. *University of California Publications in American Archaeology and Ethnology* 50.

Morrison, T. 1978. *Pathways to the Gods*. New York: Harper and Row.

O'Neale, L. M. 1936. Wide-loom fabrics of the Early Nazca Period. In *Essays in Anthropology*, 215–228. Berkeley: University of California Press.

———. 1937. *Archaeological explorations in Peru, part III: Textiles of the Early Nazca period. Anthropology Memoirs* 2(3): 118–253. Chicago: Field Museum of Natural History.

O'Neale, L. M. and A. L. Kroeber. 1930. Textile periods in ancient Peru. *University of California Publications in American Archaeology and Ethnology* 28: 23–56.

O'Neale, L. M. and T. Whitaker. 1947. Embroideries of the Early Nazca period and the crop plants depicted on them. *Southwestern Journal of Anthropology* 3(4): 294–321.

Orefici, G. 1988. Una expresión de arquitectura monumental Paracas-Nasca: El Templo de Escalonado de Cahuachi. In *Atti Convegno Internazionale: Archeologia, Scienza y Societa nell'America Precolombina*, 191–201. Brescia: Centro Italiano Studi e Richerche Archeologiche Precolombiane.

———. 1993. *Nasca: Arte e Societa del Popolo dei Geoglifi*. Milan: Jaca Book.

Paulsen, A. C. 1965. Huaca del Loro revisited: The Nasca-Huarpa connection. In *Investigations of the Andean Past*, ed. Daniel H. Sandweiss, 98–121. Papers from the First Northeast Conference on Andean Archaeology and Ethnohistory. Cornell University: Cornell Latin American Studies Program.

Petersen, G. 1980. *Evolución y Desaparición de las Altas Culturas Paracas-Cahuachi (Nasca)*. Lima: Universidad Nacional Federico Villareal.

Phipps, E. 1989. Cahuachi textiles in the W. D. Strong collection: Cultural transition in the Nasca Valley, Peru. Ph.D. diss., Columbia University.

Proulx, D. 1968. Local differences and time differences in Nasca pottery. *University of California Publications in Anthropology* 5. Berkeley: University of California Press.

———. 1983. The Nasca style. In *Art of the Andes: Pre-Columbian Sculptured and Painted Ceramics from the Arthur M. Sackler Collections*, ed. L. Katz, 87–105. Washington, D.C.: Arthur M. Sackler Foundation and the AMS Foundation for the Arts, Sciences and Humanities.

———. 1989. Nasca trophy heads: Victims of warfare or ritual sacrifice. In *Cultures in Conflict: Current Archaeological Perspectives*, ed. D. C. Tkaczuk and B. C. Vivian, 73–85. Proceedings of the 20th Annual Chacmool Conference. Archaeological Association. Calgary: University of Calgary.

———. 1989. A thematic approach to Nasca mythical iconography. *Bollettino del Museo Internazionale delle Ceramiche in Faenze* 75(4–5): 141–158.

Reiche, M. 1968. *Geheimnis der Wuste—Mystery on the Desert—Secreto de la Pampa*. Stuttgart-Valhingen: Selbstverl.

Reinhard, J. 1988. *The Nazca Lines: A New Perspective on their Origin and Meaning*. Lima: Editorial Los Pinos, Lima.

Roark, R. P. 1965. From monumental to proliferous in Nasca pottery. *Ñawpa Pacha* 3: 1–92.

Robinson, D. A. 1957. An archaeological survey of the Nasca Valley, Peru. Master's thesis, Stanford University.

Rossel Castro, A. 1942. Sistema de irrigación antigua de Río Grande de Nasca. *Revista del Museo Nacional* 11(2): 196–202.

———. 1977. *Arqueología Sur del Perú*. Lima: Editorial Universo S.A.

Rosselló Truel, L. 1960. Sobre el estilo de Nasca. In *Antiguo Perú: Espacio y Tiempo*, 47–88. Lima: Editorial Juan Mejía Baca.

Rowe, A. P. 1984. Textiles from the Nasca Valley at the time of the fall of the Huari Empire. In *The Junius B. Bird Conference on Andean Textiles*, ed. A. P. Rowe, 151–182. Washington, D.C.: Textile Museum.

Rowe, J. H. 1956. Archaeological explorations in southern Peru, 1954–55: Preliminary report of the fourth University of California archaeological expedition to Peru. *American Antiquity* 22(2): 135–151.

———. 1960. Nuevos datos relativos a la cronología del estilo Nasca. In *Antiguo Perú: Espacio y Tiempo: Trabajos Presentados a la Semana de Arqueología Peruana 1959*, 29–45. Lima: Librería-Editorial Juan Mejía Baca.

———. 1962. Alfred Louis Kroeber, 1876–1960. *American Antiquity* 27(3): 395–415.

Sawyer, A. R. 1961. Paracas and Nazca iconography. In *Essays in Pre-Columbian Art and Archaeology*, ed. S. K. Lothrop, 269–298. Cambridge: Harvard University Press.

———. 1979. Painted Nasca textiles. In *The Junius B. Bird Pre-Columbian Textile Conference*, ed. A. P. Rowe, E. P. Benson and A. L. Schaffer, 129–150. Washington, D.C.: Textile Museum and Dumbarton Oaks.

Schreiber, K. J. and J. Lancho Rojas. 1995. The puquios of Nasca. *Latin American Antiquity* 6(3): 229–254.

Seler, E. 1923. Die Buntbemalten Gefässe von Nazca. *Gesammelte Abhandlungen zur Amerikanischen Sprach und Altertunskunde* 4: 160–438. Berlin: A. Asher & Co.

Silverman, H. 1977. Estilo y estado: El problema de la cultura Nasca. *Informaciones Arqueológicas* 1: 49–78. Lima: Museo Nacional de Antropología y Arqueología.

———. 1987. A Nasca 8 occupation at the Early Nasca site: The room of the posts at Cahuachi. *Andean Past* 1: 5–55.

———. 1988. Cahuachi: Non-urban cultural complexity on the south coast of Peru. *Journal of Field Archaeology* 15(4): 403–430.

———. 1993a. *Cahuachi in the Ancient Nasca World.* Iowa City: University of Iowa Press.

———. 1993b. Patrones de asentamiento en el valle de Ingenio, cuenca del Río Grande de Nasca: una propuesta preliminar. *Gaceta Arqueológica Andina* 7(23): 103–124.

Steward, J. H. 1961. Alfred Louis Kroeber 1876–1960. *American Anthropologist* 63(5, pt .1): 1038–1060.

Strong, W. D. 1954. Recent archeological discoveries in south coastal Peru. *Transactions of the New York Academy of Sciences Series* 2 16(4): 215–218.

———. 1957. *Paracas, Nazca, and Tiahuahacoid cultural relationships in South Coastal Peru.* Memoirs of the Society for American Archaeology no. 13. Salt Lake City: Society for American Archaeology.

Tello, J. C. 1917. Los antiguos cementerios del Valle de Nazca. In *Proceedings of the Second Pan American Scientific Congress*, ed. G. L. Swiggett, vol. 1, 283–291. Washington, D.C.: Government Printing Office.

———. 1942. Origen y desarrollo de las civilizaciones prehistóricas andinas. *Proceedings of the 27th International Congress of Americanists, Lima* 1(2): 589–720.

Townsend, R. F. 1985. Deciphering the Nazca world: Ceramic images from ancient Peru. *Art Institute of Chicago Museum Studies* 11(2): 117–139.

Uhle, M. 1914. The Nazca pottery of ancient Peru. *Proceedings of the Davenport Academy of Sciences* 13: 1–16.

Wolfe, E. F. 1981. The spotted cat the horrible bird: Stylistic change in Nasca 1–5 ceramic decoration. *Ñawpa Pacha* 19: 1–62.

Yacovleff, E. 1932. La deidad primitiva de los Nasca. *Revista del Museo Nacional* 1(2): 103–161.

# INDEXES

## 1. GENERAL INDEX

This is a standard-term index of authors, institutions, rivers and landmarks, other seriations and seriation terms, artifacts other than ceramics, and incidentals. Objects and features referenced here include only the actual objects found and not painted representations of the objects that may be in the ceramic designs.

**S**



**T**

## 2. PLACES AND SITES

All archaeological sites, cities, and valleys mentioned in this volume are included in this index, including sites referenced in the comparative material of each figure.

## 3. KROEBER SERIATION

This index is an outline of Kroeber's seriation system referenced by provenience. Beginning with Strong's Paracas period, which is antecedent to Kroeber's phases, it references all pottery figures to one or more of his designated chronological stages, including and ending with post-Kroeber Late Period (Ica) pottery found during the Field Museum expedition.

## 4. NAZCA POTTERY SHAPES

All the pottery figures in the volume are here referenced by Kroeber's vessel shapes and by provenience. Where two shapes are equally possible, a vessel is indexed as both; where no shapes are correct or where Kroeber was silent, it is indexed as "unclassified."

## 5. NAZCA POTTERY DESIGNS

Pottery figures are here referenced by primary designs. These are not necessarily Kroeber's classifications, as he describes rather than categorizes Nazca art. Details of the designs are to be found at each figure and in indexed discussion.

Where two designs are equally possible, a vessel is indexed as both; where two designs are equally conjoined on a single vessel they have been given their own category; where no design is certain, the vessel has been indexed as "undetermined," and any design that has no recognizable realistic elements has been characterized as "abstract."